THE POWER OF AFRICAN CULTURES

First published 2003
by the University of Rochester Press

The University of Rochester Press
668 Mt. Hope Avenue, Rochester, NY 14620, USA
and at Boydell & Brewer, Ltd.
P.O. Box 9, Woodbridge, Suffolk 1P12 3DF, UK
www.urpress.com

ISBN 1–58046–139–5

Library of Congress Cataloging-in-Publication Data
Falola, Toyin.
 The power of African cultures / Toyin Falola.
  p. cm.
 Includes bibliographical references and index.
 ISBN 1-58046-139-5 (Hardcover : alk. paper)
  1. Africa—Civilization.   I. Title.
 DT14 .P68 2003
 306'.096—dc21

                                                      2003011478

British Library Cataloguing-in-Publication Data
A catalogue record for this book is available from the British Library

Designed and typeset by Straight Creek Bookmakers
Printed in the United States of America
This publication is printed on acid-free paper

THE POWER OF AFRICAN CULTURES

Toyin Falola

UNIVERSITY OF ROCHESTER PRESS

Frontispiece. African culture: A tightly woven basket. Abidjan, Côte d'Ivoire.

To two colleagues,
James Sidbury and Denise Spellberg:

"The area covered by your life is not as important
as what you build on it."

"TODAY IS NOT GOOD, BUT TOMORROW WILL COME."

—A TSHI PROVERB

"TOMORROW IS PREGNANT, WHO KNOWS WHAT IT WILL DELIVER."

—AN IGBO PROVERB

"YOU KNOW HOW MUCH YOU HAVE PASSED THROUGH; YOU DO NOT KNOW HOW MUCH YOU STILL HAVE LEFT."

—A YORUBA PROVERB

CONTENTS

ILLUSTRATIONS

ACKNOWLEDGMENTS

"BE GRATEFUL TO THE TREE SO THAT IT MAY YIELD MORE FRUITS."
—A SHONA PROVERB

The chapters in this book were originally written in response to public lectures, mainly in the United States, from 1995 to 2002. As I revised many of them, I tried to retain the tone and content, and the simple, sometimes conversational, tone of the original pieces. I deliberately minimized the number of notes, which sometime create obstacles to the readers, but I have provided a comprehensive bibliography for those who might wish to further explore many of the issues. The chapters are all united by the theme of culture.

The audience for the public lectures shaped the orientation of the chapters: a mixed crowd comprising students, faculty, and members of the public. As those who give public lectures realize, balancing the interests of one's peers in their discipline and those of others is always tricky. One can be too academic and alienate the audience, and one can be too simplistic and come across as too low-key and casual. Striking a balance entails a careful combination of old and new ideas, and the use of language in an accessible manner. The chapters have, again, been modified or revised to satisfy the needs of a diverse audience. I can only hope that the interests of students, colleagues, and the general readers will all be satisfied. And I should pray that scholars who review the book for academic journals read this acknowledgment and keep the author's audience and objectives in mind. This is not a monograph targeted to a handful in one's sub-field, but a work broadly defined to satisfy those with a somewhat decent knowledge of African societies, as well as students and non-African audience interested in learning about the continent.

My teaching and research continue to complement one another. As I thank my students, I also have to thank those who continue to help me in various parts of Africa in the never-ending task of seeking answers to multiple problems and questions. In the last five years, I have established valuable new contacts in South Africa, Botswana, Algeria, Egypt, and the Gambia. The list of new friends and homes is too long to present here. In

Austin, my graduate students remain my good friends, and we continue to learn from one another. A circle of friends and colleagues is helpful in giving comments on the various essays. Some asked for more, others for less; some were satisfied with the essays, and others wanted more information and comments. I thank all of them, as I take both the credit and criticism for the final product.

Among those who deserve special mention are colleagues and professors who invited me for public lectures. Universities and academic associations operate in highly competitive settings where committees debate for hours on end whom to invite and the topics to impose. Each lecture has added to the list of friends, strengthened older friendships, and promoted camaraderie in a truly global manner. At the risk of offending a number of very good people, I have to single out a few individuals in order to express my gratitude. Chapter two was made possible by the invitation of Professor Roger Louis who, as the president of the American Historical Association, asked me to participate in a plenary session at the 2001 conference in San Francisco. Professor Joe Miller kindly agreed to present the paper on my behalf, as I had to travel outside the United States on rather short notice. The third chapter was made possible by an invitation from Professor Eliot Fratkin of Smith College in 1999. I was a guest of Dr. Grace Thompson in South Africa where I spoke about development issues that formed the core of chapter four. Chief Tokunbo Dosumu-Awolowo, Nigeria's ambassador to the Netherlands, invited me to give a keynote address at a conference in October 2000. I chose the opportunity to speak on the politics of culture. Again in the Netherlands, at the invitation of the Institute for the Study of Islam, I engaged the topic in chapter seven. This was modified and expanded when I addressed the Council of Foreign Relations in New York in December 2001, thanks to the invitation of Professor Gwendolyn Mikell. At the University of New Hampshire, where I spoke about language in December 2001, the organizers were members of the history faculty. Dr. Jonathan Reynolds arranged the lecture for the University of Kentucky in April 2001, in addition to radio and television interviews where some of the issues in chapter eleven were discussed. The chapter on ethnicity was presented in three locations. The first part was in Berlin, Germany. The extensive one on the Yoruba was at Queens' University, Kingston, at the kind invitation of Professor Bruce Berman. Issues relating to historiography, gender, and environment, not all fully developed as chapters, have been presented at various lectures.

I have received generous comments from a number of people, graduate students and professors alike, as well as two readers chosen by the University of Rochester Press. I cannot but single out Tayo Alabi, Ann Cooper, Erin L. Dominguez, Tyler Fleming, Beverly Garland, Ann Genova, Matthew M. Heaton, Kirsten Walles, and Jackie Zahn. Sarah Freligh, a friend I have yet to meet, was kind in breathing more life into the manuscript. I am grateful to Abdul-Rasheed Na'Allah for contributing the poem in Pidgin in chapter 9. Ashley Rothrock prepared the index with care and attention. And I am grateful to Dr. Segun Fayemi for his evocative photographs and for allowing me to use them.

The impressive crowds at the lectures, the engagements, and the intellectual exchanges at the dinners, all inspired me to publish the essays. "Knowledge is better than riches," proclaim the Efik of West Africa, and I am able to offer the little that I know in the following pages. In offering so little, I have probably ignored the Yoruba warning: "Do not attempt what you cannot bring to a good end." Perhaps there is no good ending to many of the issues raised in this book.

Many suggestions for further reading are made in the endnotes throughout the book. The mention of a source or sources for these readings is by no means exclusive; there are many other sources treating these subjects as well.

Toyin Falola
The University of Texas at Austin

1

INTRODUCTION

"IF YOU KNOW THE BEGINNING WELL, THE END WILL NOT TROUBLE YOU."

—A WOLOF PROVERB

The major aim of this book is to present the relevance of culture to Africans in the modern era. The definition and meaning of culture are broad: values, beliefs, texts about the beliefs and ideas, multiple daily practices, aesthetic forms, systems of communications (e.g., languages), institutions of society, a variety of experiences that capture Africans' way of life, a metaphor to express political ideas, and the basis of an ideology to bring about both political and economic changes. Even nature does not escape inclusion in the definition of culture, disregarded, as some analysts do, as being in opposition to culture. To many Africans, nature is understood in part as a religious agency—to talk about nature is to talk about culture. The complexity of past traditions is inscribed into the notion of contemporary modernity.

The cathects of meaning and relevance associated with culture are multidimensional and eclectic, such that to many Africans, culture is really the single word that explains and justifies most things, from the organization of private domains to complicated political institutions. It is treated as a package of social heritage, with all the knowledge and skills vital to survival and reproduction. This book reflects this eclecticism. It reflects changes as well: culture evolves, adapting itself to new circumstances and environments. New ideas come from the outside, to replace older ideas or to be blended with existing ones. Culture and society can be fluid, reflecting an ongoing adaptation. Society and its culture can regress or progress.

Figure 1. The future begins here. Aiyetoro, Nigeria.

Culture is a dynamic process, and Africans have had to deal with the multiple changes and their outcomes. The book reflects the tension between old and new cultures. Islam, Christianity, colonization, Westernization, industrialization, and modernization are common themes in the analysis of contemporary African cultures. Rapid changes have followed the introduction of Islam, Christianity and others mentioned in the preceding list. Ideas and beliefs have been reshaped, and material culture has seen significant changes in the use of imported items. Western-oriented schools have become the source to socialize youth, and new occupations create new gender roles. If traditional cultures privilege the wisdom of elders, modern cultures favor the skills of a Western-educated elite. While traditional economies favored large families, modern economies can only support smaller ones. New ways of thinking and new lifestyles have followed the encounter with the West. Discussions and debates have been equally intense about how to respond to the changes, what to accept, and what to reject.[1]

Culture is an agency of power. If poor technology and devastated economies have painted a negative picture of Africa's powerlessness, one sees something contrary in the cultures where people have shown the capacity to be creative, to be active in seeking alternative solutions to various problems, and to adapt to imported ideas and objects. More importantly, culture has been the main source to construct identity and to reinvent the nation and ethnicities in the face of colonial imposition and the subsequent changes that followed. Similarly, culture opens the window to understand social classes and elite behavior, to socialize its members, and to reproduce established practices and values. States and individuals pursue goals on a permanent basis. Such goals are shaped by values derived from various sources.

The African elite, irrespective of their location and sources of ideas, regard culture as the number one tool in creating a difference between Africans and non-Africans, consolidating national and ethnic identities, addressing most of the issues associated with the European encounter, evaluating the impact of foreign religions and cultures, and seeking enduring answers to contemporary problems of economy and politics.[2] From the discussion on slavery to the introduction of new implements to the peasants, Africans emphasize the role of culture in African history and its quest for development. One may argue, without any fear of contradiction, that without understanding the African discourse and uses of culture, it will be difficult to understand many other issues and aspects of African affairs.

Cultures, rather than "culture" in a sense that may convey a misleading notion of homogenous practices and values, is more appropriate in characterizing the diversity that is represented by Africa. With over eight hundred recognizable cultures and languages, we are confronted with various values, dialects, philosophies, and worldviews. Modern Africa is divided into many countries, each at varying levels of political and economic development. Some countries are big (e.g., Nigeria and Egypt); some are poor; the ideologies of economic and political management have not been the same; they use a variety of European languages; and the ties that each country maintains with the outside world is partly influenced by the European power that colonized it in the twentieth century. In addition, the political system varies from the stable to the unstable, from the democratic to the dictatorial. Different areas are subject to varying degrees of Western or Islamic influences, while some groups are still closer to their traditional practices. If Africa is poor, it has its tiny element of rich people with "high culture," such as men with access to power, military generals, and successful entrepreneurs. Geographical diversity also leads to cultural variations. There is the big divide between the Maghreb states (Tunisia, Algeria, Libya, Morocco, and Egypt) with their Arab and Islamic cultures and the rest of Africa, known as sub-Saharan. To the Maghreb states, the Middle East is more important than Africa.

Yet, as Africa moves to the present era, certain unifying patterns and common trends are discernible.[3] To start with, as the African elite began to define traditions during the nineteenth century, they began a process of identifying the common elements in African ideas, values, norms, and beliefs. Thus, people divided by languages, such as the Luo and the Maasai of East Africa, can have their languages traced to the same language family (the Nilotic, as identified by the linguist Greenberg); they share practices such as pastoralism as the principal occupation, initiation ceremonies for young people, and the formation of age-grades. As chapter three indicates, the attempt to use past histories and traditions to forge a national and continental unity has also led to an emphasis on the common aspects of culture, in spite of diverse ecosystems and multiple languages. Time and again, many African elite have pointed to a psychology of oneness that only Africans can feel, similar to the personal experience of elders who are bonded to their grandchildren. Africans who have met outside of the continent experience a bonding on first contact that Ndabaningi Sithole of Zimbabwe described in 1955 as "consciousness of a kind."[4] In a land filled with whites, the few blacks turn Africa into a common identity and a racial marker. The "consciousness" has become more than an identifier of blackness, but also an ideology of politics which partly influenced the creation of the global Pan-Africanist movement. In other practical terms, many African scholars have provided a catalogue of what is common (and unique) about African culture from skin color, the way they greet, a respect for elders, communal ownership of land, food cultures as essential to their religions (e.g., the belief that hills, rivers, and other major features of the environment have spirit-forces). As we move to the contemporary period, Africans experience events and problems that are similar.

Colonialism and Culture

Colonial rule is regarded as yet another shared experience, as almost the entire continent was subdued by European powers. The colonial experience transformed African cultures to an extent that some became strangers to the traditions of old, suffering alienation in the process.[5] To many others, it called for profound adjustments to new realities as they benefit or suffer from the consequences of the imposition and spread of alien ideas. What made the colonial experience unique was the very difference between the European conquerors and their culture and their African subjects and their culture. The Europeans were able to give more of their culture to Africans, using a variety of means and institutions. Indeed, adaptation and adoption of foreign cultures went on as if Africans had a limited number of options. European technology, science, and medicine were at an advanced stage, but as they introduced these and others, it was not with a motive beneficial to Africans. The missionaries added to the creation of new culture with their active work in evangelization. Western education came with evangelization, but along with that was the division of society along ideological lines ("civilized Christians" in opposition to "primitive traditionalists"), religious lines (one Christian sect against another; Christians against Muslims), and power (elite against non-elite; church leaders against the congregation).

The linkages between colonialism and culture are not always obvious, but they are not hard to delineate.[6] If Europeans regarded the colonized Africans as the "primitive Other," the colonial experience enabled Africans to construct themselves as a terrorized race, raped and exploited by the patriarchal, powerful "White Other." The colonial encounter enabled Europe to define itself in ways different from Africa, to fall on language, food, race, and habits to construct ideas of superiority to the colonized.[7] The so-called high culture connotes authority, refinement, and civilization, in opposition to so-called primitive cultures of Africa. Colonialism served to create and reinforce this dichotomy between high and primitive cultures, between elitist and popular cultures.

The nature of colonial power and administration affected African cultures. The German influence was small, as it did not retain its colonies—Tanganyika, Namibia, Kamerun (later known as Cameroon), and Togo—for any significant length of time. So too was the Italian influence, being limited only to Libya. The Portuguese had a greater impact in the colonies of Cape Verde, Guinea Bissau, Angola, and Mozambique. Race relations were damaged by the transfer of land from Africans to Portuguese settlers. The Portuguese also granted about one percent of their African subjects the status of *assimilados,* so-called privileged Africans, who spoke and wrote Portuguese and who had accepted Portuguese laws and renounced indigenous customs. In the vast Congo, the Belgians did not encourage the spread of Western education. They limited the training of Africans in higher education to a handful and ruthlessly exploited and dehumanized Africans. The French were more idealistic, with an agenda to turn a number of Africans into French citizens. The assimilated Africans were required to be well educated, able to read and write in French, and become Christianized. It was not until after the Second World War that citizenship was extended to all their subjects, while the aim of assimilation was minimally pursued. Pursuing a policy of Indirect Rule, the British assumed that their culture and those of their subjects were different and hard to reconcile. Indirect Rule did not mean an indifference to culture. British officers learned local languages, left many Muslims to practice their religion, and allowed the Anglican Church the freedom to spread the gospel. Irrespective of the administrative system, cultural changes followed, with Africans accepting many aspects of Western civilization and questioning a number of others. As many changes were forced upon Africans, coping with those changes was never easy. Indeed, a large number were traumatized by such experiences as relocation to cities, forced labor, and engagement with new religions and education systems.

The success of the European conquest was largely dependent on technological superiority, one that exposed the underdeveloped science and technology in Africa. Almost immediately, the issues surrounding technological superiority became part of Africa's agenda of modernization and negotiations with its future and modernity. From the ordinary mirror to the complex truck, products of technology are, at the same time, objects of culture. They are not just statements about consumption, but also the reality of power. Guns and control cannot be divorced from the larger project of colonial and political domination. The conquest of Africa brought prestige to European countries. Wealth came with it, as European companies and businesses profited from the economic exploitation of Africans. Thus, as the European powers used their wealth and power to subordinate Africa, modernization and resistance to it became a cultural project.

Changes during the first half of the twentieth century were similar in many areas, enabling Africans divided by space and ethnicity to begin to formulate the concept of a united continent and to develop the culture of resistance and liberation. In the terror and disarray attributed to colonialism, Africans also found powerful ideas of redemption. Thus, colonial culture was ambivalent: it connoted suffering and salvation at the same time. There was a sense of suffering in the political order that gave power to European strangers, in new economies that transferred wealth abroad, and in new social changes that disrupted established kinship systems. But there was also salvation in the creation of a new Western-educated elite that began to be active and rigorous in the formulation of ideologies for development and the vigorous search for modernity. The political elite now preside over the countries created by the colonial governments, and the majority of the territorial boundaries have been retained.

Anti-Colonial Experience

The struggle for independence, as well as the nationalism that it generated, is treated as a shared experience. Colonial subjugation and the European encounter before it[8] never rendered Africans completely unable to create alternative cultures as well as formenting combative cultures of nationalism and resistance. Major milestones in the struggles for independence were often seen and celebrated as a collective achievement for the continent, as in the case of Ghana's independence in 1957 and the coming to power in 1994 of Nelson Mandela of South Africa. Problems and tragedies both served the purpose of energizing Africans, as in the case of the Italian occupation of Ethiopia in the 1930s. Where independence involved armed struggles, Africans followed the events and sought the means to make contributions.

Even a rather brief history of anti-colonial struggles will show how patterns and features of such conflicts were indeed similar, thus providing a historical tool to deploy to build an idea of an African unity. Colonial changes and reforms instigated anti-colonial protests from the very beginning of European rule. If Africans realized that conquest was hard to stop, they never gave up the struggle for better wages, access to education, jobs, and facilities. Where lands were expropriated by European settlers, the people demanded a return to their land. The educated elite were assertive in seeking reforms, and they adapted European-style politics by establishing political associations to create effective pressure groups. The continued grip of the colonial authorities, the Great Depression, and the Second World War affected many colonies and ultimately radicalized their politics. In the 1940s, Africans were no longer seeking reforms but an end to European rule. There was a new set of aggressive leaders, a larger number of the African population had become politically active, and many new political parties were established. The European powers had to grant a series of concessions, if only to minimize large-scale protests and violence. Intense post–World War II nationalism was widespread and ultimately brought independence to many countries between 1957 and 1969. The inherited European political systems collapsed in most of these countries, and the failure of contemporary politics provides yet another context in which to understand the continent. The search for alternatives to Western ideas has put African culture at the center of many discussions.

Many analysts who have studied the collapse of the European empires in Africa have cited the ability of Africans to use culture as a tool of resistance as one of the reasons for Africa's success. The elite of the colonial era, and even the few educated ones before them, realized the impact of Western contacts on their peoples and traditions. An initial acceptance of many of the changes gave way to doubts and criticisms of what they were accepting and how their indigenous institutions were being damaged. As early as the nineteenth century, serious thinkers began to talk about the need to restore traditions and use them to empower Africans.[9] To bear African names, eat indigenous food, and wear local attire were seen as powerful anti-colonial statements. Since then, the need to reclaim a lost identity has been a recurrent theme in African affairs. In constructing a new future for Africans, one of the constant appeals by the African elite is for them to turn to their culture. As W. E. Abraham argues in his well-read book written in the glorious years when many African countries obtained their independence, Africans should turn to their heritage and should avoid "fruitless comparisons with other continents."[10] Few people disagree that culture is important in seeking answers to Africa's economic underdevelopment.

Culture and Development

The colonial past and the global present are permanently inscribed in Africa's contemporary events, forcing many people to raise and question ideas about Africa's place in a changing world order. Again, issues of culture tend to dominate the discussion, as Africans seek ways to avoid permanent domination or to use the weapons of culture to resist and protect themselves. Not only do many Africans stress the unifying aspect of culture, they also emphasize both the tangible and intangible aspects of culture, development and identity. Those tangibles such as languages, stories, religious sacrifices, and initiation ceremonies provide the means to understand the intangibles such as values and ideas. The simplicity of material objects, like the hoes and machetes used in farm work, lead not only to discussions on technology but to the contribution of Africans to civilization. Are ideas and values superior to material cultures and technologies, if indeed both can be separated? Many Africans have loudly said "yes," simply to make the point that economic and technological backwardness does not mean a lack of civilization or cultural inferiority. Aimé Césaire, the guru of the Négritude movement, opened one of his most cited poems with lines to celebrate the simplicity of material culture, cheering for those who never invented or discovered anything.

As if to underscore Césaire's view, many analysts have shown how the nonmaterial aspects have shaped many things that Africans do. How people relate to one another, define morality, perceive social hierarchies, accumulate and spend wealth, and divide and reward roles are influenced by culture. As their ideas change, as a result of European imperialism, the spread of Islam and Christianity, urbanization, and other forces, so too do they modify or adapt their practices to meet the needs and expectations of new realities.

Postcolonial history has not always vindicated Africans, now in power, who, under colonial rule, expressed the desire to be free of colonial misrule and oppression. As an extension of the colonial period, the postcolonial era has shared many of the legacies and political cultures of the first half of the twentieth century. African leaders have yet to overcome the conceit and problems associated with colonialism; instead, they have added new problems. Some of the major problems that the African elite have contributed to the underdevelopment of the continent are discussed in the chapters on politics, political economy, and ethnicity. Thus, one can talk of the culture of politics as well as the politics of culture.

To elaborate on the interaction between culture and politics, it can be said that Africans are not different from other groups and races when it comes to making demands on their governments and political leaders. As in other parts of the world, people are organized on the basis of interest, race, gender, ethnicity, and class. This is where culture comes into the picture. A common organizing framework in Africa is around religion and group. An ethnic group is, at the same time, a cultural group making demands on its representatives, political leaders, and government to seek the means to improve the lives of its members. Conflicts and competitions are endemic, as various cultural groups clash over their demands and interests.

An ethnic group doubles as a source of identity affirmation (a cultural unit) and an agency of power (politics). What sustains the group is history and tradition. Established cultural habits in food, attire, literature, and music are put to good use to socialize members into the group, encourage marriages among group members, and generate a feeling of respect. Each generation produces a leader that champions the cause of the ethnic group and reinvents older traditions to keep the members of the group together. But there is always a political motive: ethnic leaders unite group members in order to derive economic and political benefits, engage in cooperative or dangerous relations with rival groups, and fight for power and resources. Identity is connected to politics in clearly defined ways. Recent colonial experience encourages the need to further politicize identity, and to invent new ways of dealing with European powers as well as fellow African groups.[11]

In exploiting ethnicity for politics, the modern educated elite play a crucial role. Again, the elite are astute in manipulating culture to the maximum advantage. They occupy the front ranks in the defense of ethnic interests. Ethnic cultures and history are projected by the elite as part of a broader political mission to assert their own personal and collective self-interest. Since the claim to leadership also involves an agenda of modernization, the elite cleverly use access to Western culture as a source of power and prestige. Being able to use European languages, have jobs, and behave as civilized in Western ways are all part of the ability to use cultural capital and good incomes for political ends. The elite represent a distinct group within the ethnic, merging social and cultural ideas with the political to empower themselves and the entire group. Western education is a marker of success, while ethnicity is the boundary of operation to exclude others from power and resources of the nation.[12] Elite behavior may not necessarily conform to the logic of established political theories—constitutions and laws can be broken to justify the pursuit of ethnic interests; corruption can be accepted or defended to prevent an ethnic member from being embarrassed by outsiders; and rules of politics and elections can be broken just to get one's ethnic member into power. As with friendship, elitism and ethnicity open the door to abuse and incest.

The political strategies and tools created by an elite are not always perfect, even when they are workable. The African elite have yet to create the culture to sustain the viability of an ethnic group in modern politics. As elite members compete, they make ethnicity itself fluid and competitive, beneficial, and dangerous. Among those who easily threaten the age-old obligations of kinship and ethnicity are elite members who travel abroad, relocate within their countries, marry nonethnic members, and weaken the solidarity of the ethnic group. Western education is not enough to unite the elite, who can be divided by religious affiliations, generation, and age, as well as class privileges. Interethnic relations involve complex negotiations between the various representatives of each group. Differences do emerge on strategies and goals, making it very difficult for the elite to agree, leading to various splits and alliances among members of the same ethnic group. Thus, there is a culture of disagreement and violence even in ethnic politics.

Africa and the Wider World

Africa was able both to export and import cultures. The migration brought about by the trans-Atlantic slave trade created the consciousness of a diaspora, one of cultural alienation, cultural retention, and cultural synthesis. The African diaspora has survived, and some of the links between the blacks in the diaspora and Africa continue till today. In the United States academy,

Africa is viewed as an "area study" or part of "Black Studies," broadly defined. Some scholars do not see the link between Africa and African American studies. Irrespective of how the academy is structured, Africa is part of the consciousness of the diaspora. Without the trans-Atlantic slave trade, the number of blacks outside of Africa would be much smaller. As blacks, Africans cannot avoid the association with racism, while marginalization and poverty continue to bring to the forefront issues of human rights and equity in the global system.

The slave trade was not the only factor in Africa's linkage to the world economy. Other forms of trade—the spread of Christianity and Islam, Western education, and colonialism—all contributed to connecting Africa with the global world. External contacts were strong, bringing goods, ideas, and cultural influences from various places. The consequences have not always been positive. As in the case of the colonial encounter, external contact brought economic exploitation, racism, the cultural bastardization of Africans, and political subjugation. But there have been changes that can be positively adapted to modern societies, such as the spread of the universal religions of Islam and Christianity, Western education, and modern science.

On the whole, Africa has been less than successful in exporting its cultures. Rather, it has received more from the outside in a way that has led to a constant review and modification of its indigenous cultures. The continent's labor and goods have been massively exploited, but with limited gains to its people. Its share of world resources is small; and many of its countries are poor. As chapter four shows, its dominant economic feature is underdevelopment. If there are domestic reasons that sustain this underdevelopment, they are matched by the contributions of the external world. Capitalism is the ideology of the world system. As far as the Western powers are concerned, the relevance of Africa lies in what it can supply—its minerals, crops, and cheap labor—and what the Western countries can buy to benefit their own industries and merchants. During the Cold War, ideological considerations favored the spread of capitalism in order to prevent Africa from adopting socialism or befriending the Soviets. The bargaining power of Africa in the international economic system is weak, and its reliance on foreign technology means that it also has to accept a variety of foreign cultures. In addition, its policies, whether in economics or politics, are influenced by external circumstances. Colonialism, the Cold War, and the current emphasis on globalization have served as major constraints to limit the number of options available to African leaders.

Africa has also been less than successful in translating foreign policy goals to economic development and political stability. More than forty years after the independence of many of African countries, they still cannot find any footing in the international system. Africa's anti-colonialism and anti-apartheid policies paid off in the eventual liberation of southern African countries and Portuguese-speaking countries, where independence was delayed much longer. Africa's neutrality in the Cold War was ineffective. The gains from participation in many world bodies have always been small. With respect to trade, the benefits of foreign investments are usually exaggerated—the profits hardly leave the shores of the foreign investors, leaving Africans to deal with the crumbs.

Irrespective of the outcome, Africa cannot disengage itself from international politics, but it must continue to seek the means to benefit from it. Today, ideological options are limited, and anti-Western rhetoric has been toned down, but the desire for autonomy and economic and political power remains strong. In shaping its foreign policy, culture and economic concerns have to be paramount in order to decide what to import and export, and to participate in international issues significant to their interests.

Organization and Relevance

This book brings out the salient elements in African culture and its link to the economy, politics, power, and elitism. The various chapters consider issues of cultural survival and relevance to Africa and the African diaspora, some cultural forms, and their enduring meanings. The division of the world into "traditional" and "modern"—Africa and West—is, at the same time, a cultural project.[13] When Africa is treated as "inferior," a process of mental and technological domination is involved. When Africans reject their categorization of inferiority, a cultural project of self-affirmation is implied. Chapter two discusses how Africans perceive their engagement with the West. Anti-colonialism and anti-Western hegemony, in part, have been expressed in cultural and intellectual terms. The end of the colonial era has not necessarily changed many of the perspectives analyzed in chapter two. To those who blame the West for the underdevelopment of Africa, colonialism and neocolonialism are still treated with condemnation.

In the chapter on development and politics, the colonial encounter looms large. Chapter two also examines how the African elite in different eras have examined the impact of this encounter. The colonial experience transformed African cultures in various ways. For one thing, the continent became peripheral, subordinated to metropolitan powers and ideas. A new elite began to accept or reject assimilation to metropolitan cultures. Christianity spread, the landscape was altered in many ways, and many old traditions were changed. A set of colonial texts and ideas began to emerge to justify colonial conquest and erase the memory of resistance to domination. The African elite were forced to respond to colonial conquest and its antinomies, as analyzed in chapter two.

The primary concern of African people, as well as the governments, is to overcome underdevelopment. Economic issues are linked to culture and the necessity to overcome Western domination. Culture and environment remain very much connected, as various African groups cope by creating occupations where they live and by using material objects suitable to their areas. Chapter three underscores the role of culture in development. In chapter four, the scope is broadened to a number of economic concerns that Africa must deal with, even when they are not necessarily posed as cultural issues. Underdevelopment cannot be understood strictly in economic terms but in political and cultural ways as well. Capitalism, class, and culture are interwoven. The ways people make and spend money are in part dependent on values. Imported items have greatly affected how Africans understand development and seek progress. Items associated with modernity are not just the privileges of the rich or the elite; a revolution of rising expectation has produced a culture of demand as well as resistance to bad governments and leaders that do not offer economic benefits.

Politics is central to all other issues. After suffering all forms of exploitation from European control, independent African nations emerged in the second half of the twentieth century. The optimistic expectation in the 1950s was that Africa was the frontier of development. The reality today is different. Power, economy, and corruption are linked to a political culture that regards politics as a lucrative business. There are the practical problems of manpower, particularly those with the experience to manage modern nations. There is poverty and the scarcity of resources to transform the people rapidly. Worse, the nations are still rather fragile, and the competing leaders have been unable to meet the challenges posed by loyalty to ethnic groups and religion. Chapter five examines the culture of political instability. Here, two trends are discernible. On the negative side is the clear evidence of misrule and mismanagement, constructed around corrupt practices and personality. Attaining legitimacy has been difficult in view of the persistent failure of regular elections and the culture of clinging to power at all costs. On the positive side is the evidence of a culture of resistance and a civil society that sustains the demand for progressive politics and policies. African people have been resilient in coping with bad leaders, but at the same time are relentless in seeking change. Violence is not uncommon as a form of resistance, not to mention countless cases of noncooperation with the state and acts of sabotage. The main beneficiaries have been military officers who use access to guns to take power, retain it, and grossly abuse it. Democracy is a culture that evolves over time. An antimilitary and antiauthoritarian culture has to emerge, with an empowered and enlightened electorate. Contestants have to believe that laws governing the transfer of power deserve respect. Ethnic leaders have to subscribe to a notion of legitimacy that will accept those in power, even if they come from other ethnic groups.

The issue of ethnicity in politics, treated in chapter five, is elaborated in chapter six with Nigeria as a case study. Members of an ethnic group use origin stories, myths, history, and religion to create a powerful identity that unites them in a way that enables them to see one another as a united people. As in the example of the Yoruba in chapter six, an ethnic group as large as twenty million claims a common origin from one ancestor: Oduduwa. Identities, based on culture and history, affect politics. Indeed, the invention and reformulation of ethnic identities represents the careful use of culture to engage in politics. The pattern is clear: modern Africa is created upon a layer of old indigenous cultures and nationalities. The European powers manipulated the ethnic and cultural diversity to advantage, using them to promote a policy of divide and rule. As Africans inherited power, they were faced with the task of uniting their people, but they have not been successful to date. Loyalty to an ethnic group is often stronger than loyalty to the country itself. Where warlords emerged, as in Liberia, Rwanda, and Somalia, the ethnic or clan leader is more important to his people than the "national" leader. But there is a profound contradiction in this culture of loyalty and nationalism. The "national" leader is held accountable for all the ills of society, and he is expected to provide what the people want—jobs, education, health services, and other "good things of life." The clan or ethnic leader may be held to a lower standard of expectation—he is a "good man" but for the "national leader" who frustrates his ambitions! If the requirements of ethnic loyalties are clearly spelled out and adhered to, that of the national is not—thus, there is no commitment to the national institutions, and symbols of the nation such as the flag and the anthem have little or no meaning. Contending with ethnic problems is compounded by the politics of managing scarce resources. Who gets what may depend on where people come from. One group tries to dominate the others to obtain major economic and political advantages.

Religions of all varieties and traditions remain one of the most significant components of African cultures. Whether defined by their contents, symbols, culture encounters, sources of power, or authority, religions affect most aspects of African life and society. As chapter seven on Islam shows, religions play a major role in politics. So strong is the impact of religions in shaping perceptions and values that they ultimately engender conflicts, since everybody cannot think alike or respond to issues in the same way. As chapter eight shows, modern Africa has had to encounter global religions, a process that has initiated far-reaching changes. Africans are used to religious encounters and change. After the introduction of Islam and Christianity, Africans began a process of adaptation. Islam has witnessed reforms and revolutions; Christianity has witnessed schism. Examples of millennialism are not uncommon, as religious communities look forward to a greater future led by messiahs. Many religious leaders have created syncretic movements, taking ideas from the past and present to create something new. Older religions have struggled to revitalize themselves, and traditional religions have been sustained in the modern world by neotraditionalists who insist that the indigenous traditions of the past remain the best and most useful for moving Africa forward. Many of the changes involved clashes of cultures, African and Western, and the ability to creatively blend imported cultures with local ones. Christianity and Western education are powerful forces that have transformed African cultures. To the assimilated elite, African indigenous religions and many aspects of culture are inferior to Western-derived ones. Success has been defined in Western terms, along the lines of career and social mobility by the avoidance of a so-called primitive African milieu, and the condemnation of villages and rural cultures. Nevertheless, the impact of indigenous religions can still be seen in contemporary worldviews on most issues and controversies. At the time of Africa's independence, indigenous religions were strong in many areas. And although considerable decline has set in, many aspects continue to survive while some religious leaders do in fact experiment with creative blending of multiple religious traditions.

Language is central to the organization of society, intergroup relations, and a host of cultural practices. Chapter nine dwells on the role of English in the modern society. Most Africans continue to use their indigenous languages which make it possible to continue with established cultural practices. The elite profit from the use of European languages. A creolization process is at work, as indigenous and European languages are combined, as in the example of "pidgin" discussed in the chapter. There can be no doubt as to the relevance of the European languages. From the point of view of the elite, they are the ideal media for the members to interact and to reach out to a wider world. Indeed, many have won international praise and attention in various disciplines and creative literature and art. Africans divided by countries, ethnicities, and indigenous languages are united by their ability to speak English, French, or Portuguese. The attempts to construct modern nation-states are linked to the use of European languages: a variety of economic and political policies depends on the ability to read and use sources derived from Europe. In spite of the growing importance of European languages, African governments and the elite have not given up the search for alternative indigenous languages. In North Africa, the use of Arabic is successful, as is the extensive use of Swahili in east Africa. In other countries, political instability has made it harder to choose one of the indigenous languages as the official one.

Many institutions of society reveal gender inequalities, including the exploitation of women and their marginalization in many political and economic sectors. Chapter ten reviews the historical and contemporary realities of African women. The number of elite women has been expanding, although they still function within a prevailing notion of male dominance. The chapters on ethnicity, gender, and language manifest the relationship between culture and social organizations. One can see how culture influences intergroup relations, social status, and hierarchies. Cultural experience also shapes individual personalities in a way that influences their attitudes toward birth, marriage, and death. As aspects of culture change, instability can be introduced and new regulations can emerge to mediate social relations.

In the final chapter, the relevance of Africa in a "black world" is shown in how African cultures have traveled to other parts of the world, and how blacks in the Americas and Europe regard Africa as their homeland. The connections give race and culture the power to shape people's minds and generate responses that take various forms. Slavery, racism, and poverty have linked Africa with the rest of the black population in other continents.

As all the chapters show, culture is powerful, and its impact can be seen in all spheres and sectors of society, from Africa's past to its present. A number of analysts believe that development will come only when Africans create a distance from their older traditions. Not a few scholars and policy experts have called upon Africans to throw their traditions into museums and see issues not as Africans, but as individuals, a suggestion that is based in part in a belief in Western market ideologies.[14] Those who are disappointed with the slow pace toward modernization see a good explanation in African culture as the obstacle.[15] Africans are presented as hedonists who,

Ogot. Many covered the wide gamut of cultural institutions—from law, religions, language, and customs to political theories. A national consciousness touching upon issues of race and identity formed the central concern of a host of others, such as Edward Wilmot Blyden, Attoh Ahuma, Bandele Omoniyi,[2] Léopold Senghor, and Africanus Horton. Formal Western education generated considerable interest, and all of them had something to say about it, in part because they were created by it and in part because the changes they envisaged rested on access to formal education. Some authors covered virtually all topics, refusing to make distinctions between the academic and nonacademic, the political and the philosophical, the religious and the secular. Political philosophers such as Nkrumah, Cabral, and Senghor combined ideology with sociology to advance political discourse. All the writers were shaped by the events of their age and the need to respond to different phases of the expansion of the European frontiers and empire. In what follows, I will identify the major phases and the leading ideas and themes that were produced during the nineteenth and twentieth centuries.

Responses to the European Incursion

Most of Africa was conquered between 1885 and 1900. However, Euro-African relations had preceded this period, with a number of well-established European settlements and trade colonies along the coast. In such places as Lagos and Cape Coast (now in Ghana), European traders and the representatives of governments and missionaries had interacted with Africans. European contacts with Africa dated back to the fifteenth century, and relations were dominated by the trans-Atlantic slave trade until the nineteenth century. The consequences of the slave trade were devastating, even long after its abolition. During the nineteenth century, European explorers visited Africa to find out about places and people; missionaries from different church organizations visited to spread the gospel; traders came in large numbers to procure palm oil, palm kernels, peanuts, cotton, and other products; and European administrators and military officers began to control a number of places along the coast. Traders and missionaries pressured their governments to impose colonial rule so that they could benefit from increased interactions with Africans. The interest in profit and evangelization merged in the idea that both were needed to "civilize" Africa and to produce a new generation of Africans who would liberate their people from so-called barbarism.

Few as they were, members of the African elite began early to reflect on the encounter with Europeans and the conquest that took place in the last quarter of the nineteenth century. The leading opinions varied from accommodating the changes to multiple forms of resistance. The expanding European frontiers also instilled among the African elite the need to understand their own traditions and history, partly in an attempt to negotiate with the invaders or to resist some of the changes they sought to introduce. Resistance narratives and protests took several forms: they consisted of several phases, generating cultures of liberation from the European encounter, and producing the first set of modern African heroes.

The Pre-Conquest Era

The initial reaction of many of the African elite to the growing European presence was not necessarily hostile, although there were those among them who had reservations about the spread of European culture or who simply wanted the European presence to be limited in its duration. The contacts in the first half of the nineteenth century were presented as humanitarian—to end the slave trade, promote commerce, and spread Christianity.[3] The French later added assimilation to their culture, as well as the message of freedom and equality to the humanitarian agenda. Liberated slaves were settled in Sierra Leone and Liberia; missionaries preached the gospel and involved Africans as "native agents." Many of these agents accepted the argument that commerce and Christianity would lead to the development of Africa and that they themselves would serve as both the agents of change and the new leaders of a transformed continent. Thus, in areas with a concentration of African elite members (e.g., Freetown, Lagos, and Monrovia), the most common reaction to the European expansion was that of acceptance. Africans with positions in the government, church, school, and business, all regarded themselves as successful and respected by their European colleagues: they were happy with the European presence and even wanted their impact to extend to the hinterland. If people of mixed parentage in Senegal desired assimilation to French culture, the African elite in Lagos, Liberia, and Sierra Leone were cultivating European lifestyles.[4] From their writings and lifestyles, it is clear that the majority regarded the European expansion as beneficial to the modernization process. They advocated a role for themselves—the elite as the agent of change; they wanted Christianity and Euro-African trade to flourish, they were eager for the spread of Western education, and they were eager for the coastal cities to experiment with European-style political systems.[5] Among the notable figures of this era were the Rev. Samuel Crowther, the first African to become an Anglican bishop in 1864, and Dr. James Africanus Beale Horton (1835–82), the physician and author.[6] Rev. Crowther was an effective agent in spreading Christianity. He occupied a central role in the translation of the Bible into Yoruba, and he believed that a greater European presence was good for Africans. Horton looked for secular reasons to support Europeanization: he believed Africa needed modern medicine, a formal school system, and a host of new ideas.

Christianity and the Bible shaped the minds of many of the pioneer elite, offering ideas that they had to confront, modify, or reject. They were essentially products of missionary schools, and many among them were also liberated slaves resettled in the West African countries of Sierra Leone and Liberia.[7] The modern African countries were yet to be created, but the vision of a large Africa was a driving force among them. The pioneer elite were mediators and brokers between Africans and Europeans. They sought to interpret Europe to Africans without a Western education, and at the same time to interpret Africa to the Europeans. While maintaining closeness to African cultures, they were also learning and imbibing European ways of life. They acquired European languages, which became a source of power in their mediating role. The "Victorians" among them dressed like the English, listened to European music, and even tried to practice monogamous marriages. With their Western education and Christianity, they regarded themselves as agents of civilization to change their people. However, they believed that it was equally important to stay close to their people, in addition to sharing important elements of African culture. Not only did they participate in African culture, but many of the elite even regarded it as part of their role to present and defend the culture to Europeans.[8]

Influential pioneers such as the Rev. Alexander Crummell and Edward Blyden were originally from the Americas, and they and others added the idea of race as a means to understand Afro-European relations. For Crummell, the earliest of the major thinkers, and some others such as the Rev. Samuel Johnson, the expanding European frontiers in Africa were a blessing. The elite in areas influenced by the British tapped into a Victorian worldview to analyze the African situation. They believed that through international trade and Christianity, Africa would see significant changes within a short time. Why did this early pioneer elite support the expanding European empire, even justifying the need for it? For many of the liberated slaves, exposure to Western education and Christianity provided new ways of looking at Africa. Crummell and a few others interpreted African history in theological terms: God would use the abolition of the trans-Atlantic slave trade and domestic slavery and relations with Europeans to bring progress to Africa.[9] We can also see early examples of comparative history and society, as those who had seen Western societies, notably the liberated slaves, began to envision Africa through the lens of the West, linking a desire for change with the European expansion itself. For the missionaries among them, the creation of a European empire would enable them to spread the gospel.

The believers in European expansion regarded the role of the new states and governments created by Europe as different from the established indigenous African ones. Their writings reflect a simplicity in their understanding of the nature and motives of European expansion, perhaps a good indication of the success of the missionaries to turn the pioneer elite into European-minded Africans. The states that the Europeans would construct in Africa, according to Crummell, for instance, would be firmly based on morality grounded in Christian principles. The so-called morally superior European nations would transform Africa by promoting Christianity, maintaining justice, providing education, ensuring law and order, and creating "national growth." The moral state would not fight unjust wars, would train Africans in correct behavior, and would spread the use of English. Crummell believed that Africans had a "pliable and plastic nature" to absorb the values of Europe and to learn English, which they required before individuals and nations could grow by becoming Christian and participating in commerce. Many of the pioneer writers witnessed the expansion of the European empires and had to modify their ideas to cope with the new reality. It was clear that they had not fully factored into their thinking the motives of European expansion, and they had expected rapid changes from which many Africans would benefit. To those who regarded colonial imposition as immoral, they were unable to fully deal with the issue of how an immoral system could engender a moral one.

The Conquest Era

After 1885, relations changed based on colonial domination, which lasted in many areas till the 1960s. This changed the attitude of the African elite. The move toward colonial domination marginalized their status and power, as more and more Europeans began to replace them in government, business, and church. No longer regarded as allies, they began to be dominated as subject people, in a way not significantly different from the treatment meted out to farmers and traders whom the elite themselves had treated as inferior. If they had earlier regarded increasing European expansion as beneficial, the elite began to rethink their orientation, indeed, seeing the need to become anticolonial if they were to retain their own influence. Samuel Crowther, the epitome of success for Africans, lost his influence in the 1880s, attacked by European missionaries who regarded Africans as inferior. Europeans now dominated not just the church but trade, the professions, and civil service. The era of conquest coincided with the growth of European racial arrogance, which deeply offended and radicalized the African educated elite. And as colonial rule became established, it was more than clear that the power which the African elite had hoped to exercise would not be given to them.

The conquest and the changes that came with it have dominated the consciousness of Africans and have formed the core issues around which the African elite can discuss the past of their people, as well as the future of a modernized Africa. Africa was both a victim and a beneficiary of European industrial and technological advancements. In dealing with the European empire, Africans had to confront multiple issues of colonial domination, and the spread of new cultures, ideas, and institutions. Through trade, Africa contributed labor and raw materials that significantly fueled Europe's growth. Colonial rule brought the products and knowledge of European science, technology, and industries. Christianity spread rapidly in the nineteenth and twentieth centuries, adding to the changes of the period. Many new European ideas and institutions spread in different areas and with varying consequences; new economies emerged that promoted the cultivation of cash crops for export and the exploitation of minerals by foreign companies; physical changes included the growth of old and new cities, the building of railways, roads, hospitals, and telecommunications; and Western education—the most desired of all the changes—also spread, although not at a pace that was ever fast enough for African aspirations.[10] In sum, modern Africa, as we know it today, with the countries and their boundaries, political and judicial systems, languages and other attributes, was the creation of Europe and of creative responses by Africans.

The elite had to respond to the aforementioned changes, whether or not they approved of the European conquest. Alexander Crummell died in 1898 and did not see the outcome of the European expansion. He was aware of the economic exploitation of Liberia, but he thought that African control of the government would improve the situation. Other members of his generation reacted differently to European imperialism. Two of the most distinguished pioneers were Dr. James Africanus Beale Horton (1835–82) of Sierra Leone and Edward Wilmot Blyden (1832–1912). Horton is now regarded as the "father" of contemporary African thought. He rejected the characterization of Africans as an inferior race, and he believed in the capacity of Africans to govern themselves. Trained in Edinburgh as a doctor, he saw many virtues in Anglo culture, and he firmly believed that Africans should convert to Christianity, adopt the English education system, and cultivate a Victorian lifestyle.[11] Blyden was far more distinguished and prolific, and his writings cover a wide range of subjects from race, religion, and culture to philosophy.[12]

That race would be a critical part of the thinking of the pioneer scholars was no accident.[13] Many of the writers interpreted the issues along the color line. They experienced slavery, and some, like Crummell, were staunch abolitionists. Not a few were also deracinated, having no ethnic group in Africa with which they could identify. They read a number of European racist texts, including those presented as biology and anthropology,[14] and they felt a need to counter them either by defending the black race or by demonstrating their ability to change. The ideas of two Europeans, James Hunt and John Gobineau, circulated most widely: both argued that race influenced culture and that black racial endowments and cultural achievements were distinct and inferior. The African elite rejected these notions of inferiority and were eager to identify the contributions of blacks to world civilization.[15] Those who were deracinated, like Blyden, were interested in the larger African and diaspora contexts, exploring in general how blacks could transform their lives and construct distinct societies along different lines from the European world. Blyden's impact lasted for quite a while— he enunciated the idea of race equality, with each race making a distinct contribution to world civilization. According to Blyden, the Europeans contributed to science and technology, and Africans to the spiritual and moral spheres. He compiled a list of "African geniuses," and he celebrated Egypt as the cradle of civilization. Blyden pointed out that everything Europeans criticized Africa for (such as polygyny, slavery, and human sacrifice) had also existed among them. As if to anticipate the scholars of the dependency school of the twentieth century, Blyden blamed Europeans for Africa's underdevelopment and its alleged racial inferiority:

> The permanence for centuries of the social and political states of the Africans at home must be attributed, first, to the isolation of the people from the progressive portion of mankind; and secondly, to the blighting influence of the traffic introduced among them by Europeans. Had not the demand arisen in America for African labourers, and had not Europeans inaugurated a regular traffic with the coast, the natives would have shown themselves as impressible for change, as susceptible of improvement, as the natives of Europe.[16]

Next to race in importance was the issue of power. A number of elite members wondered why Europeans should usurp the power of the chiefs. In British colonies where a policy of indirect rule enabled the colonial officers to govern in partnership with indigenous chiefs, the attacks on the colonial empire focused on how the power of the chiefs had been undermined. In colonies where the chiefs were excluded from power, the elite criticized the concentration of power in European hands.[17] The elite were also critical of the colonial policies on land. The colonial powers were criticized for seizing communal land, enacting laws to dispossess people of their land, or encouraging European settlers to appropriate for themselves the most fertile land. The contest (and writing) over land became a form of nationalist expression that led to protests in Ghana and Nigeria in the early years of colonial rule, and to rebellion in Kenya and South Africa during the struggles for independence.

Nowhere was early cultural rebellion better expressed than in the church. If Crowther accepted his ill treatment with dignity, many others chose the path of rebellion. Pioneer Christian leaders founded independent churches in order to accommodate African leadership and make Christianity more adaptable to local situations. The use of African languages in hymns and the production of musical dramas were effective in combating European cultural domination. The movement toward the creation of independent African churches generated its own intellectual tradition, known as Ethiopianism, which spread in many parts of Africa where Christianity had been introduced. In South Africa, Christianity radicalized a number of black elite members who took to anti-European writings, staged plays, and established independent churches.[18] Independence religious movements also emerged in east Africa. In west Africa, Attoh Ahuma, Mojola Agbebi, and Bishop James Johnson (alias "Holy Johnson") distinguished themselves by calling for the indigenization of Christianity.[19] Ethiopianism and other radical ideas of the nineteenth century created the origins of modern African nationalism. The pioneer cultural nationalists supplied ideas and inspiration to their successors, who added "political nationalism" to create a body of anti-colonial discourse during the twentieth century.

Nationalist Expressions

European rule was consolidated in the early years of the twentieth century. By the end of World War I, the grip in many places was firm, and several officers could not have contemplated that European rule would ever come to end. Africans who had insisted upon self-determination changed their tone to request reforms. The move toward independence came much later, in the 1950s, as Africans became more assertive in their demands for the transfer of power. The political arena broadened to include many in the African elite who organized themselves into political associations, trade and students' unions, cultural and other groups to create powerful platforms for anticolonial protests and demands. The media became more combative, while the transportation revolution enabled Africans to travel more widely and to live in cities, which fueled political participation and critical writings on the colonial system. New political leaders emerged, such as Sekou Toure of Guinea, Nnamdi Azikiwe of Nigeria, Kwame Nkrumah of Ghana, and Léopold Senghor of Senegal, and all began to add to the emerging literature on African political thought.[20]

The consolidation of European rule created strong nationalist feelings among the educated Africans.[21] The consensus of opinion was that the colonial experience should be used to "think nationally." Attho Ahuma was speaking the minds of many when he said in 1911 that all Africans should be imbued with the "spirit of nationalism," and that they should struggle to maintain their Africanity. Thus, within a generation, the elite shifted from advocating Westernization to Africanity. Now forced to deal with rejection by their European peers, they began to think more about their own people and the changes being imposed on them. The elite could not fully accept all of the indigenous traditions and were, therefore, forced to make choices and compromises. While not rejecting the new changes, accommodation to the changes compelled them to study and understand their own local traditions. Power was equally as important as knowledge: the theme of self-determination was common—as would be expected, the educated elite wanted more say in the colonial administration, and after the Second World War, they wanted the complete disengagement of the European powers.

There was a small number, generally labeled as conservatives and assimilationists, who did not resent the colonial encounter and who called upon Africans to benefit by accumulating and acquiring the new ideas and changes. Notable among this group were Kitoyi Ajasa and Henry Carr of Nigeria, the politically influential Blaise Diagne of Senegal, and Lamine Guéye, also of Senegal, who succeeded Diagne, served as a deputy in the French National Assembly, and was dominant in Senegalese politics until the emergence of Senghor in the 1950s. The pro-France African elite were eager to see the spread of French culture and political institutions. Ajasa and Carr believed that the adoption of superior European institutions and ideas was necessary for the development of Africa, and they saw no need for Africans to oppose the introduction of new ideas or even the colonial agents bringing them. Africans who supported European colonialism, especially the French-speaking ones, unapologetically absorbed European culture. They might have ignored the psychological effects of rejecting African culture, but they were not anti-Africa as their critics portrayed them. They actually wanted the best for Africans, but paid attention only to how European standards could modernize Africa. They probably acquiesced for too long, as in the case of the French-speaking elite who for a long time failed to demand independence.

More than ever before, the consolidation of European rule in the first two decades of the twentieth century brought out the ideas of race more forcefully in the writings of the African elite. The leading ideas of African Americans and notable black leaders elsewhere gained widespread currency.[22] Colonialism was partly constructed on the idea of racial difference—the assumption that blacks were inferior and needed new tools and ideas to uplift themselves. [23] The African elite responded very critically to this assumption, arguing that they were not inferior even as they absorbed new ideas to improve themselves. Some were outraged by the excessive condemnation of the black race in the European-derived literature, which in some cases even formulated extreme ideas of interracial marriage as the means to develop new colors and identities, different from blackness.[24] In South Africa, race relations and the subsequent development of a policy of apartheid led many among the African elite to take actions based on race. S. M. Molema, for instance, denounced European liberalism and called for the preservation of Bantu culture in order to fight white domination. In spite of their attempts to challenge racialist ideas and create an African identity, the elite failed to free themselves from European concepts of race and nationality. Some even accepted the ideas of European racialist authors as an explanation of why African conditions were bad or why blacks lagged behind in progress and achievements. Where Europeans constructed such stereotypes as the idea of an African society that was nonmaterialistic and nonindividualistic, it was not unusual for the African elite to accept these, even when they carried negative connotations.

The tendency toward religious radicalism continued during the twentieth century. In 1903, Rev. Mojola Agbebi, one of the few pioneer African engineers and church leaders,[25] called for an end to the use of English hymns and prayer books in African churches, and for them to be replaced by African "original songs and original tunes" and indigenous instruments.[26] Agbebi wanted Christianity without what he called its "non-essentials," such as the use of European names, clothes, hymnbooks and prayer books. He saw Islam as a religion which had become African, whereas "Christianity lives here by sufferance." He made an aggressive attack on Christianity:

> While Islam is a bloodless faith and an iconoclastic creed, Christianity has been derided by some of its European friends as a bloody faith, the doctrine of shambles and the executioner's creed. European Christianity is a dangerous thing. What do you think of a religion which holds a bottle of gin in one hand a Common Prayer in another? Which carries a glass of rum as a *vademecum* to a 'Holy' Book? A religion which points with one hand to the skies, bidding you 'lay up for yourselves treasures in heaven,' and while you are looking up grasps all your worldly goods with the other hand, seizes your ancestral lands, labels your forests, and places your patrimony under inexplicable legislations? A religion which indulges in swine's flesh and yet cry [i.e., cries] 'Be ye holy, for I am holy.' A religion which prays against 'those evils which the craft and subtlety of the devil or man worketh against us,' and yet effects to deny incantation, charms or spells and satanism—a religion which arrogates to itself censorial functions on sexual morality, and yet promotes a dance, in which one man's wife dances in close contact, questionable proximity and improper attitude with another woman's husband. O! Christianity, what enormities are committed in thy name.[27]

This kind of attack on Christianity derived from its association with European imperialism and the changes that came with it. The translation of the Christian message into local idioms became part of anticolonial nationalism.

A turning point in the rise of African nationalism occurred in 1935 when Italy invaded Ethiopia, one of two African countries that had escaped colonial conquest. When Emperor Haile Selassie made his unprecedented appearance at Geneva in June 1936, to address the League of Nations, he stood as a symbol of Pan-Africanism in a way that captured the mood and feelings of blacks all over the world. His anticolonial statement which presented the Italian invasion as an act of European barbarism is now regarded as one of the most important texts of nationalism in the first half of the twentieth century. Others were even more combative in the widespread attack on colonialism.[28]

Nationalist expression after 1936 became focused on just one issue: the end of European rule, a demand that unleashed a set of ideas on what Africans would do with power. Many of the elite became nationalists and the first generation of political and bureaucratic leaders. The number of Africans in higher institutions of learning had grown, and many among them in American and European institutions established political associations to seek reforms and independence.[29] The issues that the African elite dealt with multiplied, but the relevance of the European experience was never lost. Writers such as Nnamdi Azikiwe, Kwame Nkrumah, and Obafemi Awolowo considered a host of political and constitutional options for Africa, in ways that required them to engage with Western political thought. As the majority of the elite were worried about the conflicts and problems surrounding ethnicity, they devoted their attention to the political ideas that would lead to the emergence of united nations. For example, Awolowo advocated the creation of states along linguistic lines and a federal system of government that would give power to the component units;[30] a good number of his contemporaries saw merit in a one-party state, while Nnamdi Azikiwe defended "tribalism" as a "pragmatic instrument of nation-building." They all had to contend with the issues of development,[31] as they sought ways to obtain the benefits of Western science and technology, reduce dependence on the West, and end the exploitation of Africa by foreign interests.

From the 1940s onward, practical matters began to effectively complement intellectual ones. The assertive elite began to behave in ways that rejected any idea of European superiority, and some of their writings were deliberately arrogant. From interest in African attire, names, and cuisine to the enunciation of ideas that were described as "African," the elite saw themselves as the equals of Europeans and their rightful successors. The leaders were eager to promote relations across frontiers through or by means of various schemes to create regional and continental organizations to counter the colonial division of Africa into different countries and the failure to promote linkages among them.

Renewal, Progress, and Cultural Identity

Anti-colonial writings, interest in Africa's past and history, and other forms of indigenous expression were careful and deliberate attempts to create a cultural identity for Africa and cleverly to use this identity for continental power and rapid economic and political progress within each country.[32] Members of the elite sought ideas, values, and institutions that would integrate Africans in order to empower them. For the pioneer writers, religion had served this purpose. Crummell believed in Christianity, and Blyden in Islam. Reclaiming Africa's past history and traditions was one of the paramount goals of the elite. Many rejected the association of the European empires with the beginning of development in Africa. Africa's institutions and cultures were regarded not only as having a long history but also as evidence of indigenous development. J. E. Casely Hayford of Ghana demonstrated in the 1920s that the British did not bring development to Africa. Years later, many were to argue that the colonial encounter actually undermined Africa and led to its underdevelopment.[33] Writers such as Blyden advocated a philosophy of cultural separation from the West in order to preserve traditions and use them for purposes of development.[34]

The pioneer guru in linking progress with identity was Wilmot Blyden. He invented the enduring concept of an "African Personality"—an African whose customs and attitudes were different from those of Europeans. He believed that there was an indigenous socialist philosophy which must be adapted to the modern age. Blyden's thesis was simple but seductive—Africa used to live in peace until its contact with Europeans. To regain its lost innocence and peace, it must return to its original traditions. Blyden contrasted Africa's past with a European-dominated future to argue that a society based on its own institutions was better than one influenced too much by external forces. He identified European ideas, notably individualism, class, and social values, that he believed would destroy Africa. Blyden's ideas were modified and elaborated upon by a number of his contemporaries and successors. One of the writers in the forefront of this discourse was Kobina Sekyi of Ghana, a man of multiple talents who propounded various ideas on "Africanity" and the "black soul" to distinguish Africans from Europeans. Sekyi rejected the ideas of development that would turn Africa into a caricature of the West; he attacked the rapid spread of Christianity at the expense of indigenous religions; and he called on European officers to return power to the traditional chiefs. Like Sekyi, Orisahatuke Faduma (formerly William J. Davies) advocated a comprehensive "self-knowledge" about Africa—what he called Negrology—in order to liberate the African mind and promote race pride. All the writers were unanimous in condemning any indiscriminate copying of European ideas and lifestyles.

The elite were enthusiastic about the study and presentation of African traditions, in part to counter the impact of European contacts and to attack the colonial discourse that undermined Africa. The authenticity of African culture was compared to and contrasted with European culture, which was described as new, different, and not always good for Africans. The elite reformulated the content and meaning of many aspects of indigenous cultures so that they could serve the purpose of modernization: negative elements were edited out of their writings and positive ones became models to be adopted to meet the needs of the new age. Indigenous religions and various aspects of culture occupied a prominent place. Just to mention two well-known cases: Mensah Sarbah presented the basis of Akan religion, while J. E. Casely Hayford wrote on the indigenous institutions of Ghana.[35] Sarbah called for the adaptation of traditional laws and customs to the new age, and he protested changes in taxation, land, and other practices.[36] Virtually all aspects of traditional institutions were covered in an attempt to show the glory of the past, the need for Africa to maintain continuity with its past instead of accepting all the changes introduced by Europeans, and the relevance of socializing a new generation of Africans to their indigenous legacies.

The intellectual passion to understand tradition can be seen as part of a careful African engagement with the later phases of European expansion. The encounter triggered this passion, creating a stronger sense of awareness of the self and one's tradition. Western education and ideas supplied many of the key ideas and issues to employ in looking at African tradition. The African elite began to apply concepts such as the nation, state, race, progress, and nationalism, and to adapt them to local circumstances and old institutions. Like the Europeans, many Africans regarded various aspects of their tradition as static. Those who urged the survival of traditional institutions did not always consider the changes already introduced by Europeans. Some writers were forced to make choices between which elements of the past to retain and which of the new ones to reject. In later years, some chose to write for outsiders, serving as cultural agents to present Africa to Westerners. Jomo Kenyatta's *Facing Mount Kenya* is one of the most notable examples.[37] Kenyatta presented extensive details on the culture of his Kikuyu people before the Europeans began a process of change and destruction.

In Francophone Africa, Négritude was no doubt the most important intellectual and cultural response to European imperialism.[38] It affirmed blackness as a distinct identity on its own and celebrated its contributions to civilization. Négritude became a powerful tool to articulate the ideas of Pan-Africanism that united blacks in different countries. Also, it received wide affirmation as a socialist ideology based on long-established African values. Leading poets and those writing in other genres emerged in the United States, Europe, and the Caribbean to give expression to the Négritudist ideas. Celebrated literary works by Camara Laye and Cheikh Hamidou Kane owed their inspiration to the idea of Négritude. Aimé Césaire of Martinique became one of the most notable figures, a poet of considerable stature whose works are among the most cited in the Pan-Africanist movement.

These writings and discussions led to some concrete actions and political activities, all to minimize the agonies of the European encounter, to improve on the legacies of the colonial era, and to reshape Africa in the image of its elite. Pan-Africanism led to the creation of the Organization of African Unity, motivated by a desire by Africans to "control their destiny"; promote "freedom, equality, justice and dignity"; take steps to develop their economies; and consolidate their independence. Cultural activities were organized in various places and times, in part to counter the spread of European cultures. There was always condemnation of Africans who called for the adoption of Western cultural practices.[39]

The Revolutionaries

Some peculiarities emerged in a number of African colonies, leading to an interpretation of the European encounter in ways that were more radical and combative, and arguably less forgiving of and sympathetic to even the most positive of the changes introduced in the colonial era. Where European settlers existed in large numbers, as in Algeria, Kenya, and southern Africa, relations with Africans took a more violent orientation in part because a large number of Africans lost their land and in part because the settlers were hostile to plans for colonial disengagement after 1945. In the Portuguese colonies, independence was delayed until the 1970s, and was marked by violence and prolonged warfare. In South Africa, the apartheid policy damaged race relations and radicalized the black elite. In these areas, a number of Marxist and radical scholars emerged to offer a perspective different in some ways from those of the cultural nationalists. Notable examples include Sekou Toure of Guinea, Amilcar Cabral of Guinea-Bissau, Agostinho Neto of Angola, Edouardo Mondlane of Mozamibique, and Nelson Mandela and Steve Biko of South Africa. There were of course socialist-oriented thinkers in other areas (e.g., Lamine Senghor, Majhemout Diop and Abdoulaye Ly of Senegal), and a few, such as Lamine Senghor, actually emerged long before the Second World War.[40] As early as the 1920s, Lamine Senghor had questioned the need to collaborate with the French and called for a revolution to liberate all colonial subjects and others living under oppression. Even in countries where the political leaders were more conservative, as in the case of Nigeria, there was always a tiny but vigorous socialist revolutionary group.[41]

Should Africa take to violence to attain political freedom? Many of the revolutionary writers were forced to deal with this question, as is evident in the works of Kwame Nkrumah, Tom Mboya of Kenya, Julius Nyerere of Tanzania, the Rev. Ndabaningi Sithole of Zimbabwe, Nelson Mandela, and Amilcar Cabral of Guinea Bissau. The growing ranks of post–World War II revolutionaries were joined by Frantz Fanon in the 1950s. The critique of the colonial encounter became more devastating, and Fanon's writings were the attractive gospels of the left.[42] Fanon and the South African elite linked violence with overcoming racism and attaining freedom—self-determination would be hard, they argued, in a racialized context, and violence was a means to resolve conflicts and colonial race relations. For want of a better name, a "Fanon school" was created, with an intellectual orientation that combined class and culture to understand the reality of the European encounter. In this line of thinking, the encounter was a form of cultural domination which dehumanized Africans and destroyed many of their institutions. Africans were divided into social and class categories—natives and civilized; elite and peasantry; poor and rich—in a way that promoted antagonistic divisions in society. To the members of the Fanon school, violence was justified not just to terminate European rule but also to restore the dignity of Africans as human beings.

According to the revolutionaries, Africa needed to reject many of the legacies of the European encounter. They were critical of all elites and the social classes they represented, and they envisioned a new society based on different methods of distributing the nation's resources. The writers linked ideology with society, as in the work of Nkrumah.[43] They all advocated a socialist approach to Africa's development, although their suggestions varied widely. Followers of Leopold Senghor regarded Négritude as a form of socialism; Nyerere saw African kinship as a form of socialism; and Kenneth Kaunda came up with a concept of "humanism" that blended Christian principles with African kinship ideology.

A small group, more combative in their writings, accepted orthodox Marxism, and sought to introduce to Africa some forms of Marxist, Marxist-Leninist, and Maoist ideas. Among the most distinguished members of this group are Majhemout Diop and Abdoulaye Ly of Senegal, Nkrumah, Cabral, and Sithole. They all supported the peasantry and the poor in the expectation that colonially created social classes would disappear and that members of the political elite would ultimately give way and lose power to the majority of the population. Nkrumah became hugely famous for his revolutionary ideas on political independence as crucial to Africa's new beginning and growth. He called for a central government with authoritarian powers to revolutionize the economic system, change some of the limitations imposed by extended families, and end corrupt practices.[44]

Like Fanon, the revolutionary writers regarded the end of European power with a great deal of skepticism. They regarded independence as a mere change of personnel—from white officers to black—without the nec-essary changes in economic and political structures that would transform Africa. To the revolutionaries, those Africans who inherited power from Europeans were too trusting of their European allies and too corrupt to become the agents of progress.[45] Nkrumah foresaw that Africans would merely enter a stage of "neocolonialism" if they failed to change the eco-nomic and political structures inherited from the colonial powers. The most celebrated theoretician in this regard has been Cabral, who, like Blyden many years before, linked culture and ideology to formulate ideas about Africa's liberation.[46] Cabral argued that aspects of African culture that stand in the way of socialist revolutions should be abandoned, while he saw nothing wrong in creating a synthesis of "universal cultures" to develop science and technology in Africa. Now the icon of the African Left, Cabral emphasized the need for theories to understand the dangers posed by the European empires in Africa, as well as the crucial role of violence and revolution both to end the empires and to handle their legacies. Cabral regarded imperial-ism as an act of political violence and economic plunder. For Africans to deal with imperialism, Cabral argued that they needed a revolution to free themselves from all forms of European domination. He was dismissive of the elite, whom he regarded as parasites on the society and collaborators with Europeans to exploit their own people—a committed African could only be a revolutionary socialist. Like Fanon, Cabral was not opposed to violence, which he saw as necessary to establish a people-oriented, antico-lonial liberation movement and ideology. Cabral thought that the African elite assimilated into European culture must be re-Africanized by immers-ing them in local culture and insisting on their participation in the libera-tion movement. Very rarely did the revolutionaries have the opportunity to put their ideas into practice because they never attained power; and when they did, the results did not lead to the economic and political develop-ment of their countries.

The Academic Response

In part because of the presentation of many of the aforementioned issues as scholarly and "objective" by the university-based elite, it is important to devote some space to their views, although they tend to repeat what non-academic scholars had said before the 1940s. While they focus on many specific issues and use multiple sources, the political agendas and intellec-tual ideologies remain essentially the same: Blyden and K. O. Dike, the celebrated pioneer historian, were separated in time, but not in motives and aspirations.

The majority of African universities were created after World War II as part of the vigorous attempt by the colonial powers to reform the system and meet some of the demands of the African elite. The climate was one in which Africans were expecting political autonomy and an end to European rule. Consequently, the first generation of African university students as well as the few African scholars radiated considerable enthusiasm. The number of educated Africans began to increase rapidly.[47] The academics inherited vibrant intellectual traditions such as Négritude and an assertive political agenda that sought complete freedom. The scholars built on this, further popularizing the interest in Africa's past and responding to the challenges offered by generations of Eurocentric scholars.[48] The orientation was to liberate scholarship from colonial control: art, literature, music, drama, and other fields were used to promote the precolonial heritage and creative African responses to European culture. The universities began the process of "decolonizing" educational curricula by adapting indigenous culture and ideas to Western academic models. African universities and their products were expected not just to contribute to rapid development but also to enhance the dignity of Africa. They were eager to promote the contributions of Africans to world civilization, as well as the activities of their leaders and political heroes.

Scholarship began to promote cultural liberation from Europe and to show resentment towards colonialism. Négritude continued to supply inspiration to French-speaking scholars, and many of their vibrant ideas can be found in the leading journal, *Présence Africaine.* Everywhere, the writers were influenced by notions of patriotism. Through various genres, the past was presented as innocent, with Africans living a happy life until the Europeans violently intruded in their lives. It was important, many argued, for Africans to find the means to become reconciled with their European conquerors, but they must definitely assert themselves.[49] Wole Soyinka, Chinua Achebe, and Ngugi Wa'Thiong'o, to mention the leading pioneers, demanded immediate cultural independence. Economic planners were also eager to factor indigenous cultures into their development paradigms and planning models. The main argument in all the literary works and economic projects is that Africa has a prestigious humanistic tradition which can be adapted to modern circumstances.

Historians have occupied a leading role in the analysis of the European empires in Africa. Like the nonacademic writers before them, they have been preoccupied with issues of identity and progress.[50] Writing during and immediately after the colonial era, historians regarded Africa's precolonial past as the starting point from which to embark upon any historical reconstruction. In 1953, like many nonacademic writers such as Blyden before him, K. O. Dike, the pioneer academic historian, made a case for the recovery of the history of pre-colonial Africa if contemporary Africans wanted to liberate themselves from European domination and govern themselves.[51]

It was within the context of acquiring self-identity and liberation from European domination that the African scholars developed their perspective on the European expansion. Academic scholars wrote in ways similar to their predecessors or borrowed models and ideas from Islam and Christianity to present indigenous religions and to analyze the nature of indigenous politics and warfare. Also, academic scholars catalogued all the major changes of the colonial era and evaluated them, with approaches ranging from the radical ideas that the colonial experience brought total destruction, to moderate approaches which saw the era as a mere episode in a long history. The most common approach was to draw a balance sheet of negative and positive changes.[52]

Arguably the most ideological response in recent times is the body of literature on Afrocentricity in the United States. If scholars in Africa have limited themselves to presenting the "African perspective," some other scholars have created an Afrocentric movement that puts Africa at the center of all academic discourse. The intellectual hero of the Afrocentric movement is Cheik Anta Diop of Senegal, the famous scholar who emphasized the relevance of the antiquity of Africa, celebrated all the kingdoms Africans created, and credited Africans with considerable mental capacity for creativity. The Afrocentric movement continues to vigorously critique the European conquest of Africa and its consequences according to an outline provided by Diop, who argued that Europeans dismembered African nations, overthrew and destroyed their civilizations, and created a false notion of progress.

Conclusion

To be sure, the responses by the African elite did not cover the entire range of the African encounter with the European empires. The members of the elite, however, supplied the texts with which to understand the complexity of this encounter. But they were not just interpreting their age to generate texts for future historians; they were also trying to acquire power. Western education, even when limited to the ability to read and write, empowered many. The vocabulary of politics increased, politics focused on anticolonial activities, and aspirations revolved solely around the issues of nationalism and development—mobility for the individual and progress for the society. Many used the engagement with the European empires for self-actualization. In realizing their own goals and ultimately acquiring prestige and power, the African elite were doing some of the very same things for which they criticized Europeans. If Crummell wanted the use of English and Horton advocated the spread of English culture, it was partly to create a tiny minority that would dominate others.

Although the elite criticized the European powers, the nationalism unleashed by colonial rule rewarded them in many ways. That self-interest was part of their motivation is hard to deny.[53] Even the most extreme demands for Africanization did not go as far as to suggest that Europeans should give power back to the indigenous rulers when independence approached. If the Europeans undermined the power of these local chiefs, the elite were to do the same when they found themselves in power. The demands of many among the elite—economic development, formal education, political reforms—were mostly based on their ambitions for power and privilege as a Westernized group. Not only did they use European experience and a European style of journalism to fight the empire, they also constructed a notion of progress based on European standards. Without the power and privilege of Western education, the elite would have been unable to acquire dominance. Thus, we encounter in the elite and their writings evidence both of idealism and of contradictions: what they wanted for their society and the narrow self-interests that guided them. To the Africans whom they represented, the idealism was impressive, especially as it promised them many good things of life following the dismantling of the European empires. But as independence became a reality, the contradictions manifested by the elite became part of the problems that compromised the post-colonial world order, which undermined their ability to implement the ideas they had forcefully expressed in previous years.

The sources and range of ideas were rich and multiple. Some drew ideas from the Western body of knowledge to which they were exposed. The academics regarded themselves as part of a growing community of scholars, thus sharing and debating with their colleagues in different parts of the world. Even the nonacademic intellectuals drew from their Western backgrounds and disciplines, such as history, theology, and law, to understand Africa. Some were connected with the Pan-Africanist ideas of Marcus Garvey and W. E. B. Du Bois, as in the case of Kwame Nkrumah.[54] European and American books, essays, and media strongly influenced the African elite. The elite were aggressive in appropriating European intellectual ideas, even to explain the traditions they claimed as theirs. Racist ideas were attacked, while ideas regarded as useful to liberate Africa from Europe were appropriated. The early pioneers drew from Christian liberal traditions of equality and the promotion of commerce and individualism. Their successors were secularists who broadened the range of their ideas and sources, which angered the European officials who regarded them as dangerous. European ideas of nationalism and development took deep root and were forcefully expressed by the elite, contributing to the fall of the European empires in Africa.

Most were certainly impressed with indigenous ideas and institutions, even when they advocated change along Western lines. They created a synthesis of local and external ideas to understand the European empires. In so doing, whether they accepted or rejected Western culture and changes, they relied on many aspects of imported ideas and philosophy. Only a few among the elite advocated a total adoption of indigenous cultures, although they all rejected any suggestion of complete imitation of European culture. The elite used their power to create a cultural synthesis that they hoped would modernize Africa. However, there were differences of opinions on how to adapt European cultures to Africa. Africanus Horton made a case in the 1860s for the adoption of European culture in a politically independent Africa. Blyden used the problems of African societies and cultures to justify European imperialism. To further complicate the issue, writers who focused on their ethnic groups, such as the Yoruba Samuel Johnson, wrote in such a way as to justify ethnic nationalism in modern plural societies.[55] There was a great deal of ambiguity in all the projects of cultural synthesis. What each author wanted was an arbitrary selection from old and imported cultures—for instance, one person might praise polygyny, another might condemn it; one might suggest the adoption of Christianity, another the adoption of Islam. This ambiguity resulted in part from the problems of defining culture and identifying its contents, not to mention the difficulty of constructing a new society in an era of rapid changes.

Clashes between the elite and Europeans were normal. If Europeans had come to Africa with the notion of racial superiority and the so-called mission of spreading civilization among so-called primitive people, the majority of African elite members behaved as if they had no other option than to challenge them. Indeed, by the 1940s, the elite had come to recognize that all the colonial powers were vulnerable. If the Europeans had thought that Africans only needed limited skills and education to work in subordinate positions, the African elite sought the means to create greater economic opportunities and prestige. If Europeans believed that they had little to learn from their African subjects—the traffic of ideas was expected to move in one direction, from the superior to the inferior—the struggles for independence and violent liberation movements were to shock them.

The elite were interested both in evaluating the impact of the European empire and at the same time seeking ways for Africa to develop and benefit from the lessons of the encounter. No one denied the changes—everyone had lived through them. And those who survived the colonial period not only adapted to the changes, but they also began to add to them in ways that built on the European legacy. Televisions, Coca-Cola, and thousands of imported items are part of what now define contemporary Africa. From the modern economy to politics, the legacy of the past is plainly visible. Africans might not have been happy with what the colonial civil service accomplished, but they wanted the service to remain to be under their control. Western-style democracies, labor organizations, architecture, banking and commercial practices, and many other aspects of Western culture have become accepted. Even the notorious colonial army was inherited, but it immediately became, after independence, the most powerful of all the modern institutions, with ambitious military officers who have never hesitated to organize coups and countercoups. The educated elite benefited the most from the encounter with the West—they received a Western education; they inherited power; and they accepted many Western ideas, even becoming committed to using many of them to change Africa. By accepting modernization, they had to understand Europe and adopt many of its standards.

Regarding the opportunity for Africa to benefit from the European encounter, opinions varied widely, but three patterns emerged. A tiny minority called for full-blown Westernization, that is, Africa should fully adopt Western institutions, technology, and values. Another minority went to another extreme: Africa should restore all its traditional institutions, notably its family practices, religions, laws, and customs. The majority tended to call for a careful blend of the indigenous with selected foreign practices. The ideas of the majority seek to reform Africa. In seeking reforms, the African elite may be anti-colonial, but definitely not anti-modernization. The elite accepted, and at the same time rejected, many of the changes associated with European expansion in Africa. But because they are not anti-modernization, the African elite, old and new, inevitably have to deal with the changes and legacies that accompanied the European expansion. Today, the concept of African consciousness is not hostile to the adoption of Western pop culture, a thinking that has expanded the access point between Africans and Western countries. Indeed, pop culture has enabled ordinary Africans to circumvent the state and schools to make contacts with Western cultures.

In recent times, whenever the elite are disappointed with the performance of African leaders and they see abject poverty around them, they do not hesitate to criticize the leaders,[56] and some even regard the colonial era as the golden age of Africa during the twentieth century. A few analysts, certainly depressed by the conditions in Africa, have even called for the recolonization of Africa. Today, we cannot criticize European imperialism in Africa without also criticizing the African elite that managed the post-colonial world. Many African elite now distance themselves from military generals and other members of the military in the formal political system. If we are now characterizing the current problems of Africa in part as a failure of the intellectuals (in particular, those attached to state power) and their imagination for any number of reasons (inadequate recognition of the pitfalls of nationalism, neocolonialism, corruption, development, and the various obstacles to Pan-Africanism), scholarly attention should also make more visible the non-elite voices, histories, and movements, without relegating non-Western alternatives and traditions to static categories.

Notes

1. Although the context and themes identified in the chapter are broad, most examples are drawn from west Africa.

2. On the career and writings of this unsung writer, see Hakim Adi, "Bandele Omoniyi: A Neglected Nigerian Nationalist," *African Affairs* 90 (1991): 581–65.

3. See Philip D. Curtin, *The Image of Africa: British Ideas and Action, 1780–1850* (Madison: University of Wisconsin Press, 1964).

4. Michael J. C. Echeruo, *Victorian Lagos: Aspects of Nineteenth Century Lagos Life* (London: Macmillan, 1977); Kristin Mann, *Marrying Well: Marriage, Status, and Social Change among the Educated Elite in Colonial Lagos* (Cambridge: Cambridge University Press, 1985); and Karin Barber and P. F. de Moraes Farias, eds., *Self-Assertion and Brokerage: Early Cultural Nationalism in West Africa* (Birmingham, England: Birmingham University Center of African Studies, 1990).

5. Robert W. July, *The Origins of Modern African Thought: Its Development in West Africa during the Nineteenth and Twentieth Centuries* (New York: Praeger, 1967). See also Henry S. Wilson, ed., *Origins of West African Nationalism* (London: Macmillan, 1969); and Rina L. Okonkwo, *Heroes of West African Nationalism* (Enugu, Nigeria: Delta, 1985).

6. On Horton, see Christopher Fyfe, *Africanus Horton, 1835–1883: West African Scientist and Patriot* (New York: Oxford University Press, 1972); and Davidson Nicol, ed., *Black Nationalism in Africa, 1867: Extracts from the Political, Educational, Scientific, and Medical Writings of Africanus Horton* (New York: Africana, 1969).

7. See J. F. Ade Ajayi, *Christian Missions in Nigeria, 1841–1891: The Making of a New Elite* (London: Longman, 1966) and his "Nineteenth Century Origins of Nigerian Nationalism," in *Tradition and Change in Africa: The Essays of J. F. Ade Ajayi*, ed. Toyin Falola (Trenton, N.J.: Africa World Press, 2000), 69–84.

8. See Jean Herskovits Kopytoff, *A Preface to Modern Nigeria: The "Sierra Leonians" in Yoruba, 1830–1890* (Madison: University of Wisconsin Press, 1965); and E. A. Ayandele, *The Missionary Impact on Modern Nigeria, 1842–1914: A Social and Political Analysis* (London: Longman, 1966).

9. See Alexander Crummell, *The Future of Africa, Being Addresses, Sermons, Etc., Delivered in the Republic of Liberia* (1861; reprint New York: Negro University Press, 1969). On Crummell, see Wilson J. Moses, *Alexander Crummell: A Study in Civilization and Discontent* (Oxford: Oxford University Press, 1989).

10. The literature on the changes is large. For an overview, see Toyin Falola, "Africa," in *Cambridge Illustrated History of the British Empire*, ed. P. J. Marshall (Cambridge: Cambridge University Press, 1996), 347–56; and Toyin Falola, ed., *Colonial Africa, 1885–1939* (Durham: Carolina Academic Press, 2002).

11. Among Horton's numerous writings, see *West African Countries and Peoples, British and Native* (1868; reprint, Nendeln/Lichtenstein: Kraus, 1970); and *Letters on the Political Condition of the Gold Coast* (1870; reprint, London: Cass, 1970).

12. Among Blyden's leading works are *Christianity, Islam, and the Negro Race*, 2nd ed. (London: W. B. Whittingham, 1888); *The African Problem and the Method of Its Solution . . . Delivered at the Seventy-third Anniversary of the American Colonization Society* (Washington, D.C.: Gibson Bros., 1890); *The African Society and Miss Mary H. Kingsley* (London: C. M. Phillips, 1905); *African Life and Customs* (1908; reprint London: African Publication Society, 1969). On the analysis of Blyden's work, see, among others, Edith Holden, *Blyden of Liberia* (New York: Vantage, 1966); Thomas W. Livingston, *Education and Race: A Biography of Edward Wilmot Blyden* (San Francisco: Glendessary, 1975); and Hollis R. Lynch, *Edward Wilmot Blyden: Pan-Negro Patriot, 1832–1912* (London: Oxford University Press, 1967).

13. See Akinsola Akiwowo, "Racialism and Shifts in the Mental Orientation of Black People in West Africa and the Americas, 1856 to 1956," *Phylon* 31 (1970): 256–64; G. Spiller, ed., *Inter-racial Problems* (London: P. S. King, 1911); and Franz Boas, "Fallacies of Racial Inferiority," *Current History* 25 (February 1927): 672–82.

14. On the books and ideas to which Africans responded, see Douglas A. Lorimer, *Colour, Class, and the Victorians: English Attitudes to the Negro in the Mid-Nineteenth Century* (Leicester, England: Leicester University Press, 1978); and Christine Bolt, *Victorian Attitudes to Race* (Toronto: University of Toronto Press, 1971).

15. See J. E. Casely Hayford, *Ethiopia Unbound: Studies in Race Emancipation* (1911; reprint with an introduction by F. Nnabuenyi Ugonna, London: Cass, 1969).

16. Quoted in Hollis R. Lynch, *Black Spokesman: Selected Published Writings of Edward Wilmot Blyden* (London: Cass, 1971), 142.

17. On the relationship between the colonial powers and African chiefs, see Patrick Cole, *Modern and Traditional Elites in the Politics of Lagos* (Cambridge: Cambridge University Press, 1975); David Kimble, *A Political History of Ghana: The Rise of Gold Coast Nationalism, 1850–1928* (Oxford: Clarendon Press, 1965); and Olufemi Vaughan, *Nigerian Chiefs: Traditional Power in Modern Politics, 1890s–1990s* (Rochester, N.Y.: University of Rochester Press, 2000).

18. See Jean Comaroff and John Comaroff, *Of Revelation and Revolution: Christianity, Colonialism, and Consciousness in South Africa*, vol. 1 (Chicago: University of Chicago Press, 1991); and Bhekizizwe Peterson, *Monarchs, Missionaries and African Intellectuals: African Theatre and the Unmaking of Colonial Marginality* (Trenton, N.J.: Africa World Press, 2000).

19. On the career of these men, see the books by E. A. Ayandele, *Holy Johnson: Pioneer of African Nationalism, 1836–1917* (London: Cass, 1970); and *A Visionary of the African Church: Mojola Agbebi, 1860–1917* (Nairobi: East Africa Publishing House, 1971). On the development of independent churches, see James B. Webster, *The African Churches among the Yoruba, 1888–1922* (Oxford: Clarendon Press, 1964).

20. On the activities of these political leaders, see Robert W. July and Peter Benson, eds., *African Culture and Intellectual Leaders and the Development of the New African Nations* (New York: Rockefeller Foundation, 1982). On some of their selected writings, see Wilson, ed., *Origins of West African Nationalism*; J. Ayodele Langley, *Ideologies of Liberation in Black Africa, 1856–1970* (London: Rex Collins, 1979); and Molefi Kete Asante and Abu S. Abarry, eds., *African Intellectual Heritage: A Book of Sources* (Philadelphia: Temple University Press, 1996).

21. See Thomas Hodgkin, *African Nationalism in Colonial Africa* (London: Muller, 1956); James S. Coleman, *Nigeria: Background to Nationalism* (Berkeley: University of California Press, 1958); Rupert Emerson, *From Empire to Nation: The Rise to Self-Assertion of Asian and African Peoples* (Boston: Beacon, 1960); Rupert Emerson and Martin Kilson, eds., *The Political Awakening of Africa* (Englewood Cliffs, N.J.: Prentice-Hall, 1965); and George W. Shepperson, *The Politics of African Nationalism* (New York: Praeger, 1962).

22. See Nancy Cunard, ed., *Negro Anthology* (1934; reprint, New York: Negro University Press, 1969).

23. For a critique of the ideas of race espoused by Blyden and other pioneer writers, see Kwame Anthony Appiah, *In My Father's House: Africa in the Philosophy of Culture* (New York: Oxford University Press, 1992).

24. See Joseph Renner Maxwell, *The Negro Question or Hints for the Physical Improvement of the Negro* (London: 1882).

25. See Akinsola Akiwowo, "The Place of Mojola Agbebi in the African Nationalist Movements: 1890–1917," *Phylon* (Atlanta) 26 (1965): 122–39.

26. Rev. Mojola Agbebi, *Inaugural Sermon Delivered at the Celebration of the First Anniversary of the "African Church," Lagos, West Africa, December 21, 1902* (New York: Edgar Howorth, 1903).

27. Ibid.

28. See Nnamdi Azikiwe, *Renascent Africa* (1937; reprint, London: Frank Cass, 1968).

29. See Philip Garigue, "The West African Students' Union," *Africa* 23 (Jan. 1953): 55–69; Hans Kohn and Wallace Sokolsky, *African Nationalism in the Twentieth Century* (Princeton, N.J.: Van Nostraud, 1965); Hakim Adi, *West Africans in Britain, 1900–1960: Nationalism, Pan-Africanism, and Communism* (London: Lawrence and Wishart, 1998); J. S. Gundara and I. Duffield, eds, *Essays on the History of Blacks in Britain* (Aldershot, England: Avebury, 1992); and Effiong E. B. Edunam, "Unaccredited Ambassadors: Nigerian Students as Africa's Spokesmen in the United States, 1920–1950," *Calabar Historical Journal* 3 (1985): 136–53.

30. Obafemi Awolowo, *Path to Nigerian Freedom* (London: Faber, 1947). On the career of this successful and distinguished statesman, see Toyin Falola et al., eds., *Chief Obafemi Awolowo: The End of an Era?* (Ile-Ife: Obafemi Awolowo University Press, 1988).

31. See Toyin Falola, *Development Planning and Decolonization in Nigeria* (Gainesville: University Press of Florida, 1996).

32. The linkages of these issues, as well as the various attempts have been extensively discussed in Toyin Falola, *Nationalism and African Intellectuals* (Rochester, N.Y.: University of Rochester Press, 2001).

33. Walter Rodney's book became the most influential in this line of thinking: *How Europe Underdeveloped Africa* (London: Bogle-l'Ouverture Publications, 1972).

34. See Philip S. Zachernuk, *Colonial Subjects: An African Intelligentsia and Atlantic Ideas* (Charlottesville: University Press of Virginia, 2000), chapter 4.

35. J. E. Casely Hayford, *Gold Coast Native Institutions with Thoughts upon a Healthy Imperial Policy for the Gold Coast and Ashanti* (1903; reprint London: Cass, 1970).

36. John Mensah Sarbah, *Fanti National Constitution: A Short Treatise on the Constitution and Government of the Fanti, Asanti, and Other Akan Tribes of West Africa* (1906; 2nd ed., with new introduction by H. R. Lynch, London: Cass, 1968).

37. Jomo Kenyatta, *Facing Mount Kenya: The Tribal Life of the Gikuyu* (London, 1938, reprint, New York: Vintage Books, 1965).

38. For details, see Abiola Irele, *The African Experience in Literature and Ideology* (London: Heinemann, 1981); Christopher Miller, *Theories of Africans: Francophone Literature and Anthropology in Africa* (Chicago: University of Chicago Press, 1990); and Isaac James Mowoe and Richard Bjornson, eds., *Africa and the West: The Legacies of Empire* (Westport, Conn.: Greenwood Press, 1986).

39. See Augustus Adebayo, *White Man in Black Skin* (Ibadan: Spectrum Press, 1981). For an analysis of a number of leading "cultural studies," see Peter Benson, *"Black Orpheus," "Transition," and Modern Cultural Awakening in Africa* (Berkeley and Los Angeles: University of California Press, 1986).

40. For the most accessible compilation of selected works by the members of this group, see J. Ayodele Langley, *Ideologies of Liberation in Black Africa, 1856–1970.*

41. See Tajudeen Abdulraheem and Adebayo Olukoshi, "The Left in Nigerian Politics and the Struggle for Socialism, 1945–1985," *Review of African Political Economy* 38 (1986): 64–80.

42. Most notably *The Wretched of the Earth,* trans C. Farrington (New York: Grove, 1968).

43. See Kwame Nkrumah, *Class Struggle in Africa* (New York: International Publishers, 1970).

44. Kwame Nkrumah, *Africa Must Unite* (London: Heinemann, 1963; reprint, New York: International Publishers, 1972).

45. On the critique of the African power elite, see Bjorn Beckman, "Imperialism and the 'National Bourgeoisie,'" *Review of African Political Economy* 22 (1981): 5–19; and Segun Osoba, "The Deepening Crisis of the Nigerian National Bourgeoisie," *Review of African Political Economy* 13 (1978): 63–77.

46. Amilcar Cabral, *Return to the Source: Selected Speeches by Amilcar Cabral* (New York: Monthly Review Press, 1973).

47. Peter C. Lloyd, ed., *The New Elites in Tropical Africa* (London: Oxford University Press, 1966); and Apollos Nwauwa, *Imperialism, Academe and Nationalism: Britain and University Education for Africans, 1860–1960* (London: Frank Cass, 1996).

48. For the context in which the pioneer African academics operated, see V. Y. Mudimbe, *The Invention of Africa: Gnosis, Philosophy, and the Order of Knowledge* (Bloomington: Indiana University Press, 1988).

49. For this kind of intellectual orientation in many colonial situations, see, among others, Bill Ashcroft, Gareth Griffiths, and Helen Tiffin, *The Empire Writes Back: Theory and Practice in Post-Colonial Literatures* (New York: Routledge, 1989); George W. Stocking, Jr., ed., *Colonial Situations* (Madison: University of Wisconsin Press, 1991); Homi Bhabha, *The Location of Culture* (London: Routledge, 1994.); Partha Chatterjee, *Nationalist Thought and the Colonial World: A Derivative Discourse?* (London: Zed, 1986); and Nicholas B. Dirks, ed., *Colonialism and Culture* (Ann Arbor: University of Michigan Press, 1992).

50. See Caroline Neale, *Writing "Independent" History: African Historiography, 1960–1980* (Westport, Conn.: Greenwood, 1985).

51. K. O. Dike, "African History and Self-Government," *West Africa,* no. 1882, March 21, 1953, p. 251.

52. For representative opinions, see Toyin Falola, ed., *Nigeria and Britain: Economic Exploitation or Development?* (London: Zed, 1987); J. F. Ade Ajayi, "Colonialism: An Episode in African History," in Falola, ed., *Tradition and Change in Africa,* 165–74; and Adu Boahen, *African Perspectives on Colonialism* (Baltimore, Md.: Johns Hopkins University Press, 1987). For the most elaborate case studies, see the eight-volume UNESCO series on Africa.

53. For the most devastating critique of the educated elite, see E. A. Ayandele, *The Educated Elite in the Nigerian Society* (Ibadan: Ibadan University Press, 1974).

54. See J. Ayodele Langley, "Garveyism and African Nationalism," *Race* 11 (1969): 157–72; and his extended work, *Pan Africanism and Nationalism in West Africa, 1900–1945: A Study in Ideology and Social Classes* (Oxford: Clarendon, 1973). Also, Rina L. Okonkwo, "The Garvey Movement in British West Africa," *Journal of African History* 21 (1980): 105–17.

55. On Johnson and his influential work, see Toyin Falola, ed., *The Pioneer, Patriot and Patriarch: Samuel Johnson and the Yoruba People* (Madison: Program of African Studies, University of Wisconsin-Madison, 1993).

56. See Chinua Achebe, *The Trouble with Nigeria* (London: Heinemann, 1983); and Basil Davidson, *The Black Man's Burden: Africa and the Curse of the Nation-State* (New York: Times Books, 1992).

3

CULTURAL IDENTITY AND DEVELOPMENT

No state, not even an infant one, is willing to appear before the world as a bare political frame. Each would be clothed in a cultural garb symbolic of its aims and ideal being.[1]

. . . the passion with which the native intellectuals defend the existence of their national culture may be a source of amazement, but those who condemn this exaggerated passion are strangely apt to forget that their own psyche and their own selves are conveniently sheltered behind a French or German culture which has given full proof of its existence and which is uncontested.[2]

. . . development is modernization minus dependency. . . . African culture is central to this process of reducing dependency in the dialectic of modernization. . . . What is needed is more of modernity and less of "the Western spring." A non-Western route to modernity is possible for Africa—provided African culture is fully mobilized as an ally in the enterprise.[3]

There are two ways to lose oneself: by a walled segregation in the particular or by a dilution in the 'universal.'[4]

Such commonly expressed notions as "the cultural dimension of development," "the cultural framework to guide development," "tradition and modernity," and "cultural development," to mention but a few major ones, reflect the analytical and practical linkages that scholars and policymakers have attempted to establish between culture and development in order to assert that culture cannot be ignored in the discourse on development.

49

Figure 2. Culture: An enduring legacy. Ilorin, Nigeria.

Scholars who call into question the need for cultural retention or such evidence of the survival of tradition constitute a minority.

In Africa and elsewhere, culture shapes the perception of Self and the interaction between people and their environment. It explains habits such as why people respect old age, have many children, take care of their children, work hard, take to polygyny, and support male dominance. It justifies work ethics: for example, the desire for money without having to work for it; gender division of labor; and consumption habits and accumulative styles. It defines norms of behavior, such as inter- and intragenerational relations, codes of conduct for holders of political offices, and the difference between gift-giving and corruption. It defines boundaries among people, as in the case of gender roles or relations between the poor and the rich. As a means of communication, it enables understanding, and when a foreign language is imposed, it serves to consolidate domination. It is the basis of identity and ultimately of development. Who are Africans? What are their future goals? Are they different from others? Most functions of culture, as well as the various components of culture itself, try to project an identity. Development, as it is variously defined, tries to incorporate, manipulate, and draw from cultural identity. Cultural identity, in its formation, involves the multiple issues of history, environment, values, social stratification, knowledge, power, and wealth, which are also the domain of development.

Policies of change, in order to endure and be effective, must recognize the power of history, tradition, and cultural institutions. Development has to be grounded in culture—it should capture the essence of people's lives, profit from the creative and economic benefits unleashed by cultural production, and transform traditions and institutions that may create obstacles to progress. Social and cultural factors, the so-called noneconomic forces, do drive the economic. Progress cannot be confined to the rise in the gross national product, expansion of road networks, new technologies, etc., without considering their consequences on culture and society. Conversely, a major change in technology can reshape intellectual and spiritual beliefs and transform other cultural values. The consequences can be both positive and negative: they may generate "cultural losses" or "cultural added value."

How can Africa develop without losing its identity? How can Africa use its identity to develop? Can it construct progress without a vision of its past, or can it link its future development with its historical traditions? Can it ignore its legacies of domination in dealing with the wider world? Where does its historical path since the fifteenth century lead? To what degree should imposed changes be accepted? This set of interrelated questions has dominated African intellectual thought since the nineteenth century. Africa wants to modernize without losing its cultural identity; it wants its culture to survive and progress at the same time. It has always considered the means to determine the future by turning to its past and by using its culture to operate in a competitive global setting. It seeks to relate to the

Figure 3. Celebrating African cultures through art. Calabar, Nigeria.

rest of the world by offering something other than raw materials. It hopes to break dependence by turning to culture for liberation and challenging external imposition. When solely market-oriented external ideas and programs are imposed, people are known to have resisted, not because they do not desire change, as is often alleged, but because the change cannot be reconciled with their established practices.

Three themes loom large in this discussion. The first is how indigenous patterns of intergroup relations in precolonial Africa have been used to construct an identity for Africa and create the concept of a relevant past. For as long as Africans speak of "tradition" and "culture," there is no escape from this past. If analysts of the modern era focus on doom, those who study the African past dwell on its great achievements and capacity for survival, progress, and self-transformation. Privileging the past or cultural identity does not assume any static notion of tradition or institutions, which are embedded in history and show evidence of adaptation and change.

The second is how foreign contacts and domination have created dislocations, new realities, and alternative values. The slave trade and colonial rule reduced the capacity of African culture to contribute to development. As Africa became subordinated, it was simultaneously assaulted at two levels: it was regarded as a continent without history and culture, and alien values were introduced. Cultural difference was used to justify colonial invasion while the imposition of Western culture consolidated domination. When an agenda of modernization was embarked upon after 1940, African culture was treated as separate from its development, an obstacle to the introduction of new ideas, skills, science, technology, and management. In an extroverted development model, alien ideas were introduced while indigenous ones were condemned.

The preoccupation of Africans has been to regain that which was denied, to modify that which was introduced, to reconnect culture to development, to become heirs of the past in order to create a better future, and to defend the "particular" from the attack by the "universal." Like all colonized people, Africans use culture as a tool of resistance against imperialism.[5] African leaders and intellectuals expect themselves to be vanguards of cultural change, to protect the continent from Western cultural imperialism, and to promote the preservation of culture.

The third theme I will pursue is a set of recommendations on how to use culture for identity and development in the decades ahead. The section will draw from past history and contemporary reality to identify some broad issues that require attention.

The search for cultural relevance and development is a legitimate one. The twentieth century ended, leaving Africa behind in terms of development, and preparing it for greater challenges in the twenty-first. In the era of post–Cold War politics, Africa is becoming more and more marginalized in global concerns. Within the continent itself, the quest for stability, consensus, development, and peace imposes severe burdens. Values, indigenous and foreign, combine with differences in religion and ethnicity to create problems for some countries.

The language of intellectual discourse suggests that there is a big crisis of cultural identity and development. This may imply that a previous identity has been lost or alternatively that none has ever existed. It is true that the rewards of cultural identity are many: they provide a set of values upon which to base policies; the continent can represent a difference as the basis for dealing with other continents; and if the identity comes with dignity, Africa's stature gets enhanced. The contrary, a lack of identity, is worse: the continent remains a mere geographical expression, opens itself up for more cultural bastardization, and exposes its citizens to degradation.

There is yet the other issue of how different countries within a huge continent can be expected to develop a common cultural identity, when each has its own internal problems and differences, in addition to diver-

Figure 4. The power of music. Abeokuta, Nigeria.

gent contacts that impose additional diversity. However, the number of countries now, or nations in the precolonial past, should not prevent the search for a continental identity as long as it is positive and contributes to the development of the continent. There is more profit in working toward a continental identity in addition to the national. I think it is, however, far more important to seek the means to minimize the conflicts arising from competing identities within each country and the continent as a whole.

Cultural and Historical Foundations of Identity

Today, the bond of poverty, long historical antiquity, the experience of imperialism, and the ongoing assault on Africa's collective dignity since the trans-Atlantic slave trade, to mention but a few, are part of the shared heritage of the continent and the factors which have shaped its character and defined the problems of identity and development.

In its very long precolonial history, the most important constituents of African identity were cultural in spite of the multiplicity of ethnic groups. To be sure, there was no single African culture, but there were cultures that shared many similar assumptions. Neither was there a single African nation, but a variety of nations that shared certain similar characteristics. The starting point in a discussion like this must be the framework of society. The unifying feature in most of precolonial Africa was the concept of the community. Since the time that Jomo Kenyatta wrote his famous *Facing Mount Kenya* until today, one author after another has emphasized the centrality of the ethos of community and kinship.[6] It is true that the ethos has been exaggerated and romanticized in many writings, but its importance cannot be denied. Social cohesion and intimate relations between individuals were the key to living in a society. In contrast to the individualism of the present age, "to be human is to belong to the community, and to do so involves participating in the beliefs, ceremonies, rituals and festivals of that community."[7] The community fulfilled an integrative function.

There is abundant data to demonstrate shared cultural values and institutions and to show the extensive interactions between peoples and incorporation of one group's cultural values by others, both of which reveal that culture was integral to the construction of African identity. Only a few examples are possible here. In many places, the belief in spirits, witchcraft, "evil eye," and a host of gods was common. Names and methods of worship were different, but many assumptions were common, such as the role of ancestors, the power of spirits, divination, and the worship of gods associated with nature. In folktales, the spider and the tortoise stories were common in many parts of west and east Africa, as were those of the hare and antelope in the Sudan. The themes revolved around the ogre, infant prodigy, trickster, and life dilemma. Stories of origins and other historical aspects of folktales reveal a similar attempt to explain the evolution of kingship and kinship, authority, and various political and social institutions. In historical tales, the roles assigned to hunters, warriors, and supernatural forces in creation are identical in many areas.

There is substantial data on material culture. Drums fulfilled similar functions in various societies. Dress forms were identical in some areas. For instance, in east and west Africa the wrapper and the *poncho* (*mboubou* in Senegal, *buba* in Yoruba, *danshiki* in Fulani, *babban riga* in Hausa) were worn in most places. Masquerades were found in many areas, even if their forms and functions differed. They represented ancestors and spirits, and they were used to fight witchcraft; in east Africa, they played a key role in initiation and circumcision ceremonies, and were associated with warfare, entertainment, and politics.

In the attempt to explain the similarities in many aspects of African culture, emphasis must be placed on such factors as intergroup relations made possible by trade, warfare, diplomatic relations, and migration. Take trade, for instance: because of geographical differences, there was a limit to what could be produced in an area or region. Consequently, extensive trade networks within the continent distributed the goods of one area to others. To serve trade and promote intergroup relations, lines of communication were developed. Southern Africa and the Congo/Zaire basin were connected, and both were linked with the forest belt of west Africa. The Nile Valley shared linkages with central and eastern Africa, while north Africa and west Africa were connected by the trans-Saharan trade.

Migrations within the continent provided both unity and identity. Spurred by population increase, dynastic rivalries, the search for economic opportunities, ecological changes, and so forth, a large number of people chose, or were forced, to relocate, in the process of which they contributed to the diffusion of culture and the emergence of new cultures. Important developments, such as the movement of population from the Sahara to north Africa, the spread of the Bantu language, the Oromo movements to Ethiopia in the sixteenth and seventeenth centuries, the Fulani dispersal in West Africa, and the Luo migrations to Uganda and Kenya from the Nile Valley, all had significant consequences for unity and identity. The migrations also demonstrated the fact that mobility and interregional communication were common.

The character and organization of the states made interactions within a state and between states possible. Within the state, the family, age-grade societies, and secret societies promoted interactions. Between states, the boundaries were cultural frontiers through which ideas and people were freely exchanged.

Precolonial states sought deliberate means to achieve identity. Traditions of common origins, stories of migrations, the legends about the emergence of dynastic groups and ruling houses were *political agenda* and *manifestos* to achieve identity, integration, and stability. When many states were connected in this identity construction, the motive was to create a much broader framework of relationship. Origins of dynasties and the borrowing of political institutions, the two most common manifestations of this construction, were effective in creating identity over wide regions in the continent. Finally, the establishment of the big empires and kingdoms contributed to the spread of languages and ideas and to extensive relations among the people. The big states and empires, built and sustained by high profile politics and diplomacy, imposed political hegemony and a "universalist" ideology.

External Impact

Over the years, Africa has been influenced, indeed transformed, by its contacts with other parts of the world, notably Asia and Europe. Among the most notable issues are the slave trade, the spread of Islam and Christianity, and the imposition of colonial rule. Each of these influenced African cultures and development capacity by bringing new ethos and values and introducing new systems of interpersonal relations, domination, and exploitation.

The slave trade was a sustained assault on Africa's dignity, identity, and development. It turned the continent into a victim of rape and plunder. Not only did the slave trade introduce the beginning of the marginalization of Africa, it greatly dented the image of the continent up until the very recent era. The personality and color of a black person become weak credentials in negotiating and asserting autonomy. In many areas of the world, to be black is to be inferior and unintelligent. Any meaningful search for identity must include the recovery of this dignity and the assertion of collective self-worth.

The role of the Arabs and the rise and spread of Islam after the seventh century created a new heritage and sub-identity of its own. Beginning in the seventh century, Arab groups invaded parts of north Africa and migrated to the Sahara, the Nile Valley, and west Africa. The consequences included the spread of Arab culture and Islam. So strong was the impact that Islam displaced indigenous religions in many places and Arabic became an influential language in some areas. Where Arabic and Islam have been strong, they have created conditions for unity and identity based on an Islamic ideology.

Christianity has spread rapidly since the mid-nineteenth century. As its rapid spread coincided with the colonial regimes, the two have been lumped together in some literature as imperialist agencies. Christian missionary organizations provided the foundations of the modern formal education system. Western education produced a new elite that became influential in virtually all sectors of society, and that encouraged the spread of Western culture. Where it was able to establish a strong influence, it introduced many new ways of looking at the world and destroyed or modified many aspects of indigenous practices. Like Islam, Christianity demanded its own loyalty and alliance.

In countries where Islam and Christianity compete, as in the case of the Sudan and Nigeria, the problems of stability and identity have been compounded by rivalries for religious ascendancy, resulting in the desire for religious control or even for turning the state into a theocracy and imposing a religious ideology. So dangerous has the competition become that the survival of a place like the Sudan is severely threatened. The imperialism of both religions is also part of the problem of the search for identity in contemporary Africa. These two religions have constituted the greatest threat to the survival of indigenous religions. As much as possible, they suppress indigenous religions, criticize the use of their symbols, and fight against their revival.[8] In cases where indigenous religions are closely bound up with communal lives, the opposition by Islam and Christianity has also meant an attack on local customs and culture.

Colonial rule reconfigured various aspects of African identity and added many new dimensions to patterns of intergroup relations and the linkages between Africa and the wider world. Colonialism was harsh, tragic, and brutal. Colonial conquests brought subjugation and loss of sovereignty. The partition of Africa was, at the same time, a partition of identity. Nations were divided, often with dire consequences for the economy and society. Today, areas that were united in the last century are now tragically divided, sometimes hostile to one another, and located within different cultural streams. This is true of the Ewe, Yoruba, Azande, Masaai, and the Bakongo. In many areas with international boundaries that divide groups, there are constant frontier tensions.

Old identities were broken, as previous kingdoms, empires, and communities were divided and framed into new groupings. Inherited differences have been allowed to flourish, and the divided groups compete with one another. As independence drew nearer, hostilities intensified because of the desire of the elite of each region to control power and because of the politics of resource allocation. The constitutions that the colonial regimes bequeathed were very weak in resolving ethnic differences. Political parties were organized on a regional basis, and the politics of winner-take-all was accentuated.

Many aspects of colonial policies created problems. The disparity in social and educational provisions encouraged dissension and conflicts. Much cultural disintegration occurred because of the disruptive consequences of religion, the imposition of alien languages, movement to the cities, and the spread of wage income. Colonialism was destructive of culture and identity. Either by crushing what was opposed to its agenda or by modifying what was supportive, colonialism was a process of damage and disruption. Colonialism was an act of domination of one culture by another, bringing with it economic and political subordination. Imitation and assimilation of Western values were part of the responses to the fast penetration of alien culture.[9] According to the colonialists who defined culture as a stage of refinement, Africa had no culture. Some of the early Western scholars who studied Africa "in depth" were shocked to "discover" rich culture, but their aims were limited to such things as providing the data for use by missionaries. Apart from presenting the culture in static terms, some of them saw "irrationality" in many aspects of African culture.[10] When development planning was introduced after 1940, it was conceived in evolutionary stages with "the traditional phase" as the least developed, followed by a transitional phase with the ultimate phase being the replication of Western institutions. The logic was that Africa had to gradually abandon its tradition and past, to undergo a rebirth. Its tradition and culture were regarded as a "negative context," although they were capable of being successfully transformed. Development was the agency of change, a "mechanical" process benefiting from external intelligence and agencies. Not only were the plans ambiguous, they were also culturally determined, informed by a belief that progress meant Westernization.[11] These plans and the related ones that followed were not successful. It became clear that development cannot be divorced from culture; that so-called economic policies have cultural components; that models, science, and technology cannot be imported without regard to their cultural contexts; and that local ideas, histories, memory, and other cultural resources cannot be ignored when major changes in people's lives are initiated.

Past Burdens, Present Dilemma

Aspects of indigenous culture as well as Arab and Western civilizations exist, compete, and interact in Africa.[12] Since independence, indigenous culture has interacted with colonial and postcolonial cultures in creative and perverse ways: creative because it involves a lot of adaptation; perverse because the goals are acquisitive and materialistic, and it is largely imitative of Western culture. Some have characterized this latest development as the culture of dependency, with such features as unbridled materialism and individualism, lack of respect for collective values, disregard for dignity, and emphasis on money and power as the two most important things in life.

The external world is still arrogant with regard to Africa. Old stereotypes persist (the "dark continent," "savages," "jungle," "'Tarzan," "primitive"), the "traditional" period is condemned in preference for the modern, and Western culture is sold as superior.[13] External media images focus on civil wars, power rivalries, AIDS, and poverty. The marginalization of Africa, the increasing impoverishment of its people, the migrations out of the continent, the rapid transfer of foreign culture, the underdevelopment of indigenous institutions, and the bastardization of aspects of local cultures all point to the ongoing difficulties of maintaining a cultural identity and using it to formulate effective development strategies.

National identity is the bedrock of continental identity. The artificiality of the boundaries of modern countries remains a major source of tension. Many ethnic groups continue to pursue parochial identities in ways that threaten collective interests. Subnational loyalties continue to undermine national identity. Civil wars, ethnic rivalries, and religious tensions are the manifestations of deep crises. The declining economic resources in recent times are bound to complicate an already volatile situation. In moments like this, ethnic identification becomes a political strategy for gaining access to scarce resources and power. A number of suggestions, ranging from the use of education, equitable distribution of resources, use of ideology, and use of language, have been suggested to minimize the problem.[14]

The use of culture is regarded as the most creative way to forge an African identity. To be sure, most countries have had to make cultural choices involving a variety of options: rejection of some external influences, acceptance of Islamic and/or Western culture, and integration of the "traditional" with the "modern." Many countries have relied on the use of symbols to achieve inspiration or to fashion an ideology. Liberation movements used culture to create unity and anticolonial nationalism. When independence was won, culture was misused to defend decadent political habits and corruption. Examples include the devaluation of Christian names in Zaire; the criticism of the miniskirt in Malawi; and the removal of colonial names, replacing them with indigenous names for several countries, notably Azania, Malawi, Zimbabwe, Zambia, Ghana, Mali, and Benin. In spite of these changes, problems remain, arising from inconsistency in policy, the manipulation of culture to justify corruption and authoritarianism by a tiny political elite, the failure to translate change into development, the inadequacy of local symbols to acquire national significance, and the divisiveness of religion.

Strategies and Options

In the various discourses on the search for cultural identity and development, at least four major options have been suggested. The first is the radical, sometimes Marxist, call for an intense and committed nationalism which will restore African identity and development by liberating its politics and economy from the control of imperialism. Africa has to define its interests in such a way that it will control its economy, refuse to compromise its independence and integrity, and accord primacy to its culture. It must acquire power, confront other continents as equals, and transform its economy so as not to be dependent on others. According to this school, the dismantling of neocolonial institutions and structures is the first step toward creating any meaningful African identity. The radical nationalists urge a cultural revolution, involving political reeducation to overcome alienation and develop new values of liberation and independence.[15]

The second school is much older, although its voice seems to have been subdued in recent times. This is cultural nationalism as defined by Léopold Senghor, the leader of the negritude school,[16] or in many other variants. This school calls for the purity of African culture and points to the concrete achievements of the past (e.g., the building of the great kingdoms) and to the evidence that Africa has a long and proud history. Senghor advocated Negritude, based on the equality of races. He raised Negritude to the level of ideology: a revolt against colonial subordination, a reevaluation of African history, the quest for an African identity, and "the notion of a distinctive spiritual heritage of the black man."[17] Critics of Negritude have accused it of playing a "racist game," of being merely defensive, of accepting the supremacy of European culture, and of seeking accommodation with imperialism.

The ideas of cultural nationalism are not always as simple as Senghor's critics portray them. Also, there is no unanimity within the ranks of cultural nationalists on various issues, another misleading assumption of their critics who tend to homogenize all ideas associated with Negritude. There are those like Senghor, Edward Wilmot Blyden before him, and Aimé Césaire, who wanted Africa to seize on simplicity, humanism, and spiritualism to construct a new vision of change. Civilization need not be about impressive material evidence, but about humanity. Césaire's poetry has become the classic of the spiritual essence of civilization.

While accepting many aspects of "Negritude," Cheikh Anta Diop is the hero of the school that identifies the glory of Africa,[18] by pointing to great examples of civilization and taking a step further to say that Africa contributed to world civilization and influenced other cultures and races.[19] Many members of this school affirm that Africa already would have enough ideas from its past to transform the present, but for the devastation caused by the intrusion of Europe.[20]

The third school is rooted in the belief in the positive merit of alienation (the term is used here to mean a withdrawing or separation, an estrangement from traditional cultures by accepting new alien ideas and institutions). The alienation school argues that there is a need to adapt and assimilate Western culture. Abiola Irele, one of the leading apostles of alienation, has argued that this will involve "a willed movement out of the self and a purposive quest for new horizons of experience . . . as a matter of practical necessity, we have no choice but in the direction of Western culture and civilization."[21] He accepts the devastating impact of colonial rule, but warns:

> The traditional pre-colonial culture and way of life continue to exist as a reality among us, but they constitute an order of existence that is engaged in a forced march, in a direction dictated by the requirements of a modern scientific and technological civilization. It also happens to be the case that Western civilization . . . provides the paradigm of modernity to which we aspire.[22]

He recognizes the reasons for the pathology of alienation and appreciates why the brutal colonial experience has encouraged "the feeling that it is within our traditional culture that we were happiest, most at ease with ourselves, that there was the truest coincidence between us and the world: in other words that our identity was located."[23] However, to Irele, colonialism has rendered "the traditional way of life no longer a viable option for our continued existence and apprehension of the world."[24] He attacks cultural nationalists for using tradition to confuse, selecting aspects that suit particular situations, and proposing ideas that cannot solve the problems of Africa's alienation:

> It is of no practical significance now to us to be told that our forebears constructed the Pyramids if today we can't build and maintain by ourselves the roads and bridges we require to facilitate communication between ourselves, if we still have to depend on the alien to provide for us the necessities of modern civilization, if we can't bring the required level of efficiency and imagination to the management of our environment.[25]

He concludes that Africa has no choice but to move

> in the direction of Western culture and civilization. . . . If we can accept that the scientific and technological civilization which has come down to us, historically, from Europe can improve the quality of our lives, if we can accept

that our modern institutions should be based on political and social ideas articulated elsewhere, there is no reason why we should exclude from our acceptance other valuable areas of experience simply because of their association with Europe.[26]

Indeed, a few scholars have gone far beyond Abiola Irele to argue against the revival of African culture because they think that it cannot be reconciled with the ethos and demands of contemporary science and technology. In one extreme case, Marcia Towa, a Camerounian philosopher, concluded that such a subjugated culture as that of Africa is already too weakened to constitute the basis of identity and development in a modern world.[27]

The alienation school has not dealt with the issue of the identity that would emerge nor the consequences of social ruptures. Perhaps the logical outcome of alienation would be the emergence of a new identity, the Afro-Western, for want of a more creative terminology. The advocates of borrowing, however, need to indicate where to halt in order to avoid a complete revolution of identity-substitution. They also have to consider the long-term consequences of modern science and technology on African society.

Finally, there are those who suggest an aggregation of African cultures as a tool for identity construction and development. This school believes that a profile of African cultures can be established and a common culture can emerge between nations. The members of the school search for "the commonly shared ways of life" that the entire continent can identify with. Some of the features that have been mentioned include political institutions, the "prestige and acquisitive culture patterns," the role of unilineal descent groups, and of language. V. C. Uchendu has provided a profile:

> Black Africa exhibits four important notions which convey its conception of the destiny of the African. First, the African world view is *life affirming*. We do not subscribe to a philosophy of world denial of a compelling desire to abandon the now for there and thereafter. Second, African world view lays more emphasis on duty than on *rights*. In Black Africa rights are not asserted in the abstract; they reflect rewards inherent from one's performance of duties. Children who deny their parents good burial, which they can afford, cannot lay claim to their parents' wealth by appealing to the abstract "rights of man." Third, African world view emphasizes the necessity for a *countervailing power*. New gods may be acquired if the existing gods fail to match their rivals' power. Fourth, African world view is essentially a *tolerant* world view. African value systems are shaped by their world view. The basic

values found in Africa include: respect for elders which derives from the postulate of life affirmation; emphases on lineal continuity; mutual dependency; transparent living; and on maintaining cosmological balance. These basic values are supported by other values: the definition of achievement in social rather in personal terms; intense religiosity; caring and sharing within kinship groups and equality of access to opportunity without guaranteeing absolute equality.[28]

This position fully supports the revival of culture for almost the same reasons as the "Negritude" school: culture restores pride, provides the basis of identity, enhances the struggle to attain mental liberation, and provides the framework for development. The importance of this school lies in its powerful argument that African culture remains relevant in the modern era and has to be integrated into all aspects of cultural life.[29] The problems with the school are that it has given little thought to the integration of Islamic and Western cultures that have spread over the years and the adequacy or otherwise of all the institutions and traditions of the past. A more attractive suggestion is that of Kwame Gyekye, which is that only the positive aspects of the past should be identified, retained, and used for present purposes.[30] Although his catalogue of what is "negative" and "positive" may not generate a consensus, his criteria of selection appear sound, that is, "the fundamental nature of a set of pristine values and attitudes and the functionality of past ideas and institutions in the setting of the present."[31]

Panacea for the Twenty-First Century

Africa cannot be isolated from the rest of the world. Neither can it refuse to draw lessons and ideas from other peoples, cultures, and civilizations. Borrowing should, however, be adaptive, creative, and discriminating. The continent should be in a position to reflect on its own destiny, its identity, rather than existing as a dumping ground for discarded ideas from other parts of the world, as an imitator, and as a second-rate place. Against the background of the spread of Western and Asian cultures and of increasing globalization, there is a strong need to consider the following issues:

1. the correction of negative images about Africa, as in many radio and television stereotypes in the West and the emphasis on the negative such as warfare and famine;
2. the need to identify and promote what is African;
3. the determination of aspects of the past that are still relevant;

4. the reconciliation of many different cultural choices and their consequences for economy and politics; and;

5. the integration of cultures drawn from different historical experiences
and formations into a coherent policy to change the future.

Africa has to confront the wreckage of the slave trade and colonialism. It has to seek the means to achieve "cultural autonomy," but without
isolating itself from the rest of the world. The similarities in culture represent a huge asset that has to be promoted and used for identity and development. A number of practical solutions may be offered here. African countries have to take deliberate measures to remove the obstacles that make
communication and travel difficult within the continent. Members of the
nations that have been divided should be encouraged to interact and promote their culture and identity. National sovereignty is important but this
should not be promoted at the high cost of dividing people who want to
come together and share relations. More has to be done to make successful
the integrationist projects like the Economic Community of West African
States and the Central African Economic and Customs Union. The success
of the integration unions will minimize the divisive influence of colonial
boundaries, integrate economies and peoples, and foster greater interaction. Frontier tensions that divide countries must be removed. The newly
created African Union and the countries involved should pay attention to
the role of boundary crises and their impact on unity and identity. Boundaries should be decolonized, not by new divisions but by a mental attitude,
and demilitarized to reduce tensions to the minimum. Regional and continental integration should serve development needs, such as the expansion
of the market, greater mobility of goods and people, and a reduction in
dependence on the West. Some countries and regions are in a position to
play leadership roles in the integration effort: South Africa and Nigeria can
provide economic leadership; east Africa can promote the use of Kiswahili;
and Egypt can lead in the task of continental political integration.[32]

Culture must be kept alive. Folktales need to be gathered and used
and readapted to the television age. The cinema and other media can be
powerful agencies of cultural liberation and change. Culture has to actively
intervene in the search for identity and be employed to achieve both broad
and specific objectives. Either viewed as "programmatic" or "engineering,"[33]
culture must play a strategic role, for both political and economic ends.
Development programs must not only respect people's culture and identities, but must take these into full consideration in making new changes.
The creation of culture must also be regarded as part of development itself.

New cultural industries that emerge should, in turn, affect the economy. As simple as they appear, the crafts industries remain the best of the African cultural industries. Crafts can be practiced everywhere; the technology is accessible; the capital requirement is low; a large population of youth can be absorbed; the final products are authentic; and these industries form the basis of an indigenous technological revolution.

Africa has to understand the West to be able to confront it. Many Africans use the languages of the West without understanding the culture and civilization that go with them. Whether to combat or to befriend, there is a need for a deeper understanding of the West. It should also be understood that the impact of Western civilization and ideas is far more pervasive than many tend to assume. In the twenty-first century, the power of the market and the media will continue to entrench the hegemony of Western culture. As this hegemony takes hold, what may unite Africans in scattered locations may be the Western ideas and values that many are struggling to reject or to adapt to their environments. Ali Mazrui has suggested a strategy of "counterpenetrating the citadels of power" to create a "symmetrical interdependence." This may take the form of using raw materials to attain influence, the creation of powerful lobby groups to influence decisions on Africa, the greater insertion of Africa into the school curricula, and the globalization of African culture.[34]

Africa can diversify its sources of borrowing to include Latin America, the Caribbean, and Asia. Societies that are struggling to develop or that have created alternative models of development can offer valuable lessons. Successful examples of cultural retention and adaptation to external changes, as in the case of China and Japan, also offer models to learn from.

Adaptation has been one of the reasons for the survival and vitality of African culture. The rigid distinction between "traditional" Africa and "modern" Africa is exaggerated because there is always continuity with the past. Continuity and change are the intertwined features of the historical process in Africa. The institutions of old, such as kinship, languages, and religions, remain strong, and they affect the management of contemporary states. Asian and Western cultural influences have not succeeded to the extent of displacing all aspects of precolonial cultures. Modern-day policies must take into cognizance the resilience of these institutions and use them for progress, legitimacy, and identity.

Effective strategies have to be created to domesticate all received ideas and institutions, most notably in the areas of science and technology. Universities have to play a leading role in this, but first they have to domesticate themselves. If English and French remain as the most widely used

European languages in Africa, they can be turned into vehicles of domestication rather than as couriers of Western civilization.

Culture offers some answers to dependency. Wherever existing ideas, tools, and skills are useable or can be modified, there is no need to depend on the external. Many have advocated extensive use of indigenous languages to create the bedrock of science, as in Korea and Japan, to develop the arts and literature, to enhance communication among people, and to undercut the domination of European languages. Such widely used languages as Kiswahili, Hausa, and Arabic have been recommended for adoption by all Africans. Specialists in different disciplines have suggested how music, art, the performing arts, architecture, the cinema, agriculture, science, technology, medicine, and others can be domesticated and play crucial roles in the development process.[35] Knowledge in all these fields must keep expanding to be able to present intelligent options for Africa to move forward, promote authenticity, and avoid dislocations.

Sustainable change has to profit from the established indigenous cultural heritage and available resources and from the careful management and domestication of external ideas, science, and technology. Domestic policies will be effective if they positively transform people's lives and create a culture of democracy. Development models, whether based on local or imported ideas, must respect people, appreciate their histories and values, strengthen human rights and capacity building, and invest cultures with the power to be creative and functional. An active role in world politics and the respect of the international community will be enhanced if Africa confronts the rest of the world as an equal and stops presenting itself as a beggar. Culture, ideology, and the interrogation of past history are the essential ingredients in the package(s) of solutions for the African crisis of development.

Finally, an enormous investment must be made in capacity building in order to implement significant cultural and development programs. It is one thing to create cultural knowledge, it is another to use it in the service of development. Participation and creativity in old and new forms of culture are visible everywhere[36] but are constrained by limited funding, inappropriate cultural policies, the deliberate manipulation of culture to retain power, the focus on short-term survival strategies, the brain drain, and instabilities in economy and politics. Opportunities for capacity building are not yet lost: intellectuals must continue to insist on the connection between culture and development and to assist policymakers in devising the means to profit from modern science, technology, and communication; to empower the people and democratize society; to strengthen coop-

eration among African countries and international networking; and to promote existing and new cultures.

Notes

1. M. Marriot, "Cultural Policy in New States," in *Old Societies and New States,* ed.
C. Geertz (New York: The Free Press, 1963), 34.

2. Frantz Fanon, *The Wretched of the Earth* (London: Penguin Books, 1967), 168.

3. Ali A. Mazrui, "Perspective: The Muse of Modernity and the Quest for Development," in *The Muse of Modernity: Essays on Culture as Development in Africa,* ed. Philip G.
Altback and Salah M. Hassan (Trenton, N.J.: Africa World Press, 1996), 3–4, 17.

4. Aimé Césaire, *Lettre à Maurice Thorez* (Paris: Présence Africaine, 1956), 15.

5. On the link between culture, imperialism, and resistance, see Edward W. Said,
Culture and Imperialism (New York: Vintage, 1994); and Ali A. Mazrui, *Cultural Forces in
World Politics* (London: James Currey, 1990).

6. Among others, see E. A. Ruch and K. C. Anyawu, *African Philosophy* (Rome:
Catholic Book Agency, 1981); Jahn Janheinz, *Muntu: The New African Culture* (New York:
Grove, 1961); J. J. Maquet, *Africanity: The Cultural Unity of Africa* (New York: Oxford
University Press, 1972); and Molefi Kete Asante, *African Culture: The Rhythms of Unity*
(Trenton, N.J.: Africa World Press, 1996).

7. John S. Mbiti, *African Religions and Philosophies* (London: Heinemann, 1969), 2.
See also W. E. Abraham, *The Mind of Africa* (Chicago: University of Chicago Press, 1962),
45–46.

8. For a study on indigenous religions in contemporary Africa, see J. K. Olupona,
ed., *African Traditional Religions in Contemporary Society* (New York: New Era, 1990).

9. See N. C. Manganyi, *Being-Black-in-the-World* (Johannesburg: Ravan, 1973).

10. A major early work is P. Tempels, *Bantu Philosophy* (Paris: Présence Africaine,
1959). For easy access to the literature on the early studies and the debates they provoked,
see T. Serequeberhan, ed., *African Philosophy: The Essential Readings* (New York: Paragon,
1991).

11. See Toyin Falola, *Decolonization and Development Planning in Nigeria* (Gainesville:
University Press of Florida, 1996).

12. For the most elaborate articulation of the interaction of these three cultures and
their consequences, see Ali Mazrui, *The Africans: A Triple Heritage* (Boston: Little, Brown
and Co., 1986).

13. For the image of Africa in the U.S., for instance, see E. J. Rich, "Icons, Images,
Ideas About Africa—What is the Message?" (paper for a conference on Images of Africa,
African Studies Center, Michigan State University, May 1979); and S. S. Walker with Jen-
nifer Rasamimanana, "Tarzan in the Classroom: How "Educational" Films Mythologize
Africa and Mis-educate Americans," unpublished manuscript.

14. See D. R. Smock and K. Bentsi-Enchill, *The Search for National Integration in
Africa* (New York: The Free Press, 1975); and Gwendolen M. Carter, *National Unity and
Regionalism in Eight African States* (New York: Cornell University Press, 1966).

15. I have lumped together writings informed by different ideological expressions,
but which nevertheless fall within the rubric of my categorization: A. Cabral, *Revolution in*

Guinea, Stage 1 (London, 1965); A. Cabral, "Identity and Dignity in the Context of the National Liberation Struggle" in *Return to the Source: Selected Speeches of Amilcar Cabral* (New York: Monthly Review Press, 1973); Frantz Fanon, *The Wretched of the Earth* (London: Penguin, 1967); Frantz Fanon, *Towards the African Revolution* (London: Penguin, 1970); Frantz Fanon, *A Dying Colonialism* (London: Penguin, 1970); and Kwame Nkrumah, *Neo-Colonialism: The Last Stage of Imperialism* (London: Panaf, 1965); Kwame Nkrumah, *Revolutionary Path* (London, Panaf, 1973).

16. Other notable scholars of the school, with modifications to Senghor's, are Aimé Cesairé and Leon Damas.

17. The literature on Senghor and Negritude is very extensive. Among others, see I. Markovitz, *Leopold Sedar Senghor and the Politics of Negritude* (New York: Atheneum, 1969); W. A. Skurnick, "Leopold Sedar Senghor and African Socialism," *The Journal of Modern African Studies* 3, no. 3 (1965): 321–71; and A. Irele, ed., *Selected Poems of Leopold Sedar Senghor* (Cambridge: Cambridge University Press, 1977).

18. Cheikh Anta Diop, *The African Origin of Civilization* (Westport, Conn.: Lawrence Hill, 1974); Cheikh Anta Diop, *Cultural Unity of Black Africa* (Chicago: Third World Press, 1978).

19. See J. A. Rogers, *Africa's Gift to Humanity* (New York: H. M. Rogers, 1961); and Charles S. Finch, *The African Background to Medical Science: Essays on African History, Science and Civilizations* (London: Karnak, 1990).

20. See Chancellor Williams, *The Destruction of Black Civilization* (Chicago: Third World Press, 1974).

21. Abiola Irele, *In Praise of Alienation* (An inaugural lecture, University of Ibadan, Nigeria, 1983), 30–31.

22. Ibid, 9.

23. Ibid., 11–12.

24. Ibid., 15.

25. Ibid., 3.

26. Ibid., 25, 30.

27. Towa's view is summarized in Abiola Irele, "Contemporary Thought in French-Speaking Africa," in *African Philosophy: Selected Readings,* ed. Albert G. Mosley (Englewood Cliffs, N.J.: Prentice Hall, 1995), 281. For a more extensive discussion, see Paulin J. Hounntondji, *African Philosophy: Myth and Reality* (Bloomington: Indiana University Press, 1983).

28. V. C. Uchendu, "Towards a Strategic Concept of Culture: Implications for Continental Unity," in *African Unity: The Cultural Foundations,* ed. Z. A. Ali (Lagos: Centre for Black and African Arts and Civilization, 1988), 21–22.

29. See J. A. Sofola, *African Culture and the African Personality: What Makes an African Person Africa* (Ibadan: African Resorces Pubishers, 1973); T. Uzodinma Nwala, *Igbo Philosophy* (Lagos: Lantern Books, 1985); Kenneth Kaunda, *Humanism in Zambia and a Guide to Its Implementation* (New York: Harper and Row, 1968); and Julius Nyerere, *Ujamaa: The Basis of African Socialism* (Dar es Salaam: Tanganyika Standard, 1962).

30. Kwame Gyekye, *Tradition and Modernity: Philosophical Reflections on the African Experience* (New York: Oxford University Press, 1997), 242–60.

31. Ibid., 260.

32. See Ali A. Mazrui, "Perspective," 14–15.

33. I have used these two concepts with reference to suggestions made by Ali Mazrui, *Cultural Engineering and Nation Building in East Africa* (Evanston, Ill.: Northwestern

University Press, 1973); and C. A. Van Peursen, *The Strategy of Culture* (Amsterdam: North-Holland Pub. Co., 1974).

34. Mazrui, "Perspective," 15–16.

35. Space does not permit any extensive reviews of the various suggestions. See S. Arnold and A. Nitecki, eds., *Culture and Development in Africa* (Trenton, N. J.: Africa World Press, 1990); and Christopher Fyfe, ed., *African Medicine in the Modern World* (Edinburgh: Centre of African Studies, 1996).

36. See Mary Jo Arnoldi, Christraud M. Geary, and Kris I. Hardin, eds., *African Material Culture* (Bloomington and Indianapolis: Indiana University Press, 1996).

4

POLITICAL ECONOMY AND THE CULTURE OF UNDERDEVELOPMENT

"SIDE WITH SNAKES, NOT WITH THE RICH."
—A SHONA PROVERB

The economy is integral to culture. Even if human beings do not live by bread alone, the search for bread in Africa takes an eternity. As in the Stone Age human beings spent almost all their time seeking food, the struggle to survive consumes the majority of the population. People are poor, and poverty shapes responses to politics, leisure, interpersonal relations, and overall habits and worldview. Poverty has been on the increase since the mid-twentieth century, reflecting worsening economic and political conditions. It influences the political culture, from attitudes about corruption to the abuse of power. To the majority of Africans, the purpose of government is to provide for its people while the purpose of life is to survive and live well. They regard politics not just about distribution of power among the leading representatives of ethnic groups, but primarily about solving problems of underdevelopment. Power has failed them, development has eluded them. What can explain such a double tragedy? Power and development are linked in various ways. This chapter shows the linkage. In the process, the emerging and established patterns are also examined or detailed, showing how history and the behavior of the state and political actors shape events and affect Africans in negative ways. When Africans talk about development, what they seek is not abstract: they want a higher standard of living. Economic changes are preferred to political ones, and there are cases when

Figure 5. Food production: The dilemma of distribution. Lagos, Nigeria.

people can accept authoritarian rule if it brings the desired economic benefits and progress. Benefits and progress are not defined along traditional lines—contacts with the West have broadened the list to include all objects associated with modernity. Medicine, automobiles, good roads, access to books and the Internet, and others are now part of what a new generation of Africans want. These pursuits suggest a desire for change and even a growing addiction to materialism among the elite.

Underdevelopment

Many Africans believe that they are not doing well, but that resources are not lacking for them to have jobs, access to land, nutritious food, and other necessities of life. In other words, many tend to believe that they are poor because their governments do not care about them. It is true that the majority of the population is poor; it is equally true that development is not a top priority of many political leaders; and it should also be added that the chaotic global system is unfair to the continent. Africa operates in a hostile international capitalist environment. The majority of countries offer agricultural raw materials produced by cheap labor, but African countries do not control the demand and prices. Claude Ake has argued that development is not on the agenda of African governments.[1] It should be added that the purpose of government has been to facilitate the distribution of resources among its key members. Like the preceding colonial governments, the postcolonial administrations have been interested in ensuring that African farmers produce for external markets and, where available, that minerals are extracted for the same reasons. The public revenues created in this established arrangement are controlled by those in power, not necessarily for the benefit of those who generate them. As a government perpetuates itself in power, it regards its citizens as enemies. To the outside interests who seek to continue the pattern of the domination of Africa, it has always been easy for them to identify and collaborate with the power elite. Indeed, business interests prefer to work with a small number of highly powerful people instead of subjecting themselves to democratic institutions, which tend to be slow.

The indicators have been depressing, as the continent moved from the economic decline of the 1970s to the crisis of the 1980s and a deepening crisis since the 1990s.[2] The per-capita GNP for most countries is on the decline. Investments have not been generated at a level high enough for the majority of the population to benefit from them. All sectors have performed woefully: the growth rate, real gross domestic product, and per capita income have all fallen to abysmal levels. Schools, hospitals, and all amenities are grossly inadequate. Infrastructures continue to crumble. Revenues have declined, while the value of many currencies is grossly devalued. Realizing that the government does not take care of them, many citizens

Figure 6. Creativity and commerce combined. Oyo, Nigeria.

avoid paying taxes. Some engage in currency transactions which damage official exchange rates. Valuable commodities such as diamonds, gold, and cash crops are smuggled out of many countries in order to avoid paying dues and taxes and to earn a higher profit. Many countries are in debt to external agencies which in turn dictate to them how to organize their economies and politics. African populations are on the rise, at an annual growth rate of 3 percent. What could have been an asset for development, if resources had been managed and the creativity of the people harnessed, has become a disaster, impacting negatively on access to food and services. Almost half of the continent's population is poor. A World Bank projection in the 1990s was that Africa would have one-third of all the poor people in developing countries, a depressing number which proves that the continent is regressing.[3] Resources to educate and empower young people are limited, thus compounding the population crisis. The pressure on the environment has been devastating, as in the destruction of the savanna in the search for wood to cook or land to graze animals. Diseases, old and new, continue to be a problem. Food is scarce for a continent that for centuries used to be self-reliant. Food shortages will wreak further havoc, especially on the poor. Limited technology, poor planning, underpayment of farmers, drought, and excessive government taxes on peasants and crops are some of the reasons for the agricultural decline.

Underdevelopment has to be located in past history and current problems of planning.[4] Many countries lack adequate resources and capital to establish a viable, long-term plan. Those who have resources and capital have not managed them honestly and efficiently. In their early years as new nations, they did not have enough savings to fall back upon, a large working class to tax, or industries to create jobs. As explained below, they have relied on the rural areas, which have been overexploited without commensurate compensation. As rural areas decline, millions of people move to the cities, and once there, scramble for limited living spaces, jobs, and amenities. A number of cities have recorded annual growth rates of more than 10 percent. Although the larger share of government revenues have been spent on cities, they represent centers of poverty and underdevelopment. Violence, unemployment, and shortages of housing and water plague many cities. To overcome many of Africa's problems, policies must protect and uplift the poor, even if the elite and the wealthy are uncomfortable in the process—one cannot side with the snake and the rich at the same time, as the Shona warn us in the words of the opening proverb.

Colonial Foundations

Africa was carefully integrated into the world economy to fulfil two inter-related objectives: to supply key raw materials to feed the industrialized economies and to provide markets to distribute imported items. Using its most important assets—land and labor—Africa supplied cash crops such as peanuts, cocoa, rubber, palm oil and cotton, as well as minerals such as tin, gold, diamonds, and copper. In exchange, Africa obtained mass-produced textiles, household utensils, and other products of European industries. Its indigenous economies were altered to promote the export of goods and services. Self-sustaining economies based on agriculture were set on a course of "modernization" that was later to generate a myriad of problems. The combination of the era of the trans-Atlantic slave trade and of colonialism has devastated Africa.

Economic regimes emerged that were different, although they had similar goals. In one characterization by a leading political economist, Samir Amin, Africa fell into four zones.[5] The first was the "trade economy" noted for extensive production of cash crops, as in British West Africa. According to Amin, areas along the coast imported European goods and generated funds to run the colonial administration. The second is what he calls "white settler" colonies, similar to the first, only the emphasis was on agriculture, and fertile land was seized by Europeans who displaced the traditional land owners. The examples of these colonies include Northern and Southern Rhodesia, Kenya, and Tanganyika. The third economy, illustrated by Gabon, Central Africa Republic, Belgian Congo (now the Democratic Republic of Congo), and Congo, was controlled by "concession-owning companies." Large areas were given to companies to exploit their mineral and forest resources. African labor was brutally exploited, and the companies gave very little in return. The fourth type, "economies of labor reserves," existed in places such as Upper Volta (now Burkina Faso), Malawi, and Mozambique, whose people migrated elsewhere to work. Lacking minerals and large-scale resources to produce cash crops, the people in these countries traveled to other areas to work in mines and on farms. Thus, they can now be found in South Africa, the Democratic Republic of Congo (formerly the Belgian Congo), Zambia (formerly Northern Rhodesia), Zimbabwe (formerly Southern Rhodesia), and Tanzania (formerly Tanganyika).

Irrespective of the regimes, a number of patterns emerged. The colonial economy exploited land and labor resources. In doing so, it accumulated profits for vested interest groups and companies. Settlers took fertile land in countries where European settlements were allowed; mining companies were ruthless; and trading firms maximized profits. The government made laws to en-sure the actualization of colonial economic objectives. Economic sectors were not carefully integrated to attain any development goals.

The aim was not to make Africa self-reliant, build enduring econo-mies, and enhance living standards. Rather, the goal was to transfer wealth abroad. Established food production systems were disrupted in favor of export crops. A huge number of people were removed from farms to work in cities and mines. Many lost their lands to commercial producers and, in some countries, such as those of east and southern Africa, to European settlers. Landlessness destroyed families, impoverished millions of people, and pushed many to alienating jobs in mines and cities. Where cities grew rapidly, vices such as prostitution and alcoholism accompanied that growth. Other problems came with city culture and life: joblessness, the spread of diseases, crime, overcrowding, and competition for few jobs.

The colonial economy laid the foundation for Africa's underdevelop-ment. Throughout the colonial period, the opportunities to generate capi-tal were minimal, either because the natural resources were undeveloped or did not even exist. Instead, a mono-crop economy was pursued—one in which a country was heavily dependent on one or a few raw materials for export. The skills to manage modern economies were limited. The number of Africans with business and technical expertise was meager during the first half of the twentieth century. Industrial and technological transfer were slow, but they became part of the aspirations of a new generation of Afri-cans. The management of complex businesses was not one of those lessons imparted to Africans. It took quite a while after the end of colonial rule for many African countries to establish and compete with European investors in such lucrative areas such as hotel, banking, and airlines. The inherited economies are ones of dependence on the external world. Africa must sell its labor and resources for Western economies to survive, and, in turn, must rely on the West for modern technologies, science, and medicine.

A number of problems have persisted since the end of the colonial period. Dependence continues. While Africa has abundant resources, it is the buyers, not the sellers, who control the power. Many aspects of interna-tional trade relations also shortchange Africa. Western countries sell indus-trial products to Africa at exhorbitant prices. By purchasing computers, planes, parts, cars, and other products of technology and science, Africa buys at high prices and even imports inflation of other countries to theirs. As to their own exports, mainly agricultural products, Africans cannot pre-dict the quantity to sell from one year to another. Prices fluctuate periodi-cally, affecting their budgets and plans.

Postcolonial Africa has retained many problems of the culture of the colonial era, while at the same time creating new ones as it seeks the means to transcend inherited ones. As modern as some parts of the continent appeared during the colonial era, there was a conservative side. The importation of culture was not always extensive, due mainly to the rigidity established by some colonial powers. For instance, in the Portuguese-speaking colonies, importation of values and ideas were mainly from Portugal. Even some schools and churches socialized Africans into a world that limited their sources of ideas and values. Postcolonial Africa broadened interaction with the outside world and "democratized" the access to alien cultures, resulting in greater access to new schools and higher institutions. Those with advanced degrees have been able to travel abroad, creating what is known as the "brain drain."

Capitalism, Class, and Power

The organization of African economies affects state power and is at the root of state and bureaucratic corruption. In many countries, the predominant population works in agriculture. Essentially, they exist to be exploited by the state, which makes a profit from the sale of cash crops to external markets. Those who refuse to engage in farming and move to the cities are reserves for cheap labor. Far from being docile, aware of being exploited, and actually well-informed about national and global affairs, thanks to the power of the radio, the farmers and urban poor are limited in their ability to challenge the state. They do, of course, engage in daily protests and are mobilized to act by political forces, but the reality is that the time-consuming tasks to survive deny them the resources to fight.

A middle class exists, with members who have Western educations and jobs in the formal economic sector. As many members of this class aspire to join the highly visible political class, they tend to play politics to achieve their goals. Some among them seek a better society and criticize those in power, but they do not necessarily have the economic power to engage in long fights, which explains in part why the state is able to dominate them and punish them from time to time. Indeed, as the majority of people work in government bureaucracies, they are powerless to combat the state, and many of them simply join in corrupt practices.

The most dominant are members of the political class. Entry is competitive. The successful among them acquire businesses and some do have access to public resources that enable them to live exceedingly well. In theory, this economic power enables them to consolidate their political power. The "big men" among them live in huge palaces and enjoy luxuries that disregard the visible poverty among their people. Clashes over politics can occur among them, as some struggle to gain more political and economic power. The members are not always able to resolve their differences in peaceful ways, which results in the failure to conduct elections and the various cases of military regimes. One key element in a power rivalry is about economic control. In rent-seeking economies[6] dependent on the collections of taxes and revenues from foreign companies that extract and exploit their minerals, many key political actors collect huge bribes from the companies in addition to their corrupt access to public funds.

No country is so poor that there will not be resources to compete over. The decaying state of Zaire in the 1990s still had minerals; Liberia and Sierra Leone during the same period had timber and diamonds respectively. Chad has oil, and although the first shipment is not scheduled until 2003, there already have been conflicts over the initial royalties from oil companies. Multinational companies seeking to gain access to crude oil bribe members of the political class. Where economic partners are needed, the collaborators are among the political class. In places where foreigners are excluded from participation in some businesses, they find willing partners among Africans who may actually become wealthy in the process. Where minerals and oil are involved, foreign companies try to meddle in politics. Indeed, civil wars do not necessarily prevent them from continuing with their business. Private security forces are raised, and there have even been the notorious cases of private armies formed in Liberia and Sierra Leone just to keep business going. Even as Western countries complain of bad leadership, their companies collaborate with those bad leaders to milk their countries dry. There is an identifiable wealthy political class in all of Africa whose members profit immensely from connections to state power and Western companies.

The generation of revenue, and its disbursements, are tied to class and class interests. The cities and the elite consume more of the national revenues but contribute less than rural areas and farmers. As the economies of most countries are based on agriculture and the export of raw materials, the onus to produce is on the poorest among their people. Commodities are bought from the farmers at low prices and sold abroad at higher prices, with the government and successful merchants reaping the profit. In countries lacking minerals, dependence on the rural areas is even more intense, as the government generates most of its taxes from them. Without industries and large numbers of highly paid people to tax, the farmers become the victims. Also, as cities need food and other farm products, they rely on rural areas where the farmers continue to use traditional implements such as hoes and machetes. In spite of this, the rural areas are the least favored in the provision of amenities. Even where schools are created, the graduates choose not to live among their people and contribute to the rural community, but to migrate to the cities.

Farmers and poor people are not docile. Far from it. Realizing how much they contribute and how little they get, they often seek the means to disengage from the state or to subvert government policies. Thus, they might engage in smuggling, dilute their products, or seek the means to ignore official trade networks, all in order to make more money. When prices are low, they could decide to hoard their farm products, a move that may create inflation and reduce government revenues.

More importantly, there is a flourishing informal business which occurs outside of excessive bureaucratic control and whose participants pay little or no tax. The informal sector can be huge, more than 50 percent of the entire economies of a few countries, as in the case of Zaire and Uganda in the 1980s. Examples include a host of service occupations (singing, repairs, and maintenance), small-scale trade, and distributions in the rural areas.

The relationship between capitalism and class can best be seen in the use of power for illegitimate purposes. Corruption, the subject of the next section, should be treated as an integral aspect of the culture of underdevelopment.

Corruption

The management of Africa's economy, in spite of limited resources, increasing population, and exploitation by external forces, is affected by large-scale corruption. In other words, there is a pervasive culture of corruption in the political and economic institutions of the majority of African countries. Corruption established some of its roots during the colonial period. To start with, the political system and the rule of law benefited a handful of people in such a way that power became associated with privileges rather than service. To the African elite who engaged in anticolonial struggles, one motivation was to gain power for personal ends. Second, the colonial state failed to promote a meritocratic system; important jobs were obtained on the basis of race, and Africans were mainly in subordinate positions. After independence, a culture of patrimonialism subverted that of meritocracy. Third, the opportunities to make money from big businesses were not available to many Africans during the colonial period. Once independence came, the Africans in power cleverly diverted state funds to private hands. Fourth, the promotion of many areas of alternative cultures—mainly Western—not only threatened the indigenous products, but created the desire and expectations for imported goods.

Where resources are in adequate supply to obtain the imported items, perhaps, there can be less tension. However, since resources are scarce, one way to gain access is through dubious means. Engaging in traditional occupations constitutes a limit to one's access to imported items or objects that represent the new cultures. One way to obtain such items is through corrupt practices. Where leaders are motivated by small goals, they simply add to the perception that government is not for the people, but for a select few, and that the majority need not necessarily respect established rules.

With the departure of the colonial powers, the state becomes the best source for those in power to accumulate wealth, not only at a fast pace, but at minimal risk. In addition, since there are few individuals with sufficient wealth and savings to create businesses, the state again became the best source to generate new industries and a host of enterprises. By controlling the funds for development projects, the state becomes the best banking "source" for those interested in money. The control of state projects is of prime importance in acquiring access to wealth. These conditions breed corruption.

Indeed, the nature of the political system itself is corrupt. The political system manifests corruption. Authoritarianism and one-party system serve as agencies of corruption, with political leaders using the police and the army to destroy those who expose their bad habits. Power is used primarily to plunder; public money is used to acquire and consolidate power; and the distribution of public money to private hands is the strategy to control people.[7] Thus, government jobs can be expanded, even if the people have little or nothing to do, all in order to maintain the political system. Six people can do the job of one person, and not necessarily in any efficient manner. Thus, we have a situation in which the government creates monopolies in a variety of businesses or in the supply of water and electricity, without any of them performing very well. Nigeria, for instance, used to have almost three hundred such public-owned businesses, but few worked efficiently. The Nigerian Electricity Power Authority (NEPA) became, to the public, Never Expect Power Always. The Nigerian Airlines, with an elephant as its logo, simply became an elephant that could not fly. State banks collapse, not because they lack customers, but because they give loans that powerful people never pay back.

If corruption is limited to members of the political class, perhaps an anticorruption culture would condemn them and put them to shame. This has not been the case in many countries where corruption is becoming a way of life. There are cases where the police demand a protection fee, the postal clerk opens parcels, and the university lecturer sells handouts.[8] The widespread nature of corruption results from bad leadership, worsening economic conditions, and survival strategies. Current efforts to create democratic regimes are unlikely to reduce the scale of, and attitude toward, corruption. Indeed, elections and the process of appointing leaders and managers are themselves corrupt. So-called democratically appointed leaders are not necessarily imbued with new, anticorruption attitudes. Indeed, corruption itself will erode the credibility of democratic regimes in a way that may instigate a fresh round of military coups and countercoups.

The tragedy is that corruption is part of the culture of an established elite that is itself supposed to change the society. Initial access to Western education produced a privileged class who profited from the new knowledge and skills. Until Africans themselves began to control their countries, access to Western education was selective. By the 1940s, the elite had come to regard themselves as successors to the colonial officers. As they gradually attained power from the 1950s onward, they also developed a culture of corruption, giving jobs and contracts not necessarily on the basis of merit but of kinship and ethnicity. The elite established a strong control on state power. The assumption was that such power would be used positively to alleviate poverty, but, as it turns out, it has been to promote corrupt practices.[9]

One may argue that there is a certain level of corruption in all countries.[10] However, in the case of many African countries, the quest to hide stolen money in foreign banks complicates the situation. Corruption enables the transfer of wealth abroad. Although foreign banks and Western governments are aware of the practice, they do little to stop it since they are benefiting from money deposited in their countries. Thus, the failure to use the money to generate local investments adds to the problems created by corruption. When corruption is pervasive, as in a number of African countries, it becomes part of the culture of development. Corruption slows down the pace of development, enriches a few people at the expense of the general populace, and discourages investment, since money can be made without much work. There are cases where key political figures have deliberately turned public treasuries into private ones. Cases of African leaders keeping stolen money in foreign accounts are well known, even when their countries are heavily in debt. Corruption damages the efficiency of the bureaucracy, even if it occasionally provides the opportunity for civil servants to make extra money and do their paperwork to satisfy their benefactors.[11]

External Intervention: Debts and Structural Adjustment

Africa does not operate its economy independent of external markets and power. Its modern economies were established during the colonial period. Independence from European powers, as important as it was, did not bring about economic liberation. Indeed, independence was merely a legal document which did not ensure political stability, democracy, or development. It is practically impossible for many African countries to be autonomous for a variety of reasons: resources are limited to transform their economies; politics are unstable; and the pressure by external powers is tremendous. Most economies are small and rely on Western countries for the supply of many items, even essential ones for domestic use. So successful was the colonial era in fostering a culture of dependency that only a few countries such as Nigeria, Zaire, and South Africa (to limit examples to sub-Saharan Africa) have the population and resources to overcome dependence.

The success of the West has not necessarily translated into success for Africa. To the contrary, the development of the West may entail the underdevelopment of Africa, as the slave trade and the colonial encounter have shown. In the postcolonial era, the relationship between Africa and the West has been characterized as neocolonial, a situation whereby former colonial powers use different political and economic strategies to maintain control. In modern economies, Western companies have the edge in the competition for the production and marketing of goods. Thus, there are cases of imported goods that have destroyed local production, even of food crops such as rice. Members of the African political elite are recruited as agents to serve the neocolonial interests of Western countries. On one hand, Western governments criticize Africans for a long list of problems, yet, on the other hand, their companies seek the means to profit from Africa, even in situations of chaos. Western banks keep the stolen money of African leaders; Western companies use large-scale bribery to pave the way to secure fat contracts. Access by Africans to the latest products of technology is constrained by resources. Terms of trade are always unfavorable, as the goods that Africa exchanges with the West generate less income compared with the imports. African currencies are hard to convert and many are not freely traded, thus forcing them to keep their reserves outside the continent.

As postindependence African countries complicate their economies by mismanagement, faulty planning, and corruption, they sink deeper and deeper into dependence on Western countries. The ability to generate internal revenues is constrained, due to excessive reliance on one or two products for export. The hope in the early years of independence to secure external support in the form of foreign aid was an illusion. Such aid—now called development assistance—has always been meager or hard to secure. Even when some countries are lucky, the end result is not always positive. External investments are hard to come by, and even when they exist, the benefits can be marginal.

During the Cold War, foreign aid was an extension of foreign policy, the use of resources to co-opt a country into one ideological bloc or another. Western countries were interested not in Africa, but only in fulfilling their own economic and political missions. Arms were supplied not just to raise money for their industries, but in a rather careless manner that sustained many conflicts in different parts of Africa. The Soviets and China sold and gave arms, just as the capitalist countries did. Cold War rivalries affected African countries, which were regarded essentially as pawns by the major actors. Whenever African leaders stressed the importance of economic development, they were ignored by the superpowers interested in world domination. Always, the declared interests of Africa in international politics (resource redistribution, the end of apartheid in South Africa, global arms control, internal stability, and respect by other countries) were generally ignored by the world powers. Realizing that direct military confrontation would be ruinous to their countries, the superpowers saw Africa as one of the places where confrontation was safer. Where a country had minerals, as in the case of South Africa and Gabon, Western powers were interested in controlling them. Where a country's location was considered strategic enough for war, there was also an interest in establishing control. In the process, the survival of some countries was at stake.

The end of the Cold War has not brought positive economic changes. Indeed, things have actually gone from bad to worse. As the economy declined, the countries resorted to external borrowing. In the 1980s, money was available from many European and American banks that wanted to grant loans at high interest rates. The World Bank and the International Monetary Fund (IMF) supported the demands for loans, guaranteed many of them, and also granted their own loans as well. By 1990, the debts had mounted to the extent that close to 50 percent of the continent's export earnings were needed, not to repay the loans, but to service the interests.[12] As interests accumulated, it was clear by the 1990s that many countries would have nothing left after servicing their interests and paying wages.

External debts have resulted in external control of the economies, in many cases to a greater extent than the experience under colonial rule. The World Bank and the IMF imposed a number of conditions, known generally as the Structural Adjustment Program (SAP) meant to reform African economies so that their creditors could get their money back. So-called structural adjustment loans from the IMF could be obtained only after implementing many aspects of the imposed conditions. So stringent are these conditions that they compel not just economic reordering but the use of force to curb violent protests. One primary condition is that currencies must be devalued in order to sell raw materials at a cheaper rate. Thus, unless the countries produce more, their overall revenue may actually decline. To complement devaluation, they must take measures to "liberalize" trade. Thus, they cannot restrict imports or subsidize prices of farm products, oil, and some other goods. State-owned enterprises must be privatized, the number of the work force must be reduced, and salary increases are frozen. Governments are expected to balance their budgets, thus forcing them to severely cut their expenses. Some measures seek the expansion of existing capital for investment, such as the increase in interest rates to induce people to save. Additional aspects of the SAP are the privatization of public enterprises, an enforced free trade, and an end to government subsidies on such products as food crops and petroleum.[13]

The SAP is the kiss of death. African leaders did not just rush to the IMF and the World Bank. Indeed, many resisted for a long time before eventually taking the loans, compelled by diminishing external reserves, the failure to balance budgets, and mounting domestic and external debts. By the early 1990s, about forty countries had taken the loans, and the attendant consequences were similar. In taking the loans, these countries were consumed by the contradictions in their politics and their collapsing economies. Authoritarian leaders need money to stay in power. As their economies crumble, their ability to retain their clients and ethnic loyalists becomes a problem. However, the loans make money available but the conditions create more problems. External powers obtain greater access to official business of the governments that take loans, and their opinions become more important than those of insiders.

The loans and conditions were based on a belief that the economies would be reformed within a short duration, that standards of living would be enhanced rapidly, and that debts would even be repaid. None of these has happened. Instead, the reforms have led to violence, political decadence, and further economic decline. Food and transportation costs escalated, many small companies collapsed, and millions lost their jobs.

Anticipated savings did not materialize, and domestic loans were hard to repay because of high interest rates.

A coalition of antigovernment forces emerged as a result of worsening economies. The need to reduce the work force created large numbers of enemies. Students were radicalized by the changes in the school system which imposed tuition and reduced the size of staff and faculty. Inflation set in, reaching several digits. Thus far, they have not been able to restore the situation to normal. Food prices have been hit hard. Not only are imported foods scarce and expensive, local produce is costly as well. The cities, ever relying on the rural areas, have been hit with high food costs. The withdrawal of various subsidies also affects the cost of fuel, gas, electricity, and water. With more and more people out of job and with rising inflation, antigovernment feelings run high. The civil society becomes not only bitter but better organized. Most governments initially responded with coercion and violence, throwing critics and members of the opposition in prison and forcing many into exile.

Politics and society become highly unstable and violent. In the 1980s and 1990s, protests, strikes, food riots, and demonstrations by students became a regular occurrence in most countries. The problems arising from the SAP led to various changes in politics, including the intense use of violence to check the restless population, the collapse of some governments, and a change in leadership in some others. The basis of patrimonialism was affected. As enough money was not available to buy people's loyalty, even those who identified with a government began to complain. Ethnic solidarities weakened in some instances, as the political patrons were unable to meet the needs of their own people. The bureaucracies, too, were badly affected. The failure to recruit additional members, the wage freeze, lack of promotion, inflation, and reduced access to corruption all brought grievances and frustrations. Civil servants who were expected to work for the state turned against it. Teachers, usually underpaid, became further impoverished. The legitimacy of political leaders was eroded, their credibility undermined. By the late 1980s, various governments in many countries, from Algeria in the north to South Africa in the south, had to deal with too many challenges. Demands were intense for the creation of multiparty democracies, economic and political reforms, freedom of speech, and new leadership. Changes began to come in the 1990s, as many countries began to allow the creation of many political parties and to even allow elections. A number of governments collapsed, as in the case of Ethiopia and Somalia; and apartheid ended in South Africa. Loans and the programs to save them from economic decline created greater troubles and political woes for the regimes.

The SAP has collapsed, but not the agenda of international agencies and Western countries to control Africa. The current ideology of globalization shares much with imperialism. The domination of Africa remains: it is still an unchanging goal of taking as many minerals and raw materials as possible from the continent. The profit from military hardware remains tempting to companies who sell them to African countries. As Africa owes a lot to foreign banks, it exposes its economy to external control. Due to the media, Western popular culture keeps spreading, thus instigating more and more demands for foreign goods. Globalization has brought both gains and pains.[14]

Ideologies and the Culture of Change

The African elite has always debated the options to move the continent forward.[15] Each option is a combination of cultural, economic, and political strategies. Essentially, the desire is to minimize dependence on former European colonial powers and Western markets, develop diversity in domestic economies, and become influential actors in world politics. During the Cold War, there were attempts to behave in the international system as neutral nations. As members of "nonaligned nations," many African countries joined others, notably India, to avoid entanglement in the East-West rivalries. In reality, nonalignment was unsuccessful.

Some options are along the colonial/Western option, in cases where they choose the capitalist ideology. The aim is to create free enterprise and use public funds to generate development in those areas that are considered crucial.[16] As shortage of capital is massive, the government becomes the source of funding, thus creating government-controlled, centralized businesses. In many cases, the government itself creates and manages the businesses. Such public-controlled companies often become inefficient monopolies which disregard the rules of capitalism. They can vary from airline services to the provision of a transportation system at the local level. In the majority of cases, the enterprises are a drain on limited government revenues, they run at great losses, the managers are corrupt, and the workers are not necessarily productive. Political considerations tend to be more important than the economic, with the result that the enterprises hardly survive unless they are continually funded by the government.

Until the collapse of the Soviet Union, there were non-capitalist, non-Western options, most notably socialism. European countries were implicated in the underdevelopment of Africa as colonizers and economic partners. The alternative was to avoid them by trying the Soviet or socialist options. The strategy was to minimize Western domination by limiting the level of investments and capital that can be repatriated and establishing greater state control on the economy. A variety of socialist-oriented ideologies emerged in such countries as Tanzania, Mozambique, Angola, Guinea Bissau, the Republic of Benin, and Burkina Faso. Non-economic options were added to the economic ideologies. Until the wave of democratic movements in the 1990s, the overriding political philosophy was authoritarianism.[17] The assumption was that a dictator would hold the country together and make quick decisions to change the country. This did not happen.

Either in the search for new ideas or to meet the challenges of Westernization, many Africans have turned to culture for an answer. The ideas are so many, sometimes so confusing. To a number of Islamic elite, Africans must prevent the penetration of Western cultural practices. Indeed, some advocate the use of old Islamic laws, such as the Sharia, to ensure the survival of Islamic practices that are perceived to be favorable to development in a stable social and political environment. A secular-oriented group counters the views of the Muslim elite by advocating dynamic changes. A number of pro-socialist thinkers want a society that will become egalitarian, even if traditional cultures of patriarchy will be abandoned. To the pro-secularists and leftists, the changes can mean the adoption of Western values. Perhaps the most popular ideas are those that seek a clever blending of indigenous cultures with the modern desire of Africans for political and economic emancipation. Such thinkers as Julius Nyerere and Leopold Senghor have devoted considerable time to providing details on how African cultures can become useful to the modern age.

Ideologies have had difficulties in the effort to resolve the various problems and contradictions involved in moving Africa forward. In a manner that is both clear and engaging, Richard Fredland has created a list of the "dilemmas of development." Among them are:

> How does a leader minimize internal conflicts: urban-rural, traditional-modern, interethnic?
> How does a leader obtain the resources to satisfy the material needs without a tax base and without making crippling external commitments in exchange for funds?

How does a leader assure adequate political allegiance while fostering openness?

How does a leader procure technical expertise for his system while keeping the revolution of rising expectations under control?

How does a leader economize while providing the trappings of sovereignty?

How does a leader afford to send knowledgeable, but undertrained bureaucrats for further training, risking that they will become threats to his government or be "brain-drained" to a richer locale?

How does a leader manage this dilemma: Improving the health of the people may lead to a famine if food production is not increased, but population can be reduced by letting people suffer and die.

How can a program of sustainable development be devised to protect future development possibility while at the same time satisfying the pressing demands of an eager populace?

How does a leader further African unity while protecting national interests vis-à-vis neighboring states?

How does a leader reconcile the European background prevalent in most colonies with economically desirable austerity of traditional society?[18]

As Fredland discusses all the options, it is clear that many of the strategies adopted as well as the ideological context are not always effective. The power of charisma (as in the case of Julius Nyerere and Kwame Nkrumah) combined with that of ideology (either of the left or right) has not transformed the continent. Almost all the ideologies have promoted a culture of political statism, which involves the use of state power to accumulate and distribute public resources. Economic ideologies became part of the agenda to create a political culture with various forms. One form has been that of patrimonialism, which allows members of the political class to use state power to enrich themselves.[19] Another is that of personalistic rule, with those in power using public money to buy political support and loyalty.[20] And there is bureaucratic corruption which spreads to most agencies of government, with civil servants collecting bribes before performing their services.[21]

As Africans enter the twenty-first century, the most popular choice is that of a free market, but the results so far have not been as rewarding as anticipated. Efforts have been renewed to attain capital accumulation, institutional reforms, and growth in productivity, all in the attempt to reduce poverty.[22] Foreign investments and exports have declined, and the most notable area of growth has been in the population sector. As poverty rises, Africans will be forced to rethink development strategies and review the impact of the global system on their continent. Africans have to determine the kind of society and community they want to create and keep reevaluating the role of culture in development and in their future.

Is Something Wrong with African Cultures?

In this concluding section, I want to return to my main concern of the role of culture. Many of the issues above have been interpreted by some scholars in strictly economic terms, while others have added the cultural element. Thus, there are attempts to explain corruption and underdevelopment as a function of culture. Since the European encounter with Africa, a number of analysts, including Africans, have seen culture as the primary reason for Africa's backwardness. Ignoring the majority of Africans, scholars and experts have gone ahead to recommend what they should do and what areas of culture to abandon. In a mockery of the imposed development agenda, Janheinz Jahn thinks that Africans are regarded as disposable items and always ignored in the debates about their own future. As Jahn says, the tone is always that of a command: Africa must follow many prescribed changes without any comments. [23]

From a long list of negative comments on African culture, dating back to the nineteenth century, it is clear that the presumed solution lies in the adoption of Western methods to make Africans more efficient in production and time management and more oriented toward consumption. The assumption is that the West is successful because of the spirit of materialism and that of efficiency. To the advocates of cultural change, Africans need to be more competitive and eager to take risks; they need to respect and manage time more carefully, create opportunities for individual talents, and create more capital that will be spent on development rather than consumption. Still on track, Africans are accused of always being concerned with the present to the extent that they are unable to delay gratification and provide savings and capital for entrepreneurial use. Positive values of social cohesion are regarded as negative, cultural negotiations as social chaos. The entire range of past traditions is called into question, as in the remark by Manthia Diawara that such traditions do pose a threat to modernization,[24] and that the baggage of the past brings down the present. Apathy, hedonism, irrationality, fatalism, disregard for efficient use of time and space, lack of diligence, and laziness are part of the catalogue of criticisms directed at Africans and their cultures.[25]

Religions have been heavily criticized for constituting obstacles to development. From the standpoint of many analysts, only Christianity seems adaptable to Western capitalism. Traditional religions and Islam have been regarded as standing in the way of progress and are often contrasted with Asian religions which promote the ethics of hard work. It is hard to evaluate the impact of religion on development. Both traditional religions and Islam have shown their ability to unite communities, organize charity organizations, help the poor, assist with trade, and enhance the management of commercial networks. With respect to Islam, several case studies have actually seen it as a powerful engine for change—a religion that fosters courage and entrepreneurship.[26] There are, however, cases when conflicts between religions have led to violence and destruction to various aspects of the economy.[27]

The target of most attacks directed at Africans has been the poor farmers in the rural areas and the urban poor. They are often presented as lazy and lacking in wisdom, thus constituting obstacles to development. There is no firm data to suggest laziness on the part of the African poor. Indeed, the farmers work as much as possible to make a bare existence, while the urban poor struggle for survival on a daily basis. Labor is cheap, and the poor offer themselves for cheap employment just because opportunities are limited. The poor suffer without hope, labor without gains, and tend to think that only the power of invincible forces can help them. The perception is that one's future depends on luck, not necessarily on what one does with the brain and hands. The development potentials of the poor have to be harnessed, rather than their being tirelessly criticized.

It is also clear that many analysts assume that Africans are governed by an old social order. As the chapters in this book show, cultures are varied, ever changing. Where changes have been sudden, many Africans experience conditions of anomie, a feeling that they are not even Africans anymore. In many areas, ancient cultures have given way to new ones and ethnic culture have been eroded, but new ones are not necessarily well established. Colonialism came with a high price: Africans had to adopt many aspects of European cultures, even when they did not like them. Enduring legacies of the colonial period remain, such as the taste for imported items. Indeed, each acceptance of a foreign idea or way of life may result in the importation of foreign goods. Thus, to become a Christian involves buying the Bible and hymn books; to go to school means the same. Consequently, culture spread also promotes foreign and local businesses to sustain it. Colonialism and the engagement with the West has equally led to the spread of European languages, notably French and English. To succeed and be mobile, one must be able to use one of these two languages.

The essence of the aforementioned examples indicates that Africans have continually adopted change and adapted to imposed circumstances. Urban Africa is not governed solely by traditional values, but by a combination of cultures from various sources. It is also the case that rural Africa is not primarily dependent on age-old traditional resources. Far from it. The majority of Africans know about products of technology and science, and a variety of imported goods. The revolution of rising expectations—a well-known idea—does not affect just a handful of Africans with Western educations. The expectation and desire for better products, services, and imported items do lead to changes in the culture of taste, the management of household income, the choice of occupations, and even a decision to migrate to new areas. The cities are looking more and more like Western ones, in their look, at least, if not in their management and opportunities open for the residents. As Africans avoid the land, become cut off from a number of kinship members, and accept foreign impact, they are becoming more Western than Africans. Thus, in a sense, the issue is not whether old cultures should be abandoned, but to what extent Africans should go in the process of borrowing. Indeed, cultural nationalists have struggled to find the means to minimize the excessive Western influence, leading to the promotion of a variety of cultural programs, an ideology of blackness (such as Négritude), and others. In spite of this, the spread of Western culture, especially popular culture, continues to make steady progress.

In many cases, when experts ask Africans to give up their culture in order to develop, they are saying that adaptation is not enough, that the creative combination of ideas and values are inadequate, and that only complete Westernization will work. During the colonial era, one area regarded as a great obstacle was the communal land tenure system which discouraged commercialization, contradicting the capitalist notion that the entrepreneur should have as much access to land as needed. As the land tenure system responded to the changes, it brought suffering to those who lost farmlands and who had great difficulty buying land in urban areas. Attention was then turned to the organization and use of labor, again to make them receptive to capitalist ideology. While many with education and skills benefited as wage earners, millions had to suffer displacement, endure hardship in the cities, and suffer from the lack of adequate job opportunities.

African economies are not diversified enough to absorb the number of people who are ready to work, in contrast to precolonial agrarian economies that sustained the majority on their farms. Part of the attack on culture involves an attack on rural life, characterized as dull and primitive. Development tends to be defined as the minimization of the role of agriculture, even in the African situation where this is where the majority of the population are able to make a living. In spite of all the ideas and the changes based on Western examples, an industrial revolution is yet to occur. For this to happen, as some argue, Africa has to import almost all its elements, including the educational and creative essence. Africans are also expected to abandon aspects of cultures that interfere with the injection of foreign capital, that regard the activities of foreign companies as imperialist, and that limit access to land and labor by entrepreneurs. It is expected that ethnicity must give way to a culture of meritocracy, and generous habits must be exchanged for a materialistic culture of acquisition. All arguments about the necessity of cultural transplantation tend to be misleading, ignoring the basic fact that recipients redefine what they receive to accommodate certain established values. The new imports may not even work as expected, thus forcing the creation of new methods and ideas. Whether it is Western education, religion, or leisure, Africans have had to deal with their limitations and to fall back on established indigenous ones either to fill gaps or simply to fill the void.

No society remains static, nor can any society afford to remain static. Africa is no exception, but many changes are necessary. The culture of an inferiority complex in relation to the West, fostered by the slave trade and colonial rule, must give way to a culture of equality. Africa has to overcome the obstacles created by neocolonial relations. The culture of politics must change in favor of democracy: fair, free, and regular elections; stability, the empowerment of people; and the participation of many people in the management of public affairs. Institutions of government have to be reformed to legitimize them in the eyes of the people. The concept of power has to change from one of authority to one of service. Africa's long-established cultural institutions are less dangerous to progress than the persistent Western exploitation of the continent. However, exploitation would be harder to achieve without the collaboration of a greedy political elite. Changes in education, labor, households, and other areas will have great impact on economic and political institutions. African cultures will continue to witness transformations arising from external influences as well as changes in production and distribution mechanisms, education, health, and families. Cultural transformations will have both negative and positive impacts, and some societies may not be willing to accept those changes if they are perceived as too damaging to established traditional institutions. Development is a process; Africans have made many mistakes in the past, but the opportunities for the future are limitless. There is no final destination point, but the goal is to bring progress to the majority of the people in a way that they can have access to the basic necessities of life. In the challenges and quest to attain progress, it is wishful thinking on the part of scholars that old cultures will die completely in the process and that established values will be discarded because of bread and machines. It is the values and ideas that people want Africans to disregard that will ultimately make development and new changes acceptable, adaptable, and workable.

Notes

1. Claude Ake, *Democracy and Development in Africa* (Washington, D.C.: The Brookings Institution, 1996).

2. See OECD and African Development Bank, *African Economic Outlook* (Washington, D.C.: The Organization for Economic Cooperation and Development, 2002); UNDP, *Human Development Report* (New York: Oxford University Press, 2000); and R. Cornwell, "War and Decline in Africa," *Africa Insight* (Joahnnesburg) 21 (1991): 74–77.

3. World Bank, *World Development Report* (New York: Oxford University Press, 1990), 229.

4. On the theories and problems relating the concept of underdevelopment, see C. Leys, *The Rise and Fall of Development Theory* (London: James Currey, 1996).

5. Samir Amin, "Underdevelopment and Dependence in Black Africa: Origins and Contemporary Forms," *Journal of Modern African Studies* 4 (1972): 503–21.

6. On rent-seeking societies and the impact on politics, see A. O. Krueger, "The Political Economy of Rent-Seeking Society," *American Economic Review* 64 (1974): 291–301; and John M. Mbaku, "Military Coups as Rent-Seeking Behavior," *Journal of Political and Military Sociology* 22 (1994): 241–84.

7. See Catherine Boone, "The Making of a Rentier Class: Wealth Accumulation and Political Control in Senegal," *Journal of Development Studies* 26 (1990): 425–49.

8. On the widespread nature of bureaucratic corruption and its impact, see D. J. Gould, *Bureaucratic Corruption and Underdevelopment in the Third World: The Case of Zaire* (New York: Pergamon Press, 1980); D. J. Gould and T. B. Mukendi, "Bureaucratic Corruption in Africa: Causes, Consequences and Remedies," *International Journal of Public Administration* 13 (1989): 427–57; and John M. Mbaku, "Bureaucratic Corruption as Rent-Seeking Behavior," *Konjunkturpolitik* (Berlin) 4, no. 38 (1992): 247–65.

9. E. Harsch, "Accumulators and Democrats: Challenging State Corruption in Africa," *The Journal of Modern African Studies* 31 (1993): 31–48; J. G. Jabbra, "Bureaucratic Corruption in the Third World: Causes and Remedies," *Indian Journal of Public Administration* 22 (1976): 673–91; K. R. Hope, Sr., and B. C. Chikulo, eds, *Corruption and Development in Africa: Lessons from Country Case Studies* (London: MacMillan, 2000); V. T. LeVine, *Political Corruption: The Ghanaian Case* (Stanford, Calif.: Hoover Institution, 1975); and P. Bardhan, "Corruption and Development: A Review of the Issues," *Journal of Economic Literature* 35 (1997): 1320–46.

10. A. Heidenheimer, M. Johnson, and V. T. LeVine, eds., *Political Corruption: A Handbook* (New Brunswick, N.J.: Transaction Publishers, 1990); A. Aderinwale, ed., *Corruption, Democracy and Human Rights in Southern Africa* (Abeokuta, Nigeria: African Lead-

ership Forum, 1995); John M. Mbaku, *Bureaucratic and Political Corruption in Africa: The Public Choice Perspective* (Malabar, Fla.: Krieger, 2000); G. C. S. Benson, S. A. Maaranen, and A. Heslop, *Political Corruption in America* (Lexington, Mass.: Lexington Books, 1978); M. McMullan, "A Theory of Corruption," *Sociological Review* 9 (1961): 181–201; K. A. Elliot, ed., *Corruption and the Global Economy* (Washington, D.C.: Institute for International Economics, 1997); S. Rose-Ackerman, *Corruption: A Study in Political Economy* (New York: Academic Press, 1978); and R. Williams, *Political Corruption in Africa* (Brookfield, Vt.: Gover, 1987).

11. On the consequences of corruption, see, among others, D. H. Bayley, "The Effects of Corruption in a Developing Nation," *The Western Political Science Quarterly* 19 (1996): 719–32; H. H. Werlin, "The Consequences of Corruption: The Ghanaian Experience," *Political Science Quarterly* 88 (1973): 71–85; J. S. Nye, "Corruption and Political Development: A Cost-Benefit Analysis," *The American Political Science Review* 61 (1967): 417–27; M. Clarke, ed., *Corruption: Causes, Consequences and Control* (New York: St. Martin's Press, 1983); and K. Gillespie and G. Okruhlik, "The Political Dimensions of Corruption Cleanup: A Framework for Analysis," *Comparative Politics* 24 (2001): 77–97.

12. World Bank, *World Development Report.*

13. See P. Engberg-Pedersen, P. Gibbon, P. Raikes, and L. Udholt, eds., *Limits of Adjustment in Africa* (London: James Currey, 1996); and Thandika Mkandawire and Charles C. Soludo, eds., *Our Continent Our Future: African Perspectives on Structural Adjustment* (Trenton, N.J.: Africa World Press, 1909);

14. See Frederick Cooper, "What is the Concept of Globalization Good For? An African Perspective," *African Affairs* 100 (2001): 189–213.

15. See C. Young, *Ideology and Development in Africa* (New Haven, Conn.: Yale University Press, 1982); and A. B. Assensoh, *African Political Leadership: Jomo Kenyatta, Kwame Nkrumah, and Julius K. Nyerere* (Malabar, Fla.: Krieger, 1998).

16. For details, see B. Grosh and R. S. Mukandala, eds., *State-Owned Enterprises in Africa* (Boulder, Colo.: Lynne Rienner, 1994).

17. See chapter 5 in this volume. See also J. K. Nyerere, *The Arusha Declaration: Ten Years After* (Dar-es Salaam: Government Printer, 1977).

18. Richard A. Fredland, *Understanding Africa: A Political Economy Perspective* (Chicago: Burnham, 2001), chapter 8.

19. See chapter 5 in this volume and R. A. Joseph, "Class, State, and Prebendal Politics in Nigeria," *Journal of Commonwealth and Comparative Politics* 21 (1983): 21–38; and R. Fatton, Jr., "The State of African Studies and the Studies of the African State: The Theoretical Softness of the 'Soft State,'" *Journal of Asian and African Studies* 24 (1989): 170–87.

20. See R. H. Jackson and C. G. Rosberg, *Personal Rule in Black Africa* (Berkeley: University of California Press, 1982).

21. See John M. Mbaku, "State Control, Economic Planning and Competition among Interest Groups for Government Transfers in Africa," *The Journal of Social, Political and Economic Studies* 16 (1991): 181–94; and John M. Mbaku, ed., *Corruption and the Crisis of Institutional Reforms in Africa* (Lewiston, N.Y.: The Edwin Mellen Press, 1998).

22. See Jean-Claude Berthélemy and Ludvig Söderling, *Emerging Africa* (Washington, D.C.: The Organization for Economic Cooperation and Development, 2001); OECD, *Reform and Growth in Africa* (Washington, D.C.: The Organization for Economic Cooperation and Development, 2000); *World Bank, African Development Indicators, 1996* (Washington, D.C.: The World Bank, 1996); World Bank, *Human Development Report, 2000*

(New York: Oxford University Press, 2000); and John M. Mbaku, *Institutions and Reform in Africa: The Public Choice Perspective* (Westport, Conn.: Praeger, 1997).

23. Janheinz Jahn, *Muntu: African Culture and the Western World* (New York: Grove Weidenfeld, 1989) [originally published in Germany in 1958 by Eugen Diederichs Verlag], 235.

24. Manthia Diawara, *In Search of Africa* (Cambridge, Mass.: Harvard University Press, 1998), 56.

25. See Patrick Chabal and Jean-Pascal Deloz, eds., *Africa Works: Disorder as Political Instrument* (Oxford: James Currey, 1999).

26. See Alusine Jalloh and David E. Skinner, eds., *Islam and Trade in Sierra Leone* (Trenton, N.J.: Africa World Press, 1997); Alusine Jalloh, *African Entrepreneurship: Muslim Fula Merchants in Sierra Leone* (Athens: Ohio University Center for International Studies, Monograph in International Studies, Africa Series No. 71, 1991); and Mahir Saul and Patrick Royer, *West African Challenge to Empire: Culture and History in the Volta-Bani Anticolonial* (Athens and Oxford: Ohio University Press and James Currey, 2001).

27. Toyin Falola, *Violence in Nigeria: The Crisis of Religious Politics and Secular Ideologies* (Rochester, N.Y.: University of Rochester Press, 1998).

5

THE CULTURE OF POLITICS

**"A PERSON WHO TOOK NO OATH IS NEVER
GUILTY OF BREAKING ONE."**
—AN IGBO PROVERB

When Africans complain about aspects of bad government and political instability such as corruption, the failure to relinquish power after holding it for so long, authoritarianism, dictatorship, and military regimes, those outside the continent—especially people in stable political systems—tend to wonder why there is no revolution or how the people can be so tolerant of their leaders. Africans want a revolution, and they have been demanding one for a long time. Africans are not tolerant of their leaders—on the contrary, an uncountable number have lost their lives in the quest for change. Violent changes have occurred, but without revolutionary changes. Disappointments have not necessarily led to any mass resignation to the system. Civil society is now even stronger; cyberpolitics and warfare use all the resources of the Internet to build political connections and demand far-reaching reforms; and university students have organized countless numbers of protests. However, in many countries, the louder the complaint, the worse things become; the greater the protest, the greater the brutality by those in power. The bottom line remains the same: politics is unstable and the government is antidevelopment. We all should ask: what is wrong with Africa?

With political instability as the context, this chapter explores a number of core issues in political culture. To start with, it is impossible to understand contemporary politics without understanding past and present cultures in such areas as the beliefs and conventions of Africans, their religions, philosophy, established practices for power relations, social stratification, and concepts of power and the "big man." Ideas and values are not

Figure 7. Politics: The world of elders. Lalibela, Ethiopia.

constant, and they have responded to historical changes. The chiefs and kings of the nineteenth century ruled in the context of an economy and political ideologies which have been modified in the twentieth century. A new generation of African elite emerged during the twentieth century. Colonial rule changed the nature of African ethnicity. When the European empires crumbled, the first generation of African leaders that managed the postcolonial states were largely unsuccessful. Dictators and single parties emerged, changing political practices in a way that induced more abuses and corruption. Thus, when we refer to the past, it involves both the elements indigenous to Africans and the impact of colonial rule as the most recent background to contemporary history.

Second, there are parallel political institutions complementing and competing with one another. Modern Africa inherited Western political institutions without abolishing all of its traditional ones. However, most countries are yet to clarify what they want to retain, reform, destroy, or improve upon in their inherited indigenous traditions. Unfortunately, as they manage to acquire Western institutions, they often do so through the incorporation of indigenous ideas and conventions. Thus, some selfish modern African presidents who refuse to relinquish power base it on the argument that the old African king was on the throne for life. But are the king in traditional Africa and the president in modern Africa the same? It is therefore important to examine the past in Africa's present.

Third, politics and violence are bedfellows. Indeed, violence has been the most assured means to effect change, transfer of power, and reforms. The state uses violence to govern: it coerces people into obedience, and the role of the police and army is primarily to force people to behave in certain ways. The state monopolizes violence—those in power control the army and police, weapons, and other means used to govern by force. Opposition forces, knowing full well that those in government do not believe in negotiations, take to violence to make their points. Since those in power do not wish to relinquish it, the best way to get rid of them is generally through violence.

Fourth, politics is not simply about power and governance—a full understanding must incorporate the social and economic components. In Africa, the primary motive of politics is the pursuit not of public good, but of personal interest. Power is the best access to wealth. In many countries, the best business is that of politics, and the most successful entrepreneurs are politicians with access to state funds who spend them recklessly and invest little. Contest for power is not necessarily about choosing which of competing policies to pursue, but about opportunities to make money. To lose a contest is interpreted as a colossal failure of business and investment. And if the business collapses, what does the man eat? So strong is the connection between power and wealth that it is no exaggeration to say that many wealthy Africans have acquired their fortunes through connection to state power. For as long as politics remains profitable, so too will it be competitive in a destructive manner.

Finally, the nature of politics affects that of the overall economy, which has been grossly undermined. The political class, in seeking and consolidating power, consumes the bulk of the resources necessary for development. Military rule, one-party regimes, and other forms of government rely on a political strategy of patrimonialism, a culture which favors the recruitment and bribery of clients in order for the patrons to stay in power. Rather than develop a village, political leaders spend the money on a few representatives of the village in order to silence the majority. Rather than develop the nation, the leading members spend more time figuring out how they will share their country's resources, playing the "politics of the belly."[1] Patrimonialism brings down an economy: corruption erodes the fabric of society; and the maintenance of an ever-increasing number of loyalists consumes so much money that ultimately the state is bankrupted.

The Past in the Present

African societies are old. The longest phase in their history is still the precolonial (before 1885), and the so-called modern era is less than a hundred years old in most places. In their long precolonial history, Africans established states, political systems, and statuses, and generated surpluses which were distributed through the networks of politics and economy. Even today, many Africans continue to draw their values from the established political and social institutions of old. When new changes are introduced, they make sense of it by relating them to the past or adapting them to what they already have. The norms and ideals of politics, as well as the attitudes and behavior of political actors, show the stamp of the past. The modern African politician receives and entertains his guests in ways similar to a nineteenth-century chief. The resolution of conflicts through the use of violence or nonsecular agencies has been consistent for decades. Concepts of power have not necessarily been modified in spite of different political systems.

The most basic authority was the family, with a head who enjoyed a wide degree of power.[2] In some sense, the power of the family head mirrored that of the state. The head, usually a man, was senior by age and associated with wisdom and respect. He was an effective manager of resources and people, as he allocated responsibilities and took care of the people's needs. While performing secular functions, he also had a nonsecular one: the family head mediated between his people and their ancestors, and he ensured that family deities were propitiated at regular intervals. While he derived his authority from eldership and religion, sanctions could be imposed if he abused his power, and the belief was that the ancestor and gods could punish him in various ways, most especially with a series of bad harvests.

Above the family were clans, villages, states, and empires governed by all kinds of political systems. Some of the concepts of power and responsibility resembled those of the family head. Although rulers presided over small or big states, the bases of authority were varied. There were those who derived power from priestly duties—the control of community shrines enabled them to exercise secular powers. Where a state was large, military power was needed, in addition to management skills. Irrespective of the basis of power, the chief or king exercised authority, sanctioned by the gods. Regarded as the "father" of all, he had the support of ancestors and gods. His performance and health affected those of the community—if there was no rain or the harvest was poor, these misfortunes were blamed on him. Indigenous rulers were expected to govern with the interests of the community in mind: they were the custodians of the land; they had to respect religious priests; and checks and balances prevented autocracy.

Some of the institutions have survived, if not in their structures in all cases, then in their symbolism and ideas. Many have changed so substantially that there is even nothing "traditional" about them anymore as we move into the twenty-first century. It is important to stress that continuity and change have characterized African political culture. Even during the precolonial era, evidence of great changes occurred, as in the rise of the military to power during the nineteenth century.[3] From time to time, new men of ability, wealth, and status could emerge, and the system had to recognize them. Warrior-leaders established new dynasties and kingdoms, and governed with modified laws, as in cases of leaders such as Sundiata of Mali or Shaka the Zulu. Changing commercial networks could also provide opportunities for some people to accumulate wealth, thus enhancing their chances to acquire influence and status, as exemplified by the entrepreneurs in the Niger Delta during the nineteenth century. New powerful men often emerged to challenge the existing order, and might cause the downfall of an old dynasty, wars, and migrations to establish new communities.[4]

The successful introduction of Islam and Christianity also affected politics and the political culture, as ideas were drawn from both religions. For instance, Islam promoted the centralization of power, as established kings and chiefs borrowed ideas from it to give themselves more power. As a literate religion, Islam gave birth to the use of clerics and the conduct of

diplomacy based on written documents. Islamic laws spread, complementing indigenous ones. Islam was also the basis for many jihads in African
history. Where the jihads were successful, as in the case of the Sokoto jihad
of the nineteenth century, they transformed politics and society in many
revolutionary ways. The legacy of Islam can be seen in the modern politics
of north Africa, and areas with large Islamic populations such as Senegal,
Nigeria, and Sudan. In these places, Islamic laws are used, Muslims are in
power, and the competition with Christianity is intense.[5]

Christianity promoted the creation of a new elite whose members
argued that the acquisition of Western education was necessary to be in
power and to develop a modern vision of progress.[6] From the very beginning, Christianity and the elite it produced were subversive of tradition
precisely because they demanded secular politics and the construction of
Africa in the image of the West. Missionaries and many of their African
converts even prepared the way for the colonization of Africa in the last
quarter of the nineteenth century. During the twentieth century, the Christianized elite controlled the bureaucracies and government in many countries.[7]

When the Europeans conquered Africa, it was not "one Africa" but
hundreds of nations governed by kings and chiefs, or just elders in the case
of areas with village governments. When the Europeans left Africa, the
number of countries was about fifty, and power was given to a new generation of African elite produced in Western formal schools. In many places,
chiefs, kings, Imams, priests, and priestesses survived, with varying degrees
of power over their communities. In a colonial situation, Europeans had
the ultimate power. Where a system of indirect rule was instituted, as in
British colonies, the idea was to manipulate traditional chiefs and kings to
work for the colonial governments. In other places, the colonial officers
exercised power in a direct way, ignoring and undermining the indigenous
power elite. If the chiefs and kings lived among the people and saw the
representatives of lineages on a daily basis, the colonial officers maintained
a distance from the people. The wielders of the ultimate power lived outside of the continent; and their representatives and agents in the continent
issued instructions. Africans had to cooperate, collaborate, or resist the
government. The dominant political value revolved around exploitation:
the primary motive of the colonial power was to cheat and exploit Africans;
and the primary duty of Africans was to resist.[8] Government was perceived
as the enemy of the people, a view that remains current today.

The new educated elite were successful in displacing the Islamic and
traditional elite from power and influence from the 1940s onward. Cars,
coats, ties, radios, and many other imported items replaced indigenous

objects of status, such as horses and clothes. Wage labor ensured more money on a regular basis. The tension between the representatives of old and new elite remains, and this takes many dimensions. The educated elite form political parties that compete vigorously, exploiting religious and ethnic differences in society in order to gain power. In analyzing the contributions of the educated elite, one has to combine their self-interest with the expressed concerns for the improvement of their countries.

In running the modern governments, it is necessary to understand what has survived of the past and what requires retention and modification. There have been two contradictions. On one hand, nowhere do the traditional chiefs enjoy as much power as before. Indeed, the destruction of their power (and even of the institution) began during the colonial period. The attitude of the colonial government varied, but in all, the traditional power arrangement was substantially damaged.[9] After independence, chiefs and kings wanted some restoration of traditional power—the demand has continued till today in some countries such as Uganda, Ghana, and Nigeria.

On the other hand, modern governments based upon Western political systems or authoritarian military regimes see the kings, chiefs, and elders as keepers of ancient traditions and values. Modern leaders manifest a desire to keep this culture and traditions, using, in part, the agency of chiefs and kings. If it were possible, the chiefs and kings could be kept in a museum, open during the day and locked at night. However, as human beings presiding over existing parallel institutions, the chiefs and kings remain visible, even if some are no more than symbols of a dying past. Modern rulers do not govern well, thus instigating a permanent search either to replace human beings in power or to change the system entirely. Should power go back to the old chiefs or should the old political system be revived for modern Africa? The debate as to how best to integrate traditional chiefs into modern politics continues. Many argue that rather than revive traditional chieftaincy systems, it is better to focus on strengthening democratic forces. Chiefs, they argue, represent families and narrow interests, and the society that gave them relevance is no more. In addition, they argue that chieftaincy has been corrupted and commodified. There are others who make a case for the involvement of traditional chiefs, based on the survival of chieftaincy practices, the respect accorded to chiefs in local communities, the possibility of using the institution to build cohesion in society, and the need to learn from some of its enduring values.

The old and new elite intermix in some clever ways, as the representatives of both seek to manipulate one another.[10] Thus, a modern military general is an honorary chief; a highly trained, highly educated civil servant can retire from his job to become a king; politicians seeking power consult with traditional chiefs for support and may visit "witch-doctors" in the middle of the night for magical power; many in power depend on marabouts (Islamic charm makers) and traditional diviners to know their future and political fate; and chiefs beg the representatives of the modern political institutions for more money, more power, and better access to the corridors of power. The interactions take other forms: military generals have removed from power the traditional chiefs that disagree with them, and many chiefs have been dethroned, forced to go into exile, or downgraded. In view of the changes in the last one hundred years, how traditional is the institution of chieftaincy, and can the concepts derived from traditional politics be applied to the modern era? If democracy assumes that the masses will have power—at least through the ballot box—why does the African system continue to be about the excesses of "big men" who are hard to dislodge from power? These are questions that the continent has yet to address fully.

In spite of all the changes, elements of the past have survived. Chieftaincy has just been mentioned, and many continue to seek titles for the prestige it confers. Religious leaders enjoy tremendous influence and respect. Without formal power, religious leaders are still able to speak to millions of people and shape their worldview and politics. Households are managed by heads who have to respond to the local and national economy and politics.

Another enduring feature has been the marginalization of women in politics. Women play limited roles in modern politics. Almost all the important political positions are held by men, and Africa has yet to produce its first woman head of state. Women in elective legislative offices are few. In many countries, there is not a single woman in the cabinet; in places where there are women in cabinet positions, the number is few and the agencies are not necessarily the key ones. The key institutions of female power in precolonial societies (such as age grade associations and guilds) do exist, but they have become merely symbolic and their activities mainly cultural. Some do exercise power in cities, but the influence does not extend to the national level.

There are some cultural forces at work against the acquisition of formal power by women. In Islamic areas, the justification is found in religion, with some religious leaders saying that women cannot hold important secular positions. There is a pervasive conservative tradition that women should be subordinate to men. If men acquire power, the woman should "embroider" it by serving as the hostess. A woman aspiring to power is criticized for being too assertive, and her independence may be perceived as a threat both to her family and society. In the words of Daniel arap Moi, Kenya's president, in 1985, "God made man the head of the family . . . challenging that was tantamount to criticizing God."[11] The speech could well have been written for him by a woman, as many also think along this line, having been long accustomed to patriarchal culture. Thanks to the school system, the church, and the media, the ideology of female political subordination is firmly established to the extent that many women actually talk like Moi. In spite of the demand for change by many elite women, there are those among them whose main concern is not politics but the acquisition of privileges within the household and a focus on the training of their children.

But not all women accept the conservative agenda and ideology. In most countries, various organizations have emerged to challenge the status quo. Among the results of the incessant demand for political involvement have been the appointment of some women to high positions, the creation of agencies solely devoted to women's issues, and changes in law to ensure that women have more equitable rights to inheritance when their husbands and parents die. Notable examples include the mandatory involvement of women in the cabinets of states and federal governments in Nigeria; the women's bureaus in Zimbabwe, Lesotho, Kenya, and Cameroon; and the mandatory appointment of ten women to the Tanzanian legislature.[12]

Authoritarianism

Modern politics has witnessed the collapse of democratic institutions and attempts to institute authoritarian regimes. The failure of democratic regimes has taken many forms: military regimes, one-party states, and even a one-man personal rule. In all, one sees an extensive use of and dependence on violence. In cases where the state declined or collapsed, "warlords" often emerged, men who profited greatly from instability. Politics often relies for survival on the culture of violence; for instance, the military uses force to take over power. As an avenue to make money, politics is exceedingly lucrative.[13]

The history of Africa during the twentieth century was marked by authoritarianism. The repressive colonial rule by white officers gave way to oppressive rule by Africans until small democratic gains were made in the 1990s. For more than thirty years, Africa saw leaders of shady and shoddy character, including brutal dictators such as Mobutu Sese Seko of Zaire, Idi

Amin of Uganda, Sani Abacha of Nigeria, many military officers, self-appointed life-presidents, and monarchs appearing no better than clowns. To be sure, there were some civilian governments, even if of temporary duration, as in the case of Nigeria in the 1970s, and committed revolutionary governments, but the general tendency was toward authoritarianism.

Authoritarianism did not just appear all of a sudden. From the very beginning of modern politics, that is, at the stage when African countries obtained their independence, things went wrong. The alien European institutions lacked the local cultures and leadership to sustain them. The best lessons that Africans had, and one which they learned very well, was about dictatorship. Colonial leaders were powerful and authoritarian; and their mission was to plunder. Africans inherited this backward notion of power and of antidevelopment. The colonial state lacked any legitimacy based on the public—the independent states moved in this direction as well.[14] Lacking legitimacy, the colonial state depended on violence, with the use of the army and police to force people into obedience—thus, independent African states acquired this political culture as well. Force was the sole determinant of power in the colonial state, and excesses on the part of leaders were not necessarily punished. Indeed, if civilian colonial leaders survived the army, the modern state could not, as African soldiers used violence to put themselves in power. If the colonial state built powerful central institutions, the African leaders who inherited power similarly expropriated power and abused it. Like the colonial officers, African leaders regarded power as an avenue to wealth in order to maintain themselves in power, pay the police and army who protected them, and repress citizens who demanded changes to their lives.[15]

The first generation of leaders who inherited power from the colonial governments had to grapple with a myriad of problems, some of which were created for them and new ones that they created for themselves.[16] To rally the people against the colonial powers, they promised too much of the good things of life. Indeed, some were tempted by exaggerated economic figures of savings and foreign reserves to imagine that many things were possible within a short period of self-government. Once in power, they realized that they could not fulfil their promises. Rather than find a clever way of presenting the problems to their people, they turned their people into "subjects," enemies to deal with. The support base weakened, and the use of violence became a preferred option to solve problems. Continued economic decline further eroded the basis of political power. Many more Africans needed jobs, millions moved to the cities to create unbearable pressure on social services, and organizations emerged to make more aggressive demands for change.

If the pioneer leaders criticized the colonial governments and ended in power in the final outcome, they chose instead to combat and destroy opposition forces in order to retain power. Rather than divert money away from the police and army to provide food and amenities, they actually began to spend more money on defense and security. As more subjects became "enemies," so did the various governments intensify their campaigns against their own people. The list of enemies is the same in all the countries: university students, trade unions, peasants, and opposition political parties. The origins of radicalism were during the colonial period, when a number of protest organizations emerged. Many were, in fact, active in the politics of anticolonial nationalism, but were excluded from power at independence, as in the case of the radical Union des Populations Camerounaises in Cameroon.[17] Radicalism continues to be a vibrant political culture in Africa.

Always believing that their vision of their country's future is more patriotic and better than that of those in power, opposition groups can be relentless in criticizing the rulers. They attack their governments through strikes, demonstrations, critical commentaries in newspapers, and other "radical" activities. Those in government, eager to remain in power and permanently insecure, reply with violence. Rather than engage in productive dialogue, they resort to force as the solution. Knowing full well that violence is inadequate to retain control, those in power rely on politicized ethnicity for survival—they consolidate their power by manipulating ethnic loyalty. While speaking about national unity, they eagerly build their ethnic base in order to have a reliable constituency.

Irrespective of the political arrangement, authoritarianism manifests similar features. There is a "big man" at the top with almost absolute power. The big man and the government mean the same thing; his private wealth and that of the state are combined. He and his cronies centralize all powers, even the most mundane. Opposition forces are destroyed, eliminated, or crippled. Living in perpetual fear, the big man lives in a cage, but with all the attributes of an angry lion. He governs by distributing largess to his followers and destroying all his opponents. The populace is traumatized, and the people survive by pretenses, faking laughter to avoid being jailed. The big man may preside over a one-party system, but the most notorious among them are military generals in power who are accountable only to themselves. As there are few or no democratic institutions, civil service agencies are co-opted into governance, and ideas are presented not as options but as mandatory policies to pursue. People become experiments to test undigested ideas. All formal government sectors are inefficient, corruption becomes institutionalized, and hard work and creativity do not necessarily get rewarded. To reward members of his ethnic groups and followers, the big man will give contracts to loyalist businessmen and women. The police and army can be expanded to include people from the same ethnic group as that of the big man.

Although there are organs of government, they do not necessarily operate in isolation and with checks and balances. Paramount is the executive, whose key members control all power, govern by decree, and ignore the legislature where it exists. The executive stretches its hands into all matters, even those connected with small local governments. By being the major distributor of state largess, the executive controls the economy and the means to gain entry into the principal political offices. In some countries, members of the executive branch can also be the most wealthy, thus combining political and economic power. The police, the judiciary, the army, and the legislature (where it exists) all are accountable to the big man. The police and army perform crucial roles, and they are expanded rapidly to take care of protests and monitor opposition groups. In some countries, as in Nigeria, the defense budgets for many years was far more than what was spent on social services or education, even when the nation was not at war. Similarly, countries such as the Sudan and the Democratic Republic of Congo have huge budgets for the police and army. The bureaucracies expand, not necessarily to improve efficiency and bring the government nearer to the people, but to create jobs for many more people and perform basic routine services. The bureaucracies are not independent actors or agents, and they are an integral part of corrupt political machines.

In concrete terms, authoritarianism and centralization developed into one-party regimes or military rule led by one strong man. The strategy is always to disempower all opposition forces and leaders, reduce the political space to a manageable unit, and prevent the rise of alternative political parties and social movements. Laws can be made to outlaw other political parties and the formation of new ones, constitutions are in place to prevent the emergence of new parties, and electoral laws favor only the members of the political party in government. As Aristide Zolberg notes, where it is possible to co-opt members of opposing parties into the ruling government, this will be done, otherwise force will be used to destroy the opposition forces.[18] After this destruction, the party in power takes measures, not only to consolidate itself, but to become the only one with the resources and the means to govern. Examples of countries that have experienced one-party rule are many: among them are Ghana, Guinea, Tanzania, Kenya, Cameroon, Uganda, Côte d'Ivoire, and Mozambique.

Personal rule is not necessarily secure or autonomous. Where there are minerals and raw materials needed by external companies, foreign governments may become involved to protect multinational companies. The authoritarian leader and his agents may become subordinates of the foreign power, taking notes and dictation. When they run their economies and acquire extensive external debts, they become more subservient to external powers and use extensive coercion to subdue their restless population.

There are domestic enemies and opposition forces as well. Dissent is not tolerated; the police and secret service monitor critics and opponents. However, the system is unstable. As the big man enjoys his power and wealth, he incurs the jealousy of his associates who want to be like him, even if they pretend to seek positive changes and put an end to corrupt practices. Palace coups are not uncommon. If unsuccessful, the revenge is bloody, just to warn others never to nurse similar ambitions unless they have prepared their graves. But as the gross economic mismanagement, failed policies, and waste of national revenues drive more and more people into poverty, opposition leaders have a large number of angry and willing people to recruit. The radicalization process cannot be halted, despite the heavy-handedness of state power. Even when the ruler has tried to use all available means to retain power, there are cases of states that have declined or collapsed altogether.[19]

In the 1990s, warlords emerged in countries such as Sierra Leone, Congo, Sudan, Liberia, Angola, Somalia, Rwanda, and Chad. The phenomenon continues in some areas and will certainly occur again when central institutions of power either collapse or weaken. Instability may unleash long periods of violence, with a few warlords emerging as "commanders." These commanders can be motivated by ideologies (as in the project of ethnic nationalism), by personal ambition for power, or by a desire for money where there are resources to exploit and sell. The longer the violence, the greater the chance to internationalize the conflict and seek external resources or support. The activities of warlords do not necessarily make wars "illegitimate," especially where there are issues of ethnic and religious divisions to negotiate; in other words, not all wars are over minerals, but long-standing political problems. The problem is that the activities of warlords have led to the depiction of many wars as irrational, organized by robbers and bandits for personal self-aggrandizement. Not all African political leaders and warriors are "uncivilized bandits" using wars to make money.

Warlords profit from political instability, turning it into advantages to create "chiefdoms." In such places, the emergence of warlords was preceded by wars, conflicts for power, or even the collapse of the states. Some warlords wish wars never to end, as they benefit from what has been characterized as the "market of violence," a situation of permanent lawlessness. Warlords protect areas with minerals such as gold and diamonds, or timber, collecting "protection fees" from miners and multinational companies. Where local and international relief agencies work to supply food, medicine, clothes, and water to refugees, warlords divert some of these to themselves, obtaining basic items of survival without working for them. They also organize raiding expeditions to kidnap opponents and steal (even from poor farmers), all to add to their resources.

The more profits they accumulate, the more they stand in the way of a return to the rule of law. They provide temporary stability in the areas they control, while some among them either negotiate peace with their competitors or gain dominant power over the country. To be sure, a few among them are "freedom fighters," either championing the cause of the country or of an ethnic group within it. Warlords can be so successful as to become autonomous of the state and international agencies. They create organizations to procure arms, train soldiers, and produce and run small markets. Where a state still functions, it can exist in competition with warlords, as both compete for control, using violence.[20] Those who control the state and their rivals keep fighting until one force is strong enough to subdue the other. Meanwhile, each benefits from the violence by exercising raw coercive powers; by setting up units to fight but also to rob opponents, smuggle arms, fuel, and food; and by creating external propaganda in order to raise money.

Whatever stability or economy does exist rests on the creative ability of the warlord to use violence and to mobilize the resources to coerce those under his control. Development comes to a halt as the economy becomes "privatized" in a few hands. If minerals do not constitute the sole reason to instigate a war, access to them provides opportunities to feed and reward soldiers, buy guns, and even pay for diplomacy. Charles Taylor of Liberia used timber exports to finance his wars, and the warlords in central Africa profited from diamonds. Without a state in place, warlords as leaders do not have to be accountable or evaluated on their contributions to development. Unlike a government, they do not need to build schools or roads; their main task is to maintain the loyalty of their followers and soldiers.

In some situations, as in the case of Somalia, warlords are not necessarily illegitimate leaders. In Somalia, where the clan forms the basic social unit, a warlord derives legitimacy as a political leader. Where the state is in decline or has collapsed, contestants for power can manipulate their ethnicities for legitimacy. Connections to fragile state power can also provide a source of legitimacy, as in the case of rival leaders in Rwanda, Congo, Chad, Liberia, and Sierra Leone during their political crises and conflicts.

After reviewing the performance of men like Sani Abacha of Nigeria, Idi Amin of Uganda, and Mobutu Sese Seko of Zaire, many so-called analysts attribute authoritarianism and warlordism to Africans' lack of intelligence. However, it is the analysts who lack the intelligence to understand this complex set of characters. These rulers and others like them are so politically astute that they understand the intricate process of acquiring power, and they have the skills to retain power. Having acquired power, their notion of what to do with it may be backward, or they may be interested in staying in power only because of greed. They are all consistent in using the police and army to destroy opposition forces and possible contenders to their thrones—yet more evidence that there is method in their so-called madness.

There is rationality as well in the arguments that they put forward to justify authoritarianism, even if their styles are flawed. To start with, they inherited an authoritarian model from the colonial government, a good foundation on which to erect a centralized structure of power. In the political climate in which many of them operate, it is much easier to move toward centralization than decentralization and democracy. Next, authoritarianism and centralization provide easy answers to deal with opposition forces and diverse cleavages—it is faster for the leaders to kill their enemies than to engage in dialogue with them. The option of dialogue, as they understand it, is too time consuming, and the result is unpredictable. The monopolization of power in a centralized state forces the majority of the population to obey policies, even when they disagree, and to look to one major avenue for resources.

Other arguments relate to the need for stability and development. To the multinational companies in search of business and investments, the strong man with centralized power is easier to negotiate with. The companies can identify whom to bribe and can assist in facilitating the transfer of stolen money to Western banks. As Wunsch and Olowu point out, international aid agencies support centralized governments in the belief that they can implement policies faster and also manage foreign aid.[21] From the point of view of the governments and their supporters, a centralized government and authoritarianism are necessary to prevent secession, daily political protest, and the ultimate collapse of the government. The argument is that without the big men, ethnic and religious leaders would rip the nation apart. Also, in order to develop without wasting scarce resources, it is argued that a centralized authority will make decisions faster than democratic regimes. In the final analysis, centralized authoritarian systems have brought more pain than gain.[22]

Military rule is another manifestation of authoritarianism, a variant of a one-party state led by a powerful big man. Samuel Decalo's summary of the phenomenon of military rule in Africa is cogent:

> If during the 1960s the coup d'état emerged as the most visible and recurrent characteristic of the African political experience, by the 1980s, quasi-permanent military rule, of whatever ideological hue, had become the norm for most of the continent. At any one time, 65 percent of all of Africa's inhabitants and well over half of its states are governed by military administrations.[23]

The trend began in 1953 with the rise to power in Egypt of Gamel Abdul Nasser, and by the 1980s, it had become a routine occurrence. The number of unsuccessful coup attempts cannot be known, while only a handful of African countries escaped military intervention.

The educated elite of the colonial era, regarding themselves as the successors to colonial officers, did not anticipate this development. After all, recruitment to the army had concentrated on members of the lower class and those lacking the privilege of access to Western education. As the countries attained independence, the armed forces were expanded partly in order to protect those in power against opposition forces. The military became involved in politics, at first indirectly by protecting those in power. However, with the weapons in their control and with ambitions for wealth and power, military officers seized control of the government.

In many countries, early military coups were welcomed. The failure of the government to provide for its people, solve problems of poverty, and fulfil the promises made during the decolonization years all worked in favor of the military. The civilian politicians who rely too much on the army have done so at great risk to themselves—as officers realize the advantages of power, they prefer to move from the back seat to the front row. Excuses to seize power need not even be invented; as most countries have serious economic and political problems, the conditions for change are permanent. Thus, on assuming power, irrespective of the country or the time, military officers have used almost the same reasons to justify their actions: the need to promote national unity, stabilize politics, provide social services, and develop the economy. The Marxists among them add just one more item to the list: the minimization or elimination of dependence on

Western powers. Personal ambitions are easy to disguise in a number of cases, although they become apparent soon after the officers are in power.

All the evils of politics combine in military regimes, far worse that one-party regimes and far more brutalizing than the majority of corrupt civilian authoritarian governments.[24] Mobutu started as a military leader, later to "civilianize" himself. Idi Amin of Uganda has become a legend of patrimonialism and dictatorship. Abacha of Nigeria tormented his people. Military rule is not the same. Many military leaders adopt the well-tested patron-client relationship in a one-party state and can be "benevolent" in rewarding their associates and maintaining a semblance of political stability. Some others are very reckless, using excessive coercion and distributing largess to only a few insiders.

Whether benevolent or harsh, military regimes set back the hands of the clock on democracy and nation building. The reality of power is grossly distorted, and the mechanisms for building enduring democratic institutions are undermined. The military leader is more than just the typical big man; his power may approach that of the old pharaoh, except that he is not divine. When forced by internal and external pressure to "democratize," the military leader throws off his uniform, announces himself as a "civilian," and continues to govern as before. Quick and clever to co-opt members of the overthrown civilian government into power, the military ruler follows a similar economic path to that of his predecessor and with the same result: economic stagnation. As the big man, the military leader consolidates his power by becoming the patron. With the government bank under his control, he gives money away without any regard for accountability. He is also an ethnic leader, and his followers are expected to be loyal clients. Their tastes are huge, and their ability to consume expensive imported items lack any sense of proportion. To them, the real exercise of power lies in the ability to induce fear.

Imperialism and Its Aftermath

African leaders have autonomous powers in certain areas, but they are also mere pawns in others. Any analysis of the culture of politics must situate Africa in a global context, in order to see how the entire continent itself is marginalized and exploited by external interests. For a long time, the West has contributed to the failure of stable politics in Africa—even committed leaders have been removed or killed when they stood in the way of Western economic and political interests. When we talk about political failures, we sometimes mean no more than the failure to manage inherited political institutions. At independence, many countries received foreign constitutions, formulated in partnership between colonial authorities and the African educated elite. The elite had not been privileged to run a government, and their knowledge was limited to ideas about how the constitutions of other lands worked.

Africa has long been incorporated into the Western capitalist world. The brutalizing experience of the trans-Atlantic slave trade lingers till today. Western racism and the perception of inferior African race grew with the slave trade. The stereotypes of those years are being repeated even today. The damage caused to group relations has not been fully repaired. The lack of respect often manifested in modern politics can be traced to this experience as well as the wars and kidnapping expeditions. The exchange of human beings for luxury items promoted a culture of consumption, which has grown worse.

The nineteenth century witnessed further penetration by the West, as European powers imposed colonial regimes that lasted in many areas till the 1960s, and much later in other countries. In many ways, the foundation of modern Africa was laid in the colonial economy and politics. The boundaries of Africa were drawn, as new supranations were imposed on preexisting ones. What was paramount in remaking Africa was the interest of their conquerors and the pattern of their conquests. Whether one African is French-speaking and the other is English-speaking has nothing to do with choice but foreign conquest. Some countries are small (Gambia) and some are huge (Sudan); some have access to the sea and some do not. Some are poor and some are rich. Nigeria, for instance has about a quarter of the African population, making the country and its problems larger than those of most others. The modern boundaries have not been without liabilities. To start with, there has been no self-sustained loyalty or nationality to give its citizens a notion of belonging. The older nations that are submerged in them continue to retain their identities. Intra-ethnic trade relations have been destroyed in some cases.

Colonial rule was about the politics and reality of subjugation. The economies were reoriented to serve external interests. Very quickly, Africa became dependent on the West. Societies that were previously self-reliant for their basic needs and food have now become dependent on others. Various aspects of the colonial economy were later to create political problems. Nearly everywhere, conditions for social and economic inequalities were created—those with access to formal economies, Western education, and good jobs did very well. Since the mid-twentieth century, creating opportunities for the poor has been a major challenge as the rich continue to maintain their privileges. The urbanization process and the concentration of modern amenities in the cities instigated widespread migrations away from the rural areas.

Western political institutions were dispatched to Africa in the first half of the twentieth century. However, there were serious contradictions. Whereas the European countries claimed to be democratic (with the exception of Portugal), they practiced rigid autocratic control in their colonies. A few years prior to their departure, the European powers began to introduce democratic constitutions and practices, yet the speed of the departure was such that new practices had no time to take root or to become domesticated.[25] The idea of voting and the power of representatives of the people were introduced in many parts of Africa in the 1950s.[26] Many of the Africans that inherited power lacked the experience to manage modern states. The Portuguese left with bitterness, following a series of wars they waged to hang on to their colonies;[27] the Belgians gave a scant notice, and the Congo collapsed within weeks. Bureaucratic and technical skills were not imparted to the majority of Africans, and only the British and French were able to train a small number of Africans in business and management practices.[28] With little or no regard for Africa's established institutions and culture, initial governments were established on the models of Europe. Thus, the French transferred the idea of separate organs of government and a powerful president, and the British that of a Westminster parliamentary model with the parliament choosing the prime minister. In practice, none of the foreign models worked as anticipated.

The colonial state,[29] full of tensions and contradictions, was not a desirable foundation to inherit. To start with, and as noted above, a new educated elite emerged. In this, there were various problems, one of competition between a traditional elite and the new one, yet unresolved today. Second, the provision of education—to create elite members—was both inadequate and unequal.[30] As previously noted, the manpower for development was in short supply, even nonexistent in many areas. In some countries, as in the case of Nigeria, the concentration of manpower and elite was in the south. Where the distribution was lopsided, it created a basis for political conflicts. Regions with a small number of elite complained of being dominated by those with a larger number of educated people, and the situation was worsened by elite arrogance which associated Western education with civilization. Third, there was the problem of ethnicity, discussed below. Fourth, a linkage was established between politics and violence, not to bring about any revolution, but to subject people to authoritarian control.

The colonial state, based on the use of force, promoted a culture of violence. The use of forced labor, the payment of taxes, the supply of raw materials, and other activities were made possible through the use of force and severe sanctions. By and large, African governments have improved on the colonial methods of governance by force. Violence was also part of the politics of transfer of power to Africans in the last years of colonial rule. Examples are too numerous to cite, but they include the following: the Mau Mau protests in Kenya in the 1950s; the riots in the Gold Coast in the late 1940s; the protests in Malawi in the mid-1950s; the long wars in Algeria in the 1950s; the brutal wars in all the Portuguese colonies; and the anti-apartheid struggles in South Africa.[31] All these established a culture of violence in politics, and even today, riots and rebellions are common features of African life and politics.

The termination of European rule has not put an end to European influence in Africa. As Segun Osoba noted in an essay on Nigeria's decolonization, the goal of the British was to transfer power to politicians who were not hostile to them.[32] A similar strategy was used in many other colonies, just to ensure that an end to European rule would not mean an end to the pursuit of European interests in Africa. When it was clear that anticolonial nationalism would become stronger and many more Africans would be radicalized, the option adopted by the British and French was to seek compromises with conservative leaders in order to negotiate the transfer of power without destroying established political and economic relations. Indeed, in some countries, as in the case of Cameroon, those who inherited power played minimal roles in the nationalist politics. Their accession was possible because the European powers did not want radicals and socialists in power.[33] In a similar manner, foreign companies pursued strategies to retain control after independence, suggesting regulations that would favor them,[34] and in some cases (as in that of the Congo) actually pressuring Western countries to be involved in the selection of those in power.

With pro-European leaders in power, the policies in independent Africa did not depart significantly from the colonial ones, leading Kwame Nkrumah of Ghana to describe the situation as neocolonial. The colonial economic structure was sustained, as raw materials continued to be sold in exchange for imports, while development plans revolved mainly around the protection of private property.

African countries entered their independence era during the Cold War. Leading the pro-capitalist groups, the United States interpreted African politics from the imperatives of the Cold War. Thus, the United States would support only moderate, pro-Europe leaders. For a long time, the United States and its allies supported the minority regimes in South Africa, in part because of the trade in minerals. As bad as the Portuguese colonies were in treating Africans, the lack of support from the U.S and many other Western countries was far worse. Radicalism in Africa and socialist tendencies were interpreted by the United States and its allies as support for the Soviet Union and communism. Rather than see the expansion of the Soviet influence or anything resembling communism, the United States preferred to support authoritarian leaders, including such notorious figures as Mobutu Sese Seko of the Congo.[35]

Global politics began to be altered in the 1980s with the collapse of the Soviet Union and the emergence of the United States as the only superpower. Russia lost interest in Africa, and it cooperated with the United States in a number of conflict areas. Countries that had received military and financial aid during the Cold War began to lose them, as in the examples of Angola and Mozambique. In the post–Cold War era, Africa acquired more debt. Neoliberal politics and an economy promoted by the World Bank and the International Monetary Fund (IMF) seek a minimalist government that interferes little in the economy. Poor Africans are expected to engage powerful local and international markets partly on their own terms, with the minimalist state collecting taxes from them. The Structural Adjustment Program (see chapter 4) created big troubles. Foreign aid declined, and former clients of the Soviet Union and the United States lost their privileges. France began to reduce its support for its client states, forcing the governments to respond to demands for an end to one-party regimes. In Somalia, Sierra Leone, Rwanda, Burundi, and a few other countries, major conflicts broke out, leading to changes in power politics. External powers create their own problems, but the domestic ones are more devastating.

Ethnicity and Conflicts

African identities are formulated by religion and place of birth, both of which affect politics. The issues of religion and ethnicity are discussed in chapter 6, with a detailed case study on Nigeria. Here, some salient features are highlighted. Political leaders often regard themselves as ethnic leaders.[36] Consensus is hard to build and national resources are difficult to share, if competitors represent established ethnic groups. For self-mobility and in pursuit of the interests of the ethnic group, politics becomes an occupation in itself. In the popular American and European media, ethnicity is referred to as "tribalism," and Africans are presented as belonging to various "tribes" with some governed by so-called warlords, as in the case of Somali political leaders.[37]

Africans have always been divided into various groups, autonomous nations, and states, even before the European conquest. Mainly farmers and thus tied to their lands, their loyalty revolved around the community which offered the greatest protection to all individuals. Elders and leaders were near—to those who lived in big kingdoms, the representatives of kings did not disturb the land tenure system. Older identities were based on kinship and clans, and were later broadened into ethnic identities during the twentieth century. Indeed, missionaries and colonial administrators contributed to the invention of many "tribes" and the emergence of "tribal leaders" who developed the ambition to lead their people. What becomes a major problem in the contemporary world is that these divisions make it difficult to build powerful countries and stable politics. For this failure, Europeans and Africans have to share the blame.

To start with, the colonial powers chose to regard Africans as "tribal," promoting ideas that were particularistic rather than nationalistic. Uneven development and opportunities later generated tensions. The spread of Western education, urbanization, the location of hospitals and amenities, and many others of the desired new changes did not extend to everyone. In places where these changes were concentrated in just one part of the country, as in the coastal areas in west Africa, the other areas felt marginalized. The need to overcome marginalization contributed to the politicization of ethnicity. Advantages and lack thereof were interpreted in ethnic-cum-regional terms.[38]

The contributions of Africans to ethnic problems began during the colonial period. Many began to accept and internalize the ethnic divisions. As anticolonial protests intensified, political leaders and ambitious politicians began to see themselves as future leaders. To capture power, they had to build political parties to compete and present manifestoes. They began to talk of presiding over independent nations. However, this nationalism generated its own contradictions. To start with, the notion of the nation was one introduced by the European powers. The colonial powers created the new countries, but did not unite all the people, and they did not promote any ideology of oneness among the people. African leaders did accept these conditions, saying only that they would improve upon them. But as nationalism developed among Africans, it was characterized by the domination of a new set of educated elite.[39] The number of elite members was small, which meant that they were appropriating the voices of others as they spoke on their behalf. Knowing full well that their small number was inadequate to fight the Europeans, the elite sought the means to connect with other members of society, not necessarily as partners, but as leaders. They needed a large following to justify the formation of political parties, compete with one another, and show that their ideas had mass appeal. If the elite had concentrated on building alliances along occupational and social lines, perhaps stronger nations would have emerged. Rather, what they found most profitable was to seek identification with ethnic groups: a leader would mobilize members of his own group. As the leader consolidated his power, he presented his rivals in other ethnic groups as enemies, not as competitors seeking power. The ambitions of leaders would turn into rivalries among ethnic groups. Thus, the nationalists who struggled for independence were not united, and their strategies were definitely divisive.[40]

After independence, the ethnic cleavages are consolidated, leading to civil wars in Nigeria, Sierra Leone, Liberia, Chad, and other places. The nationalism of the colonial era could not be sustained. Once the "enemy"—the colonial power—disappeared, Africans turned against each other. Those in power, the representatives of ethnic groups, came into conflict with those outside of power, who often represented other ethnicities or ideological cleavages. Conflicts have become endemic. As stated below, the politics of clients and patrons means that those who desire wealth need power. The fight is not about protecting national interests, but self-interests to secure influence, positions, and money. Perhaps, if the industrial and manufacturing bases were well developed, employment in them and the economic activities that they would promote could have created diversions from politics. But resources have always been scarce in most countries, and those few are controlled by government. Thus, the government creates the majority of the jobs, and recruitment can be based on ethnic origins. More than half of the resources generated by African governments pay the wages of those working for them, which means that they simply collect public revenues to pay themselves. Civil service jobs have grown in many countries, accounting for more than half of the total number of wage earners.

The fight for control of government is crucial indeed, and it can be organized along ethnic and religious lines. It is not unusual to form political parties along ethnic lines.[41] Those in power tend to reward areas where they come from with roads, universities, and a host of other amenities. Those outside of power mobilize members of their ethnic groups to make vigorous demands and to interpret denial as deliberate marginalization, even punishment. Since the state controls the majority of resources, it is hard not to read ethnic interpretation into its distribution. Those who control the state often do so on behalf of an ethnic group and often use resources to consolidate power.

Ethnicity is linked to prebendalism—a culture of using power to steal money—and more generally to a patron-client political culture. The ethnic leader is the distributor of largess, derived from the state, to an army of followers drawn from the members of his ethnic group. This linkage developed in the very early years of independence. The pioneer politicians lacked the financial resources to organize political parties and mobilize their people. Many had their eyes on public funds to do this, but they were also eager to overcome poverty. While they criticized European officials, they were envious of their lifestyles and possessions. To many of them, their jobs and wages were inadequate to imitate the Europeans. Again, the remedy was to seek power. Once power is achieved, the accumulation of wealth is presented in collective terms—the corrupt leader steals not just for himself, but on behalf of his ethnic group. The presentation is not necessarily rational, but sentimental. The leader presents his success and wealth as the embodiment of his "nation"—in other words, the ethnic leader must not be poor or powerless. Then, there is sharing—part of what he steals, he gives back to some of his people. And of course, members of his group derive access to jobs and privileges through the leader. Thus, corruption is justified by the necessity of meeting ethnic needs and responsibilities.[42] The leader has a safety net when accused of or arrested for corruption: his people rise to his defense. His fall and humiliation may be treated as a collective disgrace.

The leader is a patron who regards the government as an opportunity to distribute resources to his loyalists, that is, the clients. As the patron monopolizes power and resources, he is clever enough to understand that he needs many clients to survive attacks from opposition forces. Members of his ethnic groups are rewarded in many ways: recruitment to the police and army; admission to major courses in the universities; contracts to businessmen and women, travel abroad, etc. A network of political relations emerges, looking like a pyramid, with the head of the country on top. Below him are other lower-level "patrons" and middlemen, well connected to the leader and other tiers of government.

Ethnicity is not without its positive elements. In the formation of early political parties, the manipulation of ethnicity, in spite of its risk to collective national interests, made it possible to reach millions of people within a short period. The early leaders did not have sufficient resources, and communications facilities were undeveloped. Through ethnicity, word of mouth traveled rapidly from one village to another. Once the members of an ethnic group accept a leader, his legitimacy is affirmed. If ethnicity has allowed the building of a one-party centralized state, it has at the same time provided the platform to organize opposition to state power. Because a number of ethnic groups are excluded from power and the distribution of state resources, leaders emerge among them to force the political arena to open up.[43] In some instances, such opposition has led to wars and secession, and even ethnic cleansing, as in the case of Rwanda and Burundi.

The resurgence of ethnicity has to be located in the failure of modern nation-states to generate their own nationalism to hold their citizens together. People can understand what their ethnicity does for them, or what ethnic leaders can do for them in the context of political patrimonialism. However, many citizens tend to present the state as either irrelevant or useless, one that is unable to meet their needs or even manage successfully the revenue at its disposal. If the state is useless, the citizens do not necessarily work toward making it "useful," but seek alternative ways to live and survive without it. Thus, corruption becomes endemic.

The justification of corruption by many people is based on the belief that if those who manage a government are corrupt, they do not have any moral right to tell others not to take to similar practices. Related to this is a strong belief that survival in a mismanaged state requires some elements of corruption or, at the minimum, violation of state laws. If one's salary is not enough, it is strongly believed that a person is entitled to do whatever it takes to survive, even if it means that the overall interest of the nation will suffer. Also, there is no need to respect laws. Those in power are not guided by the rule of law and are not accountable. Why, then, should the citizens obey rules? If a criminal was caught in the neighborhood, rather than hand him over to the police who may release him after collecting bribes, why not impose mob justice on the spot?

In the process of creating an alternative set of rules, mob justice, and pursuing various survival strategies, Africans may fall on ethnicity, religion, and other forms of identity to create institutions not controlled by the state. Thus, the police and vigilante groups may coexist; banks and informal credit associations may flourish in the same community; and private and public schools may take care of education. Africans cannot be fully disengaged from the state, as some have argued, but they can take steps to ignore the state and find ways to confront the police and the tax collectors who have the power of coercion.

Conclusion

By the 1980s, political repression had driven many people to the walls: at a point of no return they either died or fought. Dictators and military generals had killed so many, blood rivulets turned into rivers.[44] Then came changes in the external world that created their own pressure. Political revolutions occurred in eastern Europe and the Soviet Union, and Africans began to seek an extension to their continent. Leadership and democratic institutions became thoroughly discredited in many countries, and the African people returned to their past and cultures to seek alternatives.[45]

It is clear that politics in Africa has been very disappointing. Current democratic experiments have come with violence, political assassination, an increasing level of poverty, and bitter rivalries for power. There are constitutions, but the actions of those in government are not necessarily based on them. The rule of law and accountability are ignored. Mechanisms to transfer power are still very complicated: each election is marked more by violence and accusations of fraud than by the genuine wishes of the people to elect the representatives of their choice. Corruption remains atop the list of the culture of politics.

In spite of this, the political arena remains vibrant, civil society is active, and responses to globalization are strong in calling for an equitable distribution of world resources. Areas of greater challenges lie in understanding how the majority of Africans are coping on a daily basis, playing cultural politics to survive, attacking and manipulating the state and its agents, and continually seeking the means to have better governments. The culture of politics is changing, as various components of civil society challenge the hegemonic order and call for reforms and revolution. The pressure for change comes from within. Poverty is so endemic that the best solution is not just in economic reforms, but in changing the nature of politics. Many realize that without good leaders and stable politics, their contract with poverty will be eternal.

The widespread expectation is that power should be used in the service of the people. Democracy is defined broadly to mean economic progress and the enhancement of people's living standards. Thus, we have the preface to cultural politics: the rejection of the status quo and the creation of an alternative democratic arrangement. Next is the awareness of poverty, and the need for poor people to become more politically active. Thus, we have the culture of political engagement, as people not only define their needs but analyze the actions to take. Where religion and ethnicity remain strong, they constitute the sources of identification, and culture is used to consolidate groups and their identities. As these identities struggle, they create oppositional cultures. Religious identities have been used to mobilize followers in Senegal, Algeria, Sudan, and Nigeria.[46] Women all over Africa have resorted to gender politics. In South Africa, race-based politics focuses on blackness as a cultural category to make political demands.

Some significant changes have occurred since the 1990s.[47] Dominant power-holders were challenged in South Africa for many years until the system was reformed in the early 1990s. If those in power praised themselves and the democratic apparati that they presided over, members of different social movements disagreed and called for a redefinition of leadership, power, and democracy. Nongovernmental organizations flourished, all providing opportunities for protests, and demanded an end to corruption. Civil servants, tired of being accused of complicity with bad governments, also wanted major changes. Trade unions and university students questioned the neoliberalism of the IMF and the World Bank, and demanded more democratization. Professors migrated to other continents, and those who stayed behind joined various pressure groups to ask for rapid improvements in politics and the economy. In most countries, the call was for democracy, multiparty politics, and a transfer of power through the ballot box, all in a nonviolent political arena. Africans were tired of corruption and began to focus on accountability. Foreign governments and lending institutions were also eager to see changes. Thus, elections were held in many countries in the 1990s (e.g., Nigeria, Ghana, and Zambia) and many states began to experiment with multiparty political systems.

As Africa enters the twenty-first century, it appears that the gains from the democratic changes are being exaggerated. The new leaders are expected to bring rapid economic benefits, end corruption, be assertive in international politics, manipulate globalism to Africa's advantage, end dependence on the West, and empower their citizens. None of these is happening in many countries, as a number of long-standing conditions remain. Neocolonialism is alive and well, and globalism is still about the exploitation of Africa. Ethnic and religious identities and nationalisms remain vibrant. The cancer of corruption has not been removed.

Africa no longer has a choice but to change the culture of politics. There must be accountability and the rule of law in a multi-party democratic framework. Given the multiethnic and multireligious composition of most countries, there is indeed no choice but to decentralize power, give autonomy to local communities, and encourage productive political competitions. Age-old attitudes about politics must give way to one that values service. The primary concern must be on the strategy to overcome poverty, to give power to families and villages, and to empower women who consti-tute the majority of the population and who have suffered for too long. All these changes may ultimately involve complicated dialogue and struggles. As the middle class continues to increase and acquire survival means inde-pendent of the state, perhaps many will organize to offer successful chal-lenges to the monopolization of state power by members of the political class who lack the vision and ideas to transform the continent.

Notes

1. This is part of the title of a well-cited book on African politics, Jean Francois Bayart, *The State in Africa: The Politics of the Belly* (London: Longman, 1994).

2. For an overview of African cultures, see Toyin Falola, ed., *African Cultures and Societies before 1885* (Durham, N.C.: Carolina Academic Press, 2000).

3. Toyin Falola and Dare Oguntomisin, *Yoruba Warlords of the Nineteenth Century* (Trenton, N.J.: Africa World Press, 2001).

4. The literature is fairly extensive on precolonial changes. See J. F. Ade Ajayi, ed., *Africa in the Nineteenth Century until the 1880s,* vol. VI of the UNESCO General History of Africa (Berkeley: University of California Press, 1989).

5. On the legacy of Islam in modern politics, see Toyin Falola, *Violence in Nigeria: The Crisis of Religious Politics and Secular Ideologies* (Rochester, N.Y.: University of Roches-ter Press, 1998); and Jeff Hastings, *Religion and Politics in Africa* (London: Zed, 1996); and Rafiq Zakaria, *The Struggle within Islam* (London: Penguin, 1988).

6. See E. A. Ayandele, *The Educated Elite in Nigerian Society* (Ibadan: Ibadan Univer-sity Press, 1974); and Toyin Falola, *Nationalism and African Intellectuals* (Rochester, N.Y.: University of Rochester Press, 2001).

7. On the impact of Christianity, see Falola, *Violence in Nigeria*; Lamin Sanneh, *Christianity in West Africa: The Religious Impact* (Maryknoll, N.Y.: Orbis, 1983); Adrian Hastings, *African Christianity* (New York: Seabury, 1976); and David B. Barrett, *Schism and Renewal in Africa* (Nairobi: Oxford University Press, 1968).

8. An overview of colonial rule can be found in *Colonial Africa, 1885–1939,* ed. Toyin Falola (Durham, N.C.: Carolina Academic Press, 2002).

9. See Kofi Abrefa Busia, *The Position of the Chief in the Modern Political System of Ashanti* (London: Oxford University Press, 1951); Michael Crowder and Obaro Ikime, eds., *West African Chiefs: Their Changing Status under Colonial Rule and Independence* (Ile-Ife: Uni-versity of Ife Press, 1970); Kwame Arhin, *Traditional Rule in Ghana: Past and Present* (Accra, Ghana: Sedco Publishing Ltd., 1985); and Olufemi Vaughan, *Nigerian Chiefs: Traditional Power in Modern Politics, 1890s–1990s* (Rochester, N.Y.: University of Rochester Press, 2000).

10. See Toyin Falola, "Elite Networking: Traditional Chiefs in Modern Nigeria," in *African Networks, Exchange and Spatial Dynamics,* ed. Laurence Marfaing and Brigitte Reinwald (Berlin: Lit Verlag, 2001), 269–80.

11. Quoted in Kathleen Staudt, "Women's Politics, the State, and Capitalist Trans-formations in Africa," in *Studies in Power and Class in Africa,* ed. Irvin L. Markovitz (New York: Oxford University Press, 1987), 50.

12. A separate section of this book is devoted to the issue of gender and politics. See chapter 10.

13. Among the useful literature on politics in Africa, see Naomi Chazan, Robert Mortimer, John Ravenhill, and Donald Rothchild, *Politics and Society in Contemporary Africa* (Boulder, Colo.: Lynne Rienner Publishers, 1992); Stuart N. Eisenstadt and René Lemarchand, *Political Clintelism, Patronage, and Development* (Beverly Hills, Calif.: Sage Publications); Robert Fatton, Jr. *Predatory Rule: State and Civil Society in Africa* (Boulder, Colo.: Lynne Rienner, 1992); and Robert H. Jackson and Carl J. Rosberg, *Personal Rule in Black Africa* (Berkeley: University of California Press, 1982).

14. See Zaki Ergas, ed., *The African State in Transition* (New York: St. Martin's Press, 1987); Basil Davidson, *The Black Man's Burden: Africa and the Curse of the Nation State* (New York: Times Books, 1992); and Chinua Achebe, *The Trouble with Nigeria* (Enugu, Nigeria: Fourth Dimension, 1985).

15. For a devastating critique of the leadership, see George B. N. Ayittey, *Africa Betrayed* (New York: St Martin's Press, 1992); George B. N. Ayittey, *Africa in Chaos* (New York: St Martin's Griffin, 1998); Arthur Nwankwo, *African Dictators: The Logic of Tyranny and Lessons from History* (Enugu, Nigeria: Fourth Dimension, 1990); and Samuel Decalo, *Psychoses of Power: African Personal Dictatorships* (Boulder, Colo.: Westview, 1989).

16. For politics in the 1960s, see René Dumont, *False Start in Africa* (London: Deutsch Ltd., 1966); Martin Kilson, *Political Change in Sierra Leone* (Cambridge, Mass.: Harvard University Press, 1966); René Lemarchand, *Political Awakening in the Belgian Congo* (Berkeley: University of California Press, 1964); Stanislav Andreski, *The African Predicament* (New York: Atherton Press, 1969); D. K. Fieldhouse, *Black Africa, 1945–1980* (London: Allen and Unwin, 1989); and Bob Flitch and Mary Oppenheimer, *Ghana: End of an Illusion* (New York: Monthly Review Press, 1966).

17. See Ehiedu E. G. Iweriebor, *Radical Politics in Nigeria, 1945–1950: The Significance of the Zikist Movement* (Zaria, Nigeria: Ahmadu Bello University Press, 1996).

18. Aristide Zolberg, *Creating Political Order: The Party States of West Africa* (Chicago: Rand McNally, 1966), 66–76.

19. See Zolberg, *Creating Political Order*; Crawford Young and Thomas Turner, *The Rise and Decline of the Zairian State* (Madison: University of Wisconsin Press, 1985); and I. William Zartman, ed., *Collapsed States* (Boulder, Colo.: Lynne Rienner Publishers, 1985).

20. See Georg Elwert, Stephan Feuchtwang, and Dieter Neuberts, eds., *Dynamics of Violence* (Berlin: Duncker and Humbolt, 1999).

21. James S. Wunsch and Dele Olowu, *The Failure of the Centralized State: Institutions and Self-Governance in Africa* (Boulder, Colo.: Westview, 1990), 44.

22. See C. Hoskyns, *The Congo since Independence* (Oxford: Oxford University Press, 1965).

23. Samuel Decalo, *Coups and Army Rule in Africa: Studies in Military Style* (New Haven, Conn.: Yale University Press, 1976), 147–48.

24. For the evaluation of military rule, see Toyin Falola et al., *The Military Factor in Nigeria* (Lewiston, N.Y.: Edwin Mellen Press, 1994); Thomas Cox, *Civil-Military Relations in Sierra Leone: A Case Study of African Soldiers in Politics* (Cambridge, Mass.: Harvard University Press, 1976); Samuel Decalo, "Modalities of Civil-Military Stability in Africa," *Journal of Modern African Studies* 27 (1989): 547–78; Robin Luckham, "The Military, Militarization and Democratization in Africa," *African Studies Review* 37 (1994): 13–75; Isaac J. Mowoe, *The Performance of Soldiers as Governors* (Washington, D.C.: University

Press of America); and Pat McGowan and Thomas H. Johnson, "African Military Coups d'Etat and Underdevelopment: A Quantitative Historical Analysis," *Journal of Modern African Studies* 22 (1984): 633–66.

25. On colonial disengagement, see, among others, J. D. Hargreaves, *Decolonization in Africa* (London and New York: Longman, 1988); J. Ayodele Langley, *Pan-Africanism and Nationalism in West Africa, 1940–1945: A Study in Ideology and Social Classes* (London: Oxford University Press, 1973); and J. Ayodele Langley, *Ideologies of Liberation in Black Africa, 1856–1970* (London: Rex Collins, 1979).

26. See Fred M. Hayward, ed., *Elections in Independent Africa* (Boulder, Colo.: Westview, 1987).

27. See G. J. Bender, *Angola under the Portuguese* (London: Heinemann, 1978); B. Munslow, *Mozambique: The Revolution and Its Origins* (London and New York: Longman, 1983); B. Davidson, *The People's Cause: A History of Guerillas in Africa* (London and New York: Longman, 1981); A. Isaacman and N. Isaacman, *Mozambique: From Colonialism to Revolution* (Boulder, Colo.: Westview, 1983); and D. Martin and P. Johnson, *The Struggle for Zimbabwe* (London: Faber, 1981).

28. See Richard Hodder-Williams, *An Introduction to the Politics of Tropical Africa* (London: George Allen and Unwin, 1984).

29. On its analysis, see Crawford Young, *The African Colonial State in Comparative Perspective* (New Haven, Conn.: Yale University Press, 1994).

30. See P. C. Lloyd, ed., *The New Elites of Tropical Africa* (London: Oxford University Press, 1964).

31. For case studies, see B. Berman and J. Lonsdale, *Unhappy Valley: Conflict in Kenya*: Book 1, *State and Class*; Book 2, *Violence and Ethnicity* (London: James Currey, 1992); J. Hanlon, *Beggar Your Neighbors: Apartheid Power in Southern Africa* (Bloomington: Indiana University Press, 1986); and Rosemary Galli and Jocelyn Jones, *Guinea-Bissau: Politics, Economics, and Society* (London: Frances Pinter Publishers, 1987).

32. Segun Osoba, "The Transition to Neo-Colonialism," in *Britain and Nigeria: Exploitation or Development?* ed. Toyin Falola (London: Zed, 1987), 223–48.

33. See *Radical Nationalism in Cameroon: Social Origins of the UPC Rebellion* (Oxford: Oxford University Press, 1977). On the nature of French control after independence, see Patrick Manning, *Francophone Sub-Saharan Africa, 1880–1985* (New York: Cambridge University Press, 1988).

34. See Sarah Stockwell, *The Business of Decolonization: British Business Strategies in the Gold Coast* (Oxford: Oxford University Press, 2000); and Thomas J. Biersteker, *Multinationals, the State, and Control of the Nigerian Economy* (Princeton, N.J.: Princeton University Press, 1987).

35. Among useful studies on this subject are: Christopher Clapham, *Africa and the International System* (Cambridge: Cambridge University Press, 1996); John H. Harbeson and Donald Rotschild, eds., *Africa in World Politics: The African State System in Flux* (Boulder, Colo.: Westview Press, 2000); and Philip Nel and Patrick J. McGowan, eds., *Power, Wealth, and the Global Order* (Cape Town: University of Cape Town Press, 1999).

36. For case studies, see B. J. Dudley, *Parties and Politics in Nigeria* (London: Macmillan, 1968).

37. "Tribe" has negative connotations, referring to small societies that are described by Westerners as uncivilized and dangerous. Africanists opt for "ethnicities" or simply use the names by which the groups call themselves. For a discussion of the problems of using

"tribe" to define Africans, see David Wiley and Marylee Crofts, *The Third World: Africa* (Guilford, Conn.: Dushkin Publishing Company, 1988), 63–65.

38. For details on these issues, see Thomas Hodgkin, *Nationalism in Colonial Africa* (New York: New York University Press, 1957); O. Nnoli, *Ethnic Politics in Nigeria* (Enugu, Nigeria: Fourth Dimension, 1980); Donald L. Horowitz, *Ethnic Groups in Conflict* (Berkeley: University of California Press, 1985); and Pade Badru, *Imperialism and Ethnic Politics in Nigeria* (Trenton, N.J.: Africa World Press, 1998).

39. See J. S. Coleman, *Nigeria: Background to Nationalism* (Berkeley: University of California Press, 1958); and P. Gifford and W. R. Louis, eds., *Decolonization and African Independence* (New Haven and London: Yale University Press, 1988).

40. See William Tordoff, *Government and Politics in Africa* (Bloomington: Indiana University Press, 1984).

41. See Toyin Falola, ed., *African Politics in Postimperial Times: The Essays of Richard L. Sklar* (Trenton, N.J.: Africa World Press, 2002); and Joseph Rothchild, *Ethnopolitics* (New York: Cambridge University Press, 1981).

42. On the link between corruption and power, see Joseph S. Nye, "Corruption and Political Development: A Cost-Benefit Analysis," *American Political Science Review* 61, no. 2 (1967): 417–27.

43. See J. Markakis, *National and Class Conflict in the Horn of Africa* (Cambridge: Cambridge University Press, 1987).

44. See Morag Bell, *Contemporary Africa* (New York: John Wiley and Sons, 1986); Olusegun Obasanjo, ed., *African Perspectives: Myth and Realities* (Washington, D.C.: Council on Foreign Relations, 1988); and Wole Soyinka, *The Open Sore of a Continent* (New York: Oxford University Press, 1996).

45. For some useful literature on this period, see Walter O. Oyugi et al., eds., *Democratic Theory and Practice in Africa* (Portsmouth, N.H.: Heinemann, 1988); Sanford J. Ungar, *Africa: The People and Politics of an Emerging Continent* (New York: Simon and Schuster, 1989); Jennifer Whitaker, *How Can Africa Survive?* (New York: Harper and Row, 1988); and Thomas M. Callaghy, *The State-Society Struggle: Zaire in Comparative Perspective* (New York: Columbia University Press, 1984).

46. See J. O. Hunwick, ed., *Religion and National Integration in Africa* (Evanston, Ill.: Northwestern University Press, 1992); Donald Rothschild and Naomi Chazan, eds., *The Precarious Balance: State and Society in Africa* (Boulder, Colo.: Westview Press, 1988); and Gus J. Liebenow, *African Politics: Crisis and Challenges* (Bloomington: Indiana University Press, 1986).

47. For works that capture the changes of this period, see Larry Diamond and Marc F. Plattner, eds., *Economic Reform and Democracy* (Baltimore, Md.: Johns Hopkins University Press, 1995); Larry Diamond and Marc F. Plattner, eds., *Democratization in Africa* (Baltimore, Md.: Johns Hopkins University Press, 1999); Goran Hyden and Michael Bratton, eds., *Governance and Politics in Africa* (Boulder, Colo.: Lynne Rienner, 1992); Michael Bratton, *Democratic Experiences in Africa* (Cambridge: Cambridge University Press, 1997); John W. Harbeson and Donald Rothchild, eds., *Africa in World Politics: The African State System in Flux* (Boulder, Colo.: Westview Press, 2000); Christopher Clapham, "Democratisation in Africa: Obstacles and Prospects," *Third World Quarterly* 14 (1993): 423–38; John F. Clark and David Gardinier, eds., *Political Reform in Francophone Africa* (Boulder, Colo.: Westview Press, 1997); and Richard L. Sklar and C. S. Whitaker, *African Politics and Problems in Development* (Boulder, Colo.: Lynne Reinner Publishers, 1991).

6

ETHNIC NATIONALISM

"IF YOU CHASE AWAY A COWARD AND YOU DON'T GIVE HIM ROOM TO FLEE, HE WILL SHOW YOU HIS STRENGTH."

—A HAUSA PROVERB

Ethnicity is a big issue in African politics and a way to understand many aspects of African culture and society. In this chapter, I move from broad generalities on ethnicity to the specific, drawing from the data on the national (Nigeria) to the subnational (Yoruba). The idea is to explore the nature of the problem of ethnicity at the level of both ideas and history, including its complicated minutiae which involve the role of tradition in modern politics. Both national and ethnic identities have been invented and reinvented. National identities are newer, created mainly during the twentieth century: the modern countries were colonial creations, and since independence, various governments have tried to foster a feeling of national consciousness. Ethnic identities are much older. The Yoruba, Zulu, Somali, and others had existed long before European conquest, living in villages, cities, and kingdoms. The groups remain today, reorganized into different modern countries and constituting the basis of identities different from that of the nation-state.

To start with the bigger picture, ethnic nationalism is very much widespread in Africa. It involves a commitment to an established cultural group, the old nation and identity that were constituted in the past and reinvented for modern purposes. Ethnicity is one of the most effective and least costly means of uniting a group to fight for their rights and demand privi-

Figure 8. African youth in the New Religion. Children's church service, Parielles, Senegal.

leges and justice. From wars to secession crises, ethnicity has been the most potent agency for seeking freedom and autonomy from rival political leaders and ethnic groups. Ethnicity is an agency of self-assertion, allowing members of a group to stand for their rights or even to complain that their share of the economic and political resources of a state are grossly inadequate compared to those of other groups. A group mobilizes ethnic nationalism to protect itself from other groups: it seeks equality and parity with other ethnic groups in access to modern education, contracts, jobs, and other opportunities.

Whether it is regarded as invented, imagined, or real, ethnicity is about creating a strong and unified identity among a group of people. In cultural terms, the members of an ethnic group strongly believe that they are united by history, tradition, and customs. Over time, a consciousness emerges that all the members of the group are "one." In practical terms, the consciousness and historical memories are used as tools to further unite the group and exclude outsiders from certain beliefs and rituals. In social terms, an ethnic group is an organized network, with members intermarrying with one another, celebrating the rites of passage, and creating a community with values acceptable to its members. In political terms, an ethnic group becomes a political identity within the nation, led by recognized leaders who seek changes to the collective group and rewards for individual members. The leaders will keep alive ancient traditions and develop a manifesto on the modern aspirations of their people. Norms, beliefs, politics, and historical memory are all merged to consolidate the ethnic, in part to be able to advance a strong political agenda. Those among the group who are interested in politics learn to mobilize fellow members to establish political associations.

The politics and identity of an ethnic group are not necessarily stable. Members engage in conflicts with one another, as component units and social classes within a group may compete. There are local politics within cities and regions that create intra-elite and intra-ethnic tensions. Both the creation and the use of ethnicity are flexible. Until the twentieth century, many groups had existed for a long time without necessarily developing the solidarity and politics to compete and negotiate with other groups. The politicization of ethnicity is usually accomplished by a tiny number of individuals interested in power and wealth, who manipulate the group for their own agenda. Ethnicity contains both old and new elements of identity, politics, and culture. The old comprises values and histories of the past, long cohabitation in the same region, and a number of shared social practices. The new is the manipulation of the old to foster a consciousness of oneness as a group. As various studies have argued, the new elements began during the colonial era when different groups were set against one another by European powers in order to "divide and rule" them.[1] Where it suited their politics, European colonial powers created new ethnic groups by identifying them as such and giving them a label. Over time, the people developed an identity and consciousness as one group.

To draw on the examples that form the core of this chapter, the Yoruba see themselves as the descendants of one ancestor: Oduduwa. The ancient city of Ile-Ife is regarded as the common homeland, the origin of the kings and rulers that governed other Yoruba towns. Using history and common cultures, the Yoruba constitute a major ethnic group in modern Nigeria. Yoruba leaders use the concept of Yoruba "peoplehood" as a form of collective identity and "corporation" to fight for and defend many interests, including social, religious, cultural, and political ones. Where politics is ethnicized, the question that Yoruba leaders pose is: what can the country (Nigeria) do for the Yoruba?. As other ethnic groups seek to also maximize their advantages, tension and conflict inevitably arise. But the Yoruba do not just live in their homeland of southwestern Nigeria: they travel to other places, and other groups live among them. Yoruba migrants in other parts of the country and other groups living among them often see politics through an ethnic lens. The first case study explores the issue of migration and ethnicity, and the second is about Yoruba ethnicity in the politics of modern Nigeria.

Case Study 1: Homeland Politics and Ethnicity

Internal Migrations

For centuries before the British conquest of Nigeria in the last years of the nineteenth century, the people who occupied the Nigerian region had interacted on the basis of trade, war, diplomacy, and marriage. The Hausa long-distance traders could be found in southern Nigeria buying kola nuts in exchange for cattle products. Yoruba traders moved to the north, in search of horses and natron. The Niger and Benue rivers served as avenues of transportation and communication. During the nineteenth century, the Islamic jihad led by Uthman dan Fodio extended southward, establishing the Ilorin emirate in northern Yorubaland. Islam spread to the south, thus creating a religion that was transnational. Christianity was introduced to different parts of southern Nigeria during the nineteenth century, and it spread northward, notably to the areas of the middle belt.

The established patterns of intergroup relations were further sustained and extended during the colonial period. The railway network ran from Lagos, through the interior of the Yoruba to the north, and then southward, passing through Enugu to terminate in the city of Port Harcourt. Roads were constructed to link hundreds of villages and towns to the railway lines. Goods and people moved more than ever before. Islamic missionaries joined their Christian counterparts in moving to various places. Internal trade saw massive movements of traders in all directions. In the south, colonies of Hausa traders could be found in virtually all major centers. Southerners, too, moved to the north in large numbers. Educated southerners worked as clerks in the civil service and railways in the north. The informal sector in the north also opened to the southerners who worked as repair men, food vendors, beer sellers, operators of night clubs, and merchants.

In postcolonial Nigeria, trade, the civil service, schools, military, police, and federal establishments, all served to move people beyond their homeland. In the 1970s, the military regime created the National Youth Service Corps that compelled university graduates to work outside of their homelands for a year immediately upon graduation. Fresh university graduates crisscrossed the country. In the 1980s, the new federal capital of Abuja was established. There were movements, but what about ideas and perceptions about ethnicities?

Migrations and Stereotypes

The assumption was that, as Nigerians interacted, so would the people know one another and develop a commitment to the country. That assumption has been tested and found to be flawed. Nigerian nationalism has not been promoted or enhanced by these migrations. Indeed, thousands of ordinary people have lost their lives since the 1950s. When the Action Group, one of the country's early political parties, sent a delegation to the north in the 1950s to campaign for self-government, the trip provoked violence in the city of Kano. In 1966, thousands of Igbo lost their lives and property following the military coup of that year. A massive migration back to their homeland in eastern Nigeria followed, and the country fought a civil war from 1967 to 1970. It was to prevent another war that the government took a number of measures in the 1970s to let Nigerians travel around and live in places other than their states and places of birth. Federal colleges were established to draw students from various parts of the country, and a considerable amount of money was spent on new roads.

The crises since the 1980s have shown that the efforts of the 1970s and related ones have not been successful. During this period, the hostility between Christians and Muslims in the north has degenerated to a series of riots that have claimed hundreds of lives and the casual destruction of many churches and mosques. Communal conflicts have also occurred, targeted at small-scale merchants in a number of northern cities. In 1999, the Igbo in the east retaliated against the attack on their people, destroying mosques and killing many northerners among them. In Lagos, Ile-Ife, and Ibadan, the Hausa and the Yoruba have clashed over the control of markets.

All these conflicts have had disturbing consequences. First, people feel insecure living away from their cities and groups. Two, as people run back home, they carry with them negative feelings about their hosts. Third, the commitment to the development of a united Nigeria is always questioned. It is common for people to advocate secession and to struggle to put the representatives of their regions and ethnic groups in power. Fourth, as I have developed elsewhere, conflicts and hostilities are expressed in the use of negative words and stereotypes in private discussions and print media.[2] Thus, the Yoruba are described by other groups as cunning; the Hausa and Fulani are regarded as power hungry; and the Igbo as aggressive and untrustworthy. In what follows, I will elaborate on how migrants based away from their homelands understand the reality of their regions and how their views are dominated by fear and negative perceptions. I will focus on three dominant issues: the tension generated by religion, the control of federal power, and the competition for trade.

The Shari'a Controversy

Nothing has been more divisive than the introduction of the Shari'a in some northern states since the late 1990s. To the northern Muslim migrants in the south, the Shari'a is necessary. To the southern migrants living in the north, the Shari'a is unjust and an attack directed at them. The Shari'a is an Islamic legal code, with Islamic judges drawing from the Quran and Hadith to impose punishment for a variety of civil and capital crimes. Theft can be punished by cutting off the hand, and alcohol consumption by public flogging. Women and men are separated in public spaces such as transport vans and schools.

Southern Christians in the north are very much opposed to the Shari'a, and many have interpreted its introduction as an invitation to leave the region. Northerners in the south think that the people have the right to live in any society they deem fit and see the attack on the Shari'a as unnecessary. The controversy has led to many violent clashes in northern cities and a call to divide the country. In April 2001, a pro-Shari'a group in Kano city, the Haisa, embarked upon violent acts to press home their point that Shari'a laws should be implemented: they set fire to a guest house, a number of restaurants, and hotels.

The introduction of the Shari'a has undermined the power of the federal government, which has been unable to stop it or assure the southern migrants that their lives and property are safe. The Shari'a controversy is unlikely to go away for a long time, and many riots should be expected in the future, as people hold passionate positions, either for or against the use of Islamic law.

The Shari'a is not the only issue that raises problems. Northern Muslims in the south look to the Sultan of Sokoto for religious leadership. In the south, they build and operate their separate mosques, thus using religion to solidify their identity. The implication is that the authority of southern Islamic leaders is not respected. Thus, they will respect only the days chosen by the Sultan for the Eid-el-kabir prayers.

The expansion of the frontiers of Islam and Christianity, as well as the growing assertiveness of their members beyond their "original homeland," is yet a source of problems. Hundreds of mosques and churches have been destroyed since the 1980s. Migrants complain that they are being persecuted for their religions. The most common complaints are from the north where Igbo and Yoruba Christians, with the support of Christian indigenes, believe that they are permanently under siege. Angry words circulate on a permanent basis. One does not know which event or statement will create problems. For instance, in February 2001, the Israeli ambassador to Nigeria visited the northern state of Gombe to address the Shalom Club, a small group of members who had worked or studied in Israel. The visit led to bloodshed (many were injured and about ten people were killed) and destruction of property, including a Baptist church and two hotels. Some Muslim groups regarded the visit as more evidence of the assertiveness of southerners and Christians among them.

The Power Controversy

Where should the president of Nigeria come from? How many federal ministers are Igbo? Did enough people from the Ijo in the Niger Delta obtain federal contracts? Who distributes the licenses to drill for oil? How many army generals come from the north? These and other questions are important to migrants and ethnic leaders. All groups complain of marginalization, as their politicians and businessmen seek more power and opportunities.

To the southerners, the northerners have a monopoly of power. In general, the discussion about past military leaders, notably Generals Ibrahim Babangida and Sanni Abacha, is usually unpleasant. Both are regarded as kleptocrats who bled the country dry. Abacha is described as evil and murderous, in part because of the way he treated the famous Yoruba politician, Moshood Abiola, who won the 1993 presidential election that was later annulled by the military. As far as the southerners were concerned, the northern politicians depended on coups and bribery to compete and survive.

Political parties hardly resolve the various crises over power. At the very best, a political party tries to consolidate itself by falling back on ethnic manipulation. The game is to ensure that the majority of the members of one ethnic group, at home and in other parts of the country, belong to the same political party. Party chieftains are interested in appointments and contracts, and the competition among them is always very bitter.

It may be argued that migrants and their hosts, and indeed all ethnic groups, have yet to come together to discuss all the problems that people complain about. Although Nigerians have traveled and interacted for centuries, the concept of a united country is a recent development. The British failed to bring them together in the first half of the twentieth century. Soon after independence, they fought a civil war.

The Abuja Controversy

In the 1970s, the military decided to replace Lagos as the capital and look for a new location. Lagos was considered small, hard to plan, and congested. When Abuja, in the middle belt, was chosen, the government's propaganda was that it was a neutral place. As building began in the 1980s, the new capital provided opportunities for politicians and businessmen to make huge sums of money in corrupt deals. The history of the city has also become part of national politics and what migrants talk about with passion.

To start with what may appear a simple matter: the politics of street naming. In Nigeria, "big men" and those who think they are successful want streets to be named after them. It is not unusual for someone to live in a street named after him. To the big politicians, the most prominent roads should be named after them. The Yoruba in the north regarded the street named after the late Chief Obafemi Awolowo, their most successful politician during the twentieth century, as insignificant. They attribute the slight to Awolowo's opposition to the relocation of the federal capital. After making a prophetic statement that the building of Abuja would promote squandermania, Awolowo concluded that "If Abuja does not ruin Nigeria, Nigeria will ruin Abuja."

A second problem is the perception by southerners that Abuja has enabled a class of northern contractors and politicians to collude to divert public funds to private pockets. Abuja is part of the "Triple A" that bedevils Nigeria's economy: Abuja, the Ajaokuta steel complex, and the Aladja steel complex, all expensive projects with questionable results. Southern migrants pose the question: why is the north using federal money to underdevelop the country? Hotels, private residences, and apartments are all very expensive in Abuja. Government officials and politicians with access to state money have used it to build homes which they rent to their colleagues and others. Hotel bills are indirectly paid for by the federal government. Those who do not benefit and live at the margins of society worry about the waste.

Third, religious and moral leaders talk about the moral decadence of Abuja. In the perception of migrants, Abuja is a city of sin. They have a point. The official corruption is too clear to be missed. As accommodation is so scarce, many young women are driven to live in the streets and become prostitutes.

Fourth, contrary to the belief that everybody would feel at home in a new federal capital, southerners have complained that Abuja has emerged as a Hausa-Fulani city. Southern migrants point to the various mosques, the elegance of the central mosque, and the Arabic impact on the architecture. A southern lawyer remarked in an anti-Abuja piece in the weekly *Tell Magazine* of March 19, 2001, that "Abuja has been pretending to be the capital of Nigeria. In reality, it is the North's preparation for an eventuality; and their agents, the military, have left no one in any doubt about this."[3]

The Market and Revenue Controversies

Ultimately, the struggles over politics and Abuja are also about resource distribution and development. Who gets what in the federation? How is oil money allocated to states and local governments? Who gets the lion's share of the market? If politics is the most lucrative business in town, who controls politics and the economic rewards that come from it? Irrespective of how the question is posed, there is always an economic undertone to the political crises. I want to examine two recent cases that people talk about, one on the national issue of resource distribution and the other on a local issue of control of city markets.

To start with the local one, the allocation of market spaces in such a competitive city as Lagos has led to inter-ethnic conflicts between migrants and their hosts. Similarly, the control of the informal economy by southern migrants in northern cities has generated many complaints and riots. In the south, the competition is waged over the allocation of market stalls in areas where trade is profitable. Southerners also want to compete with the northern migrants in the lucrative cattle and kola nut trade. In the case of the north, southern migrants control many modern aspects of commerce. As they become more and more successful and fail to integrate or even become Muslims, they antagonize their hosts. Cultural difference is so noticeable that it often leads to hostility and violence, as in all the cases of Christian-Muslim riots.

With regard to the federal issue, Nigeria depends on oil revenues. The bulk of the oil resources are located in an area to the southeast of the country. If the country had followed the principle of sharing the revenues with the areas that produce the resources, the southeast would be the most developed place on the entire African continent. The demand for a greater share of oil revenues by the Ogoni and others in the Niger Delta is not just a common discussion among their migrants in other parts of Nigeria, but it has also received international attention, relative to the problems of environmental damage by multinational oil businesses.

In general, southern migrants complain that the north is benefiting too much from southern oil wealth. The perception is that the north contributes little to federal resources, but takes the lion's share. As far as the northern migrants are concerned, sharing the revenue is part of the price for living in a large country. And when the northerners are provoked, they claim that they, too, can stand on their own as an independent country without oil money. Their agriculture and trade, they claim, should be enough to sustain them.

The current controversy is over the ownership of oil resources found offshore of the littoral areas in the south. The southern states claim that the resources belong to them, but the federal government wants them as well. While northerners say that such offshore oil resources belong to all Nigerians, southerners say that this is not so. There is yet a voice that advocates free enterprise, which would enable all Nigerians with the capital and skills to have access to all resources, thus minimizing government control. To quote Lucky Igbinedion, an entrepreneur and the current governor of the Edo state in the southwest:

> Resource control is not defined by oil alone. It covers all natural resources—solid materials, cash crops, everything. It is a pure capitalistic doctrine. It is the ability of an individual . . . to have the freedom to exploit the natural resources that abound in our country. I've always maintained that somebody from Kano can go to Delta and strike oil, and it should belong to the Kano man and not to the Delta State government and not to the federal government but to the Kano man who will bring in his capital as long as he pays his royalties and taxes to the state. This is what we call resource control. It is not only for the oil-producing states. It is a national issue that has been misconstrued and politicised. People just misunderstand what resource control means because oil is the mainstream of our revenue. In Plateau State, you have tin and columbite. In Kebbi State, you have gold. I should be able to go to Kebbi and exploit gold, and it should be mine. That is resource control. It is the freedom of the individual to exploit his potentialities and capitalise on the commercial capability of such natural resources.[4]

Northerners reject this kind of statement, saying that is a way for southerners to dominate them with their skills and capital. As many northerners have said, if southerners are this ambitious, why not divide the country along professional lines: southerners should go into business and administration, and northerners should control power.

A number of issues are clear from the migrants' perception of the various realities already discussed. First, every group has a perception that other groups are hostile and will take advantage whenever it controls power or the market. The political leaders make the loudest noise, although it is not always clear whom the leaders represent and what the size of their following is. While certain opinions are commonly expressed, there is no consensus regarding the solutions to problems. The common suggestion in the last five years is that there should be a national conference of all ethnic groups to discuss the politics and future of Nigeria. When such a conference is convened, it is more than clear that its resolutions will have little or no effect on the large problems facing the country.

Second, most people put the blame on the federal government. Even when a riot takes place at the local government level, it very quickly becomes a national issue that involves the federal police and government. The strategy of blaming the center has enabled many to overlook the gross mismanagement and reckless abuse of power at the state and local government levels.

Third, although Nigeria is a federal state, it is clear that the component units lack the power and resources to act independently of the center. Nigeria actually runs like a unitary state, with a few people at the center dictating policies and distributing the revenues from oil.

Fourth, a culture of discussion and debate is yet to take firm root. When migrants feel marginalized or cheated, mediation strategies are insufficient to resolve the matter which often degenerates into violence. And when violence does occur, not only do people die, the survivors are thrown into panic, rushing to the motor parks with the few possessions they can grab, to run to their places of birth.

Finally, there is a growing desire for democracy. The future of Nigeria may be uncertain, but it is not hard to figure out what migrants and others want. High on the list of wishes are freedom from all forms of political dictatorship, the right of migrants and all nationalities to autonomy, fair elections to ensure genuine political representation, and a restructured federation that will give all nationalities a high level of freedom to determine their progress. Thus far, no government has been able to aggregate these wishes and create a program that will make migrants comfortable and secure whereever they may find themselves.

Case Study 2: The Yoruba in Nigeria

Nigerian politicians since the early 1990s have turned the Yoruba into the principal focus of national discourse. Having struggled since the 1950s, the Yoruba political class has now had its turn to have one of its own as the country's president. The Igbo expressed the view that the Yoruba had actually benefited more from the system than they claimed. The northerners' support for a southern candidate was partly because of the political crises that the military had created and the need to use a pro-north candidate to retain control.

Calculations based on ethnicity remain deep, very much as before, only slightly altered to give the Yoruba greater visibility. This reverses the long trend that privileged the north and its quest for political domination, the short-lived fear of Igbo domination in the 1960s, and the secession and civil war that followed from 1967 to 1970. The rise of Chief M. K. O. Abiola in the early 1990s, his victory in the 1993 elections, and the subsequent annulment of these elections by the military regime of General Ibrahim Babangida dominated Nigerian politics for the rest of the decade. The rise of Abacha to power met with organized opposition among the Yoruba and the pro-democracy movements. During Abacha's tenure, various Yoruba groups not only emerged to advocate democracy; but some wanted secession or, at the very least, the renegotiation of the basis of the federation to give power to the different nationalities to shape their own policies, free of a powerful center. The discourse of democracy put ethnicity at its very center. It was no longer how a group of nationalists from different parts of the country would govern and bring progress, but how the representatives of the component units would share power and resources along ethnic lines. The assumption was that the military generals and politicians would always represent ethnic interests, and in this kind of arrangement, the north would always seek domination at the expense of others. If a number of Yoruba politicians had advocated forging alliances with the northerners, many now regarded them as "dangerous enemies."

Abacha's death in 1998 paved the way for a military disengagement that resulted in 1999 in the victory of a Yoruba, Olusegun Obasanjo, as the country's president. Since his coming to power in May of that year, there has been a spate of interethnic and intercommunal rivalries, two of which pitted the Yoruba against the northerners. The Shari'a has been being declared as state law in some northern states, a development that some interpret as an attempt to destabilize the Obasanjo regime. Is there a backlash to the growing influence of the Yoruba in politics? Will the east and north create an anti-Yoruba alliance? Has the emergence of Obasanjo benefited the Yoruba? Should Obasanjo govern as a Yoruba or a Nigerian? These are some of the questions that politicians and analysts pose that reveal that the understanding of politics is still very much conditioned by ethnicity.

This section explores the historical and contemporary development in the formation of Yoruba identity and how this intersects with Nigerian politics. The premise is that contemporary ethnic politics can best be understood against the background of past events. The massive support that Abiola received was in part because of the previous ordeals of Awolowo from the 1950s to the 1980s, especially his efforts at becoming the country's leader. The lack of support by the Yoruba for Obasanjo during the elections was due to the widely held belief that he did not favor the Yoruba when he was the head of state in the 1970s, that he represented northern interests, that he worked against Awolowo in the 1970s, and that he was lukewarm in his support of Abiola in the 1990s. The support for him now that he is in power is partly based on the fear that northerners will prevent a Yoruba from succeeding. Having failed to prevent Obasanjo from winning the elections, preferring for their favorite son, Chief Olu Falae, the Yoruba now lend their support to him because they interpret anti-Obasanjo sentiments and campaigns as anti-Yoruba.

The Ethnic Factor

The role of the Yoruba in politics has been shaped by five interrelated factors:

1. The manipulation, by Yoruba politicians, of Yoruba and Nigerian history for specific ends presented as collective interests. In other words, political leaders operate as the representatives of an ethnic group.
2. The promotion of a pan-Yoruba consciousness and cultural exclusiveness built on the myth of Oduduwa, the progenitor of the Yoruba people. In other words, political leaders and representatives subscribe to the historical narratives that regard all Yoruba as the descendants of one ancestor.
3. The use of ethnocentric traits (e.g., common language, boundaries, beliefs, and group identity) for interethnic competition in a plural society. The Yoruba politicians act on the assumption that the Yoruba constitute one single nation and that their interests have to be protected against those of competitors from other ethnic groups.
4. The claim to early contact with Western education and Christianity which, from the colonial period onward, became significant criteria in access to jobs, business, and politics; and arising from this,
5. A stronger claim to modern civilization than any other group in the federation.

Indeed, on the basis of the last point, many members of the ruling class used to argue during the colonial period and immediately after that the

Yoruba were better qualified than any other group in Nigeria to provide the leadership for the country and serve as the agents of modernization. According to this belief, not only would the Yoruba transform themselves, they would disperse to transform others, and their leaders would use their modernization to move Nigeria forward. In 1947, Awolowo, the most important Yoruba hero of the twentieth century, justified the claims of the Yoruba to the preeminent leadership position partly on the basis of their exposure to superior Western culture, and the varying degrees to which Western civilization and education had infiltrated the different ethnic groups. As Awolowo stated, with some measure of confidence:

> In embracing western culture, the Yorubas take the lead, and have benefited immensely as a result. The Efiks, the Ijaws, the Ibibios, and the Ibos come next. The Hausas and Fulanis on the other hand are extremely conservative, and take reluctantly, the Western civilization. . . . And if the race is to be swift, in spite of their lower cultural background, the Ibos or the Ibibios would certainly qualify for self-government, long before the Hausas.[5]

All the claims of the Yoruba to leadership have not gone unchallenged, and certainly not this statement. The leaders of the other groups hardly agreed with this claim. For instance, Chief Nnamdi Azikiwe, equally as ambitious as Awolowo and also regarded as the leader of a rival ethnic group, the Igbo, also articulated the belief in the superiority of his own group:

> The God of Africa has especially created the Ibo nation to lead the children of Africa from the bondage of the ages. . . . The martial prowess of the Ibo nation at all stages of human history has enabled them not only to conquer others but also to adapt themselves to the role of preserver. . . . The Ibo nation cannot shirk its responsibility.[6]

If Awolowo limited himself to Nigeria, Azikiwe went further regarding the Igbo as the leaders of Africa. These men and others made new claims in later years, all leading to a similar conclusion: a particular ethnic group must lead the country for its own sake and that of others. As this belief shaped the nature of political competition, it is important to identify its outcome:

1. Building a pan-Nigerian consciousness or nationalism to sustain the Nigerian nation-state is complicated, since there are competing ethnic nationalisms. Secession and the advocacy of separate developments are strong examples of the clash of nationalisms. The belief in a superior-inferior relationship makes consensus building more difficult.

2. Building strong and viable networks of political associations and mass-based political parties is difficult, as the challenges of ethnic loyalty may undermine them. It has always been a convenient game to use one ethnic group against the other and to disguise class and self-interests as ethnic.

3. If the representatives of the large ethnic groups are interested only in themselves and their groups, the resolution of divisive issues and the protection of minority interests are difficult, if not impossible. Decisions may reveal self-interest, rather than common interest, thus laying the foundation of a future crisis.

4. The political elite regard the manipulation of ethnic loyalty as the cheapest and most reliable strategy to acquire and consolidate power. The ethnic identity is manipulated to lay claim to leadership. At the same time, the political elite fall back on this same identity to prevent the underprivileged members of their own group from creating alliances with members of other groups, since the "Others" have been portrayed as rivals, enemies, competitors, and people with negative attributes. Would Nigerian politics have been different if poor Hausa, poor Igbo, and poor Yoruba had been united in the politics of change?

The Agency of History

As with other Nigerian groups, Yoruba identity is rooted in history. Ethnocentric characteristics were formed during the precolonial period, ethnicity was accentuated during the colonial period, and profound conflicts occurred after the country's independence from the British in 1960.

The interactions among the various Yoruba polities during the precolonial period continue to have relevance in modern politics. The Yoruba did not build one political kingdom or empire, but the various subunits had strong contacts with one another. The factors that promoted the contacts in the past (for peace and war) have been activated in the modern era to build a pan-Yoruba consciousness. While there were various Yoruba groups in the past, each with its own political authority and boundary, in the context of contemporary politics, it is convenient for the political class to occasionally forget this in the agenda of forging a Yoruba "nation" strong enough to compete with the other equally large and viable "nations." The narrative is intended to underscore two interrelated points:

1. the importance of the states formed by different Yoruba groups, and their relationship to one another;

2. the attempts by a few states to expand at the expense of others, to extend their territories and "nationalities." Boundaries were occasionally adjusted, and people were forced to migrate from one area to another.

I want to begin my analysis with the historical past that has been used to provide much evidence for Yoruba unity in the political present. I will isolate the historical evidence that now constitutes the political "memory" of the Yoruba intelligentsia. It is the "memory" of this past that enables the contemporary intelligentsia to create a basis for Yoruba regional unity in modern Nigeria and to have a strong foundation for articulating a Yoruba identity. A selective reading of the past does not ensure that present politics will unfold as planned. There is also evidence of warfare and rivalries among the Yoruba, which some may recall when it serves modern politics.

Territory, Territorial Sovereignty, and Citizenship

Two major criteria have been used to create a "Yoruba map": language and the migration of dynastic leaders from Ile-Ife. Language, of course, may indicate that there are other cultural affinities. The second criterion includes all areas whose legends claim that their founders migrated out of Ile-Ife. Thus, in Nigeria, to limit ourselves to one country, the Yoruba occupy most of the southwest. To treat the Yoruba-speaking areas as a unit can be justified only on the basis of cultural and linguistic similarities. These similarities have been further promoted by modern politicians who talk of a common historical experience and the emergence of a standard Yoruba language. Yorubaland was never a single sociopolitical unit. But what geographical labels did the precolonial people invent for their territories and by what name(s) did they refer to themselves? In addition, were they conscious of such labels and names, and willing to defend them in the face of threats, both internal and external, to destroy the body of ideas or meanings which the labels and names represented? Were the Yoruba conscious of their ethnicity and identity?

The answers to these questions reveal the emphasis on groups (such as the Ekiti, Ijebu, and Egba) rather than on a single "Yoruba nation." Groups had their territories while citizenship was defined in relation to the membership of a state within a group. Land, an aspect of territorial sovereignty, was communal, and no pan-Yoruba authority ever emerged to control all the land. Territorial sovereignty and citizenship were not defined in a pan-Yoruba framework, since there were different autonomous groups and city-states. These states did not even evolve into a loose political federation. The ruling classes in the different states forged ties with one another, but certainly not a relation in which one of them assumed an overwhelming control over the others. It was the British who made the *Alaafin* of Oyo superior to many kings before the 1930s, and it was the modern political party of the Yoruba, the Action Group, that made the *Ooni* of Ife superior to the others from the 1950s.[7] Every oba was sovereign in his domain, and he, together with his chiefs and lineage representatives, constituted the leading members of the political class. The exception was when imperial control had been imposed, and the territory became a vassal to another kingdom, as in the case of the Old Oyo empire that was able to dominate a number of other groups.

Several sovereign city-states belonging to different groups dotted Yorubaland. Each consisted of a large city surrounded by outlying villages of varying sizes. The city was like a metropolis, with a network of adjoining farmlands, hamlets, and villages. Some of these city-states were large, like Oyo, the metropolis of a huge empire and the largest in the eighteenth century, and Ibadan, the largest in the nineteenth century. The majority were medium-sized, like Owu, which was destroyed in 1826, Ondo, Ile-Ife, and Ilesa. Others include the Egba states before the nineteenth century; the Ekiti states and a host of others such as the Iyagba, Owe, Oworo, and Dumu in the northeast; and Ijaye and Ikale in the southeast.

The claims to differing autonomy and sovereignty depended partly on the nature and pattern of state formation among the Yoruba. Sources do not mention the formation of one Yoruba nation but rather of several states and groups. Some, in fact, describe pre-Oduduwa communities, that is, autochthonous communities that existed before the imposition of dynasties with a connection with Ile-Ife and/or before a process of political centralization. State formation in Yorubaland is associated in myths with the activities of Oduduwa and his "children." These myths do not mention the unity among these "children" as establishing a single nation, but rather a host of nations. One inference that could be drawn from the myths is that political centralization did take place in various states at different historical periods. This was, however, a process which involved many people over a long period of time. Those who established dynasties maintained control over large territories. Many names were given to these states. Some of these names derived from the features of the environment such as hills, rivers, soil, and vegetation, and others from the personal experiences of the dynastic founders or even of the entire migration of a people.

Expansion took place until boundaries were established with another city-state belonging to the same group or a different one. The commitment to, and the struggles over, boundaries again indicates the place of different groups and of a state-oriented territorial sovereignty in Yorubaland. A state had its territory in which the citizens, who in turn belonged to recognized lineages, had their own share of land. A ruler held control of the territory and was recognized by other rulers as having the power and sovereignty; his power was limited to this territory. There were traditions to legitimize claims and the limits of expansion.[8] As the *Owa* of Ilesa put it in 1882, "[T]he boundaries of each state were well defined and regarded as sacred, so that nothing could induce any one to intrude into the territory of another."[9] Hills, footpaths, streams, and other physical features were used as demarcations. Diplomacy, treaties, and rituals were also used to strengthen the agreements on boundaries. These boundaries separated areas of jurisdiction and interest. When these were threatened, disputes arose between states.[10]

Sovereignty had relevance at the microlevel of the city-state and group. So, too, did citizenship. The people used their towns or groups to identify themselves. For instance, a person from Owo saw himself as an *Omo Owo* or shortly as Owo (Owo's citizen) and would not define himself in a pan-Yoruba context. Strong group tendencies gave rise to, and probably promoted, parochial tendencies and cultural variations. The widespread definition of being a Yoruba, instead of an *Omo Owo,* began to gain currency in the nineteenth century.

The mode of production recognized the central role of households. Production mechanisms depended on local initiatives and the use of local raw materials.[11] The point here is not to suggest that there were no economic interactions, but that the mode of production could function, as a system, at the level of the community connected to a regional network.

The same was true of the political system. Each state was sovereign and constituted a recognizable territorial unit. Its government was also sovereign, and its rulers were the symbols of the state. They exercised judicial, executive, and legislative powers. The political system of the states rested on a combination of the lineages, various associations, and the paraphernalia of a central authority. At the lineage level, the *Baale* (or *olori ebi*), that is, the lineage head, was in charge. He exercised a penal authority limited to fines and minor impositions, and chastisement. Associations included age-grades and trade guilds, both of which exercised moral authority on their members. The institutions of the central state's authority were dominated by the *oba* and the chiefs, both acting in a council.[12]

The institutions of government were replicated in many areas, but the pattern of authority showed variations. Oyo represented the model of an empire, with a powerful monarch. The Egba formed a loose confederation; the Ife a centralized provincial administration; and such other states as the Ekiti, Ijebu, Ondo, Owo, and Awori lacked large central political organizations. New changes were introduced during the nineteenth century.[13] The military became preeminent in politics, primarily because of the insecurity of the age. The military had new ideas for government, arising from their crucial strategic functions and substantial wealth. Because they owed their prominence to their exploits in war, they tended to have little regard for monarchical institutions. New ideas were put into practice in Ibadan, where a military aristocracy was established; in Ijaye, which had a military dictatorship; and in Oke-Odan and Abeokuta, where a military federation was practiced.[14]

Centrifugal Tendencies

The various Yoruba states maintained close relations with one another. The dominant ruling class in each state also had a strong interest in promoting centrifugal tendencies primarily to widen its base of power. In the first place, the myth of Oduduwa and of a common ancestry was popularized partly to strengthen the link between the ruling class and to prevent, as much as possible, the emergence of a counterhegemonic force which could destroy the dynasties and royal families. The myth also reinforced the ownership and control of territories as well as of land. The affinal relationship referred to below served as a further justificatory ideology; so did the exchange of gifts, and diplomatic practices and exchanges. Secondly, intergroup relations widened the network of markets and trade, thus increasing the avenues for profit by enterprising members of the ruling class as well as the peasants. Thirdly, and more importantly, wars were fought to subjugate neighboring and distant polities. This facilitated the accumulation of extensive booty in goods and men, as well as considerable access to gifts and tribute. These massive gains have been clearly demonstrated in the case of Ibadan,[15] as well as in the activities of the leading war heroes of the nineteenth century.[16]

The factors affecting intergroup relations were diverse: trade, migrations, diplomacy, and war. Migrations within the Yoruba region were common, brought about by such reasons as flight from wars and political upheavals and the search for new and better abodes. The nineteenth century witnessed massive migrations which had the effect of altering the map and the demographic composition of the region.[17] Such migrations allowed for borrowing and the spread of culture. The diffusion of artifacts and aspects of social institutions represents major evidence of the impact of intergroup relations and their integrative role in the Yoruba region. For instance, the

Egungun-Oyo (Oyo masquerade) spread from the north to the south and northeast during the nineteenth century. Similarly, the *Orisa-oko* (the cult of farming and fertility) and *Sango* (the deity of lightning and thunder) spread from the Oyo to other Yoruba groups. Other institutions emanated from other areas and spread to the Oyo; one example of these was the *Epa*-type masquerade headpieces.

The ruling dynasties in the various states forged relationships with one another by promoting "brotherhood relations." The cordial relations among them were sometimes explained in affinal relationship. Several of the royal families (members of the ruling class) claimed Oduduwa as their ancestor. These "children of Oduduwa" constituted the dynasties in a good number of kingdoms. The number of these "children" has been variously put at between seven and twenty-one.[18] Intergroup relations among the kingdoms were fostered by this myth of common origin. This was occasionally demonstrated in coronation rituals when some of the kingdoms appealed to Ile-Ife for the symbol of power for their new rulers.[19] Some claimed secondary relations with the sons of Oduduwa, that is, the founders of their kingdoms were children of the sons of Oduduwa. For instance, the Akure and Osogbo dynasties claimed a blood relationship with the Owa of Ilesa (a "son" of Oduduwa), while Iwo claimed a connection with the son of a female *Ooni* of Ife. The rulers who claimed to have been born of the same mother had common rituals to celebrate her. There were cases when the ruling dynasties in contiguous communities claimed a common descent from the same mother. In situations like this, members of the ruling class regarded themselves as siblings and forged deep relationships. This "blood" relationship was used to justify other important unifying steps, such as the exchange of gifts, the custody of one another's princes for effective training, the exchange of visits by chiefs, and trade relations.

Affinal relationships were also used to prevent conflicts among the members of the ruling class in the same state. Two or more ruling houses existed in most Yoruba towns. Marriage ties could cement relationships among them. The use of marriage, however, cut across states. As a political strategy and to widen the network of relationship, princesses were betrothed to princes and chiefs in other states. Examples of this strategy are many and well narrated in various traditions. The rulers of such states treated one another as "cousins" and their people as "kinsmen." When the products of such marriages grew to acquire political power, intergroup relations were further strengthened because of their dual loyalty to two states.

The conjugal and affinal ties between rulers affected how their subjects related to one another. The people followed their examples of exchanging sons and daughters. The notions of security, safety, and "kinsmen" were implied in such exchanges; in other words, they were exchanging with people in states where it was safe to do so. The network of social and blood relationship was, therefore, wide.

Though the several wars of the nineteenth century destroyed a good number of these affinal relationships, they were still remembered and also occasionally served to prevent large-scale hostilities and total destruction of communities. Ibadan, which built the most effective military machine in the century, occasionally considered this factor. It did not attack most Oyo-Yoruba states because their people were regarded as kinsmen. Even when Ijaye—the rival Oyo-Yoruba state—was attacked in 1860, the attack was undertaken only after prolonged deliberations.[20]

Concrete diplomacy was used to back "brotherhood relations." The Yoruba, like most other African people, were conversant in the art and practice of diplomacy.[21] There were several conventions: diplomatic agents were recognized; the status and power of different diplomats were known; political agents were exchanged; the inviolability of the person of the diplomatic agent was recognized; diplomatic communications were generally immune from interdiction; and symbols and signs were used as the secret language of diplomacy.

War was yet another factor which brought communities together. Successful imperial wars put separate states and subgroups under a common political umbrella. The Oyo were able to achieve this in the seventeenth and eighteenth centuries when they established an empire whose territorial extent was very wide.[22] Most of the vassal colonies enjoyed autonomy, but the king of Oyo had to ratify the appointment of their *Oba* or *Baale*. In addition, the *Oba* and *Baale* went to Oyo to obtain their titles and the Alaafin could also depose them. They appeared periodically at Oyo where they re-affirmed their loyalty in front of the Alaafin. The orders emanating from the king of Oyo had to be obeyed, and the Oyo's political agents resided in the colonies to monitor local developments.

Among the other factors contributing to cohesion were the blood and social relationships among the members of the ruling class in the various cities and villages; Oyo's military might and ability to subjugate and coerce the colonies; and the domination of commerce, which enhanced the economic power of the metropolis at the expense of the colonies. Finally, many areas were linked by roads, which served as arteries of trade and communications.

If the preceding evidence points to opportunities for solidarity among the Yoruba, there is also evidence of alliances forged with a number of other groups within Nigeria. The groups on the periphery as well as in the border zones inevitably had to interact with their neighbors. All the Yoruba subgroups had contacts with other non-Yoruba in the west African region. Both forms of interaction revolved around diplomacy, trade, cultural ties, and wars. The contacts were also well developed and encouraged the diffusion of ideas, goods, and people. They were promoted by ecological differences, the necessity of mutual interdependence, the benefits from a wider commercial and economic network, and imperial desires. Only a few examples can be cited. Oyo's relations with its northern neighbors, notably the Nupe and Bariba, prompted many exchanges and occasional conflicts. The economic integration of Yorubaland into the Hausa commercial network was very deep.[23] Hausa traders brought goods of diverse origins to Yorubaland in exchange for kola nuts and other products. The Benin expansion into the area of modern Ondo and Lagos states from the sixteenth to the nineteenth centuries was equally significant. There is more evidence to show that the Yoruba did not limit interactions to fellow Yoruba groups. Long-established relations have continued to this day, in spite of new boundaries, new administrative centers, and ethnic rivalries.

Manufacturing Yoruba: An Idea and Consciousness

If the idea of a united Yoruba can be contested, many factors remain which the modern intelligentsia have used to forge the consciousness of a Yoruba nation. In spite of differences, "Yoruba" can refer to cultural similarities and those of social formations with communal boundaries. There are myths and events that can generate ethnocentric pride and construct an identity.

The most vigorous attempt to create the "Yoruba nation" began during the nineteenth century. It was during that century that the use of the name "Yoruba" to refer to all the subgroups became popular. Names such as Aku, Nagun, Anago, Olukumi, and Yoruba had been used by neighbors and European visitors to describe various Yoruba groups.[24] Yoruba became the most popular name. Its popular usage began in Sierra Leone, when the missionaries were interested in studying African languages, including that of Oyo. By the 1880s, Yoruba had become a common usage among the educated elite.

More important than the name was the Yoruba consciousness, which developed among the liberated slaves in Sierra Leone and which they imported into Nigeria from 1838 onward.[25] From these returnees and the products of missionary education introduced in the second half of the nineteenth century, there emerged an educated elite. This elite was interested in key positions in the church and civil service, in dominating commerce, and also in sharing power with the "traditional" elite.[26] They perceived Europeans as opponents who stood in their way of achieving their ambitions. One way to overcome the threat posed by Europeans was to promote ethnocentric values, partly to strengthen intraclass unity and partly to provide ideological rationalization for some of their enterprising moves to indigenize the church and set up businesses of their own.

Several ethnocentric values assumed great importance. The myth of a common origin was popularized to create a pan-Yoruba identity and destroy the group loyalties which the nineteenth century wars had effectively consolidated. Language, too, became another factor in the effort to emphasize the similarities in Yoruba culture. Yoruba acquired a written form, becoming one of the earliest languages in the country with standard alphabets. Although it was the Oyo-Yoruba dialect that was chosen, other groups accepted it, and it became a school subject as well. The standardization enabled the language to unite all those who could read and write. Whether one was Ijebu or Egba, the standard language was available for dialogue.

From 1875 till the end of the century, some Yoruba elite promoted Ethiopianism, that is, "African nationalism expressed through the medium of the church."[27] Ethiopianism and other aspects of missionary activities and reactions to Europeans engendered cultural nationalism and ethnocentric values. During this period, the Lagos press became virulent; the educated faction advocated several reforms and changes, including the establishment of an African university, and respected Yoruba "scholars" emerged. From among the latter, a flourishing Yoruba historiography was born, culminating in the writings of Samuel Johnson. Patriotism to the Yoruba underlay most of these writings. In the last words of his monumental work, Johnson spoke for the elite of the nineteenth century who had accepted a common Yoruba identity and hoped for progress in the twentieth century:

> . . . that peace should reign universally, with prosperity and advancement, and that the disjointed units should all be once more welded into one under one head from the Niger to the coast as in the happy days of ABIODUN, so dear to our fathers, that clannish spirit disappear, and above all that Christianity should be the principal religion in the land—paganism and Mohammedanism having had their full trial—should be the wish and prayer of every true son of Yoruba.[28]

Johnson's desire for unity was expressed against the background of the century-old civil war among the Yoruba and the need to enjoy peace and an economic boom. Johnson's successors also desired unity, but in the context of ethnic competitions in a colonial and postcolonial setting.

Beyond the Ethno

During the twentieth century, ethnocentric values gave way to ethnic rivalries, as the former became transformed in the service of the latter. There is one decisive explanation for this big leap: British rule. The colonial period introduced far-reaching changes which have, in many ways, laid the foundation of many future problems and challenges.[29] Colonialism certainly accentuated group differences, encouraged the formation of classes which benefited from promoting group differences and hostilities, and introduced measures which made it difficult for Nigerians to achieve political integration and rapid economic development.[30]

The Yoruba elite began to articulate and manipulate a common consciousness of the Yoruba identity in relation to other ethnic groups. This tendency engendered competition with others and was expressed in interethnic conflicts and interethnic discrimination in job opportunities and access to national resources.

The development of ethnicity owed much to the colonial policies and programs which created new class structures and relations. The dominant class in the colonial era, which subsequently inherited power in 1960, benefited from the manipulation of ethnicity for private ends. It was not difficult for them to do so because the British did so much to promote divisions along ethnic lines. Okwudiba Nnoli has studied some of these measures and has shown how ethnicity was deliberately politicized for private ends.[31]

A genuinely nationalist, pan-Nigerian political party had not emerged by 1960, when the country obtained its independence. Rather, what the country had during the crucial era of decolonization were parties organized along regional and ethnic lines. In the case of the Yoruba, a far-reaching political expression of ethnic solidarity occurred in 1945 with the formation of a cultural-cum-political society known as the Egbe Omo Oduduwa (the descendants of the children of Oduduwa) by Awolowo.[32] One of the aims behind it was to manipulate the idea of Yoruba identity and consciousness in order to compete with other Nigerian groups. It held its inaugural meeting in Lagos on November 28, 1947, and subsequently couched its aims in an ethnic context. These included, inter alia: the fostering of the spirit of cooperation, unity and brotherhood among the descendants of Oduduwa; the coordination of educational and cultural programs among the Yoruba; the discouragement of "intra-tribal prejudice among descendants of Oduduwa whom for linguistic differences failed to recognize themselves as branches of the same stock"; and the importance of striving for the preservation of "traditional monarchical form of government of western Nigeria as to fit in properly in any future political set up for the government of Nigeria."[33]

From 1945 onward, the Egbe designed a host of strategies to pursue its aims and compete with other ethnic groups, notably the Igbo (who also had the Ibo State Union) and the northern intelligentsia, who, in 1948, also established a cultural-cum-political union known as the Jam'yyar Mutanen Arewa (The Association of Peoples of the North). Certain aspects of the Egbe's strategy were built on ethnocentric values. It created the Oduduwa National Day, an annual event held on June 5, during which youth engaged in athletic competitions and thanksgiving services held in churches and mosques.[34] The Obas and chiefs were mobilized, and many of them identified with the aims and activities of the Egbe. As a political strategy, the Egbe justified the need for chiefs in any new political arrangement. The prominent members of the Egbe went further, acquiring honorary chieftaincy titles from different Yoruba kings, thereby forging an alliance between the educated and the traditional elite. Finally, the Egbe took an interest in the propagation of Yoruba history and culture. As part of this, it established a literature committee to encourage research into Yoruba history and culture, and it commissioned individuals to examine specific aspects of the past. It was the Egbe Omo Oduduwa that later constituted the core of the Action Group (AG), a political party with a substantial Yoruba base.[35]

Chief Obafemi Awolowo and the Limits of Yoruba Ethnicity

Awolowo dominated Yoruba politics from the 1950s until his death in the 1980s. He succeeded in two major ways: the consolidation of ethnicity and the "modernization" of the Yoruba. He took the essential elements of Yoruba history that brought them together during the precolonial era and refined them into a political and cultural ideology. Under Awolowo, all Yoruba, now children of one ancestor, Oduduwa, should turn from a large family into a political party. It was as if Oduduwa had passed the baton to Awolowo to continue the great work of unification. This was the ultimate ethnic game, and Awolowo had to confront Ahmadu Bello and Nnamdi Azikiwe who were also playing the same game. In most of the "struggles"—conflicts for power and wealth—the dominant political leaders and their followers have concealed the pursuit of selfish interests by championing the cause of ethnic groups. How politicians play this game of combining self- and ethnic interests is explained by B. J. Dudley:

Political competition was seen by the elites in 'zero sum' and not 'positive sum' terms, with the players drawn . . . in a set of binary oppositions: East (or Ibo) versus West (or Yoruba); North against East, or the South against the North. In each instance, the interests of the elite were generalized by its members to be congruent with the interests of the collective. . . . Thus, Ibo elite interests were made to appear to be the interests of the Ibo-speaking peoples and . . . the interests of the peoples of the Eastern Region. Similarly the interests of the Yoruba . . . (or Northern) elite were equated with the interests of the Yoruba (or of the peoples of the North . . .). This entailed (a) that criticism of a member of the elite became . . . an attack on the collective with which he is identified; and (b) since political competition was conceived in 'zero sum' terms, that the group interest was equated with the national or rather, the 'public interests'[—]'those interests which people have in common qua members of the public'. In effect, this amounts to a denial that there could be a 'public interest' other than the interest of a particular group or groups.[36]

Awolowo was both brilliant and astute. He sought the means to create a solid constituency behind him, and to then articulate a bigger role for himself and his ethnic group in the larger national front. He was a modernizer—the second success—and arguably the country's most successful in his ability to intellectualize and execute an agenda. His premiership, from 1952 to 1959, of the western region, the Yoruba homeland constituted into a regional unit in a federal system by the British, is now regarded by his admirers as the "golden age" of the Yoruba in their modern history. A literature whose significance will be clearer in the next section of this chapter summarizes Awolowo's successes to include the following:

i.   The growth and nurture of Yoruba nationalism and civilization;
ii. The creation of the best and most efficient civil service in Africa;
iii. The creation of an authentic Yoruba middle-class that became the arrowhead of the transformation of the entire Yoruba nation;
iv. Introduction and sustenance of free and universal primary education and health service;
v.   Massive industrialization, creation of industrial and residential estates such as that of Bodija in Ibadan, and those of Ikeja and Apapa in Lagos, building of communication facilities, hospitals, pipe-borne water and opening up of the rural areas with the most comprehensive road network in Africa;

vi. Building of institutions of mass communications, like the first television station in Africa and carrying of educative films to rural areas by the regional government Information unit;

viii. Building the stadia, higher institutions of learning and public buildings that enhanced the pride of the Yoruba people as free citizens, worthy of being treated with dignity, respect and decency.[37]

The Yoruba who wanted Awolowo as the country's president believed he would successfully modernize the country and further empower the Yoruba. Awolowo lost his bid in 1959 to become prime minister. He suffered during the First Republic, as he was arrested for treason and sentenced to a ten-year prison term. The AG split so badly that it lost control of the region to a splinter party, and a state of emergency was declared in 1962. The common perception was that he had been persecuted by his northern political opponents, and this turned Awolowo into a god among his people. His stature actually rose in the 1960s, far higher than when he was in power. Following the second coup in 1966, he was released from prison, and he became a federal minister the following year. His role as finance minister during the civil war alienated him from the Igbo leadership, who expected that a Yoruba alliance would have dealt a final blow to northern domination. When Awolowo reentered politics in the 1970s, he repeated his success and failure. As before, he built a formidable political machine and party that had the Yoruba behind him. Again, as before, he lost. In the last election of his career in 1983, he lost yet again to a northerner.[38]

The Yoruba never expected Awolowo to lose the elections. He did so well in the 1979 elections, and the narrow victory of his NPN opponent had to be sustained by a controversial legal decision by the Supreme Court. Obasanjo was then in power, as a military head of state, and he was believed to be pro-NPN. Abiola was a leading member of the NPN and a critic of Awolowo. Both Obasanjo and Abiola were later to pay the price for what was regarded as a betrayal of Awolowo, although both were also to be forgiven much later.

Awolowo's failure reveals the limits of the ethnic game at two levels. The first, and the most important, is that the political actors in the other regions were also astute in consolidating their power base and using ethnicity for the formation of political parties and contesting elections. In the east and north, Awolowo was portrayed as an outsider. He was able to do well in the middle belt and the Niger Delta, minority areas. Azikiwe and the Igbo leadership successfully ensured that Awolowo would not succeed among the Igbo. In the north, the pioneer politicians successfully recreated the caliphate of the nineteenth century, using Islam to unite the north under one political party.[39] The north has been the most successful in the use of ethnicity, combining it with Islam to dominate power, during both civilian and military rule.

The second level is that there were always pockets of resistance to Awolowo among the Yoruba, a factor that was exploited by politicians and parties from other regions to justify electoral malpractices, build alliances, and actually recruit genuine supporters. The resistance among the Yoruba, largely concentrated among the Oyo-Yoruba groups in Modakeke, Oyo, Ibadan, and Ogbomoso, revealed old rivalries between groups and culminated in the rift that split the Action Group in the 1960s. There was, for instance, the hostility between two powerful kings, the *Ooni* of Ile-Ife and the *Alaafin* of Oyo. The AG had regarded the *Ooni* as the supreme Yoruba king, in line with the politics of using the myth of Oduduwa as a political ideology. The *Alaafin,* regarded by the British until the 1930s as the supreme Yoruba king, felt slighted. If the *Ooni* traditionally has sought alliance with the party in power among the Yoruba, the *Alaafin* has had to seek allies in the north. Both try not to keep the same powerful friends. Old and new rivalries have often been invoked to justify the formation of alliances between the Yoruba and other ethnic groups, as in the case of prominent members in the National Party of Nigeria in the 1970s and 1980s. Here is the fault line that weakens the ethnic solidarity: there are those who do believe that the Yoruba cannot control federal power unless they form alliances with other ethnic groups, notably the northerners. Abiola subscribed to this position—he made many friends in the north, using Islam as an opportunity to reach out. He won an election, but never achieved power. Thus, Abiola's case shows that the strategy of alliance, too, is not foolproof.

Yoruba Ethnicity in the 1990s: The Revival of "Oduduwa Kingdom"

The failure of Abiola, like that of Awolowo, was devastating to the ideologues of Yoruba unity and their claim that the Yoruba have the strongest credentials to have a son as the country's president. The manner in which the elections were annulled in 1993 was interpreted to mean that the vested interest in the north did not want a southerner and Yoruba in power. Abiola became a hero, although he was despised in the 1970s and 1980s for being anti-Awolowo and pro-Shari'a. His support for the Shari'a in the 1980s alienated him from the Christians, but they, too, chose to forgive him. As the Yoruba became louder in their cries of injustice, Abiola's supporters in the north began to abandon him. Both the military regimes of Babangida and Abacha cleverly condemned the pro-Abiola rally and protest as evidence of the excessive ambition of the Yoruba to control the federal government.

The challenges to the Abacha regime have generally been described under the rubric of pro-democracy movements, and the resurgence of Yoruba ethnicity has gone uncaptured. Yoruba ethnicity received its biggest expression in the 1990s, mainly in reaction to the annulment of the elections that Abiola won. In the expression of Yoruba ethnicity, two approaches were prominent.

The Democratic Option

There was a political path, pursued by established politicians, which ultimately led to the formation of the Alliance for Democracy (AD), the party that now controls power in all of the Yoruba-speaking states. The activities of the pro-Abacha movements were concentrated in the southwest, among the Yoruba. Many members of the National Democratic Coalition (NADECO) were leading Yoruba politicians. The Yoruba also formed an association, the Afenifere, a pan-Yoruba gathering which brought within its ranks people from different political parties and places. Strong members of the Afenifere later became influential in the AD. Until the deaths of Abacha and Abiola in 1998, the focus of the politicians was to demand the mandate of Abiola and a national conference to discuss the future of the country. When Abiola died, the politicians joined in the transition program. The anti-Abacha, pro-Abiola associations were transformed into a political party controlled by the Yoruba. So powerful did the AD become that it was difficult for another party to penetrate the areas of Yorubaland. Chief Olu Falae was the presidential flag-bearer in a two-way race with Obasanjo, a member of the People's Democratic Party.[40] Once again, as with the formation of the Action Group and the Unity Party of Nigeria in the 1970s, Yoruba ethnicity found expression in the formation of a political party.

The Autonomy or Secession Option

There have been various groups, within and outside Nigeria, seeking the autonomy of the Yoruba either as a separate country or a strong one within the federation. The denial of Abiola's presidency was regarded as sufficient reason to create a new Yoruba country or seek autonomy in a weakened Nigeria. So important did this option become that it was widely discussed in the mid-1990s, and a few organizations devoted time and attention to its articulation. I want to review the statement and argument of one such association, the Egbe Omo Yoruba (EOY). The EOY was an amalgamation of many Yoruba associations in the United States and Europe, with endorsement from leading Yoruba politicians. Notable politicians such as the late Chief Bola Ige, who served as a minister in the Obasanjo regime, General (retired) Alani Akinrinade and others have attended their meetings. The EOY has published a handbook and magazine, in addition to maintaining a web page.[41]

Using the language of redemption, agony, and hope, pro-autonomy groups saw an end to the Yoruba unless they pulled out of Nigeria or attained sufficient independence in a new political arrangement. Membership in Nigeria is regarded as a curse, and the Yoruba cannot "entrust their destiny in the hands of others."[42] According to the pro-autonomy groups, except for a brief period under Awolowo, the Yoruba have suffered enormously during the twentieth century. According to them, in the first half of the twentieth century, the British took away power from their chiefs and kings, forced them to become part of Nigeria, and "the main instruments of British colonial control, the army and the civil service, were set up and used mostly against Yoruba interest."[43] This period was followed by one of devastation, according to the pro-autonomy groups. Described by the EOY as the "years of occupation" by the Hausa-Fulani, the Yoruba were destroyed. The itemization of the consequences reveals how they perceive ethnic competition, regarding the Yoruba as victims and the Hausa-Fulani as the oppressors:

i. Like it was under British imperialism, the Yoruba people have again lost the right to be ruled by leaders of their choice. Instead, governors, state administrators and sundry local government officials are routinely appointed for them by successive coup plotters who are mainly the military front of the Hausa-Fulani occupying power.

ii. The marginalization of Yoruba people in the center(s) of power, especially in the military and security services, the civil service, the foreign service and parastatals.

iii. The decline of the Yoruba middle class. Many of them are forced to migrate to other lands, especially Europe, America and the Middle East to live as virtual second class citizens.

iv. The Yoruba people have lost their right to decency and dignity and God-given pride in their heritage, history and culture.

v. The daily looting and destruction of the resources of Yorubaland by the Hausa-Fulani occupying powers and their surrogates and henchmen have led to serious decline in the people's standard of living.

vi. The collapse of education, health services and social infrastructure which the Awolowo generation labored to build. A great culture that produced such giants as Wole Soyinka, Hubert Ogunde, Kola Ogunmola, Sunny Ade, Fela Anikulapo Kuti, Daniel Fagunwa, J. F. Odunjo, et al., has fallen into serious decline. Universities are now literally empty of intellectuals. The University College Hospital, UCH, which used to have about 60 professors in the early eighties, now has less than ten professors. The others have been frustrated out by the policies and mismanagement of the occupying power.

vii. The massive discrimination against the Yoruba people in the name of quota system and federal character.

viii. The economic dis-empowerment of the Yoruba people through massive manipulation of indices of economic growth and formulation of policies designed to destroy the industrial base of Yorubaland.

ix. The neglect and pollution of Yoruba cultural heritage, language and civilization.

x. The physical occupation of Yorubaland by troops of other ethnic nationalities who are loyal to people who have no interest of the Yoruba people at heart.

xi. Daily violation of the fundamental rights of the Yoruba people to dignity and constant brutalization by elements of the armed and security forces.[44]

The document goes further to discuss the implications of the aforementioned:

i. *Destruction of legitimacy.* Since we have been having military regimes that have no roots among the people, the concept of legitimate leadership is gradually being eroded among the people. Might is now right. The so-called governors or administrators, holding their positions at the behest of the occupying power, behave as if they own no responsibility to the people.

ii. *Destruction of heritage.* Having no emotional attachment or intellectual understanding of the heritage of the people, the so-called rulers posted from the center continue to waste even the scarce resources and heritage that they met on the ground. As far as they are concerned, the market would soon be over and the earlier and faster they grab what they can, the better.

iii. *Lack of leadership focus* Since those who are ruling are not the elected leaders of the people, they do not share the people's hunger for education, technology, science, cultural and artistic liberty, free and socially responsible press, full employment, democracy and social justice. They see any emerging pattern of independent leadership as a direct challenge to their illegitimate privilege.[45]

Arising from these depressing conditions, the Yoruba are enjoined to assert their independence and explore five options:

i. The Yoruba people must insist, with other nationalities in Nigeria, that we need to discuss the re-creation of the Nigerian state. If we must stay together, we should all agree on the terms of the marriage.

ii. The Yoruba people must accept that the destiny of the Yoruba nation is one and inescapable.

iii. the people of Yorubaland and the rest of Nigeria must elect their own leaders through universal adult suffrage and democratic institutions known to all civilized and democratic societies in the world.

iv. The political mobilization of the entire citizens of Yorubaland is the primary responsibility of every Family member so that the people can realize that only a free and democractic Yorubaland can harness its wealth for the full benefit of the people.

v. A nation's greatest resource are its people and therefore their education, health, social welfare, cultural aspiration and spiritual well-being must be the primary duty and concern of the political leadership.[46]

Autonomy and secessionist groups, like Awolowo before them, have accepted the historical evidence of Yoruba unity, and have disregarded any data on division. They regard the Yoruba as victims, and not one of the "big three" (Hausa-Fulani, Igbo, and Yoruba) who dominate the country. The failure of Awolowo and Abiola to attain power was read not as personal tragedies, but as an ethnic tragedy in which a collective nation was robbed of its well-deserved power. To these groups, the victims must empower themselves: ethnicity must not just involve a struggle with others, but an independence movement. I want to turn now to yet another group that has pushed the demand to the zone of violence.

The Oodua People's Congress

Now a radical and an "anarchist" organization, the Oodua People's Congress (OPC) started as an association to advocate unity and autonomy for the Yoruba. Founded by Dr. Fasheun, a medical doctor and politician, its mission was to seek self-determination for the Yoruba, protect their interests, and fight for their rights. Its agenda included the funding of a research center in Ile-Ife, occasional public lectures, and massive support for a leader who stands for the Yoruba. Indeed, a number of prominent Yoruba have honored the OPC with lectures and funding.

The OPC split in 1998 over the issue of the transition program announced by General Abubabar who replaced Abacha. Fasheun argued that the transition should be supported, since a Yoruba would become the president, but that the organization should not identify with any political party.

Another faction, led by his deputy, Ganiyu Adams, was against the transition. Although Fasheun was in his sixties and a veteran politician, Adams, a 29–year-old carpenter and a newcomer to politics, created a faction that grew more popular. The Adams faction became militant and antigovernment. A number of young men joined the organization, turning it from a political interest group to a radical youth movement. Adams redefined the agenda of the OPC to include fighting criminals, thus bringing the OPC in confrontation with gang members, known as the "Area Boys." To strengthen its own power as well, Adams's OPC also recruited a number of "Area Boys" to its fold, thereby transforming the organization into a "vigilante group." In Lagos, Ibadan, and Ilesa, Adams's OPC confronted criminal organizations, relying on mob popularity. According to Adams, fighting criminals is part of defending the interest of the Yoruba.[47]

With Obasanjo in power and the AD in control of Yoruba-speaking states, the belief is that either the activities of the autonomy/secession groups should end or that they should become less combative, lest the army overthrows a government headed by a Yoruba. Those who sided with for the democratic option now have the upper hand; many are in power and profiting from it, and groups such as the OPC are no longer regarded as allies but enemies.

In 1999 and 2000, the OPC was credited with killing police officers; creating havoc in different parts of Lagos; causing a market crisis that led to the death of more than a hundred people; and house burning, armed robbery, and insecurity. Regarding the OPC as a successful organization, youth in other parts of the country formed similar associations, such as the Arewa People's Congress, comprising northerners, and the Ijaw Youth Congress, all to constitute pressure groups or to champion the ethnic cause. The scenario of widespread violence all over the country became frightening to the government. So bad did things become in Lagos state that the president threatened, in January 2000, to declare a state of emergency if the state government could not check the activities of the OPC, whom he described as a group of criminals. As Adams has been able to recruit many young men and purchase weapons, it is unclear who is financing them and what the true missions have become. The police and the OPC are now enemies, and Adams a scapegoat of a state riddled with insecurity.[48]

The members of the AD are now put in the uncomfortable position of dissociating themselves from an organization that they endorsed when Abacha was in power, but which is now stigmatized as a gang. The OPC continues to use the ethnic banner and the agenda of protecting Yoruba interests. One thing that is clear is that, whenever the OPC becomes a useful tool, politicians can be trusted to move closer to its restless members.

Yoruba Ethnicity in Retrospect

Yoruba ethnicity has evolved over time, reaching its peak in the 1990s with the vigorous demand for autonomy. In their long precolonial history, the Yoruba-speaking people did not constitute a single, sociopolitical unit. Their different groups and states were autonomous units. However, the groups and states established relations with one another. Each city-state forged an identity through the use of myth. War, trade, diplomacy, and marriages fostered intergroup relations. The Yoruba also developed relations with their neighbors through commerce, war, diplomacy, intermarriages and cultural borrowing. Thus, history provides evidence of separate development and regional cooperation, thus enabling modern political actors to draw from historical materials and multiple conclusions.

The consciousness and manipulation of a pan-Yoruba identity began during the nineteenth century and ethnicity was consolidated during the twentieth century. The consciousness and consolidation owed to the emergence of a new elite, the rapid changes that accompanied colonial rule, and the incorporation of the Yoruba into modern Nigeria. A new intelligentsia, led by Awolowo, called on the Yoruba to ignore the evidence of past autonomous development and choose instead that of the creation myth, a similar culture, and intergroup relations. In other words, politics demanded that the Yoruba submerge the parochialism of their many city-states and subgroups and choose the nationalism of one Yoruba. A pan-Yoruba identity works when the Yoruba are involved in the broader arena of Nigerian politics where they have to compete. However, as they also have to organize their space and share resources, an ethnic fault line develops: the interests of different city-states and groups (e.g., Ekiti, Ibadan, Egba) can be activated. Thus, one can discern multiple layers in the construction and use of Yoruba identity:

1. at the national level, a pan-Yoruba identity is necessary in order to present a united front in a competitive system;
2. at the regional/state level, a group identity becomes important. Here the Yoruba accept their partition into the various states of Lagos, Ogun, Oyo, Osun, Ondo, and Ekiti;
3. at the group/state level, cities and villages have to compete, thereby creating the need to foster "township identities";
4. at the township level, lineages and wards create boundaries of exclusion and inclusion.

All these variations and multiple identities shape the relevance and use of history. They subject history to creativity, propaganda, and abuse. Policy options have to consider the reality of multiple identities. For instance, suggestions on confederacy ignore the fact that the values and interests of a subethnic group can assume dominance when an ethnic group acquires more power, or that new minorities can emerge in the process. Federalism, on the other hand, enables a pan-Yoruba consciousness to flourish. The emergence of a relevant ideology that would transform the Nigerian society must grapple with the problems of building a pan-Nigerian consciousness. More importantly, it has to focus on values that cut across ethnic boundaries.

Ethnicity will continue to shape the outcome of democracy. For half a century, the Yoruba have always stood behind a leader and party that represents regional-cum-ethnic interests. Awolowo's Action Group and the Unity Party of Nigeria, and the current AD, have had to seek alliances in the quest to win control of the center. In all the alliances, they have always demanded that a Yoruba would be the presidential flag-bearer. In other words, alliances have been formed to ensure Yoruba hegemony or interests. Abiola and Obasanjo, who have succeeded in winning elections, have done so by presenting themselves as the representatives of interests bigger than those of the Yoruba. Abiola consistently used his extensive connections with northerners and Islam. Obasanjo, on the other hand, presents himself as a "nationalist," as being a Nigerian before being a Yoruba. Abiola was denied power partly because of a perception that he would not serve northern interests; Obasanjo obtained power partly because of a belief that he would serve northern interests. Can a defender of Yoruba interests attain power? If so, what possibility exists for democracy to work in a multilevel society where other ethnic groups have their interests as well?

Events since May 29, 1999, when Obasanjo assumed power, have shown that the forces that created the problems of the 1990 are still in place; that the role of ethnicity and communities in politics remains strong; and that the interests of the various nationalities have not been discussed, to say nothing of being addressed. Ethnicity remains important. The self-determination of each group has to be considered, which is why the country opted for a federal system in the first place. The center has to decentralize power for ethnic groups to attain some of their aspirations. The more centralized and autocratic the center is, the more assertive the ethnic groups become. Prolonged military rule has undermined federalism and is actually responsible for the demands to restructure the basis of the federation. Economic decline and worsening living standards have called into question the relevance of the state and accentuated the need to seek alternative models to the Nigerian federation. Ethnic and religious nationalism has become powerful in the light of the failure of the Nigerian state to meet the expectations of its people.

With Obasanjo in power, the Yoruba stand to be implicated in his administration. Whether he succeeds or fails, they have achieved their long-standing dream of producing a president. If Obasanjo represents their opportunity for sustained prominence, should he, then, govern as a Yoruba with Yoruba interests in mind? This option is not open to him at a time of rising communal, religious, and ethnic nationalism in various parts of the country. The Yoruba will continue to speak of the "Oduduwa kingdom" and the possibility of autonomy, thereby retaining the relevance of ethnicity in a new millennium.

Conclusion

The chapter has noted the power and ambiguities of ethnicity as an identity and their strategies for political mobilization. It has shown that members of an ethnic group seek the means to unite, drawing on values, tradition, and historical memory in order to constitute powerful social and political units. It has also shown that leading members of an ethnic group can fight and seek alliances with other groups. Whether they are weak or strong, ethnic identities enable the survival of older cultures, the creative use of cultures for politics, the formulation of a set of universal ideas about the purpose of society and its future needs, and the promotion of a set of common ideas and values to motivate ethnic members and sustain the consciousness of peoplehood. Ethnicity has served African politics as a bargaining device available to members of different groups to negotiate and compromise. As Richard Sklar has shown with regard to Nigeria, ethnic politics is not always as dangerous as people think—it has allowed politicians to build a fast cultural and political network without spending too much money.[49]

It is wishful thinking that cultural identities constructed by ethnicity will disappear with development. To the contrary, ethnicity is becoming stronger. Rather than seek the means to destroy loyalty to the group, it is much more effective to develop complementary identities that will enable the individual to seek a balance between the group and the nation. It should be possible to be a Yoruba, a Muslim, and a Nigerian at the same time. To give the individual the option of choosing one at the expense of the other is to set the modern nation on a dangerous path that will destroy it.

Notes

1. See Okwudiba Nnoli, *Ethnic Politics in Nigeria* (Enugu: Fourth Dimension, 1978).

2. Toyin Falola, *Violence in Nigeria: The Crisis of Religious Politics and Secular Ideologies* (Rochester, N.Y.: University of Rochester Press, 1998).

3. *Tell Magazine,* March 19, 2001, 69.

4. *Tell Magazine,* April 9, 2001, 30

5. Obafemi Awolowo, *Path to Nigerian Freedom* (London: Faber and Faber, 1947), 49.

6. Nnamdi Azikiwe, *My Odyssey: An Autobiography* (London: C. Hurst, 1970), 243.

7. On the changing nature of Yoruba chieftaincy, see Michael Crowder and Obaro Ikime, eds., *West African Chiefs: Their Changing Status under Colonial Rule and Independence* (Ile-Ife: University of Ife Press, 1970); and Olufemi Vaughan, *Nigerian Chiefs: Traditional Power in Modern Politics, 1890–1990s* (Rochester, N.Y.: University of Rochester Press, 2000).

8. See the National Archives, Ibadan (N.A.I.), Nigeria, Ekiti Division, 1/1/518, Akure-Ikere boundary dispute, 1853, pp. 44–49.

9. British Parliamentary Papers, vol. 63, Nigeria, p. 68.

10. See O. Adejuyigbe, *Boundary Problems in Western Nigeria: A Geographical Analysis* (Ile-Ife: University of Ife Press, 1975).

11. Toyin Falola, *The Political Economy of a Pre-Colonial African State: Ibadan, 1830–1900* (Ile-Ife: University of Ife Press, 1984).

12. Toyin Falola and Dare Oguntomisin, *The Military in Nineteenth Century Yoruba Politics* (Ile-Ife: University of Ife Press, 1984), chapter 1.

13. Toyin Falola, "Power Drift in the Political System of Southwestern Nigeria in the Nineteenth Century," *ODU: A Journal of West African Studies* 21 (January/July 1981): 109–27.

14. Falola and Oguntomisin, *The Military in Nineteenth Century.*

15. Falola, *The Political Economy.*

16. Toyin Falola and Dare Oguntomisin, *Yoruba Warlords of the Nineteenth Century* (Trenton, N.J.: Africa World Press, 2000).

17. Toyin Falola and Dare Oguntomisin, "Refugees in Yorubaland in the Nineteenth Century," *Asian and African Studies* 22, nos. 1 & 2, 67–79.

18. Samuel Johnson, *The History of the Yorubas* (Lagos: C.M.S., 1921), 11.

19. See J. O. Olubokun, *Itan Uyin* (Yaba: Forward Press, 1952), 5; and N.A.I., Oyo Prof 2/2/1372, Yoruba Crowns, Rights and Privileges to wear crowns by certain chiefs.

20. Johnson, *The History of the Yorubas,* 335.

21. See Robert S. Smith, *Warfare and Diplomacy in Pre-Colonial West Africa* (London: Methuen, 1976); and J. F. Ade Ajayi and R. S. Smith, *Yoruba Warfare in the Nineteenth Century* (Cambridge: Cambridge University Press, 1964).

22. J. A. Atanda, *The New Oyo Empire: Indirect Rule and Change in Western Nigeria, 1894–1934* (London: Longman, 1973), 13.

23. See Paul Lovejoy, "Interregional Monetary Flows in the Precolonial Trade of Nigeria," *Journal of African History* 15 (1974): 536–85; and Mahdi Adamu, *The Hausa Factor in West African History* (Zaria: Ahmadu Bello University Press, 1978).

24. See S. W. Koelle, *Polyglotta Africana or a Comparative Vocabulary of Nearly 300 Words and Phrases in More Than One Hundred District African Languages* (1853; reprint London: C.M.S., 1963), 5.

25. For information on the emigrants, see J. H. Kopytoff, *A Preface to Modern Nigeria: The "Sierra Leonians" in Yoruba, 1830–1890* (Madison: University of Wisconsin Press, 1965).

26. See E. A. Ayandele, *The Educated Elite in the Nigerian Society* (Ibadan: Ibadan University Press, 1974).

27. E. A. Ayandele, *The Missionary Impact on Modern Nigeria, 1842–1914* (London: Longman, 1966), 177.

28. Johnson, *The History,* 642. Abiodun is capitalized in the original. He was the Alaafin in the late eighteenth century, at a time of great prosperity for the Oyo Empire.

29. For some of these changes, see Toyin Falola, ed., *Britain and Nigeria: Exploitation or Development?* (London: Zed, 1987).

30. Okwudiba Nnoli, *Ethnic Politics in Nigeria.*

31. Ibid.

32. S. O. Arifalo, "Ethnic Political Consciousness in Nigeria, 1947–1951," *Geneve-Afrique* 34, no. 1 (1986): 7–34.

33. *The Constitution of the Egbe Omo Oduduwa* (Ijebu-Ode, 1948).

34. See O. A. Sobande, *Path to Unity and Culture: Being a Comprehensive Survey of Principles and Practices of Egbe Omo Oduduwa* (Lagos, 1952), mimeo.

35. For details on the AG and the other political parties of this period, see Richard L. Sklar, *Nigerian Political Parties: Power in an Emergent African Nation* (Princeton, N.J.: Princeton University Press, 1963).

36. B. J. Dudley, *Instability and Political Order: Politics and Crisis in Nigeria* (Ibadan: Ibadan University Press, 1973), 164.

37. Egbe Omo Yoruba, *Family Handbook and National Blueprint* (Washington, D.C.: Egbe Omo Oduduwa, 1996), 4–5.

38. His career is one of the best-documented in Nigerian politics. See Toyin Falola et al., *Chief Obafemi Awolowo: The End of an Era?* (Ile-Ife: Obafemi Awolowo University Press, 1988).

39. See Toyin Falola and Hassan Mathew Kukah, *Religious Militancy and Self-Assertion: Islam and Politics in Nigeria* (London: Avebury, 1996).

40. For an elaboration of the politics of this period, see Toyin Falola, *The History of Nigeria* (Westport, Conn.: Greenwood, 1999), chapter 14.

41. *Yoruba Autonomy Alert; Yoruba Family Handbook and National Blueprint;* and *http://www.yorubanation.org/.*

42. *Yoruba Family Handbook,* 1.

43. Ibid., 4.

44. Ibid., 5–6.

45. Ibid., 6–7.

46. Ibid., 7–8.

47. Interview with Ganiyu Adams, *Tell Magazine,* January 31, 2000, 26.

48. See a detailed report on Adams and the police search for him in *The News* (Abuja), 31 January, 2000.

49. Toyin Falola, ed., *African Politics in Postimperial Times: The Essays of Richard Sklar* (Trenton, N.J.: Africa World Press, 2002), 491–502.

7

ISLAM, RELIGIOUS IDENTITY, AND POLITICS

"ONLY THOSE WHO HAVE TEETH WORRY ABOUT TOOTHACHE."
—A GBANDE PROVERB

Islam (as does Christianity) constitutes an integral part of African politics. This chapter draws on the Nigerian example to illustrate the link between Islam and politics, as well as reflect on the global relevance of Islam in the post–September 11 world. The chapter addresses two issues: what Islam means for Nigerian politics; and some considerations for understanding Nigerian Islam in global politics, in particular with reference to the United States following the attacks on the World Trade Center and the Pentagon on September 11, 2001. Nigeria has one of the largest concentrations of Muslims in the world, and Islam has played a leading role in its politics: like the proverbial mouth with teeth, there will be the occasional pains of toothache. The data on Islam is extensive, and some conclusions can be applied to many other African countries with their plural identities and complicated politics. As the chapter makes clear, Islam does not operate in a political vacuum—issues of ethnicity, power rivalry, and the ambitious search for money create their own impact on the religion itself.

To be sure, Nigeria is not an Islamic state, as it is under a democratic government with a secular constitution and the rule of law. Nevertheless, Islam is important in Nigeria, and has an impact on politics and social life. Islam is entrenched in Africa. In Nigeria, it is an old religion, with millions subscribing to the faith. In many historical periods, Islam had served as a

Figure 9. The power of Islam. Niaga, Senegal.

unifying force (as in the case of the Sokoto Caliphate during the nine-teenth century). Islam has also contributed in many ways to Nigeria's development, notably in providing the sources to organize politics and society, fostering community cohesion, and creating an ideology of change.

Without any fear of contradiction, it can be asserted that Nigeria cannot be understood without Islam. To begin with the areas of intersection between Islam and politics, first, the government's failure to promote development or enhance living standards will continue to make Islam an attractive "ideology" for organizing change and seeking better or alternative solutions to a myriad of problems. In general (as well as in different historical epochs), Islam has expressed itself as a radical religion and political ideology.[1]

Second, tensions will continue to mount in the country, and they will take various forms, including inter- and intrareligious conflicts. Within Islam, the Sufi and anti-Sufi conflicts are unlikely to disappear, and different political parties and interest groups will exploit them to gain political power to further specific interests. These can even be expressed as communal clashes as in the case of religious riots, including those of 1999 in the

Figure 10. The face of Islam. Ibadan, Nigeria.

cities of Sagamu in the south and Kano in the north. In Sagamu, the Yoruba attacked a number of Hausa (from the north), who were accused of not obeying local customs, and the Hausa retaliated in Kano by killing a number of Yoruba and forcing many of them to leave the city. Ethnic groups that migrate, such as the Igbo of eastern Nigeria, have experienced a number of communal-cum-religious conflicts outside of their homelands. Economic decline can promote such tensions and the political class can manipulate them to its advantage. Other than the use of violence by the state, there is thus far no solution to the conflicts. There is no leader of stature to mediate in the conflicts, and an alternative agenda on reforms will continue to generate debate and problems.

Third, Islamic leaders and Muslim organizations are very efficient and astute at building regional and international solidarity networks to push their claims and gain strength in greater numbers. As the power of traditional political authority represented by the emirs declines, there will be a weakened centralized institution to hold northern Nigeria together. Islam is the ideology that may create a semblance of unity. However, Islam can also rally together other Muslims beyond the frontiers of the north.

Is the secular state too artificial? Many Muslims will answer in the affirmative, and there are scholars who think that Nigeria alienates its citizens and pushes them to seek loyalties in religion, communities, and ethnic groups. Islam will continue to be relevant to power. While the Nigerian constitution prohibits the formation of political parties along religious lines, political actors will seek and consolidate power by manipulating and benefiting from several identities. These actors and their rivals will continue to use Islam and ethnicity to mobilize support.

To millions of people, the daily routines of life revolve around Islamic practices and their survival in their villages and towns. The commitment to such routines and practices is strong. The agenda of the political class is to ask the people to transcend those routines and practices and become "nationalists," or "federalists," or loyalists, that is, to move from an informal socio-political space to that of the public and formal. As Peter Ekeh points out, the zone of the formal, represented by the state and federal governments, appears both abstract and remote.[2] Securing the loyalty of the public will entail a great deal of propaganda work, far more than the conduct of occasional elections. For democracy to work, Nigerians divided by religion and ethnicity must be convinced that citizenship in the same country is important to them. The demands of religious groups may make democratic institutions rather fragile. How can a Muslim living in Ibadan, a Yoruba city, or Sokoto in the north be a Muslim and a Nigerian and be loyal to both without coming into conflict with other identities and nationalities? Various segments of the population and groups have been calling for a Sovereign National Conference to discuss the basis of the federation, the rights and privileges of each nationality and religion, a just way to share oil revenues, and a new constitution to reflect all the differences, but both the military and the Obasanjo administrations have rejected such a call, fearing that secessionists and anti-federalists may gain the upper hand. The Nigerian political class is yet to find an appropriate answer to the problems and challenges posed by pluralism, including that of religious differences and conflicts.

Islam, Elections, and Politics

On May 29, 1999, Nigeria completed a long and complicated process that brought military rule to an end, at least for now, and inaugurated what is now called a Fourth Republic. There was a First Republic (1960–65), a Second Republic (1979–83), but the Third Republic did not exist. The abortion of the Third Republic is the starting point to understanding the elections that led to the fourth. It can also be argued that the elections of 1998–99 did not produce many peculiarities of their own, as the important variables that determined them had long existed: ethnicity, religion, competition over resource sharing, minority and communal marginalization, personality and ego contests, and the prominent role of money.[3] However, if the First Republic was preceded by optimism and the Second Republic by the oil boom of the 1970s, the Fourth Republic was born during a period of great economic decline, social decay, and widespread public cynicism and apathy.

In this political ebb and flow, the role of Islam has been constant in some aspects and changing in others. Like ethnicity, it is a tool of manipulation wielded by power seekers, but also a mobilizing ideology used by those who have a genuine desire for change. If many politicians and people see in Islam a political ideology and tool, the non-Muslims seek the means to counter the power of Islam, to use ethnicity as a source of identity to mobilize themselves against possible Islamic domination, and to advocate secular institutions as the only available option to manage a modern country.

To "disarm" Islam in Nigeria, the strategies by non-Muslims have been to foster primordial identities and ethnicities; radicalize Christianity or at least "politicize" the congregations so that they will not dissociate

Christianity from politics; promote a regional concept of the south against the north; promote the spread of Western education and secular institutions, including an insistence on a modern judiciary based on English law; affirm Nigeria as a secular federal republic; and sponsor the elections of non-Muslims into power.

If a Christian, Olusegun Obasanjo, is now the country's president, it does not necessarily represent the failure of Islam, but its limitation in dominating the political arena. Nevertheless, the power of Islam as a political ideology swiftly followed the inauguration of the Fourth Republic, when the northern state of Zamfara became the first to declare the use of the Shari'a law, thereby integrating the state with religion. This chapter will also examine this crucial development, which tests the secular and democratic principles of the Federal Republic of Nigeria.

Islam has generally been linked to power, in particular in the creation of what analysts have called the "northern factor" in Nigerian politics. These geopolitics produce an irony: the north, with limited resources, without even oil, which is the source of Nigeria's wealth and power, dominates the south, where the bulk of the resources are concentrated. The north has not even acquired economic power, in spite of its leading role in politics—compared to the south, it has a less educated labor force, fewer industries, and lower per capita income. The south controls the media and bureaucracy, and has a large number of professionals. However, its power has always been one of opposition or, to use the common expression, of civil society. Not that the south wants to lose this dominant control of civil society; it wants more control of the federal government, that is, the ability to share resources. Why is the north able to dominate the political space, as alleged by the south? The answer lies in part in the ability of northern leaders to use Islam as a religious and political ideology. However, does the emergence of Obasanjo, a "born-again Christian," represent the decline of the north and of Islam? The answer lies partly in the limitation of the north and Islam to dominate the political process in perpetuity and in the assertiveness of other forces in the political arena to challenge the real and imagined threat of the north and of Islam.

Preface to the Fourth Republic

Since the 1940s, the ambition of the political elite has been to create a strong nation-state and a federal political system. This is yet to be realized, in part because the nature of political competition and a politicized economy has made access to political power a most lucrative business. The trend toward political division began during the colonial period, as British policies accentuated ethnic divisions, the nationalist movement fractured into pieces, and the federal constitution of the 1950s gave full rein to the competition among the three big regions: the north, west, and east.

Nigeria obtained its independence from the British in 1960 as a weakened and divided society.[4] The country inherited many legacies of colonial rule: a Westminster parliamentary system;[5] complicated ethnic and regional divisions that led to bitter rivalries; competition between a group of traditional and educated elite; an export-oriented economy; and a public, rather than an economic, elite that needed the control of state institutions to sustain and consolidate itself.[6] Very rapidly regionalism and political competition culminated in the fall of the First Republic, military rule, and a civil war, all during the first decade of independence.[7] The 1970s witnessed an oil boom during which the economy expanded rapidly, and produced a temporary military disengagement that gave way to the short-lived Second Republic.[8] The military regimes of Mohammed Buhari and Ibrahim Babangida governed Nigeria for most of the 1980s, and those of Babangida and Sanni Abacha the 1990s.

The 1990s was the worst decade in the modern history of Nigeria. The dictatorship of General Sanni Abacha redefined the patrimonial state by incorporating all the worst excesses of power and corruption without any regard for accountability and domestic and/or international opinions. Yet previous military regimes had prepared the ground for the emergence of General Abacha. Except for the short duration of the Second Republic, the military dominated the political scene. By and large, their role has been negative, notably marked by a civil war in the 1960s, the failure to build and foster democratic institutions of society, the failure to promote probity and accountability in government, and the gross inability to transform the economy. All the failures of the military were exposed in the 1980s and 1990s under the military regimes of the two most notorious and repressive leaders, Babangida and Abacha.[9]

The 1980s and 1990s witnessed a rapid economic decline. As before, the country relied on enormous revenues from oil, which the federal government used to control the states, distribute largess, buy political support, and pay for security forces to hunt out critics and opponents. But lacking a solid economic base and regional control of trade, and unable to generate food to feed its population, the government could not guarantee an oil-based prosperity for the majority of the population. Other major problems ensued in both decades. A Structural Adjustment Program that devalued the naira, the country's currency, increased the prices of imports, and reduced the workforce resulted in severe damage to the economy and society.[10] Although the price of oil fluctuated and foreign investments declined, huge oil revenues ensured that the economy would not collapse.[11] The naira continued to lose its value while external reserves were depleted. Military officers and privileged politicians became more greedy than ever and converted public treasuries to private ones. The embattled population sought the means to survive, as many took to migration and crime. Infrastructures crumbled, social institutions decayed, and the people lost hope.

Political frustrations, ethnic rivalries, and religious crises accompanied the economic decline. Since the 1980s, there have been many conflicts, leading to the loss of thousands of lives. Among the major ones are: the Muslim-Christian violence in the north in the 1980s, the Shi'ites' uprisings in the 1980s and 1990s, the Modakeke-Ife riots among the Yoruba, the anti-government/oil companies in the Niger Delta, the Urhobo-Itsekiri conflicts, and lately the Yoruba and Hausa riots in Lagos and Sagamu.[12]

Thus, Nigeria faced the threat of collapse in the 1990s.[13] The lessons of the civil war of the late 1960s were lost as new demands were made for secession by different groups, most notably the Yoruba. Anti-military opposition forces called for an end to military rule and for a national conference to renegotiate the basis of the federal system. The military ignored all these demands. The only major step they took was to reconfigure the internal boundaries by creating additional states, a policy that began with General Yakubu Gowon's administration in the mid-1960s. By 1998, the federal structure comprised thirty-six small states and a federal capital authority at Abuja, all weak and many unable to maintain themselves without regular federal subventions. While a number of ethnic groups had used the states to secure a sort of autonomy, their political elite viewed the state treasuries as open to them for abuse. Meanwhile, the cost of maintaining many bureaucracies had left very little money for development projects.

The grave political crises of the 1990s revolved around the ambition of General Babangida to perpetuate himself in power while at the same time initiating a fraudulent and costly transition program to a promised Third Republic. A self-described "evil genius," he engineered and manipulated political crises to advantage until he was consumed by them in 1993. He came to power against the background of the mismanagement of the Second Republic and the political authoritarianism of the short-lived Buhari regime (1984–85), but he ended with legacies far worse than those of his predecessors. He promised to govern as a liberal but became a dictator; he promised to be a "national leader" but he ended up using the north to shore up his regime and ethnicity to prevent an anti-military political coalition. Originally accused of being pro-Christian, he made Nigeria a member of the Organization of Islamic Conference, a decision that instigated a prolonged Muslim-Christian tension and the rhetoric of interreligious warfare.[14] To consolidate power, he appointed more Muslims and northerners to the Armed Forces Ruling Council, courted the friendship of religious leaders, and manipulated the appointment of a loyalist as the new Sultan of Sokoto in 1988. Babangida promised to create a new political class and culture, but neither of these materialized.

He embarked on a program of military disengagement characterized by unpredictability, a waste of government funds, and ultimately failure.[15] In an unprecedented move, his government single-handedly established two political parties—the National Republican Convention (NRC) and the Social Democratic Party (SDP). The north identified with the NRC and the south more with the SDP. The government created too many obstacles in the way of the transition, many candidates were disqualified, the rules were unstable, and the people gradually lost interest in the elections. Greater troubles came in 1993 and beyond. After the failure of a well-sponsored plan to prevent the presidential elections on June 12, 1993, not only did these take place, a victor emerged in Chief M. K. O. Abiola of the SDP. Abiola was a latecomer to the SDP, becoming a candidate after Babangida's government had prevented many others from running. Abiola was a Yoruba Muslim, a wealthy and generous philanthropist, and a friend to many military officers, including Babangida. His rival from the NRC was Bashir Tofa, a Muslim from Kano, also very wealthy. Not only did Abiola have a great numerical victory (58 percent to Tofa's 42 percent), he also won the mandate in all the Yoruba states and in four minority states in the south. Despite a poor showing among the Igbo (he won only one state out of four), he garnered a resounding mandate in the north, winning nine of sixteen states, most notably in the middle belt and northeast (among the Kanuri), both traditionally opposed to the domination of the Hausa-Fulani. Not only did Abiola win in Kano, Tofa's state, but also in three other so-called "emirate states," the heartland of the Hausa-Fulani.

Babangida and a number of the northern political class were taken by surprise by the result. Almost all their calculations had failed. Fielding two Muslims as presidential candidates was believed to be so outrageous that Christians would be alienated. However, the Christians voted for Abiola, just to oust the military regime of Babangida. There was also the expectation of a stalemate in which neither of the two candidates would have sufficient votes to fulfill the constitutional provision of the majority of the number of raw votes and territorial spread. Again, this did not happen. Some also reckoned that a coalition between the Igbo and the north would give Tofa the victory, but again they miscalculated. The north failed to provide such a coalition, and for the first time in the history of modern Nigeria, Abiola accomplished what many had thought was impossible: a national mandate. Abiola's victory showed the closing of ranks among many forces: Christians voted for him, as well as non-Yoruba, thereby showing that it was possible to overcome divisive ethnic and religious issues.

Rather than concede victory to his long-standing friend, Babangida annulled the elections before an official pronouncement could be made. This was a great error that pushed the country to the brink of another war. Babangida annulled the elections in order to retain power, having been urged to do so by a cabal of military officers and career politicians who had benefited from his regime. But they failed to anticipate the consequences, and Babangida and his loyalists were consumed by the crisis. In order to rationalize a callous decision, the Babangida regime spent its last days de-monizing Abiola and pro-Abiola supporters, and carefully orchestrating the country's ethnic divide. The Yoruba were accused of a grand desire to use Abiola to dominate politics, but this was a grand manipulation of ethnicity to undermine a political opponent. If Abiola had been a Christian, the regime would have asserted the need to defend Islam against Christianity as an additional reason. To the Yoruba, the annulment was yet another case of a northern political class unwilling to yield power to other groups. As Abiola was a Muslim, Yoruba Muslims were disappointed that northern Muslims could betray them so easily.

A long period of domestic and international crises followed. The annulment ended Babangida's long history of duplicity. Opinions were divided within the army, as some factions accused him of destroying professionalism; another faction said that he was not serious about disengagement and that he should recognize Abiola as president. The various opinions meant that there was no consensus either among the senior officers or northern politicians. However, as the anti-Abiola campaign degenerated into ethnic divisions, many northern politicians who had previously supported him began to sing a different tune. Babangida could not himself hold on to power, and a decision was made on July 7, 1993, to establish an Interim National Government (ING). Established on August 26, the ING lasted for just over two months, unable to resolve the protests that ensued in support of Abiola, especially in the southwest. General Sanni

Abacha, a northern military officer, overthrew the ING on November 17, 1993.

Nigeria moved from the expectation of democracy to political authoritarianism under Abacha. The regime portrayed pro-democracy forces and protests as "tribal" activities emanating from the Yoruba. Abiola's struggle to claim his mandate ended in his indefinite house arrest and subsequent death, and the protest for his release and the "mandate of June 12" was long and bitter.[16]

Abacha had learned all his lessons from Babangida: steal as much money as you can; use corruption to manipulate the political class; and promise disengagement but do not relinquish power. But Abacha also had his own style: be selective in cultivating your allies; accumulate billions of naira quickly as time could run out; use maximum force to deal with opposition forces; strike fear in the military officers; curtail the activities of the rank and file to the barracks; and indicate no willingness whatsoever to vacate Aso Rock, the seat of power.

The style worked for Abacha, but the political cost was high. Nigeria was isolated in international politics, lost its preeminent position in African politics, and its economy suffered further. Many opposition groups at home and abroad condemned Abacha, but they were met with severe repression. Threats of secession were openly made, especially by the Yoruba. Indeed, some groups in Lagos and the United States established the Oduduwa Republic, planning for an independent Yoruba country. The territorial integrity of the country was questioned. Why should Nigeria be one, many asked, given the collapse of the Soviet Union and Yugoslavia. Like his military predecessor, Abacha announced a transition program, but he never intended the democratic process to remove him from office. While he originally allowed many parties, only five were registered and none was allowed to challenge him. As the country prepared for a presidential election in 1998, no party was allowed to have a presidential candidate other than Abacha. A number of organizations and politicians endorsed his ambition for power, perhaps after having been paid or coerced to do so.

As is to be expected, not everybody is corruptible. A few mainstream politicians condemned his ambition as a destruction of the democratic process.[17] Students, academics, and pro-democracy movements in Nigeria and abroad vigorously attacked him for his excesses and political plans. The various demands did not stop Abacha from designing a strategy to stay in power. His tight control of the political system ended abruptly with his death in February 1998, and General Abdulsalam Abubakar immediately succeeded him. Soon after, Abiola died, anti-Abacha opposition forces lost steam, and there was a promise of a new beginning.

Politics and Political Competition, 1998–1999

Abubakar successfully executed the final transition program, but the greater force was a clique of former military officers and wealthy civilians who had their own agenda and candidates. Abubakar himself was not totally free of complicity in this agenda. He had served under Abacha as the chief of army staff and, as head of state, had refused to release Abiola from jail. The very fact that Abubakar and the serving military officers were willing to relinquish power reflects the changing political conditions at both the domestic and international levels. To start with, the long, drawn-out protests in support of democratization would not have ended without a program of transition. Jubilation followed Abacha's death, with the expectation that the military would retreat to their barracks.[18] It was also apparent that the military were unable to obtain international support for their continued stay. Indeed, pressure mounted on Abubakar not to stay long in power. Opposition forces were still in existence. There were political parties building coalitions, and communities in oil-producing areas of the Niger Delta making aggressive demands for equity. Continued military rule also meant that there would be no answer to the economic decline, because fresh initiatives were difficult in such unpredictable circumstances. Knowing that military officers in political positions would eventually leave, those with access to government funds and power abused it.[19]

In the early days of the Abubakar regime, the pressure from pro-democracy groups was to put Abiola in power. Not only did Abubakar refuse, but Abiola died. His death ended a long period of antimilitary protest. However, there was a demand for a national conference to discuss the basis of the federation and the necessity, or not, of granting autonomy to different "nationalities" in the country. The call for a national conference was stronger in the south, being a code to address the issue of northern/Islamic domination. The Abubakar regime ignored the call.

The only promise made was that military rule would end. Abubakar announced a transition timetable of less than a year, from September 24, 1998, to May 29, 1999. He not only kept to this timetable, he also did not interfere in the formation of political parties, did not manipulate the decisions of the electoral commission, did not support any of the major political actors, and was sincere in his decision to disengage.

All the political parties formed under Abacha were dissolved, but the new ones were made up of the same people, with only some adjustment within the parties. While the political parties that emerged resembled those of the past, the consensus that the president would come from the south, in order to placate them for the Abiola crisis, minimized the danger of south-north, Islam-Christian conflicts. Opposition to a southern president came from a small quarter, led by Abubakar Rimi of Kano, a former governor and minister. However, the majority of northern politicians and Muslims conceded the presidency to the south.

There was yet another major change. If previous elections and republics had been preceded by constitution-making and ratification, this would not be so. In a most unusual development, the formation of political parties, campaigns, and elections all preceded the approval of the 1999 constitution. Previous presidential-style constitutions had been controlled by the Constitution Debate Coordinating Committee in 1998. With limited public input, the committee submitted a document to the military which was ratified after a few amendments. Only a minority of Nigerians had access to the constitution. Its viability and adequacy would be tested by conflicts over religion, the resolution of human rights problems, the excessive control of the center, the marginalization of oil-producing regions, and the inability of citizens to establish state-based political parties to create conditions favorable to them without the intervention of the federal government. As the section below on Zamfara shows, the power of the federal government to interfere in Islamic laws is limited. Also, the constitutional provisions to deal with inter- and intracommunity clashes have to be tested—should the center use force or leave security matters to the state governments? For a long time, only a few Nigerians were able to see the constitution for their new republic.

The political parties and aspiring politicians did not demand a new constitution, spending their time instead on plotting to capture power. There was a demand on them to create a national political party by having offices in two-thirds of the country, and before a party could receive a final registration, it had to win 5 percent of the votes in all the local councils in no fewer than twenty-four states during the elections of December 5.

The establishment of political parties and campaigns became the monopoly of those with money. The cost of party registration and campaigns was so high that only the wealthy could mobilize the sufficient funds. Politicians looked to established party networks, alliances, and ethnic and religious constituencies to form new political parties. Some changes were actually cosmetic, as in the case of the United Nigerian People's Party that was different in name only from the former United Nigerian Congress. The north-south divide was resurrected. All the political calculations in the south were made to prevent the emergence of a northern president. Indeed, notable southern politicians took to the rhetoric of warning the north of secession and even demanding the restructuring of the federation.

Many political parties, twenty-six in all, were formed, but only nine later received official recognition and only three became very active. The parties and campaigns did not depart from the established political script. To start with, they all claimed to have a national scope, but a large number were organized along ethnic lines. Even when they eventually passed as "national parties," they were nothing more than an agglomeration of ethnic notables. Indeed, the most powerful brokers first presented themselves as men with large constituencies and followers that they could mobilize for action. The intense lobbying for power and position also precipitated the mobilization of ethnic and religious forces. Olusegun Obasanjo, who eventually emerged as the president, was attacked for lacking any ethnic base, because the Yoruba people belonged to a different political party. Obasanjo's rival wondered why someone who was rejected by his own people could become a national leader.

The nine official parties were marked more by differences in names than in manifestos. By and large, ideologies have not been a great marker of difference in Nigerian political parties, although a few have always claimed to be socialist in orientation. The leading party, the People's Democratic Party (PDP), was a centrist party. It was a great coalition of ambitious notables comprising former military generals and politicians. Its main programs touched upon agriculture and education, but many of its leading members were less concerned about development than power. The PDP has turned out to be a party without much discipline, and those who control power within it are "moneybags" who reap political profits from that money. The Alliance for Democracy (AD) has remained essentially an ethnic party of the Yoruba in the southwest. It was both an attempt to unite the former members of the Awolowo-led Unity Party of Nigeria, the anti-Abacha coalition, and pro-democracy forces. It based its manifesto on a welfare program with a promise to expand and improve on educational and social services. Its grip on the southwest is so strong that the party has produced all the governors in the Yoruba-speaking states. The third strongest party is the centrist All People's Party (APP), which has a large number of pro-Abacha politicians mainly based in the north. The other parties have been on the fringe: a few leftists formed the People's Redemption Party, which has not made any significant impact. Also with limited or inconsequential impact were the United Democratic Party (UDP), the United People's Party (UPP), the Democratic Advanced Movement, and the National Solidarity Movement.

Some analysts have criticized the high number of political parties, while some have seen them as a true expression of the democratic spirit.

Both views are misleading. The participants were not expecting a political space with many political parties, nor were they fostering democracy. Rather, a political party enabled its founder and key executives to justify their claim of representing religious or ethnic interests, and to create opportunities to negotiate with fellow politicians so that power could be distributed to as many of them as possible.

As the politicians had carefully schemed, political discourse and campaigns focused less on policies and more on personality. The major actors controlled the media pages, posing both as the representatives of various interest groups and as nationalists. One day they would talk as true Muslims or Christians; another day as defenders of ethnicities; and the next day as "true federalists." But what counted the most was hidden from the public: an extensive use of money to woo opponents and buy votes.

As money became one of the major determinants in the contest, politics favored those who had it in abundance or those who had wealthy sponsors. Since most wealthy Nigerians have accumulated their wealth through connections to state power, politics in turn favored those who had previously held power, such as retired military officers or politicians that held office or served as civil servants. The big players in the presidential elections—Obasanjo, Chief Olu Falae, and Chief Alex Ekwume—were not new to politics; Obasanjo had served as head of state in the 1970s, Ekwume as vice-president during the Second Republic in the 1980s, and Falae as the head of the federal civil service and secretary to the Babangida military regime in the 1980s. A clique of faceless, wealthy retired generals served as sponsors.

Once it was settled that a southerner would become the president, the traditional politics of north-south gave way to that of competition within the south and the choice of a vice president from the north. Within the PDP, Ekwume and Obasanjo competed bitterly, but the forces within the party and the faceless sponsors favored Obasanjo. In order to better understand these political processes, I would now like to turn to a discussion of the particular elements that have impacted them.

Muslims and Non-Muslims in a Complex Political Arena

An analytical narrative of events as presented above is not enough to understand all the forces at work. One must consider the power of Islam and Christianity, as elaborated upon, as well as other multiple identities and social classes that affect elections and politics in a way that opposes or reinforces the Islamic element. Also of importance are issues that divide people and over which they need to compete vigorously. Primordial loyalties organized around ethnicity, community, and religion may transcend the loyalty to the Nigerian state, constitution, and law and order. Primordial loyalties may also strengthen or undermine the force of Islam. I will identify both the issues and identities as they shape elections and politics in Nigeria.

Muslims and non-Muslims do not necessarily agree upon a number of major issues: the secular or non-secular nature of the Nigerian foundation; the distribution of federal positions to ambitious members of the political class; the continuation or abandonment of the English legal system; the retention of Nigeria as a federal structure; the distribution of power between the federal and state governments; the place of women in society and politics; the number of Nigerians and their regional distributions; and the number of states and local governments in the federation, etc. In what follows, I will briefly discuss a few issues that affect the intersection between Islam, politics, and elections.

The access to and manipulation of Western education has long been a source of tension. The south had an early advantage, as Christian missionaries came via the Atlantic Ocean to evangelize and promote formal Western education.[20] When independence came in 1960, the south had more educated elite than the north. To the north, this was a perceived source of domination. This disparity fueled regionalism and attacks on southerners. As the north established more Western-style schools, so too did the south, with the result that to date, the south continues to have more educated people than the north. As economic opportunities shrunk in the 1990s, the southern elite, especially the middle class and fresh graduates, have suffered more, and thousands of them have migrated to all parts of the world. To these migrants and to the jobless in the south, Muslims and the north have held the nation back and must be blamed for their predicament. As many Yoruba and Igbo in the south have said, their "nations" would have developed but for the inclusion of the north in Nigeria.

In reality, the south is more afraid of the north. For most of the years since independence, the north has produced the majority of the country's leaders, leading to the political concept of "northern primacy." After independence, the northern political class used the army to control power and distribute resources among themselves. In the 1990s, a number of northern intelligentsia were developing a political theory of domination: the east should control trade, the west the civil service, and the north political power. As if this fraudulent political theory was not enough, a tiny number of Islamic intelligentsia were advocating a possible end to the definition of the country as a secular state. When the 1993 presidential election was annulled, the only explanation that the southern elite could give was that it was yet another example of northern primacy, and the crisis quickly became one of overcoming the fear and consequences of northern domination.

The fear of domination gave rise to suggestions on zoning, an arrangement whereby each region, a cluster of six states, would produce the country's president in a rotational arrangement. It was also suggested, as in the expansion of the number of federal ministries, that the country should have many vice presidents to represent regional interests. The consideration had to do with satisfying the political gladiators without regard for the economic costs that would be involved in the process, and the consequent slowing down of development and the inability to have the necessary resources to transform the rural areas and the peasantry.

As in all societies, people can see issues from the perspectives of location, class, religion, gender, and privilege. Nigeria is a diverse society, with many ethnicities and languages, nearly five hundred. Religious pluralism and ethnic differences do undermine the process to build a Nigerian nation-state, but those divisions prevent or undermine equally the attempts by one group or religion to impose itself on the country. For instance, Muslims have been accused of wanting to impose Islam on Nigeria, but mobilization by southern Christians has suggested that there would be secession or warfare as a result. The Igbo have tried to secede but in vain. The northern political class has attempted a permanent political domination, but southern resistance has forestalled this. Thus, while the identities create problems to forging an enduring nation, they nevertheless also create the basis for negotiations between Muslims and Christians, southerners and northerners, the modern and the traditional elite.

Ethnic-cum-communal identities are strong, and they can complement or differ from the religious. Many nations had existed and flourished before the British imposition of colonial rule. While the nations have been amalgamated, the concept of a nation-state governed by European institutions has been slow either to be widely accepted or made to work. For one thing, the British themselves profited from the people's identification with their older nations, and the choice of federalism partly recognized the differences and kept them apart from one another.[21] Colonial rule consolidated ethnicities and the politics of division. The use of Islam to promote the politics of "One North" began after 1945.[22] Elsewhere, politicians resorted to the resurrection of tradition and culture to foster unity. Chief Obafemi Awolowo used the Yoruba myth of creation and their progenitor father, Oduduwa, to form a cultural organization and political party, the Action Group, which subsequently dominated Western Nigeria.[23] Azikiwe and others were able to rally together the Igbo in the east. The three ethic groups controlled the big regions of the north, west and east and often disregarded the minorities within them, leading to further agitations.

Ethnicity generates conflicts and competition. While it is a cheap way to form a political party since members of the same group can be easily reached and converted into a strong constituency, it also unleashes rivalries with political parties built around other ethnicities. Competing elites resort to ethnicity to distribute power, educational amenities, employment, etc. The purpose of controlling the center may partly be to use collective resources to benefit a group. For instance, the politics of revenue allocation has been shaped by ethnicity,[24] while different groups fight over lucrative ministries such as that of petroleum, and internal and external affairs. In 1999, a number of Igbo politicians complained that the ministries allocated to them were "yeye"—a Yoruba word for insignificant—and one minister-designate actually refused to show up for the swearing-ceremony because of this. Decisions such as the choice of a lingua franca, and location of airports and industries may be affected by ethnic considerations.

Major political decisions and problems have revolved around meeting the challenges posed by the ethnic divide. For the greater half of the first century, the strategy was to seek the means either to prevent the coming together of the various ethnic groups to form a powerful association against the British or to submerge the interest of the minorities while maintaining political balance among the Igbo, Hausa, and Yoruba. To do this, federalism was adopted. However, census became a political problem and led to competition, as each region had to inflate or contest figures. Also, the minorities, almost 40 percent of the population, were eager for freedom. In the north, where the regional government of the Northern People's Congress refused to recognize the minorities and actually attempted to spread Islam among them, the Tiv in the middle belt resorted to violence in 1960 and 1964.[25]

Following the military takeover of 1966 and the events that led to the civil war, the creation of additional states from existing ones became a strategy to contain regional rivalries. In 1967, the four big regions were broken into twelve. The twelve were later reconfigured to thirty-six in order to meet the pressure emanating from powerful ethnic interests as well as from the ambition of the political class to control state resources.[26] Other measures to minimize the destructive impact of ethnicity included the introduction of the National Youth Service Corps, which compels new university graduates to work in states other than their own, the reflection of a federal quota in universities and federal appointments, and the appointment of one cabinet minister from each state of the federation. In 1991, the collection of data for the national census did not include questions on ethnicity, arguably to underplay it. Many of these measures have not produced the desired results. Indeed, the competition for ethnic representation at the federal level has been a source of conflict that threatens the very survival of the state itself. The ultimate desire is to preside over the distribution of federal money, to allocate licenses to oil explorers, and to steal. Islam, Christianity, and ethnicity are manipulated by key political actors to obtain and consolidate the opportunity. Rivalries among states and religions can at the same time be opportunities for leading political actors to settle their scores. When their ambitions at the federal level fail, political actors move to the state level to compete with members of the same group or religion for power and control of state resources. The elite in the army use the need to minimize religious and ethnic conflicts to disguise their ambition for controlling power in order to enrich itself. The army is as divided as the larger society, but the generals maintain a faìade of interest in the concept of Nigeria and use the rigid, hierarchical structure of the army to curb the radical expressions of the rank and file.

The duplicity of the army generals is always clear in moments of danger to their rule. Babangida and Abacha manipulated Islam and ethnicity to maintain their power, while pretending to protect the integrity of Nigeria. Babangida clandestinely promoted the entry of Nigeria into the Organization of Islamic Conference, over the objections of Christians, simply to satisfy the Islamic constituency at a time when he was not trusted by northern Islamic leaders. As the OIC crisis pitted the south against the north, and Muslims against non-Muslims, Babangida manipulated the conflicts to attack his competitors for power and to silence many of them while at the same time appealing to Christians by calling Nigeria a secular state. When he annulled the 1993 presidential election and the Yoruba took to massive protests, he used other groups to attack them by saying that they wanted Abiola, a Yoruba, in power only for their own ethnic benefit. Abacha continued with this game. When the Ogoni complained of environmental pollution and marginalization, Abacha manipulated their neighbors against them and executed Saro Wiwa, one of their leading members.

As important as ethnicity is, it is not the only source of division necessary to understand politics or the place of Islam in Nigeria. In the north, in spite of its presentation of Islam as a hegemonic force and a source of unity, many violent clashes have occurred among groups and between peoples of the same city. There is the cleavage of religious difference which is discussed below. But as in other places, communal or town differences occur within regions and ethnic groups. In recent times, such differences have translated into serious disputes and violence in such places as Zangon-Kataf between the Kataf and Hausa; Ile-Ife, between the Ife and Modakeke; Warri, between the Urhobo and Itsekiri; Lagos, between the Ijo and Yoruba, etc. Christianity, Islam, and ethnicity have not put an end to division of townships and communities. The Yoruba may unite to compete with the Igbo and Hausa for federal resources, but Yoruba subgroups such as Ijesa, Ekiti, Egba, and Oyo also compete within the Yoruba zone.

The different pace in educational development, mentioned above, has created a fissure between the south and north and within both regions. Class consciousness and radical ideologies, although not fully realized, have occasionally undermined the unity of Islam and ethnicity or have provided intersecting ties that indicate the possibility of the creation of a united country.[27] For instance, in the north, the left-wing party of the Northern Elements People's Union, founded in the 1950s by Aminu Kano, which became the resurrected People's Redemption Party during the Second Republic, tried to undermine the claim to unity in the north based on Islam.[28] NEPU and its successors regarded many members of the political and religious class as exploiters and opportunists. During the Second Republic, the PRP won elections in Kaduna and Kano states, great victories that reduced the control of the established and traditional politicians in Northern Nigeria.

Military rule must be added as a source of division.[29] Within the army, the officers and ranks are divided, like the rest of society, by issues of ethnicity and religion. Professionalism has been undermined by participation in politics. But the greatest source of worry is the role of the military as a major constituency that dominates politics with its control of weapons, and established tradition of coup-making. When in power, the military sets itself in opposition to civil society, constitutes an enemy of the democratic process, and destroys the federal system of government. Whenever it is in control, the military concentrates power in the center; in the hands of the so-called commander in chief, the states become mere "command posts." Since the state governors cannot fight the commander in chief, different organizations will emerge to demand their rights or organize protests.

Islam and Christianity are two established universal religions in Nigeria. Both have undermined local religions and control much of the political and social space. The spread of both is uneven, a fact that makes religion sometimes coterminous with communal or ethnic identities. Islam is dominant in the north and competes with Christianity in the middle belt and southwest, while Christianity is dominant in the southeast. Often a north-south regional divide is also read as the Islamic-Christian divide. An ethnic category such as the Igbo in the east may also mean Christian, while Hausa or Fulani identity in the north is both ethnic and religious. Both Islam and Christianity compete for space, converts, and political domination. Leaders of religious organizations use the style and language of politics in their propaganda, quest for converts, and desire to prevent one another from dominating the political environment. In their interactions, virtually everything is political. A major case in point is the statistics as both play the numbers game: Christians claim that they number more; Muslims say the same. Official records, unreliable for most areas, put the Muslim population at 47 percent, the Christian at 34 percent and others at 18 percent. Both religions are far from homogenous in any aspect. Each is divided into factions, with competing leaders, numbering over 3,000, according to the list of those who are officially registered.[30] National politics often unite them, as in the case of the Christian Association of Nigeria (CAN).[31]

A combination of factors has made religion a powerful factor in Nigerian politics.[32] First is the failure of political leadership. As successive military leaders fail to transform the country, religious organizations seek alternative leaders and leadership models. The stress has been on morality, accountability, and spirituality. To many Muslims, Mhumar Gadaffi of Libya and Ayathola Khomeini of Iran provide alternative models to emulate. Second, the failure of institutions and structures of governance have been interpreted as the failure of the state itself. To many Muslims, the failure represents the limitations of secular institutions. Third, the Structural Adjustment Program and its failures in the 1990s instigated tensions expressed as religious conflicts. As the economy declines, more and more people see in religion an escape or a source of opposition to the state.[33] For instance, in Kano, the country's political decay and economic problems have not only drawn more people to Islam, it has also radicalized them.[34]

Fourth, religion, like ethnicity, is a source of mobilization for political actors. Once a political candidate defines himself as a Muslim and his rival happens to be Christian, politics can acquire the coloration of religious conflict. In the north, many politicians have turned to Islam for power legitimization. There have been power rivalries with Christians and bids to impose the Shari'a over a larger region. These attempts have radicalized the Christian Association of Nigeria to contest all religious symbols and what it perceives as efforts to use Islam to dominate politics.[35] By and large, northern politicians have continued to profit from Islam, using its symbols as political ideology in order to unite the region against the south and to mobilize their different constituencies.[36]

The conflicts play out in the political arena on a permanent basis. To start with, Christians have always have been afraid of Islamic/northern domination. This fear began during the colonial period both in the south and middle belt.[37] There is a pervasive fear that Islam would expand and gain greater influence by using the resources of the federal government to its advantage. No doubt, there are leaders such as Ahmadu Bello, the first premier of the north, who have had this vision, and there are still vigorous attempts at proselytizing.[38]

The fear of domination is unlikely to disappear as long as religion is part of the definition of community and ethnicity in most parts of the country. In the north, minority elements define themselves as Christians, and they have actually resorted to Christianity to solidify their identity, as in the case of the Kataf of Zangon-Kataf. At the national level, the north-south divide is treated both as an ethnic and a religious fault line.

Islam and the Northern Factor

I now want to historicize the role of the north in the politics of Nigeria, as it intersects with Islam. For most of the twentieth century, the north has tried to present the image of a "homogenous polity" in relation to the south, and there is an intellectual articulation of the thesis that the Hausa or Hausa-Fulani are the dominant members of this region.[39] There are contradictions in this self-presentation: first, it is a diverse region comprising almost two hundred ethnic groups; second, the Hausa-Fulani group has been accused of trying to dominate other ethnic groups, and the accusation has given rise to a number of riots in various places;[40] third, there are many pockets of Christian populations, notably in the middle belt; and fourth, there are left-oriented intellectuals who can be described as nationalists.

In the first half of this century, Indirect Rule enabled the north to revive the structure of the old Sokoto Caliphate. If power was diffused in the south, the old Caliphate in the north made possible the creation of a pyramidal power structure that enabled the sultan and emirs to retain much control over the people. After 1945, the south relied on the educated elite to organize, a strategy that lends itself to intense competition and fragmentation.[41] In the north, the strategy was to use the structure of the old Caliphate and prevent fragmentation. The NPC, the first party, maintained a hierarchical structure, a replication of the Caliphate, with village heads serving the emirs who controlled the Native Authorities. As Dudley explained, the strategy was not to develop "mass party organs" but to rely on traditional political elite.[42] The chief agent of the unification of the north was Sardauna Ahmadu Bello,[43] the modern politician whose ancestor, Uthman Dan Fodio, built the old Sokoto caliphate, an outcome of the nineteenth century jihad. Bello's era, 1951 to 1966, marked the apogee of northern unity. As the British were initiating their departure, the northern political class was manipulating the structure of the nineteenth century caliphate and Indirect Rule to great advantage. The symbols and ideology of Islam were used to serve political interests, Bello emerged as the number one political figure, and the Northern People's Congress became the major party. Bello and the NPC put under their command structure the emirs, local government (Native Authorities), and politicians. The emirs adapted their office to the needs of modern politics, thereby benefiting from the arrangement.[44] To the NPC and the emerging political class, the south was the primary enemy.

An early start in Western education, the emergence of a business class, better organized parties, and influential leaders such as Obafemi Awolowo and Nnamdi Azikiwe were advantages that threatened the north. Within the north itself, a small group of educated people were thinking like southerners in terms of breaking free of the control of emirs. This was another threat to the traditional establishment. The solution was to create a party that would unite the north, and bring all members of the political class under one umbrella and the leadership of Bello. The NPC used the power of a modern political party and tradition to discredit or destroy opposition forces such as the Northern Elements' Progressive Union, formed by Aminu Kano, to halt the infiltration of the north by southern leaders, and to punish Northerners who refused to toe the party line. Traditional authorities in minority areas were given power to control the Native Authorities and destroy opposition forces. Whenever a younger activist generation raised its head, the NPC would move quickly to destroy it.

Ahmadu Bello was not just moving a new political class into a modernization project, but he was very astute to clothe the change in the garb of tradition. He cleverly turned to Islam as the ideology of control, leadership, and the unity of the region. Disregarding the minorities and Christianity, Bello constructed the idea of a religiously homogenous region. He and the emirs would not be just political leaders but spiritual leaders as well. Bello established religious organizations as if they were to be the "religious wings" of the NPC with spiritual leaders under him. By far the most notable of the organizations was the Jama'atu Nasril Islam (JNI) established in 1962 to "consolidate the northern states, and make sure the north is one, and there is peace and stability in the country."[45] The JNI brought together prominent civil servants, politicians, and religious leaders to discuss Islamic issues. There was also an organization to unite Islamic preachers, the Kaduna Council of Malamai, founded in 1963, that later integrated with the JNI. About the same time, Bello embarked on an aggressive campaign to convert more northerners to Islam, one that led to anti-Islamic and Hausa-Fulani movements in a number of places.[46] Alhaji Abubakar Gumi was the first chairman of the JNI, and he remained for almost three decades one of the most influential Islamic leaders in the country, with a strong passion for the reforms and spread of Islam and the pursuit of northern interests.

Ahmadu Bello's death in the first military coup in 1966 initiated the process of fragmentation of the north. The ideal of unity and the ambition of the political class did not entirely vanish, but historical circumstances did weaken the northern front. The charismatic leader was no more; Igbo officers were in control for six months before the north regained power; soldiers, rather than emirs and politicians, became the major actors; the big north was broken into six states, later to be further fragmented; Kaduna lost its influence as the major seat of power as new state capitals emerged; and various Islamic organizations clashed with one another. The military wing of the northern political class acquired considerable influence after 1966, producing a long list of leaders: Yakubu Gowon, Murtala Mohammed, Shehu Shagari, Buhari, Babangida, and Abacha, all but one Muslims. Within six months of the accession of the Ironsi-led government, northern officers reorganized to end what they understood as Igbo domination. Yakubu Gowon was a northerner, but from the middle belt, and a Christian. Not only did he take away the power of the emirs over the Native Authorities, he also created new states, actions which weakened the internal solidarity of the north.

The southern political class continues to see the north as a united front, especially following the "warfare" of the post-1993 annulment of the elections. But the south has benefited from this weakness, as in the case of the emergence of M. K. O. Abiola as a political force, the appointment of Chief Earnest Shonekan, a Yoruba, as the president of the Interim National Government in 1993, and of Obasanjo as president in 1999. Some would regard the success of these three as evidence of the manipulation of politics by the north. In the case of Abiola, he was accepted by the northern masses, but its political class did not want him in power; in the case of Shonekan, he was regarded as a stooge of Babangida; and in the case of Obasanjo, many calculated that he would serve only northern interests. Thus, in a sense, the southern political class still does not see the north and Islam as a weakened force, but as still powerful and with a "hegemonic circle" so strong that the entire country dances to its music.[47]

The idea of a strong north as portrayed by the southern elite is always exaggerated. What the southern elite ignores is that the vigorous pursuit of modernization in the north has weakened the hold of its hegemonic class on power. New actors have emerged, with their bases in the army (as in the case of General Babangida), civil service (Chief Adamu Ciroma), and education (Professor Ango Abdullahi). The new men have often come together in circles that the southern elite derisively labeled as the "Kaduna Mafia."[48] The large number of university graduates as well as increasing urbanization has considerably weakened the power of the emirs and Sultan. The new men were partly instrumental in bringing down the Second Republic. As northerners, they were embarrassed by the shoddy performance of the Shagari government; they sought to forge new political alliances with southern politicians and ultimately instigated the military to take over power.[49]

Although the north has produced most of the military generals in power, by and large, the generals are more concerned with their private wallets than with development, and they build alliances primarily to consolidate personal wealth and power. However, the generals find it easier to identify with the northern political class than with the southern, especially when they are under threat and can manipulate ethnic divisions for selfish benefits. Abacha offered a different model: he could alienate the traditional constituency and still survive. Other than a few emirs (notably those of his home base of Kano), Abacha antagonized many traditional rulers, even removing the Sultan, the wealthy and influential Ibrahm Dasuki, in April 1996. The early incorporation into his regime of such notables as Adamu Ciroma, Abubakar Rimi, and Babagana Kingibe was rather short-lived as he replaced them months later with less politically powerful appointees. When challenged by Yar' Adua, the general and politician, Abacha's security machine descended on him, accused him of participating in a coup, and threw him in jail, where he died.

Although there are many political actors, among them a few who are indeed very powerful, none has acquired the clout, prestige, and awe of the late Ahmadu Bello. All attempts to invent another Ahmadu Bello have failed. He did not use cash to buy people and support, but royalty and an elaborate reward system that gave positions and power to his followers. The new contenders to replace Bello, such as Yar' Adua and Babangida, want to rely on the use of stolen wealth, but they cannot fool their followers nor their rivals who have no respect for them but are eager to take their cash. The various minorities—ethnic and religious—have also become more assertive. For instance, the northern Christians forged an alliance with their southern counterparts in the Christian Association of Nigeria to discuss matters pertaining to religion and politics. The creation of states has also enabled a number of minorities to gain some degree of autonomy, as did the states of the middle belt.

Political dissidence is a common characteristic of northern minorities. During the Second Republic, the Kanuri to the northeast organized themselves into the Great Nigeria's People's Party led by a veteran politician, Waziri Ibrahim, partly to reject the domination of the Hausa-Fulani and the Nigerian People's Party (NPN). Similarly, politicians in the middle belt formed the Council for Understanding and Solidarity (CUS), which forged an alliance with the Nigerian People's Party (NPP), which was controlled by easterners.

The Shari'a in Zamfara State

The question of using the Shari'a Islamic law has generated public controversy since the 1970s. In the writing and ratification of the constitutions of the Second and Third Republics, the demand for a federal Shari'a court of appeals created a political crisis, requiring the intervention of the military. In both instances, the south interpreted the debates on the Shari'a as an attempt to impose Islam on the country. There has always been a political side to the demand for the Shari'a. To start with, its most forceful advocates are not religious preachers or scholars, but a new breed of politicians. The demand for the Shari'a enables these ambitious politicians to exploit an ideology to unite the north, to halt the inroad of southern competitors to the north, and to even discredit established northern politicians who are regarded as too soft in advancing the agenda of the north. These young politicians failed in their demands in the 1970s and 1980s, opening them to charges of being either politically immature or unable to understand how to deal with southern opposition.[50] Since then, the Shari'a has continued to generate political controversy. In its last month, the Provisional Ruling Council under Abubakar did not agree on what place the Shari'a should have in the constitution. The pro-Shari'a group called for an amendment that would enable the states in favor to set up Shari'a courts in addition to the provision in the constitution for Shari'a courts of appeal.

A new, and perhaps the most aggressive, implementation of the Shari'a followed in the first year of the Fourth Republic, when the executive and legislative branches of Zamfara state extended the full jurisdiction of the Shari'a court throughout the state and over criminal issues, beginning on October 27, 1999. Governor Ahmad Sani Yerima has not only been optimistic about its achievement, he has indicated that he is prepared for a fight to defend the Shari'a. To him, it was a feat that many had thought impossible to achieve, even under Muslim presidents. Muhammad Maccido, the Sultan of Sokoto and president of the Nigeria Supreme Council for Islamic Affairs (NSCIA), endorsed the governor, saying that he "fully supports the establishment of Sharia law for Muslims and whosoever wishes to be judged by it."[51] Some representatives of Islamic countries in Nigeria visited Gusau, the state capital, to congratulate the governor.

The Zamfara Shari'a law appears to go beyond the constitutional provision that there should be a Shari'a court of appeals in any state that wants it. In a democratic structure, the federal government lacks the power of the military to issue an immediate decree to stop the action of the Zamfara government. President Obasanjo described it as unconstitutional: "Nigerian constitution does not allow any part of the country to adopt a state religion or any law that goes against the national constitution."[52] He asked the Christians not to panic.

However, the Christian Association of Nigeria (CAN) wanted Obasanjo to use federal power to reverse the decision. The state branch of CAN in Zamfara has intensified local efforts to mobilize Christian opinion against the Shari'a. In mid-November 1993, the chairman of the Zamfara State Chapter of CAN, Venerable Peter Dambo, criticized the federal government for maintaining silence over the Shari'a issue and called on the government to declare a state of emergency in Zamfara. Dambo saw an even bigger Islamic plan: "What is happening now in Zamfara State is a means to divide the country and if this is allowed to continue and manifest itself in totality, it will be very unfortunate for the nation."[53] Members of CAN advocated retaliation in the southern states where they wanted the Christians to demand the introduction of Christian canon laws. To Dambo, "If the Federal Government would not take any action to stop the implementation of Sharia in Zamfara in spite of the popular outcry and opposition by Nigerians, there is nothing wrong in the Christian states too to impose the canon laws on their citizens." In addition, CAN also threatened to go to court and called on the country's attorney general to sue the state government. Other branches of CAN and the national headquarters have taken a united stand to attack the move. To many Christian leaders, this represents the very first step to initiate an agenda of Islamization.

To Governor Yerima, the Christians are exaggerating the impact the Shari'a has on them, as it is meant to root out all moral and criminal vices among only the Muslims. According to Yerima:

> Let me make it unequivocally clear to all that we are not unaware of the multi-various nature of our society as a multi-religious and multi ethnic one and we therefore do not intend to impose the Sharia law on the non-Muslims in the state as being deliberately and mischievously falsified by some agents of blackmail, or do we harbour any ulterior motives against any group of people than our overwhelming majority Muslim citizens in Zamfara State."[54]

To deny the Muslims the Shari'a because of what Christians say, Yerima concluded, is to deny the Muslims the right to freedom and Islam.

If the governor of Zamfara gave assurances that Christians would not be affected by the Shari'a, CAN was quick to say that he was wrong and that "anti-Christian actions" were being implemented, including the refusal of motorcycle operators to carry non-Muslims. A number of CAN's branches also held or plan to hold anti-Shari'a protests in different parts of the country. They have pointed to cases of discrimination against Christians in Zamfara and other Islamic states, notably in issues of employment; the allocation of land to build churches; and the demolition of churches in Gusau, Kano, and Sokoto, ostensibly because the Christians do not have legal claims to the land.

Criticism has come from other sources, mainly among secular-oriented organizations. Pro-secular university students demanded that they not be posted to Zamfara for their national service after graduation. A women's group, Women in Nigeria (WIN), makes a pro-gender argument. To WIN, the Shari'a is an instrument of a male-dominated society to subjugate women under the cloak of religion, denying them the right to free movement and work, keeping them in perpetual servitude in a patriarchal society, and leaving them few options: "baby-making machines, pleasure objects to men and chattels."[55] WIN adds that the introduction of the Shari'a will undermine the corporate existence of the country's secularity. It has called on the Zamfara state government to repeal the law and on the federal government to ensure that the state complies. Further criticism comes from secular-minded lawyers and politicians who regard the Shari'a as a legal imposition and an attempt to use Islam to dominate national politics.[56]

To cite one example, Justice Akinola Aguda, a public figure and notable lawyer, called the Shari'a illegal, without foundation in the country's constitution, and that the end result would be to create confusion that may lead to the breakdown of Nigeria.[57] Human-rights activists see the sanctions (such as amputation for theft) as barbaric.

One power that the federal government has is to ask the Nigerian Police Force not to enforce the Shari'a. Police authorities indicated that cooperation with the state government was not assured and that it had put in place security measures to deal with violence in January 2000, when the Shari'a law came into full effect. A tension exists in that the Shari'a bill empowers the Shari'a court to authorize the police to enforce the law, but the state government does not control the federal police. According to the police chief in Zamfara, "We will not enforce any law that goes contrary and in conflict with the Nigerian law because we have sworn to defend the country and the citizens as a whole."[58] The Zamfara government thinks otherwise. The chairman of the Joint Aid Monitoring Groups on the Application of Shari'a, Dr. Atiku Balarabe, insisted that it is the constitutional duty of the police to enforce the Shari'a, since it is a law that is approved under the constitution. Meanwhile, the Zamfara government began to train monitors to report violations of the law.

The Zamfara case opens the possibility of violence not just within the state but in other areas, either in support of or against the Shari'a. The opposition by CAN will turn it into a Muslim-Christian crisis, similar to tensions of the 1980s and 1990s. CAN indicated that it will mobilize Christians to defend their rights.[59] It is at the same time challenging the continued membership of Nigeria in the Organization of Islamic Conference, and a religious crisis will follow if Nigeria is to pull out. Some branches of CAN have taken the Zamfara state to court; more than ten thousand Christians protested against the Shari'a in Gusau; some ethnic organizations, notably the Igbo ones, are warning their people to return to the south; the House of Assembly in the "Christian state" of Cross River passed a resolution that oil revenues should not be given to Zamfara. Not only has the Zamfara state refused to change its mind, the much more volatile state of Kano has similar thinking. All forty-four chairmen of the councils of local governments and many members of the state assembly have agreed to implement the Shari'a.[60] In Sokoto, Kebbi, Niger, Kaduna, and Katsina states, a similar move is underway, supported by many politicians and Islamic leaders who have made combative speeches in its favor. Support is not lacking for the Zamfara state. To the Moslem Lawyers Association of Nigeria, only the courts could decide or rule on the legality of the bill enacted into law by the Zamfara government. The pro-Shari'a group has many reasons to support the law: there should be no separation between Islam and the Shari'a; only the laws of God are legitimate; religion cannot be separated from law; Shari'a is not new in many parts of the north; it gives the right of place to God as the creator; and it promotes morality. Muslims are divided over the issue. To the Shi'ites, the steps by Zamfara are not enough because they want an Islamic society; to a number of "elders," the Shari'a will split the country; to secular Muslims, it is a diversion; and to young preachers, it is necessary. The Jama'atu Nasril Islam promises to convene a conference, but it is unlikely that resolutions will satisfy all the various groups. Meanwhile in Gusau, Zamfara's capital, indications are that some groups will take to violence in struggles to either impose the Shari'a or alienate Christians.[61] Governor Sani has warned that the decision on the Shari'a is nonnegotiable. If the Shari'a is regarded as complicating Nigerian politics, Islam is regarded by others as complicating global politics. I now turn to the latter point.

Nigerian Islam in Global/United States Politics

Since the attack on the World Trade Center on September 11, 2001, analysts have continued to focus on the role of Islam in global politics. Keeping the focus of the chapter in mind, the case study will continue to be on Nigeria, specifically in its relations with the United States. It is difficult to address the issue of the role of Islam without also asking what Nigeria's relation to the United States should be. Nigeria's deliberations about this need to understand that U.S. interests and intentions for the region (and the world) include an interest in the region's stability, vigorous trade relations that allow access to oil and other natural resources, and an unchecked neocolonialism through various international institutions. It is also important that the current debates around such bodies as the World Bank, IMF, IDB, WTO, etc. resolve themselves to promote expanded trade, stability, environmental and human rights protections, and equity. One of Nigeria's main claims for retaining a positive relationship with the United States are around its importance to regional and African stability. If U.S. interests, which are not being submitted to international processes and policies (as evident from Kyoto, arms treaty, World Court, etc.), can coincide with Nigeria's own vision of development and of its role in Africa more broadly, then there is good ground for a positive relationship. Otherwise, if the United States perceives the need for a restructuring in Africa to accelerate the rate of profit and extraction of natural resources, then Islamic fundamentalism becomes as good an excuse as any for undermining Nigeria's regional strength. Nigeria may be able to continue to pursue an ideal of secular federation that can honor ethnic and religious politics while also maintaining a pluralist political framework and discourse. While there are limits to this ideal, India is a good example of a country that has been committed to secularism and rapid industrialization, yet has moved to religious politics as a successful means of mass mobilization which has been firmly open to Western global interests. India's saving grace is the claim that it has a middle class market of 200 million waiting for Western goods and services. The extent to which Africa's attractiveness as a market can be balanced against its appeal as a source of raw materials will also determine U.S. policy in the future.

A number of issues must be factored into the consideration. To start with, Nigeria will continue to be prone to violence, which may limit investment options and create problems for its emerging democratic institutions. Conditions for violence are many—based on communal, ethnic, and social divisions. Internal chaos can be blamed on external agencies, most notably multinational companies. An articulate group of intellectuals blame Nigeria's woes on bad leaders who collaborate with American and Western interests to exploit resources and the poor to the benefit of a small group of people. How the United States will promote business without being "condemned" is crucial. Multinational companies should be careful not to exacerbate domestic challenges.

In some areas, American popular culture is portrayed as "sinful." There is a perception in Nigeria that there is an "American culture" instead of diverse cultures. Many are unaware of the cultural wars and controversies even within the United States itself. American propaganda abroad should not "homogenize" American culture, and there is not much to gain in promoting American culture as the best in the world. Vigorous attacks on some established practices such as polygamy, purdah, veiling, etc. may be counterproductive and create unnecessary enemies. Where the people are receptive to Western culture (fashion, music, films, etc.), there is no protest against the spread of American popular culture. The United States has to recognize the "cultural divide" in Nigeria and assume that every area and people do not cherish the same thing. In conducting propaganda abroad, less will be gained by selling American culture, but more can be attained by finding the means to avoid being labeled as a country of immoral infidels. The United States must accept other people's customs while preserving its own values.

It is important to support Nigeria's (and Africa's) steps towards democratization. Nigeria's recent advances in this direction are crucial for Africa's stability in general. If one is advising the United States on its policy toward Nigeria, the more publicity that can be given to Nigeria's efforts at democratization (rather than military rule) the more likely (though only mildly "more likely") it is that the United States cannot develop policy strictly according to its material interests. Nigeria has to be represented as having a crucial role in Africa's stability, which includes democracy.

The United States will continue to attract Nigerian migrants for a variety of reasons: careers, the search for economic opportunities, education, etc. The majority of migrants are from the southern parts of Nigeria, educated, and hardworking. Historically, northern Muslims have not seen migration to the United States as a serious option. Southern Muslim migrants are moderate and are not politically active. While Nigerian Islam exhibits radicalism, there is no tradition of suicide to make political points. The main reasons for migration are less religious, but more economic and social: those who want to come to the United States think that they are being prevented from doing so; those already in the country think that they cannot compete or use their skills to the maximum.

Where there is extensive poverty and political mismanagement, Islamic radicalism is unstoppable. The United States has to extend its hand in friendship and cooperation in order to promote better economic and political management. If the United States is "following the money" to stamp out terrorism, it should also provide leadership in following the corruption of African leaders who steal money and deposit them in Western banks. If avenues to hide stolen money are reduced, it can be recirculated within Africa for investment purposes. Foreign investors have plundered the continent without Western countries complaining about it. Nigerian agents have collaborated with Western interests to exploit their people. The United States can play a leadership role in the economic development of Nigeria.

The politics of Islam in Nigeria revolves mainly around a domestic agenda that is seeking greater access to resources and political influence. Islam is a way in which northern constituencies have been able to imagine national political power. Although Muslims are aware of international politics, the pressure is from the outside, sometimes to make Islam more radical.

Secular movements/organizations can be more anti-Western than Islamic ones. The differences between a collapsed state against a rogue state should also be understood. In stable states, Islam poses no danger to the

United States, and its members are not terroristic. There is no such thing as "universal Islam," Africa is different from the Middle East, and Nigeria has not produced terrorists.

To conclude with respect to both the domestic and international concerns regarding Islam and politics, many of the advantages that have defined Nigeria as a potentially great country still exist. It is Africa's most populous country, with a large percentage falling under the age of thirty, which implies that many will be restless and will continue to demand changes and jobs. It has a large number of educated people capable of generating ideas, but the economic base of a "middle class" is not there to turn them into consumers, taxpayers, great thinkers, and captains of industry. The political leadership has the ambition of dominating regional politics and leading Africa in world politics. The economy is the second largest in the continent, behind South Africa. Based mainly on revenues from oil, it is capable of being transformed, with careful management, to end massive corruption and to improve the development of agriculture. Its size and resources can turn Nigeria into a regional hegemon and a world power.

The disadvantages are all still present: an unproductive army, whose elite are greedy for power and money, may strike at any time to put an end to a fragile democracy. The military has dominated politics for decades, with very limited positive changes to show for it. The two civilian regimes generated limited stability and little growth, thereby offering an invitation for military rule. Both the military and political elite have been very corrupt and have failed to include the people in any major program. To be able to minimize the dangers posed by religious conflicts, the Nigerian state needs to become development-oriented.[62] The loyalty of the people to Islam and Christianity remains stronger than the loyalty to Nigeria. This is true of other African states as well.

Notes

1. See Habib Boularès, *Islam: the Fear and the Hope* (London: Zed, 1990); and John O. Hunwick, *Religion and National Integration in Africa: Islam, Christianity, and Politics in the Sudan and Nigeria* (Evanston, Ill.: Northwestern University Press, 1992).

2. Peter P. Ekeh, "The Scope of Culture in Nigeria," in *Nigeria since Independence: The First Twenty-Five Years,* vol. 7: *Culture,* ed. Peter P. Ekeh and Garba Ashiwaju (Ibadan: Heinemann), 1–17.

3. On previous elections, see Amadu Kurfi, *Election Contest: Candidate's Companion* (Ibadan: Spectrum, 1989); 'Lai Olurode, *A Political Economy of Nigeria's 1983 Elections* (Lagos: John West, 1990); William Miles, *Elections in Nigeria: A Grassroots Perspective* (Boul-

der, Colo.: Lynne Rienner, 1988); and Henry Bienen, *Political Conflict and Economic Change in Nigeria* (London: Frank Cass, 1985)..

4. For an overview history of the country, see Toyin Falola, *The History of Nigeria* (Westport. Conn.: Greenwood, 1999).

5. This was a gross failure, and was later replaced in 1979 with an American-style presidential constitution.

6. For details, see Toyin Falola, ed., *Britain and Nigeria: Exploitation or Development?* (London: Zed, 1987); Toyin Falola, *Decolonization and Development* (Gainesville: University Press of Florida, 1996); and Toyin Falola et al., *History of Nigeria*, vol. 2 (Lagos: Longman, 1991).

7. For details, see R. Melson and H. Wolpe, eds., *Nigeria: Modernization and the Politics of Communalism* (Lansing: Michigan State University Press, 1971); S. K. Panter-Brick, ed., *Nigerian Politics and Military Rule* (London: Athlone Press, 1970); John P. MacKintosh, *Nigerian Government and Politics* (Evanston, Ill.: Northwestern University Press, 1966); R. Sklar, *Nigerian Political Parties: Power in an Emergent African Nations* (Princeton, N.J.: Princeton University Press, 1963; reprint, Enugu: Nok, 1997); and C. S. Whitaker, *The Politics of Tradition: Continuity and Change in Northern Nigeria, 1946–66* (Princeton, N.J.: Princeton University Press, 1970).

8. See William Zartman, ed., *The Political Economy of Nigeria* (New York: Praeger, 1983); B. J. Dudley, *An Introduction to Nigerian Government and Politics* (Bloomington: Indiana University Press, 1982); R. A. Joseph, *Democracy and Prebendal Politics in Nigeria* (Cambridge: Cambridge University Press, 1987); S. Othman, "Classes, Crises and Coup: The Demise of Shagari's Regime," *African Affairs* 83, no. 333, 441–61; and Oyeleye Oyediran, ed., *The Nigerian 1979 Elections* (London: Macmillan, 1981).

9. See Larry Diamond, "Nigeria: The Uncivic Society and the Descent into Praetorianism," in *Politics in Developing Countries,* ed. Larry Diamond, Juan J. Linz, and Seymour Martin Lispet (Boulder, Colo.: Lynne Rienner, 1995).

10. Toyin Falola and A. G. Adebayo, *Culture, Politics and Money among the Yoruba* (New Brunswick, N.J.: Transaction, 2000), chapters 12 and 13.

11. See T. Forrest, *Politics and Economic Development in Nigeria* (second edition) (Boulder, Colo.: Westview Press, 1995).

12. See Toyin Falola, *Violence in Nigeria: The Crisis of Religious Politics and Secular Ideologies* (Rochester, N.Y.: University of Rochester Press, 1998).

13. For developments during this decade, see, among others, Eghosa E. Osaghae, *Crippled Giant: Nigeria since Independence:* (London: Hurst and Company, 1998); and Stephen Wright, *Nigeria: Struggle for Stability and Status* (Boulder, Colo.: Westview, 1998).

14. Falola, *Violence in Nigeria*; and Jibrin Ibrahim, "Religion and Political Turbulence in Nigeria," *Journal of Modern African Studies* 29, no. 1 (1991): 115–37.

15. For details, see L. Diamond, A. Kirk-Greene, and O. Oyediran, eds., *Transition without End* (Boulder, Colo.: Lynne Rienner, 1997); and P. Beckett and C. Young, eds., *Dilemmas of Democracy in Nigeria* (Rochester, N.Y.: University of Rochester Press, 1997).

16. See E. Babatope, *The Abacha Regime and the June 12 Crisis* (Lagos: Author, 1995).

17. "Abacha: Lar and Co. vs. Northern Elders Forum," *Post Expressed Wired,* March 31, 1998.

18. See R. Maduku, "Delusion over Democracy," *The Guardian on Sunday* (Lagos), 26 July 1998; and Ayodele Ale, "Death Knell for Abacha Parties," *TEMPO,* 16 July 1998.

19. Atedo N. A. Peterside, "Consequences of Fiscal Indiscipline on the Economy," *The Guardian,* 25 June 1999.

20. See Magnus O. Bassey, *Missionary Rivalry and Educational Expansion in Nigeria 1885–1945* (New York: Peter Lang, 1999).

21. See Okwudiba Nnoli, *Ethnic Politics in Nigeria* (Enugu: Fourth Dimension, 1980); and his *Ethnicity and Development in Nigeria* (Aldershot: Avebury, 1995).

22. Mathews Hassan Kukah and Toyin Falola, *Religious Militancy and Self-Assertion: Islam and Politics in Nigeria* (London: Avebury, 1996).

23. On the relevance of this myth in relation to the role of religion, see David Laitin, *Hegemony and Culture: Politics and Religious Change among the Yoruba* (Chicago: University of Chicago Press, 1986).

24. See A. G. Adebayo, *Embattled Federalism: History of Revenue Allocation in Nigeria, 1946–1990* (New York: Peter Lang, 1993).

25. See R. Anifowose, *Violence and Politics in Nigeria: The Tiv and Yoruba Experience* (New York: Nok, 1982).

26. See H. Ekwekwe, *Class and State in Nigeria* (Lagos: Longman, 1986).

27. See Sam C. Nolutshungu, "Fragments of a Democracy: Reflections on Class and Politics in Nigeria," *Third World Quarterly* 12, no. 1 (1990).

28. On Aminu Kano and his political parties, see Alan Feinstein, *African Revolutionary: The Life and Times of Nigeria's Aminu Kano* (Enugu: Fourth Dimension, 1987).

29. On an elaborate discussion of the role of the military, see Toyin Falola et al., *The Military Factor in Nigeria* (New York: Edwin Mellen, 1994); and Jimi Peters, *The Nigerian Military and the State* (London: I. B. Tauris, 1997).

30. See Falola, *Violence in Nigeria*; Falola and J. K. Olupona, *Religion and Society in Nigeria: Historical and Comparative Perspectives* (Ibadan: Spectrum, 1991).

31. See I. M. Enwerem, *A Dangerous Awakening: The Politicization of Religion in Nigeria* (Ibadan: IFRA, 1995).

32. See Pat Williams and Toyin Falola, *Religious Impact on the Nation State: The Nigerian Predicament* (London: Avebury, 1995); and R. Loimeier, *Islamic Reform and Political Change in Nigeria* (Evanston, Ill.: Northwestern University Press, 1997).

33. See P. M. Lubeck, "Islamic Political Movements in Northern Nigeria: The Problem of Class Analysis," in *Islamic Politics and Social Movements,* ed. Edmund Burkell and Ira M. Lapidus (Berkeley: University of California Press, 1988); and P. M. Lubeck, "Islamic Protest under Semi-Industrial Capitalism: 'Yan Tatsine Explained," *Africa* 55, no. 4 (1985): 369–89.

34. See B. Barkindo, "Growing Islamism in Kano City since 1970," in *Muslim Identity and Social Change in Sub-Saharan Africa,* ed. Louis Breener (Bloomington: Indiana University Press, 1993); and U. M. Birai, "Islamic Tajdid and the Political Process in Nigeria," in *Fundamentalisms and the States,* ed. Martin E. Marty and R. Scott Appleby (Chicago: University of Chicago Press, 1993).

35. Enwerem, *A Dangerous Awakening.*

36. See M. H. Kukah, *Religion, Politics and Power in Northern Nigeria* (Ibadan: Spectrum, 1993).

37. See Niels Kastfelt, *Religion and Politics in Nigeria: A Study in Middle Belt Christianity* (London: British Academic Press, 1994).

38. See Peter B. Clarke and Ian Linden, *Islam in Modern Nigeria: A Study of a Muslim Community in a Post-Independent State 1960–1983* (Mainz and Munich: Grunewald-Kaiser, 1984).

39. In its most subtle presentation, see the hegemonic presentation of the Hausa in Mahdi Adamu, *The Hausa Factor in West African History* (Zaria: Ahmadu Bello Univeristy Press, 1978).

40. Falola, *Violence in Nigeria.*

41. Sklar, *Nigerian Political Parties.*

42. B. J. Dudley, *Parties and Politics in Northern Nigeria* (London: Frank Cass 1968).

43. On Ahmadu Bello, see, among others, J. N. Paden, *Ahmadu Bello: Sardauna of Sokoto* (London: Hodder and Stoughton, 1986); and M. Yakubu, *An Aristocracy in Political Crisis: The End of Indirect Rule and the Emergence of Party Politics in the Emirates of Northern Nigeria* (Aldershot: Ashgate Publishing Ltd., 1996).

44. See C. Whitaker, *The Politics of Tradition: Continuity and Change in Northern Nigeria, 1946–66* (Princeton, N.J.: Princeton University Press, 1970); and John N. Paden, *Religion and Political Culture in Kano* (Berkeley: University of California Press, 1973).

45. Shehu Galadanci, foundation member of JNI, quoted in Paden, *Ahmadu Bello,* 564.

46. Kukah, *Religion, Politics and Power,* 20–24; and Paden, *Ahmadu Bello,* 569–78.

47. See Wole Soyinka, *The Open Sore of a Continent* (New York: Oxford University Press, 1996).

48. For a speculative study on this so-called Mafia, see B. J. Takaya and S. G. Tyoden, *The Kaduna Mafia: A Study of the Rise, Development and Consolidation of a Nigerian Power Elite* (Jos: Jos University Press, 1987).

49. See S. Othman, "Classes, Crises and Coup: The Demise of Shagari's Rregime," *African Affairs* 83, 333; and S. Othman, "Nigeria: Power for Profit-Class, Corporatism, and Factionalisation in the Military" in *Contemporary West African States,* ed. D. B. C. O'Brien, J. Dunn, and Rathbone (Cambridge: Cambridge University Press 1989); Forrest, *Politics and Economic Development,* 88–89.

50. See Dudley, *An Introduction,* 163; Joseph, *Prebendal Politics,* 133–36.

51. *Newswatch,* 21 November 1999.

52. Ibid.

53. *The Guardian* (Lagos), 13 November 1999.

54. *Newswatch,* 21 November 1999.

55. *The Guardian* (Lagos), 15 November 1999.

56. See the report of the forum organized by the Vanguard newspaper in the *Vanguard* (Lagos), November 15, 1999.

57. *Tell Magazine,* November 22, 1999.

58. *The Guardian* (Lagos), 14 November 1999.

59. *The Vanguard,* 15 November 1999.

60. *The Guardian ,* 15 November 1999.

61. See *The Vanguard,* 14 November 1999, on the destruction of Christian posters.

62. For the literature on the character of the African state, see J. F. Bayart, *The State in Africa: The Politics of the Belly* (London: Longman, 1994).

8

TRADITIONAL RELIGIONS IN MODERN AFRICA

"IT IS BETTER TO GO IN VAIN THAN TO STAY IN VAIN."

—A SWAHILI PROVERB

There is no need to justify including a discussion of religions in the understanding of African cultures. Increasing secularization and modernization have not diminished the importance of religions and a worldview based on indigenous cultures. Not only are values shaped by religious traditions, millions of Africans regard themselves as religious and make decisions based on beliefs, conscience, or the fear of punishment or great rewards in the afterlife. Many attitudes are shaped in part by religions. The landscape is marked by religious symbols and places of worship. Politicians manipulate religions and religious organizations in order to secure the loyalty of people and to mobilize them. Religions represent core aspects of a cultural system in addition to constituting the key component in how a group defines itself. Religious explanations for many events and problems continue to compete or supplement the scientific; a large number of intellectuals derive sources of power from religions, as in the case of Imams. Religion has provided many opportunities for change. As the preceding chapter shows, Islam and Christianity are competing religions, and their members in some countries engage in bitter rivalries for converts and power. As world religions travel to Africa with the cultures of other lands, issues relating to culture contacts and conflicts are not uncommon. Through the religious medium, Africans are able to compare and contrast Western cultures with theirs, identifying aspects to accept and resist.

In this chapter, I will discuss some of the more important issues, not only to complement the preceding chapter on universal religions, but to focus on Africa's indigenous or traditional religions. The focus is on the contemporary period, a time when African religions are no longer the major ones. The themes show the encounter of indigenous religions with foreign ones, as well as their decline and the residue of their survival. On one hand, there is evidence of the decline of traditional religions; on the other hand, there is evidence of survival and modernization. Indigenous religions have demonstrated a great capacity to redefine themselves, adapt to new circumstances, and redefine some of their practices.[1] On balance, as of today, the decay of traditional religions is more prominent than its survival. Traditional religions are far less organized than Islam and Christianity, and they lack the resources to compete with them in the changing world of the colonial and postcolonial eras. Traditional religions are certainly less aggressive in the quest to convert, which partly explains why they have also been less involved in religious conflicts in such countries as Nigeria and the Sudan.[2]

The major chapter in the story of indigenous religions in contemporary Africa concerns their encounter with Islam and Christianity. There is no doubt that the success of Islam and Christianity has undermined the indigenous religions, displacing them in some areas and making them irrelevant in many others. Christianity is now firmly established in Africa. Indeed, it is an old religion in places such as Ethiopia and Eritrea.[3] In many places, successful conversion began during the nineteenth century, and Christianity became a mass religion during the twentieth. The literature on the early history of Christianity is rather extensive, full of episodes of voluntary acceptance of Christianity, resistance to the new religion, violent encounters, and the ability of Africans to "translate the message" in a way suitable to their needs and environments. The adoption of Christianity was not without its advantages, mainly the association with the symbols and power of Europe. It brought Western education, medicine, and opportunities for work in the formal economic sectors. It enabled a number of African chiefs and kings to use religion to promote international trade and consolidate their own power. To the elite produced by the missionaries, it led to an assumption that they were equipped with the knowledge to transform Africa. It provided an avenue to build social networks in the new cities: the elite and church members could share and circulate information about jobs, social services, public policies, and other things beneficial to them. As many as the changes might have been, they did not amount to any noticeable transition from a traditional world to a modern one.

Where initial evangelization efforts failed, the missionaries came back. As Africans became converts, they became the active native agents who actually took the gospel to all nooks and crannies. No sooner did the religion spread than a synthesis with African cultures began. Dona Beatriz Kimpa Vita of the Kingdom of Kongo in the eighteenth century prefigured the history of African adaptation that is now common. A charismatic prophet, she gave birth to a movement in 1704. Along with her disciples called "the angels," Dona told the story of her death and resurrection, from a human being to her incarnation as Saint Anthony. She regarded Jesus Christ as a Congolese, and claimed to be bestowed with divine powers. With her angels wearing attire said to have been made from the same materials that Jesus wore as a child, Dona's movement gained support among Africans, especially the poor. Although it was a peaceful movement, one intent on stopping wars that supplied captives for the trans-Atlantic slave trade, she was roundly condemned by Europeans. She was crucified on July 2, 1706.[4]

Many other prophets and prophetesses followed Dona, some actually recording great successes and creating huge movements that today have become international, as in the case of the Nigeria Redeemed Church of Christ. Resistance to Christianity has also come from another angle: Islamic leaders and groups who also took advantage of local cultures. Thus, in the first half of the twentieth century, there were many cases of resistance directed at Christian missionaries and their converts. In Senegal, where the French initially pursued a strategy of assimilation which mandated that Africans seeking French citizenship become Christians, Muslims reacted with hostility, with many seeking the means to strengthen their faith rather than succumb to colonial policy. In some of these cases, the strategy of Islam was to present itself as indigenous and not associated with imperialism.

There can be no doubt whatsoever that African Christian leaders and missionary agents have transformed Christianity. They fought the race inequality within the church and devised successful strategies for creating their own independent missions. With many declaring themselves as prophets—reinventing the strategies of the biblical prophets, writing their own hymns and prayers, and demanding loyalty and devotion from their followers—African church leaders created not just race equality but local varieties of Christianity which can endure.

Islam and Christianity have both been used to define ethnic and cultural identities. Both religions have served as an agency of nationalism. Resistance to colonial powers was often expressed in religious terms or led by religious leaders. When Islam and Christianity contribute to nationalism and identity formation, they are in part responding to demands based on local needs and the aspirations of elite members.

Furthermore, Christianity has created the new social identity of an African middle class, one with Western education, aspirations of mobility defined in some modern ways, and an urban lifestyle. The role of this elite was certainly pronounced during the colonial era. With a Western education, they were able to secure wage jobs which improved their social status. After the Second World War, when European powers were transferring power, the elite benefited most significantly, inheriting power which was quickly used to build wealth. Prestige followed. Other members of society thus had a reference point to organize their lives, with the ambition of receiving a Western education and becoming mobile. Western education was the handmaiden of Christianity. The majority of pioneer schools were established by Christian missionaries in order to convert Africans and create a middle class that could work in various areas. The nature of education in the colonial era reflected the intentions of the missionaries. The emphasis was on primary education, and the initial higher institutions were geared toward the production of the clergy. Significant changes came after the Second World War, when many high schools and a few universities were established by the colonial governments. Not all elite members accepted assimilation into a Christian and Western world; many among them became defenders of African values and strong critics of imported religions. Traditionalists and the new elite have had to talk about indigenous cultures and religions.

Indigenous Religions and Cultures

Notwithstanding the perception of the converts, Christianity and Western education created a package that regarded their converts as superior to others. Missionary education repeatedly told the students that their past and religions were backward, simple, and childish, and that the primary goal of conversion was to save them. Where African religions and values had to be mentioned in the classrooms, the aim was to prevent the students from going back to them, a reminder of their pagan past. With Western culture and Christianity presented as noble and superior, the captive minds were brainwashed into despising their own culture and religions. In areas where practitioners compared religions—the new and old, varieties of old and new—as in the case of South Africa, they did so in part to justify the imposition of an economic and political order to marginalize Africans.[5] Christianity posed a serious threat to the established cultural and social order. New converts could reject the authority of chiefs and kings, ridicule indigenous religions by burning their symbols and ritual object making a mockery of masks and sacred spaces, violate norms by disregarding taboos and revealing age-old secrets, and stake a new social path by condemning polygamy and aspects of arts and culture. Even objects associated with decorations were destroyed for their association with so-called paganism.[6] Society became divided between Christians and "primitive pagans," Muslims and Christians, Muslims and non-Muslims—all with implications for politics and the economy. A christianized Western-educated elite could behave arrogantly to a "primitive pagan." Christian missionaries could criticize traditional religion as idolatry, condemn dancing and singing as being associated with cults, oppose polygamy and some other marriage practices, and take other steps that undermined older cultures and the traditional elite.

Christianity has always entailed more than religion; conversion came with exposure to Western cultures. However, if they linked religion to their own culture, the missionaries were also eager to disconnect Africans from their cultures, thereby creating a notion that religion and the nonreligious aspects of life (e.g., singing and drumming) were separable. African gods and spirits were presented as "satanic" and "paganistic;" only the Christian God was the authentic one and the Bible was regarded as the only legitimate Holy Book. Even creative aspects of African culture such as drumming, singing, and dancing were criticized. Converts were warned to avoid participation in rituals, ceremonies, and other activities that supposedly doomed their future salvation. In order to make Africans turn their backs on their culture and past, conversion was necessary, and certain symbols had to accompany it: they should bear Western or biblical names, wear Western attire, eat Western food (notably bread, tea, and an egg for breakfast), use Western languages as a routine, and travel to Western countries, notably the capital cities of Europe.

Assisted with the power of the colonial governments, the missionaries made a number of drastic changes to many aspects of African culture that they regarded as rather barbaric. Certain practices were proscribed, such as female circumcision in some parts of Africa, as well as a few deities such as the Akim Kotoku of Ghana and the cult of Dente in Togo. Laws were passed in many places banning witchcraft. Many other practices were ridiculed simply to undermine them: food habits, attire characterized as costumes, languages reduced to "vernaculars" in order to undermine their significance. There was the psychology of inferiority fostered by the very nature of colonial conquest and governance. European guns subdued African states and societies, reducing their powerful chiefs and kings to subordinate officers of European powers. Similarly, the African elite were subdued and had to accept the junior roles created for them.

Modernization in education, medicine, and social structure has undermined many aspects of indigenous religions. Where Western medicine is superior, it has reduced the number of clients that visit herbalists and other traditional healers. Technology is an area that humbles Africans. From small items such as mirrors to bigger ones like the airplane, the superiority of Western technology has translated to a belief in the idea of a superior culture/race. Christianity has exploited this to its advantage, largely by association with Western technological power. The "new" African—wearing Western attire, bearing Western names, speaking and writing in European languages, and eating Western food—can now conveniently avoid traditional religions, opting instead for Christianity or Islam.

Urbanization, too, played a role in changing many views. New cities emerged during the twentieth century, and older ones grew as well. The cities have become centers of new opportunities and privileges, in spite of the problems associated with urban living. Hospitals, schools, and economic production centers are concentrated in the cities. To many, migration to the cities is an opportunity to reject the rural, create some distance from traditional cultures, and use modern technology and new products. Cinema halls, electricity, pipe-borne water, extensive interactions with others without patriarchal supervision are all part of the package of modernity offered by cities. To agencies of modernization, such as the Christian missions and secular governments, the cities enabled them to reach millions of people with modern communication and transportation facilities. Laws could be made, and the people could be forced to comply. Newcomers and the poor saw the elite and successful city-dwellers as models to emulate. They came to the cities with their established ideas and cultural practices; however, the space and the venues to live their old ways were limited. Consequently, they explored other avenues, such as attending new churches, visiting clubs, and participating in other new city cultures. After the Second World War, new cultural practices in the cities favored the spread of Western cultures and Christianity. Consequently, urban Africa today is imitative of Western culture, even if the elements of traditional and Islamic religions remain equally strong. Churches and mosques are prominent features of the landscape. Western-style attire are fashionable for attending church and going to the offices.

The encounter with Islam and Christianity is much more than the story of the displacement of older indigenous religions. Indeed, many practitioners of indigenous religions might not have interpreted the process as that of displacement, but as one of accommodation which enabled them to add other religions to their crowded cosmos. African indigenous religions exhibit features of flexibility and tolerance which make it easier for their practitioners to welcome other religions while retaining many of their traditional values and symbols. This flexibility can be exploited, however, as in the case of Muslims who, as Lamin Sanneh notes, exploited the situation to great advantage in constructing a new society based on an Islamic view of state and religion.[7] There are even cases when an ethnic group, in response to a series of changes they originally resisted, turned around to modify their views on the spiritual and sacred meanings of water, body, religious sites, and others to accommodate secular and scientific interpretations.[8] To a number of converts, the baptism and the sermons that were regarded by the missionaries as an act of conversion were no more than mere gestures. Thus, conversion can be accepted and social changes might follow, all without abandoning the "African ways."

Indigenous religions and cultures have also been used to organize resistance by African Christians against the mainstream missions. There are many cases of the use of the elements from indigenous religions and cultures to redefine Christianity, sometimes in ways that established missions did not approve of. For instance, in the 1930s, the Gikuyu of Kenya established the African Orthodox Church, which supported circumcision and took an anti-European and anti-mission church stance. It was proscribed by the colonial government. Other churches with similar objectives have been created, and they have recorded success in drawing followers.

Even in more subtle and often disguised forms, resources are drawn from indigenous religions and worldview to understand and critique the changing world of the colonial and postcolonial era, partly in order to adapt to them and partly in order to create a defense mechanism. For instance, in a nuanced study, Luise White has used vampire stories to explain the African's understanding of the colonial system.[9] Bloodsucking stories are not restricted to this era. Even today, people continue to believe that fortune and power seekers can use other people's blood for rituals. More generally, schism within Christianity has been driven in large part by a desire to interpret the religion along an "African" way that relates things to customs, supports local leadership, accepts polygamy not as a sin, and in some cases even defends such a practice as female circumcision. The prophets of the African churches behave in many ways like the cult leaders of old: they see visions; they interpret dreams in ways that indigenous diviners may; their members can fall into a trance, a sort of spirit possession common in traditional religions; they have the power to heal by manipulating objects and symbols such as holy water, incense, ashes, and oils; many do wear white gowns, adopting the symbolism of the color white in traditional religions; they encourage the use of ritual dance in sacrifice and worship; and they claim to have the power to destroy witches and other enemies pursuing their members.

Rather than totally destroy traditional religions and beliefs associated with them, Islam and Christianity have actually incorporated many of their elements. While Islamic preachers may intensely condemn indigenous religions as paganism, one sees a lot of borrowing from indigenous medicine, charms, and literature to make Islam more attractive to Africans.[10] Songs for African gods have been adapted into Christian songs, and traditional dancing steps and drumming have also been adopted. The belief in magic and witchcraft has been appropriated by many modern churches to retain their membership and instill some fear in the congregation. The power of the church pastor to conquer a witch—in ways similar to that of the herbalist or diviner of old—is an effective strategy to demonstrate the power of Jesus Christ and the relevance of Christianity.[11] One study has documented how Luo women borrow strategies from precolonial female spirit possession to act as leaders in Christian organizations.[12] It is the ability to borrow from existing religious traditions, while criticizing them at the same time, that has partly enabled Islam and Christianity to endure. In cities where changes are most noticeable, the blending of old and new beliefs is most prevalent. Ethnic identities have been consolidated in cities, as people use ethnicity to create social networks and political associations. Where the police and the judicial system are weak or inefficient, Africans have turned to a traditional judicial system to create a new order and peace. Old music forms are reinvented. Western musical instruments such as the piano and guitar are used along with African rhythms. Songs are generally composed in African languages, with occasional code switching with European words and phrases.

Although Africans have accepted Islam and Christianity, many of the beliefs and views they express are drawn from traditional religions and cultures. The idea of God can combine elements from the Bible, the Quran, and the African worldview. The emphasis on community and ethics of behavior reveal a mix as well. The rejection of religion as abstract and the emphasis on prayers and sacrifices to solve worldly problems enable the views of traditionalists. The beliefs by Africans in sorcery, witchcraft, and destiny are so similar, irrespective of their religions. The construction of an afterlife, based on Christian and Islamic ideas, has yet to undermine a belief in the power of ancestors among groups with established practices of ancestor veneration. Respect for unseen forces, elders, and hierarchies are drawn, not necessarily from Islam and Christianity, but from established indigenous values. One observer interprets the tendencies to borrow from traditional religions as "the coming into being of 'churches' which are positive repudiations of Christianity, even though they use the scaffolding of the Christian church to erect new structures for the self-expression of the traditional religion."[13] This view may be considered extreme by a number of church leaders, but the impact of indigenous religions on (African) Christian theology cannot be disputed.[14]

Continuity with the past is pronounced in various aspects of African religions. Religious symbols and beliefs are strong, some repeating the ideas of old and some already integrated into Islam and Christianity. Where ancestor veneration is ongoing, it is part of the religious practices of old. Secret societies have been modernized in many areas and their functions redefined to enable elite members to participate and use them as networks. The magic component of indigenous religions has yet to disappear. So strong is the belief in witchcraft and magic in many parts of Africa that one might assume that changes to established ideas have been minimal. Herbalists, medicine men, charm makers, and diviners are numerous in cities, indicating the continuity of medical practices and the belief in supernatural forces.[15] Even when elite members say that their preference is for the modern, many still visit the traditional diviners and healers. Writing in the 1960s, Professor Bolaji Idowu, one of the most distinguished pioneers in the study of indigenous religions, remarked on the ability of African converts to tap into many religious sources, without regarding them as contradictory or sinful:

> It is now becoming clear to the most optimistic of Christian evangelists that the main problem of the church in Africa today is the divided loyalties of most of her members between Christianity with its Western categories and practices on one hand, and the traditional religion on the other hand. It is well known that in strictly personal matters relating to the passages of life and the crisis of life, African Traditional Religion is regarded as the final succour by most Africans. In hospitals, for example, people who, on admission, have declared themselves Christians, and indeed are 'practising' Christians, have medicine prepared in the traditional way smuggled in to them simply because, psychologically at least, that is more effective in that it is consecrated medicine with the touch of the divine healer, in contrast to the

Europeans' *mere* 'coloured water' or *mere* pills. In matters concerning providence, healing, and general wellbeing, therefore, most African still look up to 'their own religion' as 'the way.'[16]

Writing twenty years earlier, E. G. Parrinder made a similar observation, highlighting how even members of the Western-educated elite continue to believe in traditional medicine:

> Educated people attribute to witchcraft their failures in work, or seek magical protection against new diseases. They may use new types of medicine, but of a magical kind. Many have recourse both to the medicine-man and to the European-trained doctor. The medicine-man serves as a link with the village ancestors. He may interpret a patient's sickness or nightmares as due to an angry ancestor who has been neglected and demands that money be sent home to make him offerings.[17]

The methods of consultation and the type of medicine are not necessarily the same today, but the belief in witchcraft and charms remains as strong as ever. The survival of African medicine is no longer in doubt.[18] Divination systems remain strong, and diviners are almost everywhere, already creatively adapted to urban life and the needs of modern occupations.[19] In 1978, the World Health Organization called on African governments to recognize and use traditional medical practitioners. Some governments responded to this challenge, and a number of efforts have been made to reform and "professionalize" the occupation of traditional healing.[20]

The continuation of many indigenous practices means that we still can locate communities in Africa based partly on older sacred beliefs and practices. Many aspects of the beliefs have been modified, some proscribed by laws, and many have been forced to adapt to modern circumstances. Certainly, worldview and mental orientation remain shaped by older religions in aspects relating to the meaning of life, origins, death, and many ideas about the universe. There are hardly places where people do not believe in the concept of an "evil eye," the expectation of danger in association with some bad people, events, or symbols. Community festivals are widespread, such as yam festivals, masquerade ceremonies, and a variety of annual remembrances of ancient gods, such as Ogun among the Yoruba. Beliefs in spirits are as strong as ever. Where festivals are held, established practices relating to sacrifice, prayer, communal feasts, and other religious aspects do occur. Supernatural forces are believed to be everywhere. Beliefs in a number of gods may have waned in some places, but their symbols persist, as well as the invocation of their names in moments of dangers. So too do the contents and motivations of prayers, including, but not limited to, a desire to survive, overcome obstacles, live long, and have children remain as before. Religious workers and mediators, such as diviners, herbalists, and priests, all continue to be invested with power to carry prayers to gods, to use codes and symbols to cure illnesses, and to manipulate sacred objects for specific events.

The existence of this community and its retention of older beliefs and practices can be demonstrated in several ways, some so fascinating that they show the continuity in Africa's long history and the power of its changing traditions. First, where communities still subscribe to indigenous religions, the principles are similar to those outlined in many studies,[21] although suggestions that these remain pristine should be ignored. Thus, there is a belief in a Supreme Being, gods, and spirits; a universe controlled by greater forces; the need to live a moral life in order to reap rewards now and in the future; creation myths at the beginning of a very distant past; ancestor veneration; the power attributed to nature, witches, and other powerful agencies; and the need to balance the interest of human beings and nature in the development process. These worldviews continue to be shaped by the strong assumption that supernatural powers control the universe and the various human groups residing in it; and that for an individual to survive, he or she must function as part of a larger group. More than the issue of worldview is the actual survival of a number of cultural practices such as singing, drumming, art, dancing, dressing styles, and others. Where people practice their traditional cultures and religions, they no longer necessarily feel inferior, although the elite among them tend to be apologetic and defensive. There are priests and religious leaders in charge of various communities, and the power of these leaders varies from one region to another, from one cult to another, and from one community to another. Chiefship and cosmology were connected in precolonial Africa;[22] while they have not been totally disconnected, secularization has tended to undermine the power of traditional leaders, but not destroy them.[23]

In many parts of West Africa, the annual celebration symbolized by the masquerade remains rather common. This is the cult of ancestors, which plays a visible role in some culture groups, such as the Yoruba of Nigeria.[24] Where divination and witchcraft are part of the established belief system, the cults associated with them tend to have continued in many areas. Thus, the oracle divinity is still widespread in many places. The Yoruba Ifa and its priests (the Babalawo)[25] are featured in many popular dramas and television plays, revealing their influence on modern consciousness. In reality, Ifa and the Babalawo are part of the living traditions and practices. Just as many Muslims and Christians continue to patronize the Babalawo, so too is the desire to participate in cults associated with personal success, as in the case of Ogun (the god of iron) among Yoruba in such occupations as driving and blacksmithing. Where some festivals are clearly associated with the history of a town, they also tend to have survived, and participation actually cuts along religious lines. The festivals enable the community to come together, even when people are mere spectators, to renew their commitment to tradition and shared histories.[26] The festivals are marked by public singing and loud drumming in a way that strongly suggests that all attempts by Islamic and Christian missionaries to destroy indigenous use of songs and drums have been unsuccessful. Indeed, the talking drum remains an integral aspect, not just of religion, but of music and drama, even of the secularized versions. Magic and medicine are equally powerful. Irrespective of their religion and level of access to Western education, a large percentage of Africans continue to believe in many medical and magical practices associated with indigenous religions. Many people use herbs, and consult charm makers and diviners. The idea of the existence of powerful magic is generally unquestioned, even on university campuses. Be it the desire for love or the desire for wealth, it is not uncommon to find people who believe that it can be fulfilled with the use of the right magic.

Second, in modified or redefined ways, indigenous religions shape many aspects of contemporary culture. Muslims and Christians believe in witches who can be conquered, not just by the priests of these two monotheistic religions, but also by those of the indigenous religions. There is a strong belief that the manipulation of religious symbols can alter fortunes and nature. Elite and government officials have paid traditional rainmakers to stop rain during important celebrations, thereby integrating tradition with celebration and modernization. Idioms and statements drawn from indigenous religions are part of the culture of the contemporary world. Traditional roles assigned to women have largely been retained.[27] Indigenous religions have been able to adapt even to secularization tendencies, appropriating nonreligious elements to reform themselves or even to grapple with changing worldviews. Even the most visible frontier of secularization, the cities, still show the evidence of indigenous religions in the importance accorded to herbs and charms, priests and diviners, and many premodern worldviews that regulate interpersonal relations.

Third, indigenous religions have manifested the ability to modernize. Some elements of religious practices have been presented in such a way to accommodate Muslims and Christians. Thus, in some Yoruba cities, Christians and Muslims have participated in community festivals, reenactment ceremonies of kinship rituals and power, and even some events associated with the honor of gods. In the celebration of the rites of passage, old and new religions are combined in ritual performance, songs, and many aspects of social arrangements. Burial ceremonies remain the ultimate unifier, as members of the community, however divided by religions, unite to honor the dead and participate in burial rites.

Modernization can also be seen in the way that indigenous religions present themselves to the public, a process of self-fashioning that is geared toward appealing to younger people and the elite. Some are imitative of Islam and Christianity, as in the building of permanent and modern temples for gods. Shrines of makeshift objects and huts are giving way to "temples." Some ancient shrines have been modernized, with awe-inspiring artistic decorations, for example, as in the case of Osun Osogbo in western Nigeria. Where some gods are "international," largely because of their spread during the trans-Atlantic slave trade, some attempts are being made to ensure their survival and standardize elements of worship in order to make them more appealing. Osun, Sango, and Ogun, all Yoruba gods, are examples of deities that are constantly being modernized in west Africa, South America, and the United States.[28] For instance, a popular book on Ogun, the god of iron and occupations associated with it (e.g., hunting, war), claims that its contemporary worshippers number more than forty million.[29]

Fourth, thanks to the school system, indigenous religions are taught in schools, especially in universities as part of religious studies, anthropology, law, or sociology. While the schools are not useful for conversion, they have been able to present indigenous religions in the context of history, comparative religions, and cultural development. It is actually in schools that many youths learn about indigenous religions for the first time; in other words, it becomes an academic than a practical reality. But even as an academic enterprise, many have become excited with the new knowledge, asking their teachers why Africans have abandoned their own gods in preference for imported ones. According to the late Professor Bolaji Idowu:

> Often, they want to stop their teacher and ask him to say precisely in what way the imported values are better than the indigenous ones, and why 'we' cannot bring back the religion of our forbears to its own, refining it, if need be.[30]

The development in universities reflects a much broader attitude of government officials and secular policies, especially in non-Islamic areas.

Many African governments, in the quest to assert themselves and claim a connection with Africa's past, have supported the revival of some aspects of indigenous religions and cultures.[31] They funded programs to revive some of these aspects, allowed radio and television stations to document and broadcast festivals and worship, sponsor communal festivals, and even organize various competitions among youths in schools and towns.

Still, on modernization and change, elite practitioners of indigenous religions have been embarking upon various moves to universalize and propagate their beliefs. Many methods are being employed. Some are seeking the means to simplify the religions and make them adaptable to the modern era. Beliefs are being codified in written forms, in a way that the essentials of a religion can be communicated and the teaching of priests can be standardized. Godianism, a religion distilled from African indigenous religions, is one example, with its leader being able to write speeches and present his religion as one based on a "holy book."[32] Godianism attempts to reduce the pantheons by stressing a belief in a Supreme Being. Varieties of Godianism exist in several parts of Africa, each with its own leader and creed. There are examples that even preceded Godianism, such as the Church of Orunmila among the Yoruba, the Aruosa Church among the Edo, and the National Church of Nigeria and Cameroon. Some die rather quickly, to be replaced by other leaders and organizations. What unites them is simply the quest to adapt indigenous religions to the modern age. Some have priests (even calling them reverends and preachers), hymn books, temples, and an order of service. Books and articles now exist that explain the various religions, even the activities of secret societies.[33] The imitation of Islamic and Christian practices also includes the use of modern media and technology to preach and present the faith. The Islamic and Christian "God" are substituted with African ones, and local languages are used to preach and pray. Sacrifices, including the use of animal blood, are integrated with worship. The move toward modernizing African religions includes rejecting imported religions, empowering Africans to assume spiritual leadership, and creating opportunities for the elite to have alternatives to Islam and Christianity.

Certainly, the elite converts to indigenous religions are not as ashamed as their predecessors, who, on conversion to Christianity, distanced themselves from "paganism." Though few in number, the elite converts are willing to associate freely, convene conferences, and seek time and space in the public arena. More importantly, they can communicate the principles of their religions. Today, we have not only scholarly books on indigenous religions, but also practical-oriented books, hymnals, handbooks on a variety of subjects, and meditation books. Western technology and education are being used to modernize and commercialize old religions. Similarly, many diviners and herbalists, with or without a Western education, have become better organized to regulate their profession, standardize the training of new recruits, commercialize alternative medicine, and seek government recognition for their trade. Herbalists demonstrate their craft for a fee, just as masquerades now do even in secular events, and attend public conferences.

Fifth, as many societies witness problems of crime and social decadence, especially in the cities, there are increasing calls to borrow certain elements of indigenous religions to maintain the social and moral order. Disappointed by what contemporaries see as the moral failure of their age, rebirth based on religious principles has always been suggested as an option. To quote Parrinder for the last time:

> The greatest danger in African religious life is that the old should disappear, without some new religious force to take its place. Unchecked individualism, self-seeking, corruption and materialism are the great enemies of modern Africa. Yet the past has been so thoroughly impregnated with religion and its ethics that it is difficult to see how an ordered society can be established without them.[34]

He was writing a long time ago, too long for him to know that Islam and Christianity would become religious forces, but without the ability to establish "an ordered society" that could satisfy the majority of Africans. Even a number of Christian and Muslim leaders are driven, no doubt by frustration, to call for the revival of many older values that are believed to be positive. Analysts and policymakers who describe themselves as "neotraditionalists" also seek ethics in indigenous religions to counter the perceived negative impact of changes coming from abroad. There is hardly a consensus on the values and ideas that are to be retained, as analysts pick whatever they find enduring and suitable for present needs. From the point of view of this chapter, the fact that they are engaging in such a discussion is an indication that they wish to keep the religions alive in the public and intellectual arena. As to the specifics, many agree that an ethical system based on the overall welfare of the community is much better than the contemporary idea of individualism. As analysts point out, in the past, the sins of the individual were visited on the kin members and groups, thereby putting pressure on people to avoid such serious crimes as stealing, adultery, and murder. An individual in trouble was not only punished, but members of his or her family would suffer a similar fate. They all could be ostracized, banished from the town, asked to perform elaborate sacrifices, and requested to pay heavy fines.[35] In contrast, modern societies, ignoring the teaching of indigenous religions, stress individual success and the acquisition of wealth and power to the detriment of society. While analysts are correct about the merits and relevance of group identity, it remains unclear how elements of the past can be duplicated in a competitive modern economy.

Finally, traditional religions show that they are still of practical value, not just for the individual but for political leadership, mass-based politics and war. The link between religion and nationalism is mentioned above, but there is also a link between religions and contemporary politics and war. That many politicians and political leaders use charms is no secret. Indeed, many boast about it and do in fact threaten their opponents with the possession of powerful magic to destroy them. All wars and major conflicts in Africa have involved a reliance on traditional powers of magic and religious priests. Commenting in 1988, a Mozambican minister remarked that the liberation wars by his people against the Portuguese demonstrated not just the survival of traditional religions, but its linkage to the power structures:

> We didn't realize how influential the traditional authorities were, even without formal power. We are obviously going to have to harmonize traditional beliefs with political project. Otherwise we are going against things that the vast majority of our people believe—we will be like foreigners in our country. I think we are gathering the courage to say so aloud. We will have to restore some of the traditional structures that at the beginning of our independence we simply smashed, thinking that we were doing a good and important thing. . . . Traditional beliefs are a point of reference for all those people caught in the middle of the road between Westernization and African society. In a state of flux like a war, the beliefs become even stronger. This war of ours has certainly underlined the shortcomings of our choice to ignore those beliefs.[36]

Stephen L. Weigert has documented the validity of this remark in a study that examines the role of traditional religions and ideologies in a number of wars in the second half of the twentieth century. Weigert's five case studies—drawn from Madagascar in 1947, the Mau Mau of Kenya in 1952–63, the war by the UPC in Cameroon from 1955 to 1970, the conflicts in the Congo from 1964 to 1968, and the war in Mozambique from 1977 to 1992—are not theologically inspired, but part of anticolonial struggles. In spite of the secular motivation of the wars, traditional religions played a crucial role. Indeed, as he points out, some insurgent movements were inspired by "traditional religious and revivalist ideas."[37] Thousands of soldiers, ordinary ones and commanders, believed in the efficacy of charms and magic as bulletproof against not just bullets but also spears, knives, and machetes. In mobilizing people to fight, the leaders pay attention to religious values and traditions to generate widespread enthusiasm and support. The connection between religion and nationalism is pretty much established, either by the activities of priests and prophets who led the resistance against colonial rule,[38] the diviners and charm makers who prepared charms for soldiers engaged in various wars of liberation, or even scholars and activists who present traditional religions as alternatives to Christianity and Islam. The effectiveness of a number of insurgent movements, concludes Weigert, "was, in part, due to a creative synthesis of traditional theology and modern techniques of political and military organization."[39] Weigert concludes that:

> Modern African military history demonstrates that a substantial body of African religion and mythology has survived the impact of Western political institutions, ideology, and military technology. While bullets may never be turned into water, oppressive alien ideas and their corrupting influence on indigenous tradition continue to be diluted by those who retain their faith in ancestral spirits and institutions.[40]

The belief that the power derived from traditional religions should be combined with modern weapons remains current, as manifested in the wars in Sierra Leone, Liberia, and central Africa in the 1990s and the early years of the twentieth century. To prepare for war, a soldier may consult a spirit medium, an herbalist, diviners, and charm makers. Morale in battles is heightened by nonsecular beliefs in the ability to overcome problems. To a victorious party, success is not simply analyzed as a function of military strategy and superior weapons, but as the favorable intervention of supernatural forces. To believe in charms is not necessarily regarded as antisecular.

Because of the relevance of traditional religions to contemporary society or for the ideological reason of countering Western domination, every generation has produced leading advocates who want Africa to either reject the two universal religions or retain them without destroying the indigenous ones. Thus, we have the example of Wilmot Blyden during the nineteenth century and Léopold Senghor in the twentieth.[41] When Kwame Nkrumah became the first head of independent Ghana in 1957, he sought to recover the past by using African rituals to open official business. Libation and ritual statements were made, instead of the Christian prayer. Latter-day advocates make similar arguments.[42] In order to avoid the extinction of indigenous religions, they argue, avenues must be created for adaptation and modernization with a changing world, most especially with the imperatives of development, science, and technology.

Perhaps in the years ahead, indigenous religions will decline to a point that they become impossible to even recognize. So powerful is the ability of Islam and Christianity to convert and retain its members that indigenous religions cannot possibly launch a counterattack. Indeed, in most censuses in African countries, only a minority declare themselves as members of indigenous religions. Compared with the universal religions, the indigenous ones offer little by way of mobility and power, while the intellectual ideas that sustain them may have become anachronistic in many ways.[43] As a body of coherent system, indigenous religions cannot survive in a society based on new science, technology, and economies. Cults may disappear, symbolism may be redefined, and many practices may weaken or disappear altogether. The linkage between cults and occupations, in a way that religion has been used to give more power to men than women and establish control on some products such as iron,[44] is severely threatened and destroyed in many instances.

However, ideas, words, and views on many aspects of indigenous religions, such as magic, witchcraft, spirits, ancestors, and the agency of the supernatural, will continue to be with Africa for a long time to come, not simply because they are part of the worldview that modernity has neither challenged nor destroyed but because the universal religions have also appropriated them. Values, both premodern and modern, are still very much tied to traditional religions and the related worldview.[45] Divination practices, such as the Yoruba's Ifa, have the ability to endure, as they continue to meet the needs of individuals to understand themselves, solve personal problems, and enable them to peep into an uncertain future. While the power of kingship is in decline, the legitimacy of the institution still relies on rituals and tradition.[46] African heroes of the past—warrior-priests and mythological leaders—are still used to construct and consolidate ethnic nationalism.[47] Struggles over land are ultimately tied to local traditions and religions, while not underplaying commercial considerations.[48] The limitations of Western medicine will ensure the survival of alternative medicine. Not only will diviners and some powerful priests continue to play the role of counselors and therapists, but charm makers and herbalists will continue to have clients. The cures for misfortune, failure, "spiritual sickness," and others that are hard to explain lie not in the hands of Western-trained doctors but with traditional healers. Africans, even those with the highest educational qualifications, continue to believe that there is science and magic, and individuals are controlled by destinies. Songs, art, and literature will continue to profit from the knowledge and information derived from local cultures and religions.[49] Material culture,[50] including those with imported components, are invested with a lot of meaning derived from traditional sources. Even modern science and technology have not escaped being understood in some mythical and religious way. Moreover, both Islam and Christianity will continue to exploit the most beneficial aspects of indigenous religions to their advantage. When more and more people reflect on the capacity of indigenous religions to build community cohesion and ensure a more stable social order, they will learn to draw from its positive elements, while rejecting those that are considered inappropriate to contemporary times. Oba Victor Ayeni of Ila-Orangun, a notable Yoruba king who lived for the greater part of the twentieth century as well as a Christian convert who actively participated in festivals and the worship of the major deities, offered an intelligent and pragmatic "secularist" solution to the preservation of indigenous African religions:

> I do not wish that all these traditions should perish, because that is our history and they provide a link between us and our ancestors. . . . The way to preserve many of these cultural practices is to present them as "asa" [tradition] and not as "esin" [worship]. The supernatural elements will have to be deemphasized to attract followership. If we present and sustain these customs as a mark of our identity with the past, with our ancestors, and as part of our history and heritage, not as a religious obligation, then they will survive. The removal of the *orisa* (deity) aspects will not make many of these practices useless or irrelevant. For instance, no one will doubt the beauty, the thrill, and the amusement associated ordinarily with the Egungun Festival, even without the religious elements. It is entertaining and interesting to look at. But when you now say that this is our ancestor coming all the way from heaven, how do you want me to believe when I know that it is not true. Just say this is *egungun,* and I will respect it for that.[51]

The noted king is providing what appears to be the consensus among many Africans—the desire to escape the destructive impact of globalization, the eagerness to purge religions and cultures of elements considered negative, and the practical policy of being able to draw on a positive cultural heritage to construct a better society and attain sustainable development. Traditional religion may be dying, but efforts should be made that what remains of it should not be in vain.

Notes

1. See M. Fortes and G. Dieterlen, eds., *African Systems of Thought* (London: Oxford University Press, 1965); T. Ranger and I. Kimambo, eds., *The Historical Study of African Traditional Religion* (Berkeley: University of California Press, 1972); Thomas D. Blakely, Walter E. A. van Beek, and Dennis L. Thomson, eds., *Religion in Africa* (Portsmouth, N.H.: Heinemann, 1994); and Jacob K. Olupona, ed., *African Traditional Religions in Contemporary Society* (New York: Paragon, 1991).

2. For some recent work on the nature of religious conflicts in Africa, see Abdullahi Ahmed An-Na'im, ed., *Proselytization and Communal Self-Determination in Africa* (New York: Orbis, 1999); and Holger Bernt Hansen and Michael Twaddle, eds., *Religion and Politics in East Africa* (Athens: Ohio University Press, 1995).

3. See Elizabeth Isichei, *A History of Christianity in Africa* (Trenton, N.J.: Africa World Press, 1995).

4. For a most fascinating account of her career, see John K. Thornton, *The Kongolese Saint Anthony: Dona Beatriz Kimpa Vita and the Antonian Movement, 1684–1706* (Cambridge: Cambridge University Press, 1998).

5. See David Chidester, *Savage Systems: Colonialism and Comparative Religion in Southern Africa* (Charlottesville and London: University Press of Virginia, 1996).

6. For some examples, see the historical description of the encounter in E. A. Ayandele, *The Missionary Impact on Modern Nigeria, 1842–1914: A Social and Political Analysis* (London: Longman, 1966); M. A. Onwujeogwu, *An Igbo Civilization: Nri Kingdom and Hegemony* (Benin: Ethiope, 1985); Obaro Ikime, *The Isoko People: A Historical Survey* (Ibadan: Ibadan University Press, 1972); and J. D. Y. Peel, *Religious Encounter and the Making of the Yoruba* (Bloomington: Indiana University Press, 2000).

7. Lamin Sanneh, *The Crown and the Turban: Muslims and West African Pluralism* (Boulder, Colo.: Westview, 1997).

8. Sandra E. Greene, *Sacred Sites and the Colonial Encounter: A History of Meaning and Memory in Ghana* (Bloomington: Indiana University Press, 2002).

9. Luise White, *Speaking with Vampires: Rumor and History in Colonial Africa* (Berkeley: University of California Press, 2000).

10. See the collection of essays in Part 5 of Nehemia Levtzion and Randall L. Pouwels, eds., *The History of Islam in Africa* (Athens: Ohio University Press, 2000).

11. See J. S. Mbiti, *New Testament Eschatology in an African Background* (Oxford: Oxford University Press, 1971).

12. Cynthia Hoehler-Fatton, *Women of Fire and Spirit: History, Faith, and Gender in Roho Religion in Western Kenya* (New York: Oxford University Press, 1996).

13. E. Bolaji Idowu, *African Traditional Religion: A Definition* (London: SCM, 1973), 206.

14. Among others, see J. D. Y. Peel, *Aladura: A Religious Movement among the Yoruba* (London: Published for the International African institute by Oxford University Press, 1968); Thomas Spear and Isaria N. Kimambo, eds, *East African Expressions of Christianity* (Athens: Ohio University Press, 1999); and Emmanuel Martey, *African Theology: Inculturation and Liberation* (New York: Orbis, 1993).

15. See H. Ngubane, *Body and Mind in Zulu Medicine: An Ethnography of Health and Disease in Nynowa Zulu Thought and Practice* (London: Academic Press, 1977).

16. Idowu, *African Traditional Religion*, 206; italics in the original.

17. E. G. Parrinder, *African Traditional Religion* (London: S.P.C.K., 1968), 144.

18. Christopher Fyfe, *African Medicine in the Modern World* (Edinburgh: Center of African Studies, 1986); and M. Akin Makinde, *African Philosophy, Culture, and Traditional Medicine* (Athens, Ohio: Monographs in International Studies, Africa Series, No. 53, 1988).

19. On divination systems, see Philip M. Peek, *African Divination Systems: Ways of Knowing* (Bloomington: Indiana University Press, 1991).

20. Murray Last and G. L. Chevunduka, *The Professionalisation of African Medicine* (Manchester: Manchester University Press, 1986).

21. See Bolaji Idowu, *Olodumare: God in Yoruba Belief* (London: Longman, 1962); E. G. Parrinder, *West African Religion* (London: Epworth Press, 1961); J. S. Mbiti, *Introduction to African Traditional Religion* (London: Heinemann, 1975). J. S. Mbiti, *Concepts of God in Africa* (London: S.P.C.K., 1982); J. O. Kayode, *Understanding African Traditional Religion* (Ile-Ife, Nigeria: University of Ife Press, 1984); and O. Imasogie, *African Traditional Religion* (Ibadan, Nigeria: University Press Ltd., 1982).

22. See Randall M. Packard, *Chiefship and Cosmology: An Historical Study of Political Competition* (Bloomington: Indiana University Press, 1981).

23. See Olufemi Vaughan, *Nigerian Chiefs: Traditional Power in Modern Politics, 1890s–1990s* (Rochester, N.Y.: University of Rochester Press, 2000).

24. On Yoruba religion, see Judith Gleason, *Orisha: The Gods of Yorubaland* (New York: Atheneum, 1971); and Roland Hallgren, *The Good Things in Life: A Study of the Traditional Religious Culture of the Yoruba People* (Löberöd, Sweden: Plus Ultra, 1988).

25. On Ifa and the Babalawo, see Wande Abimbola, *Ifa: An Exposition of Ifa Literary Corpus* (Ibadan: University Press, 1976).

26. See W. R. Bascom and M. J. Herskovits, eds., *Continuity and Change in African Cultures* (Chicago: University of Chicago Press, 1959); and Ulli Beir, *The Return of the Gods: The Sacred Art of Susanne Wenger* (Oxford: Oxford University Press, 1959).

27. See W. T. Davis, "Our Image of God and Our Image of Women," *Orita: Ibadan Journal of Religious Studies* 10, no. 2 (Dec. 1976): 123–28.

28. See Joseph M. Murphy and Mei-Mei Sanford, eds., *Osun across the Waters: A Yoruba Goddess in Africa and the Americas* (Bloomington: Indiana University Press, 2001).

29. Sandra T. Barnes, ed., *Africa's Ogun: Old World and New,* 2nd ed. (Bloomington: Indiana University Press, 1997).

30. Idowu, *African Traditional Religion: A Definition,* 205.

31. The most notable example has been the 1977 Second World Black and African Festival of Arts and Culture (FESTAC) held in Lagos, Nigeria.

32. K. O. K. Onyioha, *African Godianism* (New York: self published, 1980).

33. Among others, see Kolawole Komolafe, *African Traditional Religion: Understanding Ogboni Fraternity* (Lagos: self-published, 1995); Philip John Neimark, *The Way of the Orisa: Empowering Your Life through the Ancient African Religion of Ifa* (New York: Harper San Francisco, 1993); and Afolabi A. Epega and Philip Neimark, *The Sacred Ifa Oracle* (New York: Athelia Henrietta Press, 1995).

34. Parrinder, *African Traditional Religion,* 146.

35. See Kofi Asare Opoku, *West African Traditional Religion* (Accra: FEP International Private, 1978), 78–79; J. O. Awolalu, "The African Traditional View of Man," *Orita: Ibadan Journal of Religious Studies* 6, no. 2 (1972); and Bryan Wilson, *Religion in Sociological Perspectives* (Oxford: Oxford University Press, 1982), 52.

36. Quoted in William Finnegan, *A Complicated War: The Harrowing of Mozambique* (Berkeley and Los Angeles: University of California Press, 1992), 125–26.

37. Stephen L. Weigert, *Traditional Religion and Guerilla Warfare in Modern Africa* (New York: St. Martin's Press, 1996), 2. For another useful work that demonstrates the power of community consciousness, if not fully falling on tradition, see Jonathon Glassman, *Feasts and Riot: Revelry, Rebellion, and Popular Consciousness on the Swahili Coast, 1856–1888* (Portsmouth, N.H.: Heinemann, 1995).

38. See Thomas Hodgkin, *Nationalism in Colonial Africa* (London: Muller, 1956).

39. Weigert, *Traditional Religion,* 97.

40. Ibid., 106.

41. For details, see Toyin Falola, *Nationalism and African Intellectuals* (Rochester, N.Y.: University of Rochester Press, 2001).

42. See Theophile Obenga, *African Philosophy in World History* (Princeton, N.J.: Sungai, 1998); and J. A. Sofola, *African Culture and the African Personality* (Ibadan, Nigeria: African Resources Publishers, 1973).

43. On the nature of conversion and the impact on indigenous religions, see Robin Horton, "African Coversion," *Africa* 41 (1971): 81–108.

44. See Eugenia W. Herbert, *Iron, Gender, and Power: Rituals of Transformation in African Societies* (Bloomington: Indiana University Press, 1993).

45. See Barry Hallen, *The Good, The Bad and the Beautiful: Discourse about Values in Yoruba Culture* (Bloomington: Indiana University Press, 2000).

46. See John A. A. Ayoade and Adigun A. B. Agbaje, eds., *African Traditional Political Thought and Institutions* (Lagos: Center for Black and African Arts and Civilization, 1989); Andrew Apter, *Black Critics and Kings: The Hermeneutics of Power in Yoruba Society* (Chicago: University of Chicago Press, 1992); and John Pemberton III and Funso S. Afolayan, *Yoruba Sacred Kingship: "A Power Like That of the Gods"* (Washington D.C.: Washington Institution Press, 1996).

47. See Carolyn Hamilton, *Terrific Majesty: The Powers of Shaka Zulu and the Limits of Historical Invention* (Cambridge, Mass.: Harvard University Press, 1998).

48. See Pauline E. Peters, *Dividing The Commons: Politics, Policy, and Culture in Botswana* (Charlottesville: University Press of Virginia, 1994); A. Fiona D. Mackenzie, *Land, Ecology and Resistance in Kenya, 1880–1952* (Portsmouth, N.H.: Heinemann, 1998).

49. See John William Johnson, Thomas A. Hale, and Stephen Belcher, eds., *Oral Epics From Africa: Vibrant Voices from a Vast Continent* (Bloomington and Indianapolis: Indiana University Press, 1997); and John Miller Chernoff, *African Rhythm and African Sensibility: Aesthetics and Social Action in African Musical Idioms* (Chicago: University of Chicago Press, 1979).

50. On a number of key features of material culture, see Mary Jo Arnoldi, Christraud M. Geary, and Kris L. Hardhi, eds., *African Material Culture* (Bloomington: Indiana University Press, 1996).

51. Pemberton III and Afolayan, *Yoruba Sacred Kingship,* 205.

9

ENGLISH OR ENGLISHES? THE POLITICS OF LANGUAGE AND THE LANGUAGE OF POLITICS

"FOLLOW THE RIVER AND FIND THE SEA."
—A SWAHILI PROVERB

The telling has not been easy. One has to convey in a language that is not one's own the spirit that is one's own. One has to convey the various shades and omission of a certain thought movement that looks maltreated in an alien language. I use the word "alien," yet English is not really an alien language to us. It is the language of our intellectual make-up. We are all instinctively bilingual, many of us writing in our own language and in English. . . . We cannot write like the English. We should not. We cannot write only as Indians. We have grown to look at the large world as part of us. Our method of expression therefore has to be a dialect which will someday prove to be distinctive and colorful as the Irish or the American. Time alone will justify it.[1]

The focus of this chapter is on the use of the English language and its intersections with culture, elitism, and power. Most of the broad statements should be applicable to the majority of African countries, although the data is drawn from Nigeria. To follow the use of English in Africa is like following a river that may lead to a sea. We are dealing with a situation of linguistic and cultural diversity—while English is the official language, the majority of the population uses a host of other languages to conduct their various daily activities.

As with the rise of an educated elite, we are dealing with a "new" phenomenon dating only from the mid-nineteenth century. The English language, in its association with the educated elite, developed slowly. For most of the twentieth century it was a language of the minority and it was a powerful vehicle to express nationalism during the colonial era. As the majority of the population was disempowered by the inability to use the English language, they formulated alternative strategies of survival, which included the evolution of a new form of English, the Nigerian pidgin or "rotten English." Thus, the space became crowded with the use of not one English, but various Englishes. The emerging elite and their use of Englishes also benefited the mother tongues. Not only were vocabularies invented for local languages that transformed them into written forms, nationalism began to empower them by advocating their increasing use in the school system and, after independence, by reducing the role of English as the official language in preference for local ones. The search for an alternative or complement to English as the lingua franca has become a political issue. To recapitulate before embarking on the details, the chapter will touch upon the following issues:

1. the rise of the use of English language, and its Africanization;
2. the elements of Nigerian English;
3. the development of the Nigerian pidgin; and
4. the search for a lingua franca.

The most common debates relating to the four itemized issues, always posed and answered in a polemical manner, include the following:

1. Is English the country's official language?
2. Is English a lingua franca?
3. In what ways and manner should English interact with the hundreds of Nigerian languages?
4. If the majority of those who use English as a second language may never be proficient in it, are there alternative languages to be developed, such as pidgin, or should the various mistakes in English be accommodated as a Nigerian variant?
5. How can Nigeria create a linguistic identity if language is central to the identity of many nations? Would the search for a linguistic identity not move in the direction of rejecting English? How can Nigeria enjoy "linguistic autonomy" if the English language was originally imposed on it and the country is yet to develop conditions that will empower it to either choose an alternative language or market a variant of English that it eventually finds acceptable?
6. If there is one acceptable international English, should Nigerian English be recognized in the schools and by examination bodies? If we

Figure 11. Language as a sales strategy. Accra, Ghana.

can speak of "Irish English," "American English," and "British English," why can't we speak of "Nigerian English"? If Nigerians depart from a so-called model (e.g., American English or British English) are they enriching English or bastardizing it? This is an issue that even the International Corpus of English,[2] which aims to develop some universal or acceptable standards, may not be able to handle.

7. To what extent does the use of English in the country prevent a "linguistic democracy," that is, create a situation whereby millions of people are excluded from active participation in public and civic duties because they cannot use English, since not all Nigerians have the opportunity to learn English or attain competence in it?

The History and Impact of English in Nigeria

As is to be expected, the spread of English was associated with the expansion of the West in Africa, beginning from the late fifteenth century onward. By the fifteenth century, a rather small circle of traders along the West African coast began to utilize some words in English. The effective beginning of the use of the language in Nigeria can be dated to the mid-nineteenth century, when European missionaries and officials began to arrive in large numbers. As formal schools were established, the English language became one of the most important subjects, with syllabi designed to teach communicative skills and an education based on European classical traditions.

The spread of Western education assumed a rapid pace in the twentieth century. In the south, Western schools proliferated. Developments in the north were slower, as Islamic leaders regarded Christian missionaries as a threat to their religion. However, after 1940, the north changed its attitude and also began to sponsor English in the schools. When power began to pass to Nigerians from the 1950s onward, the spread of Western schools and English became one of the most successful achievements of the era. English eventually became the official language, and it has had to interact with local languages.

The impact of English cannot be overemphasized, as it permeates various aspects of society. Originally, it began as the language of commerce, a role that has ensured for it a permanent place in society. Language and culture often spread together. In this case, English was the agent that introduced Western forms in food, attire, sports, and entertainment. Very quickly, the distinction between the city and the village, the educated and the uneducated revolved around the issue of language and culture. As villages and the uneducated represented "backwardness" or "primitiveness," the acquisition of English and European ways of life came to represent "civilization" and "modernization."

Moreover, English became the language of both the mission and the school system. The pioneers used it as a medium to teach and also as a curricular subject. Both roles have survived, even when local languages are not ignored, especially at the elementary level. Even in the north, where Hausa served as the medium in lower elementary grades, English has become important as a medium. At the secondary level, a pass in English is mandatory to secure jobs or pursue higher studies.

As the British established their political influence in Lagos in the mid-nineteenth century and subsequently imposed colonial rule, English became the language of administration and politics. For Nigerians to participate in the new institutions and agencies of government and change, the acquisition of English became a key requirement. Thus, English became associated with the needs and register of change, progress, and development. English became one of the determinants for establishing a new stratification and new hierarchies, with the result that members of the educated elite enjoyed greater visibility and dominance.

The link between English and religion remains. While Nigerian languages are the choice in many churches, English has not been abandoned for worship and sermons in many cities and in various heterogeneous settings such as college campuses and police barracks. European and American evangelists and their Nigerian followers preach in English; their sermons are quickly translated to a Nigerian language, often in a rather literal manner.

English, Elite Power, and Politics

For the emerging educated elite, English has been not just a language for communication, but also a source of power. It enhances political participation, the cultivation of elitism, and the articulation of the ideas of nationalism and progress. In other words, English facilitates self-definition and politics. The ability to communicate in English became one of the defining characteristics of this elite. And during the nineteenth century, many also adopted an English lifestyle.

During colonial rule, the elite profited from English by using it to express political demands. Nationalism and the fight for independence involved the use of English to make various demands, to formulate new constitutions, to organize political parties, and to develop new media outlets to express political positions and publicize manifestos.

The northern elite was slow in accepting this language. Originally, it believed that English and European culture would undermine the Islamic religion and the power base of its intelligentsia.[3] However, by the 1950s, the Islamic elite had come to accept the dominant role that English and Western education would play in the modernization of Nigeria. The northern elite also formed political parties and worked toward the expansion of modern education, not only to empower their citizens but to prevent domination by southerners.

In the 1940s, when nationalism intensified, the use of "bookish English" became a weapon to mobilize the masses. When Nnamdi Azikiwe joined the political landscape, part of his fame derived from his complicated and convoluted expressions. Azikiwe went back to the Victorian style of the nineteenth century to dress short statements in inflated language.

Soon after independence, the country began to be governed by the military, essentially comprising officers who were less educated than the leading politicians they overthrew. While they could conduct private transactions in Hausa and other local languages, they were more likely to communicate with people in English. A revised constitution designed to transfer power from the military to civilians assumed that federal legislators would at least be proficient enough to communicate in English. As of now, between 20 and 30 percent of the population can use English very well. The qualification for this social group includes the ability to use English with an acceptable level of competence. The connection between language and power is not peculiar to Nigeria: in other multi-ethnic African societies with many languages, those who control the use of European languages tend to argue that they are modernizers.[4]

English is much more visible in the legal system, the media, and the formal sectors of society. The print media with a national or regional orientation is usually in English. The legal codes are written in English, and the official language in many formal courts is English. Even where a Nigerian language is used for official transactions, most minutes are recorded in English. Candidates seeking elective offices may speak in a Nigerian language for effect, but they know that they have to translate what they say into English if they want the media to report them. Older and newer cities, becoming more and more homogenous, depend partly on English for their diverse dwellers and outsiders to communicate, especially in market situations.

The Africanization of English

English has been Africanized by way of innovations, experimentations, code-switching, departures in themes and styles, the impact of culture, and the numerous limitations and challenges of bilingualism. Nigerian English can claim to be part of what is now called "world Englishes."[5] Time and again, the "nativization" of English is made clear in many African literary texts. Chinua Achebe's work has been used as an example. Qouting from a commonly cited novel, the *Arrow of God* (1964), Achebe starts with an Africanized presentation of a man who wanted to send his son to church:

> I want one of my sons to join this people and be my eyes there. If there is nothing in it you will come back. But if there is something there you will bring back my share. The world is like a Mask dancing. If you want to see it well, you do not stand in one place. My spirit tells me that those who do not befriend the white man today will be saying, "had we known" tomorrow.

Then, Achebe, writing as a commentator and using non-Nigerian English, recreates the same idea in another way:

> I am sending you as my representative among these people—just to be on the safe side in case the new religion develops. One has to move with the times or else one is left behind. I have a hunch that those who fail to come to terms with the white man will regret their lack of foresight.[6]

And he compares both statements by saying that:

> The material is the same. But the form of the one is in character and the other is not. It is largely a matter of instinct but judgement into it.[7]

Language usage has taken many forms when expressing creativity, as the Indian scholar in the opening remark has noted: to create an independent canon that is both "decolonized and demythologized"; to combine two or more languages, as in pidgin discussed below; and to write English in the idioms of local languages, as in the works of Amos Tutuola.[8]

If the initial goal of the European missionaries was for Africans to receive minimal education and acquire basic use of the language, Nigerians turned English into an expression of political power. It became a vehicle to create new cultures and to impose the context of multilingualism and pluralism on a foreign language. English has had to relate with hundreds of local languages, complementing and competing with them. The need for language choice and policy inevitably arises.

As English inevitably interacted with African languages, a "nativization process" began, leading to what can be called "Nigerian English." Code-switching and loan words are manifestations of this "nativization." Two forms of "nativization" are prevalent. The first is lexical and structural (including syntactical, morphological, and phonological) features present in Nigerian languages are imposed on English. Second, the creative use of English is dependent on the reservoir of knowledge derived from local languages and culture.

A variety of Englishes has developed over time, sometimes discussed in relation to a so-called standard model. Not all variants of English are intelligible to so-called international speakers or "native speakers." Some variants have emerged in the process of interacting with one or more of the over four hundred local languages. Nigerian English can also include grammatically correct usages that employ local words as part of code-switching: "they" instead of "he" or "she" to denote respect for an elderly person; and the use of gender-neutral pronoun such as "they" when "he" or "she" is meant. As many cultures have no words for uncle, nephews, nieces, and cousins, the language of sibling (sister, brother) or "relatives" may be used instead. Prepositions may be incorrect, and the use of definite and indefinite articles can also be wrong.

Even when the English is correct by any standard, there is the issue of accent. "S" can be pronounced as "sh" in many settings and "th" as "d" in some others. There are identifiable Nigerian accents, which may be misinterpreted by non-native speakers as mispronounciation or the bad use of words and phrases. To further complicate the matter, Nigerian accents are heterogeneous. Very clearly, the Hausa, Igbo, and Yoruba pronounce many words in different ways.[9]

How the variants should be developed, especially in schools, has been a problem. Some policymakers assume that there can be only one standard English and that the variants represent errors which should be corrected. Both the public and specialists think otherwise, actually insisting that so-called errors should be acceptable. Indeed, the corpus of Nigerian Englishes is being gathered, in part to avoid penalizing students in major examinations. Ultimately, such local differences will constitute the formation of grammars and dictionaries that can standardize Nigerian English.

Essentially, three principal forms of Nigerian English have been identified: Contact English, Victorian English, and School English.[10] Contact English evolved through a creolization process involving the use of "broken English" or pidgin. "Broken English" is an attempt to grapple with the use of English with a limited vocabulary and without following the standard rules of grammar. It has been identified with coastal Nigerians who came in contact and wanted to communicate with English-speaking people. While it has been superseded by pidgin, it is still used in plays to depict local people who are fascinated with English and want to impress people with their false competence in it. Words are elongated for effect (e.g., "surprise" can become "surprisation"), plurals are confused (e.g., "he have" instead of "he has"), verbs are swapped with nouns, and pronounciations are distorted (e.g., "fader" instead of "father").[11]

With respect to Victorian English, Ayo Bamgbose associated this with the English adopted by the mid-nineteenth-century Lagos elite, whose culture has been brilliantly analyzed by Michael Echeruo. These were pioneer professionals, many of whom were liberated slaves returning from Brazil. In Lagos, they constituted the pioneer educated elite, an "upper class of civilized Africans."[12] In their language choice and style, they displayed erudition, familiarity with the classics, use of compound words, and long and convoluted sentences. Bamgbose points out that the tradition actually survived the colonial period. Just to take one example, drawn from the well-known Onitsha market literature, *Veronica My Daughter:*[13]

I must advise you Madam to let your conversational communication possess a cherified consciousness and cogency, let your entamporaness discernment and unpermited expectation have intangibility, veroness and versity. Avoid pomposity, proticity, verbosity and rapacity.[14]

Yet another example:

As I was decending from declivity yesterday, with such an excessive velocity, I suddenly lost the centre of my gravity and was precipitated on [a] macamadized throughfare.[15]

The third variant of Nigerian English is School English or the English of the school. As has already been pointed out, it began with the missionaries during the nineteenth century, based on the use of the hymnal, sermons, and the primer. The assumption was that the "natives" must be introduced to language in its basic, simplified elements. Sentences are short and straight to the point.

The consensus among linguists is that the current standard Nigerian English is derived from a combination of the three varieties. The emerging characteristics of this standard Nigerian English include the following:[16]

1. linguistic nativization: "This includes substitution of Nigerian language vowels and consonants for English ones, replacement of stress by tone, pluralization of some non-count nouns, introduction of culture-specific vocabulary items, back formation, semantic shift, different verb-preposition combinations."[17]
2. pragmatic nativization: "The rules of language use typical of English in native situations have been modified under pressure from the cultural practices of the Nigerian environment. Hence Nigerian English replicates numerous indigenous greetings: *Welcome, Well done, Sorry, Thanks for yesterday, Safe journey, How? Till tomorrow*, etc. Modes of address are formalized to reflect social status and age, with the result that offense may be taken if multiple titles (e.g., Alhaji Honourable Chief Dr. A) are abridged and someone addressed as 'My dear father' may be no more than an elder in one's village, not in the least bit related to the speaker."[18]
3. creative nativization: "It manifests itself in two ways: first, expressions are coined to reflect the Nigerian experience or world view. Expressions such as to *take in* (to become pregnant), *been-to* (one who has travelled abroad, particularly to England), *sufferhead* (a luckless person), *arrangee* (someone employed in illegal currency deals), *four-one-*

nine (a dupe) are coined. Second, authentic Nigerian native idiom is translated into English in such a way as to reflect the mood of the situation or character."[19]

4. drawing from the Bible: Many phrases and words are drawn from the Bible, and used in literary discourse as proverbs and idioms for emphasis, and to make arguments.[20]

5. the influence of "Americanism": Owing to the growing influence of the American media, movies, videos, and the Internet, American vocabulary and expressions are spreading, with a number of American ones now either being interchanged with Nigerian-English words or being accepted as alternative choices. However, teachers still have to contend with what is right or wrong. For instance, "all manuals on English teaching in Nigeria insist on the infinitive with *to* in such expressions as *help to train, enable someone to achieve,* and that it is wrong to say *help train,* and *enable someone achieve*; but these stigmatized forms are correct American English."[21]

6. descriptive labels may overlap: "Among such labels are overclarification or tautologization, rationalization, cross-interference or contamination, phrasal contraction, lexical metathesis or free collocations, semantic generalization, agglutination, arbitrariness (for example, in the selection of articles and signs), indiscrimination (for example, between formality and informality), transitivization and intransitivization."[22]

As to how to treat the acceptability of Nigerian English, opinions are divided, and the politics of what English to teach in Nigerian schools will never be easy to resolve. A tiny elite will continue to push for a so-called international variety—the variety used by the British Broadcasting Corporation or another acceptable "international model." However, the majority will opt for the promotion of "Nigerian English" with a recognizable vocabulary and grammar. The various examination boards in the country will have no choice but to accept the peculiarities of English as a second language. English lacks a so-called international norm. Indeed, it may be argued that its success derives in part from its great flexibility, the opportunity for various places in different parts of the globe to adapt the language to their own needs.

Written English may be easier to understand than spoken English. The oral English in Durham, New Hampshire, and that in Ibadan, Nigeria, will continue to differ, even be mutually unintelligible in some circumstances. But the vocabulary of English can be shared by a greater number of people, even if various national forms do emerge. A number of researchers are doing "corpus research," collecting data on "variants" used locally in Nigeria, and comparing them to model forms. A few among them have been reaching the conclusion that the "variants" should be acceptable.

English and Nigerian Languages

Nigerian languages have also benefited from English, as they have borrowed many words such as technical terms, dates, and names for imported objects. Bilingualism has become common, especially among the educated elite. This in turn has made code-switching much more widespread all over the country: English can be inserted into local languages and vice-versa. A number of loan words have become so indigenized that even locals do not know that they are foreign. Some others may be of more recent origin and recognizable, such as the Yoruba words for computer (*komputa*), television (*telifison*), tailor (*telo*), and radio (*redio*). Technical words tend to be loan words, such as the components of a car, train, or computer. Among other major impacts of English are:

1. The prevalence of "English-induced structures."
2. The sound-systems of a number of local languages are modified in bilingual situations, "leading, for example, to the introduction of non-indigenous sound patterns, e.g., English 'p' for Yoruba 'kp' in *palo* (parlour), *pepa* (paper), *peeni* (pen), or English consonant clusters in place of insertion of Yoruba epenthetic vowels: *minista* instead of *minisita* (minister), *bredi* instead of *buredi* (bread), *boos* instead of *boosi* (bus)."[23]
3. Code-mixing: English words can be inserted into a Nigerian language syntax. Ayo Banjo and others have studied this usage, noting how English syntax structures are even adapted to the Nigerian language. English loan words are used in a way that conforms to the syntax of the Nigerian language. To be specific: "an English modifier-noun structure is converted to Yoruba non-qualifier structure (e.g. *my cousin* becomes *cousin mi*), the past tense morpheme is dropped from English verbs (e.g. *he transferred his services* becomes *o transfer services e*) and Yoruba aspect markers are transferred to English verbs (e.g. *they are planning to go to London* becomes *won n plan ati lo si London*)."[24]

Code-mixing is the most commonly observed of the three, used extensively in informal and day-to-day communications in various settings. Code-mixing involves borrowed lexical items and vocabulary, so that two languages or two codes are used to produce a message. The grammar of the indigenous language is adjusted to accommodate the foreign elements of English, but the deviation from what is standard is clearly observable. These borrowed words may actually become, over time, part of the indigenous vocabulary. A few words, phrases, or terminologies in English can be inserted into any Nigerian language. For instance, it is common to hear "bawo ni matter yen"—"how is that matter?" A bilingual or multilingual person may switch from one language to the other, drawing from the following: part of an English sentence (e.g., "examine the matter" or "consider all the circumstances"); one word as verb, noun, or adjective (e.g., milk, computer, honestly, brilliant); and discourse markers (e.g., immediately, according to). Even speakers of the same language can code-mix in some circumstances: if certain words are necessary to clarify a point; when they use different dialects of the same language and code-mixing will facilitate understanding; if the facilities in their own languages are limited for what they want to say; if speakers want to use certain words in English to show status or disguise their inability to actually use English on an impressive scale; or if there is a lack of fluency in any of the two languages being code-mixed. Although the advocates of the use of standard English or Nigerian languages see code-mixing as bad, it does expand the opportunity to use language in a more creative or accessible manner. Also, it enriches the dominant language. However, there is no consistency to a code-mixed language as two people may not use one sentence or code-mix in the same way.

The Nigerian languages have benefited from their contacts and interactions with English. While borrowing words from English to adapt to modern society, Nigerian languages have retained their syntax. The major Nigerian languages will continue to expand, as more bilingual and multilingual speakers are created and as they attain greater sophistication in research and teaching at all levels of the education system.[25] At the local levels and in day-to-day transactions in many parts of the country, the language of choice will continue to be a Nigerian language. Other than in formal settings, Nigerian languages are very much in use on college campuses, government agencies, and businesses. Indeed, it is unusual for members of the same language group to converse in a language other than their own. Situations which call for the use of English tend to be formal. Where two people can use the same language (say, Yoruba or Hausa) and they speak in English, it may be an indication of tension or conflict between them. Among the Ibiobio, it may mean that one of the parties wants to tell a lie! In the cities, where multilingualism is the rule, people use English only when it is the only appropriate language to use. In the north, for instance, it is more than clear that the preference is for Hausa, even when both parties are able to communicate in English. Where migrants from the same area live in the same neighborhood, as in the "Hausa Quarters" in the south, the major language of communication among the members is their "mother tongue," and they use English or pidgin only in transactions with non-members.

It is also clear that some features of English and Nigerian languages do differ. Nigerian languages have the features of the "mother tongue": in a monolingual context, the "mother tongue" meets most of the needs of the speaker, it is the most connected with culture, and it facilitates social and occupational requirements. On the other hand, English is a "second language": the user conducts only part of her/his communication in English; and most people have to go to school in order to acquire the requisite skills in the language.

The Pidgin

Pidgin started as a language of oral communication among people with limited or no formal education, and blossomed into a vehicle to express humor in the media. Later, it was extensively used for news broadcasts, and more recently to express very serious ideas in poems, books, drama, and other important media. It is a combination of a local language with English—a creolization which can produce its own speakers and set of rules. Words are constantly borrowed from English, but packaged in ways that are different from English. The lexis may be expanded to cope with words that do not exist in local languages, like computer and biochemistry. English syntax may be appropriated for effect or simply to make sense. For instance, "make sure" becomes "mek una sure se." Pidgin can be described as a language in the process of creolization. After creolization, will pidgin de-creolize to become a language in competition with English?

As "proper English" spread, so too did pidgin. In written forms, its use was rather slow. An eighteenth-century document by Antera Duke is perhaps the first indication that English could be combined with a local language. As with other pidgins, it probably started as a "makeshift" language between two people who used different languages. Perhaps the vocabulary was limited in the beginning, but sufficient to conduct trade and a minimal level of interaction. It was perhaps the first opportunity by many Nigerians living along the coast to acquire some English words: in other words, to embark upon a process of learning another language. What emerged as "Nigerian pidgin" is a language with a Nigerian grammar and an English vocabulary. The original areas of use were Warri, Sapele, Calabar, and Port Harcourt, all areas along the coast. We may never know the history of the emergence of pidgin, but we do know that it became fairly established by the first half of the twentieth century. In the 1950s and 1960s, Frank Aig-Imoukhuede and Dennis Osadebay, two pioneer modern poets, used pidgin to compose a few poems. Soft-sell gossip publications, such as the *Lagos Weekend*, realized that pidgin gave them greater sales figures.

If pidgin started as the "English" of the underclass, its influence began to spread and become noticeable from the 1970s onward. In ways that may appear rather curious, members of the supposedly educated class, notably university students and civil servants in many parts of the south, also began to use it. In one sense, such an extensive use of pidgin is an indication of the failure of a new generation to use the English language in a proper manner. In other words, the correctness in the use of pidgin disguises the failure to be effective in English. Unlike with English, the rules of pidgin are less restrictive, can be broken without sanctions, and the user is not stigmatized on the basis of accent or word mingling. Since the mid-1980s, the quality of education has declined, even at the university level. From the mid-nineteenth century to the mid-twentieth century, the ability to speak correct English was associated with the educated elite. Indeed, the very definition of appropriate English was associated with them. At the close of the twentieth century and today, that association is no longer appropriate, as more and more educated people take to the use of pidgin.

However, if a number of elite members have taken refuge in pidgin to hide their incompetence in English, there is a tiny group that has turned to pidgin not because their English is limited but because they see it as the best means to reach a larger audience. Well-known poets, singers, and playwrights adopted the use of pidgin to communicate their ideas. Fela Anikulapo-Kuti, the country's music legend, used nothing other than pidgin. Ken Saro Wiwa, who became internationally famous following his execution by the military regime of General Abacha in 1995, also put pidgin to good use. Even in dignifying pidgin, its "ruralness" is always emphasized, as it is used to represent the voice of the semiliterate or illiterate. When educated people use it, it is sometimes to indicate a free or informal setting. Among the popular works in pidgin are those by M. J. Vasta, F. Aig-Imoukhuede, and Ken Saro-Wiwa,[26] popular plays include those by Tunde Fatunde,[27] and a book of proverbs in pidgin has also been published.[28] In these and other creative works, pidgin enables the author who is competent in English to use pidgin for humor, depict so-called illiterate characters, ridicule people, and make comments on power.

Pidgin has been successful in competing with English in different settings. First, in heterogeneous cities with representatives of various local languages, pidgin has been a better unifier than English. Thus, one can get by in Port Harcourt, Lagos, Sapele, Abuja, and Warri, to mention some large cities, by being able to use pidgin.

Second, in the electronic media, most notably the radio, the use of pidgin has ensured lively programs, grassroots ideas, and mass appeal. It sustains interesting drama series and documentaries. If acting in English requires too much memorization, the use of pidgin enables actors to be spontaneous, to add to the scripts as they go through them. State radio and television stations, notably in the southeast, use pidgin to broadcast government programs. "How Una See Am?"[29] is one such television program on public opinion. Public announcements and propaganda are often conducted in pidgin, as in the following examples:

Pidgin   Help Nigeria make your life better
English   Help Nigeria to make your life better
Pidgin   Oya! Quicki comot dat rice, sell am make all man see wack
English   Resolve now! Stop hoarding rice; sell them so that all can eat.

Third, pidgin is the language that sustains communication at the lowest rungs of the ladder in the civil service, judiciary, army, police, and government agencies.

Should pidgin be recognized as an official variant of English or an independent language? There are those who argue that a pure pidgin can be developed, with rules that all users will respect.[30] Some have even gone further to suggest that it should be adopted as the country's official language, or used temporarily as the official language pending the ratification of another one, because more people are able to speak pidgin than English. In other words, it can be treated as a "national language" since its use is more widespread among people of various ethnic groups. There are critics of pidgin, though, some saying that since it is not widely used in many parts of the north or in villages, it should not be promoted. A number of educators complain that pidgin stands in the way of the correct learning of English, makes it hard to distinguish the educated from the illiterate, and is inadequate to express great literary ideas. Linguists remain divided on the status of pidgin. To B. O. Elugbe and A. P. Omamor, it is a unique language, different from English.[31] Indeed, there are those who can use only pidgin, rather than English, as their mother tongue,. In this case, they can be treated as different from bilingual speakers who can use pidgin and English. Nevertheless, there are many English words in pidgin, as well as extensive code-switching. A. Adetugbo would argue otherwise, saying that pidgin is too closely tied to English; in other words, it is a variant of English.[32] Agreeing with this position, another linguist, E. Bamiro, has concluded that "it is a basilectal [i.e., less desirable] form" of English.[33] One thing that is clear is that in its written form, especially among educated writers, pidgin reads like English, which strongly suggests a process of decreolization.

The Politics of Lingua Franca

The role of English and the search for a local substitute have been the subject of protracted debate. This often cantankerous argument sometimes moves into the realm of politics and public policy. The problem is that Nigeria is a multiethnic and diverse society with hundreds of languages and ethnic groups. This heterogeneity creates the need to resolve a number of complicated issues in politics, culture, language, and development. Language resources are very much connected to culture, identity, national cohesion, and development. To manage these resources, clear policies have to be formulated. In Nigeria, many of the policies relate to language choice, the development of "national languages," and the place of English. We lack accurate figures on the number of Nigerians who can use English to communicate on a day-by-day basis. However, it is clear that in many areas where the population is homogenous, people tend to be monolingual. The argument of those who are opposed to English as a lingua franca is that the monolingual population is excluded from aspects of culture and development that are dependent on English.

To some critics, English is the language of domination, colonialism, and imperialism. At one level, it allows the West to dominate Africa. At another level, it enables an elite to dominate the country. Many defenders of culture and tradition think that the use of English is undermining the preservation and practices of home-grown institutions. As a fundamental agent in the creation of an elite, English is blamed for dividing society. Some of these critics call for a war against English in order to prevent the extinction of Nigerian languages, preserve the country's cultural heritage, and develop the country. They will even go further to say that the use of English causes the alienation of Nigerians from their culture, assimilates them to a foreign culture in a subservient manner, and prevents the socialization of Nigerian youth into their own culture. This cluster of "schizophrenic arguments" is based on fear: the fear that English makes Nigerians insecure in its use and adoption and that it represents a danger to indigenous resources and creativity.

A "technical" argument has also been made against English: the majority of non-native speakers can never be competent in it. The decline of teaching and competence in the use of English cannot be denied. This can be attributed to the decline in education standards in general, the lack of teaching resources, the limited opportunity to use English outside the school system, and the low morale among the population as graduates find it hard to get jobs. This argument relates to "linguistic democracy," which is that a high number of Nigerians cannot use English to empower themselves or become more competitive in the market place.

A prominent literary figure, Ngugi wa Thiong'o, has waded into the debate, calling the use of English in the first place an abnormality that is so damaging in its impact that Africans now ignore their own languages to generate relevant literature.[34] He is not alone in making a case for the use of African languages to produce literary works for Africans, although most of the celebrated writers continue to use European languages.[35] The principal justification is usually nationalism: the language most suitable for Africans should be the one their ancestors "invented."

There are those who speak in defense of English,[36] arguing that English cannot be treated as a mere guest. Some tend to suggest that there is no useful language to adopt for the nation other than English. Thus, suggestions are made to strengthen the teaching of English, based on the assumption that Nigerians actually do not have much of a choice other than to use this language for interaction, mobility, and globalization. To many, English is crucial to the country's development, for it makes it easy to import ideas in various areas, most notably in science, computers, and engineering.

There are those who argue for complementarity, that is, the promotion of English and local languages at the same time. While not necessarily dismissing many of the nationalist claims of those opposed to English, they merely argue that local African languages can be promoted and English can be "tamed" to serve the same or similar purpose as the mother tongues. To cite Chinua Achebe once again:

> Those of us who have inherited the English Language may not be in a position to appreciate the value of the inheritance. Or we may go on resenting it

because it came as part of a package deal which included many other items of doubtful value and the positive atrocity of racial arrogance and prejudice which may yet set the world on fire. But let us not in rejecting the evil throw out the good with it. . . . [T]he African writer should aim to use English in a way that brings out his message best without altering the language to the extent that its value as a medium of international exchange will be lost. He should aim at fashioning out an English which is at once universal and able to carry his peculiar experience. . . . I have in mind here the writer who has something new, something different to say. The nondescript writer has little to tell us, anyway, so he might as well tell it in conventional language and get it over with. If I may use an extravagant simile, he is like a man offering a small, nondescript routine sacrifice for which a chick or less will do. A serious writer must look for an animal whose blood can match the power of the offering.[37]

The proponents of a bilingual approach argue that the use of Nigerian languages is best in rural areas, and English should not even be used to announce government policies or assist the farmers with new ideas. Similarly, leading educators argue that Nigerian languages should be used as the medium of instruction in the early years. "It is our thesis," argued A. Babs Fafunwa, a leading educator and one-time minister of education, "that if the Nigerian child is to be encouraged from the start to develop curiosity, manipulative ability, good spatial visualization, spontaneous flexibility, originality, initiative, industry, manual dexterity and mechanical comprehension, he should acquire these skills and attitudes through his mother tongue which is the most natural way to learn. This is the way the children in Europe and America learn."[38]

The place of English and Nigerian languages in the country has raised a variety of issues, some even calling it a dilemma of language choice. Considerations involve the interjection of nationalism and ethnicity, and sometimes revive the complicated politics of division in the country. From the point of view of the government wishing to avoid political disharmony, the country has to be multilingual, and its policies and programs must reflect this reality. However, there are those who argue that English should be the only official language. Others argue that the three most widely spoken Nigerian languages—Yoruba, Hausa, and Igbo—should become official languages and be vigorously promoted. And still others go further to suggest the adoption of one language, Hausa, as the official language.

Most of the discussions, especially in the media, tend to be highly politicized. The common opinions include the following: that all Nigerian languages be developed, that all the Nigerian languages be officially recognized, and that English be promoted along with all or a few Nigerian languages. Since the promotion of languages ultimately involves the schools, funding considerations (e.g., recruitment of teachers and teaching equipment) mean that not all options can be pursued.

Attacks on the adoption of English as the official language are based on nationalistic and cultural considerations. To those who see English as a colonial language, its continued use has been a reminder of that era and a continuation of Western domination. Thus, they tend to argue that an alternative Nigerian language is desirable, adding that the use of a Nigerian language will promote indigenous cultures, promote intergroup relations, and unite the various parts of the country.[39]

When we leave polemics and considerations based on nationalism aside, there remain problems in the "conversion" of Nigerian languages to "official" ones. Some are technical: not all Nigerian languages have been studied, not all have standard orthographies, and some have not even acquired a written form. To overcome these three problems, the government has to spend more money on language research. There is also the issue of language size and the number of languages. The number is more than 400, and many of these are used by groups with small populations. The most widely used are Yoruba, Hausa, and Igbo, but there is no accurate information on the number of people who communicate in each of them. There are also minority languages spoken by large groups of people, notably Ijo, Edo, Fulfulde, Ibibio, Tiv, Igala, Kanuri, and Nupe. It is likely that 60 percent of the population belongs to the three major language groups, and Hausa probably has the most speakers. In terms of development, the three major languages are the most advanced, including the metalanguage which has been used to write science and mathematics textbooks.

Whether a Nigerian language represents a small or big group, or has technical advantages or not, has not minimized the intense discussion about a lingua franca or the political relevance of language. Most languages do accompany the definition of identity and ethnicity. As each group struggles to maintain its ethnicity and identity, it protects its language and tends to see the choice of another language in schools as an attempt at domination. Minority groups tend to think that the promotion of Hausa, Igbo, and Yoruba is grossly unfair to them. Among the majority groups, each resents any suggestion that a language other than theirs should become the official one. Thus far, there is no indication that the majority of Nigerians will accept any choice made for them by the government.

The answers to minimizing the role of English include the choice of one or more Nigerian languages, the adoption of pidgin, or even the creation of an artificial language. Only a brief review of the various proposals is possible in a short essay. The suggestions on the choice of a Nigerian language vary a great deal. Some want to use a minority language—even one that is yet unwritten—because they think that it will remove the fear of political domination associated with the choice of one of the three major languages. Of the three major Nigerian languages, Hausa is usually mentioned as the most acceptable because more Nigerians use it than any other language.

Pidgin is arguably the most popular choice after the suggestion of the adoption of Hausa. Its advocates say that it is widely used in many parts of the country, no ethnic group can lay claim to it, its grammar and phonology are indigenous, and it is accessible to both the educated and the uneducated. To the critics, pidgin has a limited vocabulary, its orthography is undeveloped, and its use is associated with the poor.

Regarding the adoption of an artificial language, the most creative suggestion has been to collapse many words in all Nigerian languages and use them to create a new orthography and national language. One suggestion is the creation of *Guosa,* a combination of twenty-two Nigerian languages made by one Igbineweka who also created a short dictionary of his new language. Linguists have criticized this for its inadequate vocabulary and absence of rules of grammar. An artificial language is also disconnected from identity and ethnicity.

A minority opinion has gone to the extent of abandoning all Nigerian languages for Swahili, a lingua franca in East Africa. Wole Soyinka argued in 1977 that Swahili was appropriate because it is indigenous to Africa, widely used in East Africa, and its grammar is developed. Not only is the suggestion unpopular, but Swahili is not connected to any identity group in Nigeria. It could be useful as a language for all Africans if there is ever a need to promote continental unity.

Indeed, because of the failure to accept one Nigerian language, the status of English is enhanced—politically, it is a "neutral language," neutral in the sense that it does not belong to any one ethnic group. The most commonly expressed opinion is that English will forever remain a complementary language to the well-established local languages such as Yoruba, Hausa, and Igbo. Policy options tend to be presented as English plus one or more local languages. Advocates of the use of English as a second language believe that both English and local languages must be developed to a level of sophistication in which they will feed one another.

Conclusion

Nigerian English is in the process of creation, an ongoing project. As the "Nigerianization" of English becomes established, the school system will have to respond to it by appropriately rewarding those who are able to adhere to its rules and norms rather than by penalizing students for deviating from so-called "international English." Pidgin will remain a language with revolutionary potential, and it is even now being exported by migrants to the United States and other parts of the world. The domestication of English will continue as Nigerians draw from their enormous resources to create adaptations, even new words. Thus, the form of English may change, if not its status. We are not sure whether Nigerian English will acquire respect within Nigeria and outside the country or whether a general perception will one day emerge that will regard Nigerian English as indigenous.

The government has also been sensitive to the politics of choosing a national language. It has come to accept that English will be the language of business and administration. "The business of the National Assembly," stated the 1979 Constitution, "shall be conducted in English language and in Hausa, Igbo and Yoruba when adequate arrangements have been made there." Nevertheless, it promotes Nigerian languages by allowing the use of Igbo, Yoruba, and Hausa for legislative deliberations, in addition to English. The National Policy on Education insists that Nigerian children should learn at least one major Nigerian language:

> In addition to appreciating the importance of language in the educational process, and as a means of preserving the people's culture, the Government considers it to be in the interest of national unity that each child should be encouraged to learn one of the three major languages other than his own mother tongue. In this connection, the Government considers the three major languages in Nigeria to be Hausa, Igbo and Yoruba.[40]

To further promote Nigerian languages, the policy on education stated that:

> The medium of instruction in pre-primary schools should be the language of the immediate community. In a multi-national school, English may be used as the medium of instruction, but the language of the immediate community should be taught in the spoken form. . . . Government will see to it that the medium of instruction in the primary school is initially the mother tongue or the language of the immediate community, and at a later stage English.[41]

The three major languages are also offered in junior secondary schools, although the representatives of minority groups complain that this is unfair to their own people. At the local levels the languages of an area are used by the government (local, state, and federal) to announce public policies and conduct propaganda. The use of English is unlikely to undermine Nigerian languages and pidgin, and the wise thing to do will be to promote them. When it comes to the formulation of national economic and political policies, conduct of foreign policy, and official meetings, English is the "official language." All the major documents and policies of the government, at different tiers, are written in English.

Other foreign languages are in use, but their numbers are small. French is taught in schools, and in the 1990s, the country made a decision to enhance its status. Nigeria's neighbors are all French-speaking, and it was believed that French would facilitate relations with people in those countries. However, there was a political motive behind the decision. The Abacha regime that made the decision was suffering from international isolation, and it wanted to use the encouragement of the French language to promote relations with France. The other foreign language is Arabic, associated with the spread of Islam. Arabic has been spoken in the north for centuries. Ajami, a combination of Arabic and Hausa, is also used. Arabic is the language of religious instruction and of communication among Islamic scholars. In view of its importance to Islam and the Islamic community, it will continue to be a major language. However, since those who are literate in it cannot compete for the majority of jobs in the formal sector, Arabic poses a limited challenge to English. Indeed, the trend among the current generation of students in Islamic areas is to learn both Arabic to fulfil religious needs, and English to be able to participate in the modern economy and politics.

English, in whatever form, will consolidate itself as a principal language. This consolidation will in part owe to the school system and the advantages conferred by the language. English is both a subject and a medium of instructions in most schools. Although the mother tongue is used in some parts of the country in the early years of elementary education, this is not so in the majority of private schools and cities where the acquisition of English is deemed essential for progress. English is crucial to how the educated elite defines itself—it will remain the language of this elite. As the members of this elite continue to dominate power and bureaucracy, they will ensure that English remains an official language, if only for self-interest.

When we include pidgin as a variety of Nigerian English, it becomes inaccurate to see only the elite as dominating the language space. Even if members of the elite complain about pidgin and other so-called "bad Englishes," the fact is that millions of people are able to communicate in them,[42] and there are scholars who argue that the emphasis on one correct model of English is nothing but an attempt to maintain class dominance.[43]

To reproduce the membership of the elite and connect the country to the outside world, English will continue to be a subject and a medium of instruction in schools. A competitive group of scholars needs it to circulate their ideas beyond the shores of Nigeria and for literary expression. English is also connected to development: it is the language that the politicians of different groups use to communicate and negotiate with one another, on the one hand, and with the public on the other. The spread of powerful media organizations such as cable television's CNN brings information and entertainment from other parts of the world to thousands of Nigerian homes.

Although English spread in Nigeria in the context of colonialism, its retention will be in the context of world trade and politics. To import and export commodities and cultures from other parts of the world, English is crucial to Nigeria. It will remain a major language in Nigeria in the context of multilingualism. The use and teaching of English in Nigeria will always be within these bilingual or multilingual systems, and attempts have to be made to marry both in a creative way. It will remain the "second language" if only for its sociolinguisitic, economic, and pedagogical importance. It will serve the dual function of being a national and international language. The politics of language will be confined to the "national role" of English while that of its international role will be largely uncontested.

Appendix: A Poem in Pidgin

I no Sabi o!

Why you dey ask make I dabaru hin face
Make i biti am so tey make hin kon dey pis for hin niker
Why be say you o, na for katakata, for dabaru na hin you dey chop
Why be say you o, na to faiti finis na for where you dey fat
Why be say you o, to comot happiness for your broder hin belle na
him dey sweet your belle,
No, I no sabi o

Me I no sabi o!
My people dey talk say,
"When we dey cry sebi we dey see."

Abi wai you kom tink say
Na de tin wey make your belle sweet
Na hin go make my belle honey
You tink say
Na di tin wey make rain rain for hammatan
na him go make am rain for rainy season,
Your korokoro eyes no even fit see una nose
No o, I no sabi

Me I no sabi o!
Me know say since wen
Our obodo kontiri dey worker to do good for hin people
Wey he want make life good for Onitsha, Ibadan, for Sokoto
No bi your katakata sef kon jam him leg for ground,
No bi you wei take bad belle kon detroy dis place
Konkobility, now you kom call make I join you
No, no bi me o. I no sabi.

—Abdul-Rasheed Na'Allah[44]

Notes

1. Braj Kachru, "Toward Expanding the English Canon: Raja Rao's 1938 Credo for Creativity," *World Literature Today* 4, no. 4 (1988): 582–86.

2. On this project, see S. Greenbaum, "Standard English and the International Corpus of English," *New Englishes* 1, no. 9 (1990): 79–83.

3. See A. Mazrui, *The Political Sociology of the English Language: An African Perspective* (The Hague: Mouton, 1975), 64–66.

4. See M. Ali Mazrui and Alamin M. Mazrui, *The Power of Babel: Language and Governance in the African Experience* (Chicago: University of Chicago Press, 1998).

5. Braj Kachru, "World Englishes: Approaches, Issues, and Resources," *Language Teaching* 25, no. 1 (1992): 1–4. See also his edited volume, *The Other Tongue: English across Cultures* (Urbana: University of Illinois Press, 1982).

6. Chinua Achebe, *Morning Yet on Creation Day* (London and Ibadan: Heinemann, 1975), 61.

7. Ibid, 62. As quoted in Braj Kachru, Foreword, in *New Englishes: A West African Perspective*, ed. Ayo Bamgbose, Ayo Banjo, and Andrew Thomas (Trenton, N.J.: Africa World Press, 1997), iii–iv.

8. See Amos Tutuola, *The Palm-Wine Drinkard and His Dead Palm-Wine Tapster in the Dead's Town* (London: Faber and Faber, 1952); and his *My Life in the Bush of Ghosts* (London: Faber and Faber, 1955).

9. For examples of how various groups differ in their accents, see E. Dunstan, *Twelve Nigerian Languages: A Handbook on their Sound Systems for Teachers of English* (London: Longman, 1969); and V. O. Awonusi, "Regional Accents and Internal Variability in Nigerian English: A Historical Analysis," *English Studies* 6 (1986): 555–60.

10. See Ayo Bamgbose, "English in the Nigerian Environment," in *New Englishes: A West African Perspective,* ed. Bamgbose, Banjo, and Thomas, 9–26. Yet another set of categories may include the following: Nigerian pidgin, English with a Nigerian accent, and English with a non-Nigerian accent.

11. For examples of "Broken English," see Ken Saro-Wiwa, *Sozaboyy: A Novel in Rotten English* (Port Harcourt, Nigeria: Saros International, 1985).

12. M. J. C. Echeruo, *Victorian Lagos* (London: Macmillan, 1977), 110–11.

13. O. A. Ogali, *Veronica My Daughter* (Ontisha: Appolos Brothers Press, nd.). Quotations cited in Bamgbose, "English in the Nigerian Environment," 18.

14. Spelling errors in the original.

15. Spelling errors in the original.

16. For details, among others, see Ayo Bamgbose, "The English Language in Nigeria," in *The English Language in West Africa,* ed. J. Spencer (London: Longman, 1971); and O. Kujore, *English Usage: Some Notable Nigerian Variations* (Ibadan: Evans, 1985).

17. Bamgbose, "English in the Nigerian Environment," 21.

18. Ibid.

19. Ibid. Bamgbose gives examples from the literary works of Vincent Ike and Chinua Achebe.

20. Ibid, 22. Bamgbose listed a few examples: "the evening is far spent, sufficient unto the day is the evil thereof, sing your nunc dimitis, the spirit indeed is willing, coming like a thief in the night, it came to pass, the alpha and the omega."

21. Ibid, p. 23. [The "correct American English" is "enable someone to achieve."] For details on Americanism in Nigeria, see V. O. Awonusi, "The Americanization of Nigerian English," *World Englishes* 13, no. 1 (1994): 75–82.

22. Obafemi Kujore, "Whose English?" in *New Englishes,* ed. Bamgbose, Banjo, and Thomas, 371. The author gives examples to illustrate the point.

23. Bamgbose, "English in the Nigerian Environment," 24. For other examples and elaboration, see Bamgbose, "Languages in Contact: Yoruba and English in Nigeria," *Education and Development* 2, no. 1 (1982): 329–41.

24. Bamgbose, "English in the Nigerian Environment," 25. See also his "The Influence of English on the Yoruba Language," in *English in Contact with Other Languages,* ed. W. Viereck and W. D. Bald (Budapest: Akadamiai Kiado, 1986).

25. For examples of current scholarship on African languages, see Ian Maddieson and Thomas J. Hineebusch, eds., *Language History and Linguistic Description in Africa* (Trenton, N.J.: Africa World Press, 1998).

26. M. J. Vasta, *Tori for Geti Bow Leg* (Lagos: Cross Continental Press, 1981); F. Aig-Imoukhuede, *Pidgin Stew and Sufferhead* (Ibadan: Heinemann, 1982); and Ken Saro-Wiwa, *Sozaboy: A Novel in Rotten English.*

27. Tunde Fatunde, *No Food No Country* (Benin: Adena Publishers, 1985); and his *Oga Na Tief Man* (Benin: Adena Publishers, 1986).

28. B. Erekosima, *African Proverbs in Special English* (Port Harcourt: Rivers State Newspaper Corporation, 1987).

29. This can be translated as "Your opinion."

30. See B. O. Elugbe and A. P. Omamor, *Nigerian Pidgins: Background and Prospects* (Ibadan: Heinemann, 1991).

31. Ibid.

32. A. Adetugbo, "The Development of English in Nigeria up to 1914: A Sociolinguistic Appraisal," *Journal of the Historical Society of Nigeria* 9, no. 2 (1978): 102.

33. E. Bamiro, "Nigerian Englishes in Nigerian Literature," *World Englishes* 10, no. 1 (1991); See also Bamgbose, "The Influence of English on the Yoruba Language," in *English in Contact with Other Languages,* ed. W. Viereck and W. D. Bald (Budapest: Akadamiai Kiado, 1986), 7–17.

34. For an extensive discussion of his argument, see Ngugi wa Thiong'O, *Decolonising the Mind: The Politics of Language in African Literature* (London: James Currey, 1986).

35. See Obi Wali, "The Dead End of African Literature," *Transition* 10, no. 3 (1963): 13–15; Edmund L. Epstein and Robert Cole, eds., *The Language of African Literature* (Trenton, N.J.: Africa World Press, 1998).

36. See Wole Soyinka, *Art, Dialogue and Outrage: Essays on Literature and Culture* (New York: Pantheon Books, 1993).

37. Chinua Achebe, "The African Writer and the English Language," *Transition* 4, no. 18 (1965).

38. A. Babs Fafunwa, "The Importance of the Mother Tongue as Medium of Instruction," *Nigeria Magazine* 102 (1969).

39. See B. O. Elugbe, "National Language and National Development," in *Multilingualism, Minority Languages, and Language Policy in Nigeria,* ed. E. N. Emenanjo (Agbor: Central Books Limited in collaboration with the Linguistic Association of Nigeria, 1990).

40. Section 1, Paragraph 8, *National Policy on Education.*

41. Ibid., Section 2, Paragraph 7; Section 3, Paragraph 15 (4).

42. See D. Jowitt, *Nigerian English Usage: An Introduction* (Lagos: Routledge, 1991).

43. See H. E. Newsum (Ikechukwu Okafor), *Class, Language, and Education: Class Struggle and Sociolinguistics in an African Situation* (Trenton, N.J.: Africa World Press, 1990).

44. I wish to thank Abdul-Rasheed Na'Allah for composing this poem especially for this book. He has provided an English summary stanza by stanza:

I cannot do it

Why will I destroy him, as you want me to do,
And become a terror in my community!

Your objectives are not necessarily mine,
I can think for myself and will act on my intentions

People like you drag our country to flames,
Nigerians, Onitsha, Ibadan, Sokoto, in dire poverty
People like you would stop at nothing.
No, I won't join you!

10

GENDER AND CULTURE IN OLD AND NEW AFRICA

"A WOMAN IS A FLOWER IN A GARDEN; HER HUSBAND IS THE FENCE AROUND IT."
—AN AKAN PROVERB

How does a man with six wives arrange love-making sessions? Can a woman, too, have six husbands? Why does female genital mutilation persist? If there is no welfare system, who takes care of widows? If societies expect all women to marry, what happens to single parents? Why do women in Islamic areas cover their faces in public? Why do African men dominate their wives? These are some of the questions that my American students are fond of posing when we address topics relating to kinship and gender. Perhaps because people want to improve their knowledge, or because they are simply amused by some of the practices, they have asked similar questions at public lectures, and I have had occasions to address the issue of polygamy at a major forum. The popular literature on African women generated by Western writers reveals only the frightening aspects, painting women as savages who are exploited by men for their maximum reproductive forces as well as for their labor. Recent literature, especially that on female circumcision, presents women as powerless victims, human beings no better than the slaves of old. From the various depictions, one cannot help but ask: Are African men evil and the African women so docile as to tolerate evil?

In this chapter, I will try to answer some of these questions within a general framework of kinship and development. In both, elements of traditions and modern cultures are clearly manifested, and I will use a few issues

Figure 12. Commerce: A woman's world. Ayorou, Niger.

as illustrations. Issues pertaining to women and culture have become central to discussions on democracy and governance in Africa, and the overall problem of underdevelopment. In other words, until women's lives are transformed in a positive manner, the continent cannot move forward.

In many parts of Africa, a clear break has not been established with the past, while changes are yet to take any firm hold. In different parts of Africa, patriarchy has long been established, and its manifestations can be found in various aspects of gender relations. A number of contemporary conditions affect both men and women in ways that create both equality and competition. In a continent where poverty is widespread, one's gender offers little or no protection against hunger, disease, and joblessness. Thus, class and elite positions may also affect the diversity of gender roles and access to opportunities.[1] Women are not docile, not from the evidence of their autonomy and struggles. Patriarchy is not about "evil," but a hierarchy that makes men more powerful than women.

Culture definitely plays a role in many of the experiences of women, as well as the hardships they complain about. Gender inequality can be rationalized by culture. Gender roles and reward allocation may be based on old beliefs. Within households, even if gender roles are complementary, men are regarded as the heads of households while a woman has relevance

Figure 13. Food gathering: A man's world. Dakar, Senegal.

as a mother and wife. She keeps traditions and kinship alive by bearing children and socializing them. As a bearer of children, she acquires respect within the household; as bearers of male children, she acquires prestige and ensures the stability of her marriage and the continuity of kinship and its traditions. Culture also affirms the power that is available to women. One area is in spirituality and religion. As ritual leaders in some cults, women have enormous power. In societies that believe in witchcraft, such power becomes an avenue to attain respect also.

The majority of African societies are patriarchal in nature. In this context, an ideology exists in support of gender inequalities and roles. Patriarchy is an affirmation of male domination, a way to stratify societies along gender lines, such that men receive more prestige and power than women. When a woman marries, she moves to the household of the man, where she is expected to behave in certain ways. This relocation may come with a loss in power, unless the husband is a king or chief, or he is wealthy, and the wife can benefit from the connection. Female circumcision and rules about virginity must have prepared her to play a subordinate role and to give the control of her sexuality to a man. She may have seen a widow who was compelled to marry a man in the household of the deceased; she could have seen her mother kneel, to show great respect, to serve food to

Figure 14. The culture of cleaning clothes: A woman's world. Mopti, Mali.

her father, and she would have seen that a boy is regarded as more important than a girl. As part of the socialization process, her mother will insist that she retain her virginity, know how to cook food that will please her future husband, and show respect. The newly wed woman will be judged by some of what her mother told (and warned) her about. She is expected not only to respect her husband, but to respect those senior to her in age and even men younger than her within the household. Her own respect will come with age and seniority. The longer she is married, the more senior she becomes, and the more respect she acquires.

The various ways to control female sexuality, sanctioned by culture, show male dominance. Women are expected to appear in certain physical ways, as in the fattening practice in southeastern Nigeria which attaches beauty to fatness. Among the Hausa in West Africa, girls are socialized to become modest and shy—they are expected to be obedient, accept the husbands chosen on their behalf, and cultivate the habit of silence. If Muslims, they can be kept in seclusion, justified by the need to prevent them from interacting with other men, mixing with "pagans," or having anything to do with people without the permission of their husbands.

Whether male or female, poor or rich, Africans belong to social groups defined by kinship, as in birth or marriage, or by non-kinship, such as occupational associations or social groups. Both old and new Africa cannot be understood without understanding kinship. Birth and marriage unite a large number of families who trace descent to one ancestor, commonly a male. In the past, laws of inheritance were governed by descent. A kinship identity was formed based on names, ritual, religion, taboos, and other markers.

The interlocking of people and the role of women are enacted within the various social groups. If women gain power, wealth, and prestige, its significance is measured within the network of the social groups. If class and other cleavages are still in the process of formation, Africa is still at the crossroads in terms of the connectivity between people—the established traditional pattern is a collectivist ethos, while the emerging capitalist-oriented one is individualistic. If women operate within the collectivist framework, certain elements of patriarchy have to be accepted. If they break loose and act independently as in a globalized world, the balance in the social group is threatened. Will they support emerging family forms of single parents, lesbianism, and others? Patriarchal-minded people prefer the consolidation of traditions to prevent the penetration of new family forms.

In precolonial Africa, the stress was on the group so that larger interests would supersede the "selfish" ones of the individual. A group could be rewarded for the achievement of one person, and it could equally be punished for the transgression of its members. In this kind of ideology, women had to conform to a group's interest. To be sure, not all individual accomplishments were discouraged—some groups, such as the Igbo of Nigeria and the Baganda of Uganda, actually celebrated individual achievement—but the premium was on meeting the challenges of group survival. Farm work, security, prevention of diseases, building houses, and other tasks in the pre-industrial past required the cooperation of many people. The socialization process was deliberate in making the individual part of the group. Ceremonies of new babies and their eventual growth involved the entire community. A child was exposed to a large number of people beyond the nuclear family, all to affirm its membership in an extensive kinship network. The child was a product of a marriage that had connected extended families of about three or four generations, all operating, in cooperation and conflict, within the framework of communal ethos.

The child would discover that he or she was one of many children belonging to the same father. He or she might also realize that not everybody that was called "mama" was the biological one, but co-wives with the actual mother. As the child grew up, he or she might begin to wonder why resources had to be carefully managed among many siblings, when fewer children would have been the wiser option. That decision, however, was not based just on resource management, but on the necessity of children for sustaining kinship and the economy. Children were necessary to sustain kinship and the economy. In the perpetual desire to link various generations, the dead ones and the unborn, children constituted the strongest part of the chain. In popular thinking, without children the kinship as a biological and ideological entity would come to an inglorious end.

Part of the experiences of modern Africa is the erosion of collectivist interests, and the forceful emergence of the attitude of the individual to become a hero to the self and to the community. Men and women now seek the means to celebrate self, although the pressure of group interests has yet to go away. How can a married man actualize self-interest in a community? The erosion has resulted in new conditions that create independence for women and others in such a way that the group cannot sanction them. One result has been migration away from the group, to faraway places outside the continent or to cities within the continent. Cities offer opportunities for jobs, to live in small apartments, to develop new friendships, and to re-create group networks in a way that can fulfill utilitarian goals. In these distant settings, the individual can decide on those aspects of the collective to pay attention to.

Western education has been a powerful agency for change. It offers not only new skills for both men and women, but also new values and ideas about how to organize private and public lives. If children raised in traditional settings did not challenge the authority of the elders, Western education leaves all ideas open to questioning. If traditional occupations were bound by specific locations, Western education can lead one to different parts of the country or the world at large. If family elders were loved for their moonlight stories, radio and television have displaced them in many areas, especially in elite homes. Where Western education has taken deep root, initiation ceremonies have been abandoned or modified.

There is also the force of new laws and regulations. The police, as the agent of the modern state, can arrest a person; the learned judge (rather than village elders) will try him; if the person is found guilty, the prison door is open, with brutal guards to keep an eye on him. A woman living a comfortable life on wage income has no relations to turn to, if the job is lost, in order to maintain the same standard of living. If the collective ethos is weakening, what can sustain such practices such as initiation ceremonies and female circumcision?

Female circumcision has become a contentious issue while male initiation has not, though some of the reasons for both are similar. In societies of old, as individuals witnessed a transition from one stage of life to another, the community celebrated and performed rituals. Initiation ceremonies were intended to introduce citizens to adulthood, and then to marriage. In some cultures, initiation could be marked with circumcision of teenagers, as in the case of the Kikuyu of Kenya and the Igbo of Nigeria. In some other cultures, circumcision could come much earlier, and marriage became the initiation to adulthood.

Male initiation rites and practices are not just about religion but about education, sports, leisure, endurance, and knowledge.[2] In places where male initiation ceremonies are declining or dying, there is the need to create secular ideas to attain similar goals. Gathering its young men together, a community was able to turn a ceremony into the affirmation of collective identity. Young men grew to respect their people and traditions, and to be in a position to defend them. Community elders would impart lessons on history and morality. And there were many advantages for the initiates: they acquired respect as adults; they had evidence to prove they could endure pain; and they were now able to marry and practice sex in ways approved of by the community.

With respect to women, female circumcision was not as widespread a practice as the Western media has portrayed it, and even where it has been more common, it is not as widely practiced as many people think. For women, initiation could take many forms, such as marriage, tattooing of parts of the body, cicatrization, and tooth removal. Where female circumcision (clitoridectomy, to use the clinical terminology for the removal of the clitoris—or genital mutilation, now the most common label, partly to attract attention to it) is practiced, the justification for it has mainly been based on tradition and the male perception of female behavior. Whether male or female, an uncircumcised individual in a number of African societies would not make the leap to adulthood, become married, and have children. In other words, the sanction was rather severe—not having children was like banishing the memory of the person's existence. The practice of circumcision is attributable also to the ambiguity of gender: at birth, a boy with the foreskin is female, while the female with the clitoris is male. According to this belief among the Dogon (an ethnic group in Mali) belief, for the child to claim its true gender, circumcision must take place.

Where the practice has survived, the tendency is to explain female circumcision as nothing but another manifestation of male dominance. Male circumcision has no effect on sexual pleasures, unlike clitoridectomy, thus fueling the suggestion that the practice was enforced by men simply to deny women similar pleasure. The belief was that women had an excessive sexual drive which could be curtailed by removing the clitoris. Those who continue to defend the practice ignore the aspect of male domination and emphasize culture: Africans are presented not as stupid people but creative beings who know what is good for them. When people who are opposed to clitoridectomy present it as barbaric (as Christian missionaries and others have done), they enable the defenders of the practice to focus on the cultural factors, to argue, as Jomo Kenyatta does in his well-read classic, *Facing Mount Kenya,* that it is an aspect of indigenous religion and culture which must survive. To destroy culture, according to the argument by Kenyatta and others, is to destroy identity. Thus, clitoridectomy is not isolated as an aspect of culture that can be modified or abandoned without necessarily destroying other aspects of the culture. In what would seem ironic, Kenya became one of the very first countries to outlaw it, though there are no ways to arrest and punish those who violate the law.

Those opposed to clitoridectomy did not question tradition, but pointed to the diminished sexual pleasure for women and a host of medical woes that circumcised women could face. In the 1990s, clitoridectomy became one of the issues that Western feminists adopted to seek change in Africa. Indeed, their attacks on clitoridectomy became a media issue, even a justification for those seeking permanent residence in the United States. In one case, a woman successfully argued that if she was to return to her native country, her two daughters would be forced to undergo genital removal.

If Africans, including women, are uncomfortable talking about the pleasure of sex (the subject is still confined to the private domain in most countries), many are willing to talk about the medical woes. Everybody agrees that it is painful—even those who do the removal will say the same thing—and some women's pain can remain for a long time. Measuring the degree and impact of pain is hard, but is the outcome worth it? Certainly not. There is also the issue of the scar that is left, a sort of permanent damage to the body. On this, opinions are divided. If that part of the body is private and always covered, who sees the scar? And the most conservative people pose the question: why look at that part of the body to see the scar?

Modern medicine has pointed to two issues that culture is unable to address. First, a link has been established between clitoridectomy and death during or immediately after childbirth. Missionaries based in Kenya in the early decades of the twentieth century had noted the high death rate during childbirth, later discovered to be connected with clitoridectomy. This may, of course, be associated with the nature and severity of the circumcision, but it is a powerful reason to stop the practice, as the death rate was lower among those who were not circumcised.

The second issue is the way the surgery is performed during the time of the AIDS epidemics. The procedure is simple but unregulated. The "midwife" lives in the community, and can use the same instrument to perform the removal for many girls, even in conditions that may be unsafe. In other words, unlike male circumcision which can be performed in a modern hospital, clitoridectomy is more or less private. Those infected may have to find treatment in a modern hospital, and there is no sanction imposed on the "midwife" in case of serious illness or death.

In calling for the abolition of any entrenched cultural practice, it may be necessary to find acceptable substitutes. A new set of values have to evolve on sexual practices and how to mark and celebrate the transition from childhood to adulthood. Here, the key may be the formal school system and a variety of social and cultural practices that will call on the creative energies and talents of the community. Changes continue to occur, even in some objectionable practices. In places where the community continues to value male initiation, the ceremony has been reduced in duration from months to days. In places where people insist on female circumcision, some modern clinics have come up with the compromise of cutting just a small tip of the clitoris, a surgery that is merely symbolic as it leaves no scar, does not affect sexual pleasure, and does not create problems at childbirth. Compromises within cultures can be politically astute and desirable as a strategy of changing established beliefs and practices.

Marriage Practices and Current Controversies

Female circumcision is not the only aspect that has generated crisis in modern culture. Aspects of marriage and family life are being debated, usually framed as a contest between tradition and modernity. Even many of the factors that ensured marriage stability in the past are being challenged. Why do people get married? Old Africa had a primary answer: to reproduce children and thus ensure the survival of kinship. New Africa, like Western societies, now adds love. As many have discovered, love cannot sustain the relationship if there are problems, especially those associated with the answer of Old Africa. Old Africa did not deny that there was love, as their stories and poems clearly show, but it was considered as merely part of the conditions to reproduce and socialize new kin members. The modern belief is that couples should love, but must have children if the love is not to fade away.

Bridewealth[3] is common in many areas to legalize a marriage and for the man's kinship to have legitimate claim to the children arising from it. The bride and her family receive goods and/or services from the bridegroom and his family. The goods are local, such as cattle and goats. The payment can just be once, while in some places an installment exchange is allowed. In some extreme cases, a poor man can offer his labor in lieu of goods, although this practice is not widespread. These days, the bridewealth includes money, imported items, and expensive goods. When family members used to constitute the principal production units, bridewealth was a small compensation for the lost labor of the woman. But the bride carried with her some of the goods to the family of her husband, notably expensive attire, thus starting her marriage life with a good wardrobe. In more ways than one, bridewealth affirms the importance of women in the community, an assured agency to transfer wealth between families. The items are shared by members of the extended families and their friends, yet another way of announcing the legality of the marriage. Those who give the bridewealth and those who share in it are expected to ensure the stability of the marriage.

Some of the traditional practices that justified bridewealth are no longer applicable to modern-day society. The legal system has developed rules and sanctions to legitimize marriages. To those in non-farming occupations, daughters are not needed in farm work, and thus, they do not impose any loss and hardship on others if they decide to marry. And as the goods and services demanded in some areas have become excessive, some analysts have seen an element of greed in the contemporary practice of bridewealth, which has become a way to exploit people rather than to cement social relationships. Traditional marriages were stable, with a low divorce rate. The sanctions to prevent divorce were strong; the necessity of returning part of the bridewealth constituted a constraint, while the control of children by their fathers assured custody only to men.

In many parts of Africa, a man could marry two or more wives, a practice known as polygyny. To cultures that practice monogamy, as well as to Westerners, polygyny is another evidence of male domination and a marriage practice not based on love. Again, the practice has to be understood in its traditional context. In an agrarian society dependent on family labor, the best way to expand production (and thereby wealth) was to have access to additional labor. A most reliable source of labor was one's children. Women, with their reproductive power, became the key to family expansion, thus playing a leading role in the creation of household wealth and overall prosperity. Thus, polygyny can be interpreted as a clever device to use women to acquire wealth and status. Where wealth is counted in people, the polygynous man with numerous wives and children demonstrates success and prestige. Where pawnship was practiced—the use of people's labor to serve in lieu of interest on loans[4]—the man with many wives and children also had access to capital that could be invested or even consumed in a way to exaggerate his success within the community.

Just as polygyny enabled men to derive maximum advantage from marriage, so too did the women turn it to a great advantage. With co-wives, each woman's domestic task was reduced. In marriages where conflicts were minimal, polygyny ensured companionship within the household, as the wives could become great friends. Co-wives offered assistance to one another in need, such as pregnant women, and more importantly the sick and elderly who needed care and attention.

Since there is limited research on the population of Africa over a long historical period, we are still unable to confirm the assertion that there were more women than men in precolonial Africa. The assumption is that warfare and the Atlantic slave trade led to a higher male infant mortality. Thus, polygyny became a clever answer to address the excess of women.

Polygyny survived the twentieth century, in part as an established marriage practice, but also as an attempt to adapt Western-style monogamy to a number of cultural practices. The number of monogamous marriages is on the rise, due in part to education, the spread of Christianity, the reduction in the average number of children a man expects to have, and the refusal of many women to enter polygynous relations. In Tunisia, polygyny has been proscribed by law. However, in many countries today, the number of men in polygynous relationship is as high as one-third of the married population.[5] Thus, the question arises: why has polygyny survived? To start with, even if European colonial officers were critical of polygyny, the economic system they promoted actually encouraged it. African economies remained agrarian, but in a way that promoted male power and changed the attitude toward land. The emphasis on the production of crops for export (such as cocoa, peanuts, cotton, rubber) led to attempts to maximize the use of land and labor. The commercialization of land began in a way that benefited men rather than women. Where traditional inheritance practices had been more equitable, men in some areas reinterpreted customs to ensure their control of land. The production of cash crops also demanded the use of labor. As with traditional economies, marriage provided an avenue to obtain labor, with many ambitious farmers resorting to polygyny as an agency of labor recruitment.

Many of the customs and beliefs that sustained polygyny in the past are still very much alive. In the majority of African communities, women are expected to marry. While the number of single parents is growing, low status is accorded to unmarried women. The pressure to marry lends itself to polygyny, even to tolerating bad marriages. Preference for male children is widespread, with the result that a married man without a son would take a second wife. Where infant mortality rate is high, the wish to be survived by children means that a man can have more than one wife. No desire is greater than to have children, if only in order to be cared for in old age. In places where great prestige is associated with large families, polygyny becomes an avenue to acquire high social standing. In Islamic communities, religion is used as yet one more justification of polygyny—the widespread belief is that a man can marry up to four wives as long as he can provide resources to support them and love them equally.

Marriage forms such as polygyny fulfill various functions in society. In cases where a man inherits a widow, say, of a senior family member, the motive is not necessarily based on sex, but on welfare—the marriage enables the woman and her children to have support within their established households. While there are other forms of polygyny (although not among educated people) which were originally intended to cope with people's welfare and maintain the survival of the kin group, widow inheritance is the most common, a form that is collectively described in the anthropological literature as *levirate*. Various customs prescribe various rules about who can inherit a widow, but in general the inheritor is junior in age to the deceased.

The desire for children is at the root of some other practices, ensuring that a man leaves a child behind. Impotency may be a problem, or even death at an early age, and the solution may be to have a woman produce children on behalf of another. Among the Zulu of South Africa, a man may marry his wife's sister, in an arrangement that anthropologists have labeled *sororate*. If the married Zulu man found it difficult to have a child by his wife, the woman's family could offer the wife's sister to produce children on her behalf. It is not only the Zulu that employed surrogate women to bear children for others—the practice existed in various versions in different places. Additionally, a dead man could have a child: a living volunteer married on his behalf, entering a sort of "ghost marriage," and the products belonged to the dead whom they claim as a father.

In some parts of Africa, as among some communities in northern Nigeria, young girls can be induced or forced to marry older men. This practice is, of course, different from the belief in some parts of Southern

Africa that sex with a virgin could cure AIDS and other sexually transmitted diseases.[6] Among the Tiv, an old practice allowed a male member of the household to use his sister or other relation in exchange for a woman to marry. In this exchange marriage, the woman was not given a choice and could actually end up with someone that she did not like.

The Changing Role of Women

It is misleading to talk about issues of exploitation and empowerment of women as if their role has been static. Evidence is clear that women's roles have changed over time, and that we now have women who are as well educated as men.[7] The distribution of power within the household has also responded to changes in society over time. During the twentieth century, traditional practices were modified or strengthened by colonial changes, the penetration of European gender values, and new developments that gave more power to men.

While patriarchy was established in most of precolonial Africa, the nature of economy and politics gave women visible roles and privileges. They were part of the agrarian societies, where the mode of production was based on the family. Age and seniority were as important as sex in allocating responsibility and sharing rewards. An elderly woman was more respected than a younger man. Girls and boys shared tasks within the household.[8] Women had established occupations, either complementing those of their husbands or operating independently. In places where women had direct access to land and other resources to establish their independent trade and occupations (as in the case of Yoruba traders of Nigeria), they were able to attain status and prestige. Even where they lacked direct access to land, the role of women in production was crucial to the survival of society—they controlled the domestic chores of cooking and cleaning; they were involved in building houses; they played an important role in rearing livestock and in a myriad of other duties vital to the functioning of the society. Reproduction is the key to the continuity of kinship and community, and women as childbearers, carry its burden and glory.

Women did all the jobs associated with men, although not in all African communities. Thus, there were women warriors in Dahomey; the Maasai women were house builders, and even served as guards to defend them; and Yoruba women were versatile traders, even in long-distance trade. In spite of these examples, it is clear that most occupations were gendered. Certain jobs were exclusive to men, such as hunting, blacksmithing, and carving. Women concentrated on domestic chores, assisted with harvesting, and processed foodstuffs. Within the family, most of these tasks were transferred to the children through a socialization process that was dependent on observation. As peasants, women were exploited. Where relations of dependence existed, as in slavery and pawnship, women, too, were exploited for their labor and sexuality.

While the distribution of power in the community favored men, in many places, women were not totally excluded from power or political influence. Indeed, one study has suggested that there was a phase of matriarchy when gender equality existed among the Owan of West Africa, and that patriarchy actually evolved there over time. The study points to goddess traditions and festivals, and indicates how the distribution of power favored women in matrilocal communities.[9] The lingering survival of matriarchy in some places has given women more privileges and influence than are reflected in some of the literature.

Elsewhere, formal and semi-formal women's organizations existed in most societies to allow participation in politics, the management of affairs specific to women, and the exercise of influence. Notable among these organizations were those by traders and market women who established guilds, secret societies, and age-grade groups. Not only were women the leaders, but they were also able to take control of matters of interest to them. The officers of the organizations were regarded as chiefs, and some titles carried enormous prestige, as in the case of the *Iyalode* among the Yoruba and the *agba ekwe* among the Igbo, both groups in Nigeria.[10]

There were kingdoms and societies such as the Serbro of Sierra Leone and the Tonga of Zambia where women could be chiefs. In Dahomey, there were women warriors and chiefs. Cases of leaders such as Queen Amina of Hausaland (northern Nigeria) and Nzinga of Angola show how some women could rise to positions of great influence.[11] In a number of West African societies, the queen mother was so powerful that she could even select the king and serve as the power behind the throne. In nineteenth-century Sokoto caliphate—the largest single political unit—Nana Asma'u, the sister of Uthman dan Fodio, the jihad leader, was a notable political and intellectual force. Some of her writings have survived, and they do attest to her strong intellect and personality.[12] During the nineteenth century, there were other distinguished women leaders such as Efunsetan Aniwura of Ibadan and Madam Tinubu of Lagos. In religion, women were members of many powerful priesthoods, as in those of a number of Yoruba gods such as Sango, Osun, and Obatala, where women were not just cult members but major leaders. Witches with "positive" power were also respected for their contributions to society. H. Henderson, in one case study, established three linkages between religion, economy and power:

> i. [There is] a strong correlation between women's important economic functions and their roles in religious functions (thus where women have important economic functions of an autonomous nature such as trade, they will form associations which will have important political and religious functions).
> ii. Where women are economically independent, there will be an elaboration of their personal cults and an invitation to those of men.
> iii. [There is] a correlation between the relatively high social position for women, and their control over personal destiny shrines (thus the greater the control women possessed over these ritual and religious objects, the greater the degree of autonomy of action they possessed in society).[13]

Status and influence represent evidence of autonomy. It is clear that there were other ways for women to gain and use their independence. The control of economic power within the household meant that successful women entrepreneurs had great voice. The stress on age and seniority brought prestige to many as they grew older. Ancestor veneration was extended to women, a confirmation of their power and prestige in the afterlife. Women were active in trade and markets, thus serving as valuable links between the farms and the households, that is, the producers and the consumers.

By the time we entered the twentieth century, much of the political and economic power enjoyed by women had been diminished. There are scholars who see a trend towards marginalization even earlier, blaming the trans-Atlantic slave trade for destroying family relationship and disturbing a more equitable gender balance.[14] According to this argument, which awaits further research, the enslavement of millions of people and the violence and death associated with the wars and kidnapping reduced the male population, creating considerable pressure on women to have more children and pay more attention to domestic duties. In the process, they lost economic and political power.

The political arrangement since the European conquest at the turn of the twentieth century has favored men. Colonial officers were male who ruled in partnership with African men. African men served as tax collectors, police, and soldiers, and in "native authorities," all agencies that ran the colonial system. The association of men with power and authority was consolidated at the expense of women. Male power was used to seize more land. As cities became important centers of new economic and social opportunities, moves were made in a number of places to limit access to unmarried women. Many were forced to cohabit with men to justify residence in cities, while rural single women were prevented from relocating to cities in some countries such as South Africa.

In colonial societies, all Africans were exploited, irrespective of gender, but men were more active because of the nature of the economy. Occupations that attracted wages, such as service in the army, police, and civil service, were mainly for men, thus providing them with more cash than women. As the school system prepared men for these marginal jobs, education and skills were provided to more men than women. Men concentrated on the production of cash crops for export, one of the primary motivations for the conquest of Africa. Either because cash crops were more lucrative than food crops or because some colonial authorities compelled Africans to grow what they needed, men took control of more land than before, pushing women to less fertile lands and crops with less market potential. Policies of land reforms favored men, as in the case of land private ownership regulations in Kenya in the 1950s.[15] Where women had been dependent on cattle, as among the pastoral farmers, changing ideas about property in a number of areas denied them access to cattle and some occupations relating to it, as male cattle owners turned the women into labor to produce wealth for them.[16]

Where minerals such as diamond, gold, tin, and coal existed, men were also recruited (or forced) to work as mine workers, even in situations where they had to leave their wives in their villages. Migration to the cities involved more men, and when their wives joined them, the wives were again pushed into less rewarding jobs. Thus, in many ways the colonial economy confined women's activities to the domestic and the marginal informal sectors of the economy. The idea of men as "breadwinners" and "wage earners" spread, while women were relegated to positions of home keepers and custodians of "petty jobs." Many women became dependent on their wage-earning husbands, who gave them only the amounts needed for housekeeping. Men dependent on farming took more land at the expense of women, married many wives in order to expand their labor force, and accumulated property and money at the expense of their wives in order to build their status and prestige. Several case studies have pointed to the exploitation of women in the colonial situation. Studies on prostitution in urban centers have shown how the inability by women to obtain jobs and survive gave them limited options other than to sell sex. Many others took to homebrewing and small jobs.[17] In villages in Cameroon, a number of men turned their wives into a cheap labor force to grow cash crops.[18]

In part to change their conditions, and in part to rid Africa of European rule, African women contributed to nationalism in colonial Africa. A few were leaders and activists who challenged the colonial state and their local agents.[19] Women leaders mobilized against the taxation of women, as well as against other aspects considered unjust to them.[20] Some joined political parties, and even acquired management power, as in the examples of Margaret Ekpo, Lady Oyinka Abayomi, Carlotte Olajumoke Obasa, Olaniwun Adunni Oluwole, and Constance Agatha Cummings-John.[21]

Gender relations that were formed during the colonial era were transferred to the postcolonial period. In spite of women's contributions to anticolonial struggles, men took virtually all the most important positions in the formal sectors. Most African countries developed centralized power structures where what people got was largely dependent on whom they knew. As most men had received a Western education, they also dominated the wage-earning sectors, thus consolidating many of their privileges. While an increasing number of girls began to go to school in the 1960s, a notable accomplishment indeed, the prevailing view was that only "gentle" occupations awaited them, such as teaching and nursing, both of which did not translate into much political and economic power.

As noted below, Africa has seen many changes, but a number of inequities persist. The perception that women are "secondary citizens" remains—the best of everything is for men, and the crumbs for women. Resources are not equitably distributed; men take more than women, although women often contribute more to production and households. Men in power and development experts assume that they can plan for women, not as partners in progress, but as recipients of favors and objects of policies and programs. Cultural stereotypes present women as weak and incapable of leadership; the belief is that their main goals should be to manage the "home front." Discrimination and marginalization can be seen in many aspects of life, and the contradictions are all clear. If women's reproductive and productive functions are so eclectic that they are actually manifest in all sectors, low rewards and hardships can be linked to gender.[22] In laws made by men, women are denied many rights in inheritance and divorce settlements. In agriculture, where they contribute a lot, women have limited access to land, credits, and opportunity to cultivate leading cash crops. In education, women are still behind men—even where access is open to both sexes, the dropout rate for women is higher in part because of pregnancies and early marriage, preference of parents to meet the needs of boys rather than those of girls, and heavy involvement in household tasks. In health they do not have full control over their reproductive ability, and their nutritional needs are grossly inadequate. The statistics for many countries put the population of women at more than 50 percent, but they constitute less than a third of the labor force.

In spite of all these inequities, women continue to struggle and to achieve considerable success in different areas.[23] Changes have come, but contradictions remain. The status of women is not the same in all countries, and even within each country changes are not uniform. A woman may receive a university degree (a great educational change), but may still be expected to do all the house chores (a traditional role). She may have power (as a civil servant), but she is not able to influence the allocation of resources, such as a male politician or military general is able to do.

The Paradox of Change

The forces of change—colonialism, Westernization, capitalism, Islam, and Christianity—do also create their obstacles, as Ifi Amadiume has brilliantly shown.[24] Take the modern economy, for instance: where capitalism is spreading, it is exploiting women similar to the way patriarchy exploited them in the past. Economies based on wages turned males into sole "breadwinners." Modernization has come with some negative baggage, as it originally invested men with more skills and power that were used in part to dominate women. Islam is not hostile to secluding women, thereby undermining their career goals, while Christianity regards men as heads of household who deserve the obedience of their wives. While urbanization is liberating, it may constrain autonomy if there are no jobs or if the jobs are menial or involve selling sex.[25] Women continue to serve as poorly paid domestics and as prostitutes in cities where competition is intense. Female poverty can be endemic, especially in cities where the cost of living is high.

At present, it is clear that men control power in most countries, dominate the occupations and the households, and manage public and private institutions to their advantage. Some studies suggest that the dominant role of men is actually a global phenomenon.[26] In the case of Africa, certain tendencies are clear. The attainment of economic stability rests on the acquisition of education and maintenance of extensive connections, both of which men have better access to than women. Without skills and education, the majority of women are still engaged in occupations relating to farming. The 1989 data by the World Bank puts the percent of the women's population in agriculture at more than 60 and the percent of their responsibility for the production of basic foods at 70.[27] The rewards are unimpressive, with the majority of women being totally unable to save or accumulate any significant wealth. Where men have control of land and its products, women suffer more hardships, as they are unable to control even what they earn.

The worldview and legal system continue to favor men—the assumption tends to be that women should occupy an inferior status. The typical husband desires an obedient wife, playing a subordinate role defined for her. The widespread opinion is that a woman's role should be domestic in nature. Many men, even in monogamous nuclear relationships, still expect many children, an average of five in some places. Thus, women still have to devote a preponderance of time to child rearing. Where women do work, the purpose is to add to the status of the husband. In matters of law, women can suffer when they lose their husbands, as their relations can take a heavy share of the inheritance. In cases of divorce, most women get little or nothing, and the custody of their children is never assured.

Modernization has been more beneficial to elite women. With diplomas from higher institutions in Africa and abroad, they are integrated into the formal sector. The more active among them establish cultural, social, and political organizations to support a variety of programs, spread literacy, and encourage many more women to go to school. Skills are being introduced to "rural women" to improve the techniques of farming, child rearing, and crafts making. Wives of heads of governments at the national and regional levels are playing active roles in popularizing some issues on politics and development, lending support to their husbands, and promoting aspects of culture.[28] Some of these prominent women have also demonstrated the abuses that can come with power and influence, as in the case of a number of Nigerian "first ladies" whose preoccupation is to make fashion statements.

Educated young women and men are no longer bound by tradition in selecting partners to marry, and elders can no longer conduct arranged marriages for them. If in the past marriage was between two families in order to establish a large kinship, today it may just be between two people to establish a nuclear family. It is not that the extended families are ignored, but the interests of kin members are not considered of prime importance as before. Established traditional practices have been adapted to modern times and to the demands of other religions such as Islam and Christianity. Thus, the parents of the bride and bridegroom are still heavily involved, and their consent is crucial; bridewealth is still exchanged, even as tokens in some areas, and the celebration is community-oriented, involving a large crowd. Where the parents interfere too much, or in cases where the community is also insisting on the specific choice of partners or how to celebrate a wedding, the couple can elope and either become married or simply cohabitate and have children. Cities, again, provide the sanctuary to the couple in love.

However, the modern nuclear family cannot escape the role of extended families. It is common to have other kin members living with couples; married people have to take care of their aged parents, who usually spend their last days with their children. Moreover, celebrations involve many people; when a man dies, the wife may have to struggle with his brothers and relatives in sharing the inheritance.

The liberty of contracting relationships and talking about love and emotion does not free the modern African woman of problems. To women in search of absolute freedom, there are substantial issues. To start with, patriarchy is alive and well. Men continue to make more money than women, creating a financial imbalance that may undermine the power of many married women. Africans still see reproduction as the main purpose of marriage. A married man without children will be pressured by relatives and friends to have a mistress who can bear children for him. Even a man with children still can be influenced by peers to have mistresses. The general perception is that having mistresses does not suggest that men do not love their wives. Bigamy laws are rarely applied, even when a man has children by his mistresses. Thus, we have to understand the meanings attached to love and relationships. In general, love is defined as responsibility and duty, a situation whereby the man fulfils his obligations to his nuclear and extended families. The worldview about infidelity tends to be forgiving of men and, certainly, critical of women, who are expected to be monogamous and faithful. An observer, a woman journalist, noted that a number of women also keep men friends either for revenge against their cheating husbands, or just for money.[29] The punishment meted to a woman who commits adultery is rather severe. Thus, while we can talk of women's independence, we should also note that marriage relationships are not necessarily egalitarian or stable.

Some countries, such as Kenya, Ethiopia, and Côte d'Ivoire, have passed laws giving women the right to inherit. As a result of the success of the pressure for changes, laws against polygyny and bridewealth have been passed in Côte d'Ivoire. In Tunisia, monogamy is sanctioned by the power of law. In Islamic Senegal, which allows polygyny, a man requires the consent of his wife before marrying a second one. Children of the elite and members of the upper class, whether they are boys or girls, receive equal access to education, and they can now be found as professionals in virtually all sectors of modern society. Elite women also tend to "marry well," thus further extending their influence and privileges.

Some conditions are in place to effect major changes in the future. Many women's organizations have pressed for increased empowerment and greater gains from development projects. Various governments have been persuaded to recognize the need to involve women in the administrations, even at the most senior cabinet levels. Educational opportunities have expanded for women, and in some areas there are more girls than boys in schools. Many are moving to occupations traditionally associated with men, such as engineering and computer programming. Development agencies now understand that it creates a greater impact on society to channel grants and resources to women. Grassroots women's organizations have risen to the challenge, pressuring the government and foreign donors to consider their plights. Their focus is not even to wait for assistance, but to mobilize their members to work for progress by forming cooperative clubs, childcare centers, and credit associations. In cities, women have struggled to control local trade, penetrate major informal economies, unite to save and build capital, organize social events, create opportunities for leisure, and use the ability to make a living to create better relationships with men.[30]

Hundreds of non-governmental organizations have emerged across the continent, and they work tirelessly to effect changes. They are heavily represented in all the major international forums on Africa organized by the United Nations and other agencies. African women representatives have been insistent on what they want: the acquisition of skills to participate in all important economic and political affairs, an end to violence and wars that kill and injure millions of women, and solutions to the lingering problems of poverty and disease. They demand changes in these aspects of culture that constitute obstacles to them: changes in the training of children at home and schools to alter the perception of women as subordinate to men; an equitable distribution of resources in such a way that women will get their fair share; programs to improve the standard of living of women in rural areas; enlightenment programs about the rights of women in society; and an overall improvement in the areas of nutrition, hygiene, and family planning. Practical steps have been taken by many women's organizations to ask young women to marry for love, divorce when things are not working well, pursue engineering and science courses, seek power, alter the legal system in their favor, play the leading role in making decisions that involve them, and control their sexuality and reproductive ability.

The struggles have to be collective, and they may even have to benefit from the age-old African ethos of group interests and consensus building.

As Catherine Coquery-Vidrovitch concludes, seeking emancipation in Western feminist terms may be tough, "in a society that specifically denies the individual in favor of the group and prefers consensus to freedom of individual choice."[31] As elite women now realize, self mobility and success does not help others. Women have to fight for power, not just legal changes that exist on paper, but the ability to use power itself in a direct manner. Dependence on men for power—as in the case of wives of governors and presidents—has limited value. African women have also been productive and active economically, and the struggle is about attaining adequate rewards and compensation.

Women have to change women, not leave things to men, who will think about themselves and the status quo. The Beijing Declaration and Platform for Action adopted in 1995 to demand various changes is 132 pages long: if Africa can implement a page a year, the progress for women, although it may take 132 years, will surely create a revolution through evolution. But eight years have already been lost!

Notes

1. See Sharon B. Sticher and Jane L. Parpart, eds., *Patriarchy and Class: African Women in the Home and Workforce* (Boulder, Colo.:Westview, 1988).

2. For some examples of initiation rituals and ceremonies, see Mary Douglas and Phyllis M. Kaberry, eds., *Man in Africa* (Urbana: University of Illinois Press, 1967).

3. Bridewealth can be a troublesome term if it is used to connote a substantial amount of commodities of monetary value.

4. Toyin Falola and Paul Lovejoy, *Pawnship in Africa: Debt Bondage in Historical Perspective* (Boulder, Colo.: Westview Press, 1994).

5. See Diane Kayongo-Male and Philista Onyango, *The Sociology of the African Family* (New York: Longman, 1984), 8.

6. This strange belief has led to a high rate of rape, even group rape, by men in search of young women who could prevent them from dying. Some mothers have also resorted to virginity testing to prevent their girls from having early sex and thus contracting AIDS. See *Sunday Tribune Perspectives* (South Africa), November 11, 2001, 4.

7. See M. J. Hafkin and Edna C. Bay, eds., *African Women in Changing Perspective* (Stanford, Calif.: Stanford University Press, 1977).

8. See Oyeronke Oyewumi, *The Invention of Women: Making an African Sense of Western Gender Discourses* (Minneapolis: University of Minnesota Press, 1997).

9. Onaiwu W. Ogbomo, *When Men and Women Mattered: A History of Gender Relations among the Owan of Nigeria* (Rochester, N.Y.: University of Rochester Press, 1997).

10. See Bolanle Awe, "The Iyalode in the Traditional Yoruba Political System," in *Social Stratification: A Cross-Cultural View*, ed. Alice Schlegel (New York: Columbia University Press, 1977), 144–95; and Ifi Amadiume, *Male Daughters, Female Husbands: Gender and Sex in an African Society* (London: Zed, 1987).

11. See Sa'ad Abubakar, "Amina of Zazzau: Exploits and Impact in the Savanna Region of Nigeria," *Kano Studies,* No. 2 (1981): 99–109.

12. Jean Boyd, *The Caliph's Sister: Nana Asma'u, 1793–1865: Teacher, Poet and Islamic Leader* (London: Frank Cass, 1989).

13. H. Henderson, "Ritual Roles of Women in Onitsha Ibo Society," Ph.D. dissertation, University of California at Berkeley, 1969.

14. See Maria R. Cutrufelli, *Women of Africa: Roots of Oppression* (London: Zed, 1983).

15. See Jean Davison, "Who Owns What? Land Registration and Tensions in Gender Relations of Production in Kenya" in *Agriculture, Women, and Land: The African Experience,* ed. Jean Davison (Boulder, Colo.: Westview, 1988), 157–76.

16. For a case study, see Margot Lovett, "Gender Relations, Class Formation, and the Colonial State in Africa," in *Women and the State in Africa,* ed. Jane L. Parpart and Kathleen A. Staudt (Boulder, Colo.: Lynne Rienner, 1989), 23–46.

17. See Philip Langley, "A Preliminary Approach to Women and Development: Getting a Few Facts Right," in *The Roles of Women in the Process of Development,* ed. Gerard M. Ssenkoloto (Doula, Cameroon: Pan African Institute for Development, 1983), 79–100.

18. Jane I. Guyer, *Family and Farm in Southern Cameroon* (Boston: Boston University African Studies Center, 1984).

19. For the story of one case now fully documented, that of Funmilayo Ransome-Kuti of Nigeria, see Cheryl Johnson-Odim and Nina Emma Mba, *For Women and The Nation: Funmilayo Ransome-Kuti of Nigeria* (Urbana and Chicago: University of Illinois Press, 1997).

20. See some examples in Bolanle Awe, ed., *Nigerian Women in Historical Perspective* (Ibadan, Nigeria: Sankore, 1992).

21. Stella A. Effah-Attoe and Solomon Odini Jaja, *Margaret Ekpo: Lioness in Nigerian Politics* (Abeokuta, Nigeria: ALF Publications, 1993); Constance Agatha Cummings-John, *Memoirs of a Krio Leader,* ed. LaRay Denzer (Ibadan, Nigeria: Sam Bookman, 1995); and Awe, ed., *Nigerian Women in Historical Perspective.*

22. For country studies that catalogue the problems, see Amadu Sesay and Adetanwa Odebiyi, eds., *Nigerian Women in Society and Development* (Ibadan, Nigeria: Dokun Publishing House, 1998); Dora Obi Chizea and Juliet Njoku, *Nigerian Women and the Challenges of Our Time* (Lagos, Nigeria: Malthouse, 1991); Simi Afonja, et al., eds., *Nigerian Women in Social Change* (Ile-Ife, Nigeria: Obafemi Awolowo University Press, 1995); O. A. Adeyemo, *Women in Development* (Ibadan, Nigeria: National Centre for Economic Management and Administration, 1991); and 'Lai Olurode, ed., *Women and Social Change in Nigeria* (Lagos, Nigeria: Unity Publishing and Research Co., 1990).

23. See Margaret Jean Hay and Sharon Stichter, eds., *African Women South of the Sahara,* 2nd ed. (London: Longman, 1995); and Iris Berger and E. Frances White, *Women in Sub-Saharan Africa* (Bloomington and Indianapolis: Indiana University Press, 1999).

24. Ifi Amadiume, *Reinventing Africa: Matriarchy, Religion and Culture* (London: Zed, 1997).

25. See Kenneth Little, *African Women in Towns* (Cambridge: Cambridge University Press, 1973).

26. See Ester Boserup, *Women's Role in Economic Development* (Aldershot, England: Gower, 1986).

27. World Bank, *Sub-Saharan Africa: From Crisis to Sustainable Growth: A Long-Term Perspective Study* (Washington, D.C.: World Bank, 1989).

28. See Maryam Babangida, *The Home Front: Nigerian Army Officers and Their Wives* (Ibadan, Nigeria: Fountain Publications, 1988).

29. Bosede Sola-Onifade, *The Nigerian Woman* (Lagos, Nigeria: Julia Virgo, n.d. [1980s?]), 41.

30. See Christine Obbo, *African Women: Their Struggle for Economic Independence* (London: Zed, 1980).

31. Catherine Coquery-Vidrovitch, *African Women: A Modern History* (Boulder, Colo.: Westview, 1994), 231.

11

AFRICA, THE HOMELAND: DIASPORIC CULTURES

"WHOEVER DOES NOT KNOW YOU CANNOT APPRECIATE YOU."
—A SWAHILI PROVERB

Africa has established a presence on other continents, due in part to the extensive forced migrations associated with the trans-Atlantic slave trade that occurred between the fifteenth and the nineteenth centuries. The scattering of blacks to the Americas and Europe created an African diaspora whose relevance remains today. To the blacks in the diaspora, Africa remains the "homeland" which has facilitated the construction of the identity of blackness. The chapter examines issues around culture and representation, showing the power of culture to unite, keep alive the notion of "Africaness," and even create opportunities to challenge negative ideas on race. Thanks to its culture, the "poor" continent is empowered by culture.

The political side of the African diaspora has generated considerable attention. Its ultimate manifestation has been expressed as Pan-Africanism which, during the twentieth century, translated into a series of major congresses and related activities demanding political rights for all blacks. The ideology of Pan-Africanism is socialism. As important as Pan-Africanism and socialism have been, they represent only one aspect of the history of the African diaspora. Various cultural and ideological areas have either been ignored or marginally addressed. Today, the politics of the African diaspora centers around demands for reparations and the scholarship of Afrocentricity. Both continue to generate controversies in some quarters.

Figure 15. A cup for the journey. Lalibela, Ethiopia.

Figure 16. The African world: A delicate balance. Near Ougadougou, Burkina Faso.

Figure 17. Portable African culture: A strong and beautiful tapestry.

But there is also the politics of culture, which generates less contro-versy and is far less visible—the use of traditions, symbols, religions, and other aspects of culture to build identity, resist dominant cultures, and project hope. In fact, greater success has been recorded in cultural struggles than in economic ones. For more than a hundred years, many have ex-pressed the ambition of turning the diaspora into a great economic advan-tage, for example, by creating transnational businesses that would empower blacks. For instance, in the nineteenth century, Bishop Henry Turner, the famous minister of the African Methodist Episcopal Church and the most renowned emigrationist of his generation, eagerly spoke of the creation of the "black capitalists" who would promote trade between the United States and Liberia and become millionaires within a few years. Muhammed Duse, a Pan-Africanist, went beyond this by actually creating some business ven-tures during the twentieth century. These and other business efforts have met with limited success. Again, the experience in sustaining and creating cultural connections has been different, with notable achievements.

Themes and Assumptions

This chapter will dwell on how culture has played a number of important functions in the diaspora, creating sources of identification among various communities, important linkages among groups and people, and ideas to uplift black people irrespective of their location. The chapter addresses a variety of issues, including the following:

1. African Imprint in the Americas and Caribbean
   From the *kente* attire of Ghana and the *abakua* music of Cuba, to the *orisa* worship of Ogun, various aspects of African culture have spread globally, serving as agencies of black representation, historical memory, visible presence in the Western world, and sources of identity. The chapter touches upon cultural aspects in American societies that have their roots in Africa in such areas as religion, music, and food.

2. Culture and Resistance
   Whether in Cuba, Haiti, or the United States, mobilizations for pro-test and change have relied on ethnicity, cultural identities, and reli-gion to resist hegemonic power. Even the politics of Pan-Africanism was reinforced by culture—the Harlem Renaissance gave a formi-dable intellectual expression to black radical politics; artists and singers

attended Pan-Africanist congresses; and scholars of international stature emerged to lend their weight to political demands. "If We Must Die," the combative poem by the Jamaican poet Claude McKay, became a slogan, a cultural code that celebrated the power of resistance. Culture has been used to create hope—the idea of transformation via the power of unseen forces and the emergence of a future hero.

3. Religious and Cultural Identities

A number of religions sustain black identities in various places (e.g., Rastafarianiasm and the reggae music of Bob Marley, Islam, "traditional religions," and others). There is also the idea of black-consciousness—Négritude—which has received intellectual expression in creative scholarship. Millennial dreams created black Messiahs such as Haile Selassie, who could save the race. Religious forces and symbols have been united to forge a mentality of oneness.

4. What Is Africa to Me?

The definition of the individual and collective self among blacks in the Americas and the construction of identity have borrowed extensively from the African connection. There have also been perceived obligations to contribute to the liberation of Africa from colonial rule and to its economic development. Educational and evangelical projects were aimed at making these contributions, based on the idea that Africa requires political, economic, and moral redemption, and reconstruction. Through Pan-Africanist ideas, black literature and cultural projects, and even tourism, the black world has been connected and occasionally invested with the notion of "oneness." As non-African blacks looked to Africa for solidarity and identity formation, so too did Africans look to the Americas for intellectual and practical ideas of redemption.

5. Knowledge Circulation

Within the diaspora, political ideas about race relations and strategies of redemption spread widely. Technical skills equally expanded. One courier agency has been the various generations of African students who study in the United States, who have been able to use the opportunity to understand politics, race relations, capitalism, and culture. In the first half of the twentieth century, the political ambitions of these students and African American political leaders converged in Pan-Africanism. As they moved from a racialized world to a colonized one, they sought the means to manipulate trans-Atlantic ideas and visions. The idea of reconstructing Africa thus involved a sense of unity in the diaspora—the transfer of black personnel and ideas from outside of Africa to Africa becomes a key component in uplifting Africa. Culture and skills merge in the project of race emancipation.

A number of assumptions that influence this chapter should be stated at the outset. First, I have used the word diaspora to refer to the dispersal of Africans to other areas (Asia, Europe, the Caribbean, and the Americas) during the slave trade and the voluntary migrations of Africans to other continents, for a variety of reasons, which have been increasing since the nineteenth century.[1] Blacks have also returned to Africa, either on a permanent basis (as in the settlement of Liberia and Sierra Leone) or on a temporary basis (as in the example of African American missionaries). We are dealing with multiple experiences, some global (the sense in which diaspora is used) and some localized within nation states, but with connections to other places (as in the case of apartheid in South Africa and the radical response to it by blacks in Africa and elsewhere). The African diaspora is a broadly defined notion, conveying a sense of globalism, but with the nation state also in mind.[2] Although academic interest in it is now widespread and vigorous, it is not a new idea. As long as blacks have been able to write and become involved in politics, they been thinking globally, in terms of situating themselves and their works in a trans-Atlantic vision and paradigm.[3]

The diaspora is a historic creation (migrations and dispersal), a mental and cultural idea (consciousness), a metaphor (to explain racial and economic injustice), a pilgrimage (the idea of a return to the homeland), an economic world system (the exploitation of black labor and a sense of collective loss), a political agenda (Pan-Africanism), an intellectual concern (academic courses and seminars), and a constructed identity (invented traditions, identity politics). Irrespective of how it is viewed, the diaspora is tied to culture in many ways: Africa is regarded as the homeland, the cultural space that belongs to all members; diaspora's boundaries are marked by culture and race, and its language is also defined by culture.[4]

Second, in all the aforementioned cases and others, culture has been used to sustain identity, empower people so that they can survive various circumstances of life, define blackness in order to build pride in the race, and preserve traditions and memory in order to develop historical consciousness. The interactions among the members of the diaspora have been fostered by various aspects of culture. Indeed, governments have sponsored such huge gatherings as the Second World Black and African Festival of Arts and Culture (FESTAC) in Lagos in 1977 to underscore the relevance of culture for global linkages. Through various avenues, ideas have circulated in the diaspora. There is the conventional one of the media. When Marcus Garvey created *The Negro World* after the First World War, the circulation reached almost two hundred thousand. But the number of those who were able to access the message was even larger—through people who traveled (for instance, merchant sailors) and took the paper to many places, including Africa, where it was read to people and the message further circulated through oral transmission. Music has equally been a powerful tool, as in the case of Bob Marley and Fela Anikulapo Kuti. Books and essays also travel widely. Garvey's *Philosophy and Opinions* (1923) became the Bible to the generation of Kwame Nkrumah, the famous Pan-Africanist and the first president of independent Ghana. Garvey in turn confessed that the book that had the most profound influence on him was Washington's *Up from Slavery.* Ideas in major books get circulated by word of mouth in a culture where orality has developed as a strategy of cultural preservation.

Third, although often ignored, black communities have historically contributed aspects of their labor and civilizations to others—to the Greeks and Romans in ancient times; and to areas where they were taken as slaves (e.g., Saudi Arabia, India, Turkey, Portugal, the Caribbean, the United States, Britain, Canada, and Brazil). Blacks, too, have borrowed ideas from others, since the traffic in borrowing is never unidirectional. Africans in the diaspora have been assimilated and integrated into host communities and have equally struggled to adapt themselves to new circumstances. In this discussion, the emphasis is on Africanism in the Americas—what Africa has contributed to both the black and white communities.

Fourth, non-African blacks have contributed to the development of the African continent in various ways. The traffic has always been impressive, including African students who studied abroad and returned home with ideas from other lands, African traders, educators, sailors, African Americans who resettled in Liberia and Sierra Leone or who worked as missionaries in other places, and Afro-Brazilians and Afro-Cubans who went to Africa. For years, many African Americans of different ideological persuasions and careers have expressed the need to contribute to the development of Africa. In understanding why there is a strong desire to do this, we see the role of identity, the power of culture. Africa is the homeland, and its people must not suffer. Retaining some cultural elements from the homeland, they also want to give back to Africa, thereby creating a brisk traffic in cultural ideas.

Finally, culture, in all its ramifications, creates the subtext of politics. Political activities such as Pan-Africanism are based on a belief that members of the diaspora share some common culture or regard themselves as Africans. The African diaspora lacks a clear unity based on one language or religion, as in the case of some diasporas. Neither do we have historical continuity in which diaspora members maintain unbroken historical links with Africa. However, there are four strong elements in the cultural unity of the African diaspora. To start with, the blackness that others deride becomes an identity marker, one in which physical appearance becomes a strong element of culture itself. Second, historical experiences have been constructed as a racial identity—such experiences as slavery, political exclusion, economic exploitation, and related conditions are treated as constituents of a collective identity. Although the experience may differ and obscure differences in gender, class, and even the relevance of race, it is nevertheless treated as a "collective" one. Third, there are cultural remnants, in ideas and practices, that members continue to associate with Africa. And finally, a point made by Ronald W. Walters, is that of imagination: "what fired the imagination was the incongruity of the European perception and treatment of Africans and the African's own perception of his native continent as an option for liberation."[5] Walters, an African American, says that he may look like a white lawyer in his three-piece suit, but Africa remains in his imagination; he is even possessed "of both spirit and imagination."[6] This imagination has given rise to deliberate projects to study African culture, identify its main elements, and choose the name "African American" to claim a link to Africa. Still borrowing from Walters, Africans in the diaspora, while not claiming to be part of the routines of African culture in Africa, base their claims on the following: "(1) their affirmation of an African heritage; (2) their participation in the diasporic aspects of pan African political struggles; (3) their continuing concern with the status of Africa and their efforts to improve it, and (4) their relationship to other hyphenated Africans in the Diaspora."[7]

African Imprint in the Americas and the Caribbean

A variety of African cultures have made an important impact on the United States, the Caribbean, and Latin America. Some have persisted and many have been transformed to produce hybrid practices. Among the notable areas are the survival of the core aspects of worldview relating to family and the work ethic, religious values, the use of African musical instruments and rhythm in the musical cultures of many areas, African cuisine, the use of African songs in religious worship in places like Brazil and Cuba, and the use of the hoe and some farming equipment in Haiti. Some gods such as Ogun, Sango, and Yemoja and the African belief systems regarding magic and witchcraft have become truly trans-Atlantic. For instance, Ogun, the Yoruba god of war and iron, is worshipped or invoked in speeches by millions of people in West Africa, the Americas, and the Caribbean.[8]

The transfer of culture was made possible by forced migrations and the nature of the relations between various cultures in the Americas. Integration is not always easy, as barriers may be created by host communities, or migrants may simply refuse to integrate.[9] Through assimilation, the cultures of the host societies have also been absorbed, in some cases completely.

It is not always possible to correlate demography to cultural retention or the degree of assimilation to host societies. Other factors do affect demography to produce many consequences. Assimilation and intermarriage take place and affect the adoption and retention of cultural practices. Education and integration to market economies can also lead to the emergence of alternative cultures, making it difficult to isolate the African agency. Where the Protestant churches are strong and exert influence on the black population, as in some parts of the United States, many have replaced their African values with Anglo-Saxon ones.

The sheer physical presence of black people in a country is itself a form of survival which may affect perception of race and the nature of domestic politics. In some countries, color difference is institutionalized, a practice which may even affect the neighborhoods in which people live in a given city. Roger Bastide noted in the mid-1960s that even where the color line is not institutionalized, there is a tendency for blacks to feel as if they are different from others, and to construct a world of difference.[10]

Where the majority of the population is black, as in Barbados, Haiti, Jamaica, and Trinidad and Tobago, the diaspora connection is plainly visible. There are countries where the degree of intermarriage is high, and people of African descent have played important political and economic roles, as in the cases of Cuba and Brazil. There are places where the demographic impact of blacks is minimal—Chile, Bolivia, Paraguay, Uruguay, and Argentina. R. D. Raltson, borrowing data from other scholars, has indicated additional categories. He regards Colombia, Nicaragua, and Panama as three countries where small, "tightly-knit" black populations have been able to maintain a respectable level of distance from other races. According to him, there are other countries where people of African origin have also not been fully integrated with other local populations—Suriname and the maroons in Santo Domingo, Jamaica, Cuba, and Haiti.[11]

With regard to culture, it is unwise to keep searching for evidence of so-called cultural purity, as if values and cultures can be retained in their original forms over a long period. Changes inevitably occur, leading to various transformations and new hybrids. Connections with Africa can, however, be clearly seen in some examples. For instance, in Jamaica the Sasabonsan cult was originally of Asante origin, later to become modified to a spirit-based cult. In 1894, the Jamaica Baptist Free Church, created by Bedward, added magic and repackaged it as Christianity. It has not been uncommon to add elements from Christianity to an African religion either to create a redefined Christianity or a redefined traditional religion. This is the power of cultural creativity at work, the ability to draw from various sources to meet one's needs and achieve spiritual satisfaction. Evidence of this strategy can be found in Haiti where the Catholic Church and African gods met and combined in creative ways. Interactions can also be multiple, as in the case of the *macumba* of Brazil, where African religion interacted with the Catholic and Amerindian observances. Where intermarriage has occurred, as in the rise of the mestizo in the West Indies where Africans (the Caribs) married Amerindian women, cultural mixing can be intense and complex.

Interest and research in cultural survival started a long time ago, with a most notable contribution from Melville J. Herskovits, who in 1941 published *The Myth of the Negro Past*.[12] Since then, the literature has been quite respectable, with some clear patterns now fairly well established. This established literature reveals a number of issues. Drawing on evidence of remnants of African culture in the United States (notably in the states of South Carolina, Georgia, and Florida) and in Brazil, the Caribbean, and Suriname, a debate ensued as to the survival or otherwise of African culture. Some scholars tend to see continuity and survival, while others see transformations and new ways of life.

In what is now known in intellectual circles as the "Herskovits-Frazier debate," Melville Herskovits argued that there is cultural survival whereas E. Franklin Frazier posited that African Americans lost their culture over time and that what is characterized as survival is an alternative culture. For Frazier, slavery was so completely destructive that no aspect of African values survived, and African Americans had no choice but to borrow heavily from white communities.[13] As more scholars joined in the debate, it became obvious that Herskovits is right to point out that cultural retention is strong, although a tiny voice continues to affirm that Frazier is right in pointing to the deculturalization of the black experience, and that Africanism should not be treated as the most notable aspect of African American culture. There are others, notably Sidney Mintz and Richard Price, who are opposed to the idea of cultural survival, but do not necessarily support Frazier either. They argue that there is more cultural syncretism in the New World, not just cultural survival, as African cultures came in contact with others to lead to the creation of new ones.[14] Research continues to focus on issues of survival and new cultural formations as well as on the impact of different ethnicities and identity on cultural practices.[15]

The list of the contributors to unearthing the evidence of survival and Africanisms is long, including Newbell Puckett, Carter G. Woodson, W. E. B. Du Bois, Guy Johnson, Lorenzo Turner, Norman Whitten and John Szwed, Sidney M. Mintz and Richard Price, Peter Wood, Lawrence W. Levine, Margaret Washington Creel, Sterling Stuckey, Charles Joyner, Winifred Vass, Dena J. Epstein, and John W. Blassingame.[16] Among the major statements by these various scholars are that: the folk beliefs of African Americans in the southern states show similarities with those of Africans in their contents and strategies of transmission; African customs have been preserved in African American philosophy, folklore, belief in witchcraft, voodoo, ghosts, and burial customs; the survival of African culture can be found in various aspects of arts, crafts, history, language, and spirituality. Detailed studies on the Gullah communities and Georgia Sea Islands reveal considerable evidence of African retention in oral cultures (e.g., proverbs, legends, songs and folktales, and speech). Those who examined colonial America see the African impact on agricultural practices such as open grazing, basketry, and rice growing. Studies on the banjo have traced it to Africa, while the impact of African Bantu languages has been established with respect to American folklore, place names, and literature.

Much of this previous research has been extended and consolidated in a book edited by Joseph E. Holloway.[17] The ten essays in the volume examine the cultural carryovers from west and central Africa in various areas, notably history, language, arts, and religion. The major zones of influence identified in this important book include the following:

History—some African groups, notably the Bantu of central Africa, created homogenous societies and cultures in some areas of the United States; southern planters borrowed from the agricultural practices of their African slaves.

Language—African Americans have retained the linguistic structures of African languages in the use of tone and tense distinctions.[18]

Religion—many African American practices are derived from Africa, such as the belief in a Supreme Being, the awareness of the spiritual world in the life of an individual, the practice of Christianity that incorporates aspects of indigenous religions, "the ring shout, the passing of children over a dead person's coffin in the Sea Islands, and the placement of objects on top of graves."[19] Detailed case studies in a number of chapters bring out other major points— Jessie Gaston Mulira traces the voodoo religion in New Orleans to Dahomey, arguing that the religion and its elements of magic, rituals, and symbols, were transplanted virtually wholesale.[20] In another examination of African American religion in Florida during the eighteenth and nineteenth centuries, the attention paid to ecstasy, funeral rites, musical styles, and rituals is traced back to Africa.[21]

Arts—African influence can be seen in African American musical forms, folklore, and artistic culture in general. The impact of the Kongo culture (from central Africa) is considerable on the aesthetic of black culture in the Americas, contributing to the emergence of the *samba* in Brazil, to that of jazz in the United States, and to a number of dance patterns such as the *akimbo* pose, baton-twirling in Mississippi, and *juba* dance (now known as the Charleston). Africa also influenced the epic heroes (Stagolee and John Henry), medicine, food, and drama. Many of these survived the Middle Passage and were practiced on the plantations. Later, slave songs became the spirituals.

In the same collection edited by Holloway, John Philips broadens the discussion to examine how African culture also influenced white Americans in areas such as food, agriculture, religion, social structure, and music. In general, the impact of Africa and blacks in general on white civilization or economic development tends to be ignored or denied. But Philips notes that some aspects of African culture adopted by white Americans are not necessarily found among African Americans or are actually more prevalent among whites (as in case of the banjo).

In isolating some of the African contributions to white America, Herskovits' short but pioneering essay remains a landmark.[22] He identifies at least five major areas:

1. music—jazz and spirituals, in both of which African Americans have distinguished themselves, have become popular American music. Adding to the banjo, Philips notes the African influence in the development of country music and the white Appalachian banjo and the development of the American washtub bass from the African earth-bow.
2. southern dialect, in its pronunciation and musical tone.
3. African spirit of respect for people, elders, and neighbors and the use of kinship idioms.
4. cuisine, such as gumbo, fried chicken, okra, and heavy seasoning of food.
5. religious behavior—to quote Philips, who paraphrases Herskovits, "European possession cults practiced a very personal form of autohypnosis,

whereas American churches engaged in a more social form of group excitation induced by the rhythms of the liturgy and the droning of the preacher. Such a trance form was characteristically African but was often found among whites who belonged to churches with large numbers of black members and in the Pentecostal sects."[23]

Philips extends this list of contributions, adding new areas that require further investigation as well as offering explanations as to how people of African descent could have imparted their culture to white communities.

What Herskovits and Philips identify are positive aspects of culture borrowing. Culture also offers the tools to create differentiation. In creating racial distinctions, the marker is not just physical characteristics but cultural ones as well, especially a deliberate creation of social boundaries. To take just one example, the combination of slavery and poverty created a culture of black inferiority in the minds of whites. It is this white belief in the culture of black inferiority that has part defined the power and identity of whiteness which makes it easier to exploit racial difference. "Without the presence of black people in America," concludes Cornel West,

> European Americans would not be "white"—they would be only Irish, Italians, Poles, Welsh, and others engaged in class, ethnic, and gender struggles over resources and identity. What made America distinctly American for them was not simply the presence of unprecedented opportunities, but the struggle for seizing these opportunities in a new land in which black slavery and racial caste served as the floor upon which white class, ethnic, and gender struggles could be diffused and diverted.[24]

The issue is even broader than this. By trying to understand blackness and castigating it, whiteness was being invented. A notion of white superiority is in essence the creation of a white culture based on "Otherness." The emergence of one culture that counters the other is the result of their contributions to one another, even if this process goes unacknowledged.

What Is Africa to Me?

Blacks outside of Africa have constructed their identity based on their African origin. Indeed, their definition of Self and its perception by others inevitably revolve around issues of race, slavery, and Africa. Historically, there has also been a strong tendency not just to borrow from Africa, but to contribute to it. For instance, part of the agenda of Pan-Africanism was to seek the means to liberate Africa from European domination and to supply the continent with ideas to transform it. For various generations of diasporan Africans, the continent has been a source of immense pride. Every era has produced leading African Americans who talk about the renewal of pride in Africa and popularize the contributions of Africa to world civilization.[25] African American consciousness of Africa is both cultural and political and can be found in the way Africa is connected to their identity, their contributions to Pan-Africanism, the dismantling of colonial rule in Africa, and the end of apartheid in South Africa.[26] Notable among these African Americans are W. E. B. Du Bois, the "father of Pan-Africanism" and one of the most prolific authors of the twentieth century; J. A. Rogers, the author of *The World's Great Men of Color*; Chancellor Williams, who wrote one of the most influential books on Africa, *The Destruction of Black Civilization: Great Issues of a Race from 4500 B.C. to 2000 A.D.*; Arthur Schomburg, an essayist and the creator of one of the most respectable archives on the African diaspora; and the highly respected Howard professor, the late William Leo Hansberry, whose lecture notes were later published by Professor Joseph Harris, an equally respected scholar. In the late 1970s, Alex Haley successfully created major public interest in his book, *Roots,* which has since led to annual pilgrimages by many African Americans to west Africa. In the same spirit, the African American National Black Arts Festival, a biennial festival, began in 1988 to bring together black artists and scholars from Africa, the United States, the Caribbean, and Latin America.

As indicated above, the connections between Africa and diasporan blacks have been expressed in multiple ways Two major areas will be discussed to illustrate the intensity and relevance of linkages in the diaspora: projects and ambitions by blacks outside of Africa to return to Africa (emigration) and the contributions of African Americans to the spread of Christianity in Africa (evangelism).

Emigration Projects and Ideas

In the nineteenth and twentieth centuries, black emigration was both a cultural and a practical project to construct a linkage between Africa and its members in the diaspora. The back-to-Africa movements grew in the United States, the Caribbean, and Brazil, indicating a great ambition by thousands of blacks in the diaspora to return to west Africa, south Africa, and the Horn.

Early emigrations from the United States were to Liberia and Sierra Leone during the nineteenth century. Before the official abolition of slavery in Brazil in 1888, a large number of Brazilian blacks emigrated to west Africa. In spite of the disappointment that accompanied this move, the idea of "back-to-Africa" continued to be expressed during the nineteenth and early twentieth centuries. The leading advocates of this idea during the nineteenth century included Lott Cary, John B. Russwurm, Paul Cuffee, Henry H. Garnet, Martin R. Delany, and Daniel Coker. A number of individuals and small missions helped to propagate the idea of emigration. For instance, the famous scholar, Dr. Edward Wilmot Blyden, represented the American Colonization Society in 1889 to urge more people to go to Africa. A few combined missionary work with emigration, as in the cases of Henry H. Garnet, who in 1881 became a resident minister and consul-general to Liberia, and Bishop Henry NcNeal Turner, who went to Africa in the 1880s and 1890s.

Some examples of the emigration projects can be offered here.[27] In 1878, the South Carolina–Liberian Exodus Joint Stock Steamship Company was able to take about 203 African Americans to Liberia. In the 1890s, hundreds of black farmers in Arkansas and Oklahoma were eager to relocate to Liberia. In 1896, Turner was able to relocate three hundred people to Liberia. Three years later, the African Development Society was established, an organization aimed at sponsoring African Americans in buying land and relocating to East Central Africa.[28] In 1900, the International Migration Society of Alabama sent about five hundred people to Liberia. This was not a good experience for all of them, and those who returned came with terrible stories of impossible living conditions, discouraging many others.

In the early twentieth century, efforts to relocate to South Africa and Ghana were unsuccessful. Marcus Garvey, born in Jamaica in 1887, was the most remarkable advocate of emigration in the early decades of the twentieth century, rising to become one of the few heroes of the Pan-Africanist movement. His career has generated an impressive array of literature.[29] So successful was Garvey that his movement—the Universal Negro Improvement and Conservation Association and African Communities League (UNIA)—was the largest after the First World War. He believed that self-help programs were necessary to liberate blacks. He moved to the United States in 1915 to develop his business and political ideas. Garvey chose the United States after reading Washington's *Up from Slavery* in hopes of learning about his Tuskegee Institute and enlisting his help in building similar schools in Jamaica. Washington died shortly before Garvey's arrival. According to Garvey, agricultural and industrial schools had to be created in Jamaica and elsewhere, a black-owned fleet of ships should be created to facilitate commerce between Africa and the Americas, and blacks must create one nation to serve all of them. Garvey chose Liberia as the focus of his emigration scheme, which promised to relocate almost thirty thousand families. The emigration project was a failure.[30] Perhaps inspired by Garvey, a few African Americans went to Ethiopia (among them William Leo Hansberry).

These cases of emigration represent examples of the "reverse diaspora," in which blacks were returning to Africa rather than leaving their continent. What did emigration mean to the participants and what did it contribute to Africa? Emigration was associated with empowerment—the ability to be free to determine one's occupation and enjoy rights and privileges as a citizen. It was associated with dignity and respect in a nonracialized environment. "[O]ne thing that the Black man has here (i.e., in Liberia)," concluded Henry Turner, "is Manhood, freedom; and the fullest liberty; he feels like a Lord and walks the same way."[31] Turner maintained that blacks could create not just a dignified living, but an autonomous culture—they should create a new nation with their own laws, customs, economies, and civilization. The supporters of emigration wondered: if blacks in the New World had Africa to go to, why live in another place where they had to beg for justice, jobs, and freedom? Garvey, who linked emigration with the creation of black business power, was able to energize a large number of blacks in Africa and the Americas. For him, blacks were suffering people who, to liberate themselves, must "claim Africa for themselves."[32] The emigrants to Africa brought with them new ideas, skills, knowledge, and culture. Again, only a few examples can be provided. In west Africa, the Afro-Brazilians emerged as a distinct cultural group during the nineteenth century. They created a trading and professional group, and altered the cultural landscape.

The Afro-Brazilians

During the nineteenth century, mixed passenger cargo lines traveled between the ports of Lagos, West Africa, and Bahia de Todos os Santos. Brazilian emigrants increased in number from 1835 onwards, settling along the coastal cities in the Gold Coast (Ghana), Togo, Dahomey (Republic of Benin), and Nigeria. They formed communities, clearly identified by themselves and their hosts, who were bearers and propagators of culture. New consumer goods were imported from Brazil, notably rum, cigars, and tobacco in exchange for kola nuts, palm oil, local textiles, and European cotton. A commercial class emerged and profited from this trade, along with an artisan class—masons, carpenters, printers, and tool repairers. Not only did the latter spread their skills among Africans, they also introduced the Brazilian architecture style to West Africa. "Brazilian Quarters" were created in a number of areas, including multistory houses copied from Bahia, a number of mosques, and a large Catholic cathedral in Lagos. In Dahomey, the common Brazilian architecture was the "Casa-Grande" structure of the Brazilian plantations and sugar mills. A number of Brazilian emigrants were well educated, and they imported books and other reading materials. During the colonial period, their education enabled them to join the civil service. Not only did they use culture to retain their identity, they also introduced their hosts to their ways of life in such aspects as folk dances and songs. As they became integrated into African society during the colonial period, they gradually lost much of their heritage and Portuguese language.

Afro-Brazilians contributed to the growth of religions. They did not belong to just one religion, and many actually took advantage of emigration to return to their old religions. Among them could be found Muslims who contributed to the building of mosques and Catholics who contributed to the building of the first church in 1879 in Lagos. Eager to retain aspects of their African culture, Afro-Brazilians contributed to the Africanization of Christianity. Many chose not to keep a distance from indigenous gods and spirits, seeking accommodation between older ways and Catholicism. While deriving or enjoying the prestige and social status brought by Christianity and its elite, they seem to have taken refuge in the spiritual powers of local gods and diviners. For the Yoruba among them, the *orisa* (gods) and *babalawo* (diviners) were as important as the Catholic saints.

Even the commercial traffic reflected this religious blending. If items of status and leisure were imported for the Afro-Brazilians in west Africa, they exported religious and cult items such as kola nuts, cowries, gourds, palm oil, black soap, carved objects to represent the gods, charms (*juju*), and many others. Demand was high, showing that many people were devoted to *orisa* worship in Brazil.

The Spread of Atlantic Ideas: The Circulation of Knowledge and Skills

Voluntary migrations of Africans to North America and other areas where black people live have broadened the interactions between Africa and other continents. Major intellectual and practical ideas about change, leadership, and political philosophy have also spread so that people can now talk of black literature, black music, and black art. Space does not permit an elaboration of all these issues, but I will identify the most persistent ones.

Hundreds of voluntary African migrants left Africa for Western countries and returned to Africa with ideas and skills. The historically black colleges in the United States such as Howard, Xavier, Fisk, Bethune-Cookman, Hampton, Lincoln, Livingston, Tuskegee, Wilberforce, and Morris Brown became dream schools for many Africans. African American churches sponsored a number of African students, and black ministers were mentors to many.

The education of Africans in the United States has helped in many ways to strengthen the linkages in the diaspora. Through education, cultural ideas and technical skills have been circulated within the diaspora. African students have served as culture couriers and keen observers of American domestic politics and race relations. In interacting amongst themselves, they have developed associations and strategies to deal with their own countries and continent. When some American-trained Africans returned to their home countries still under colonial rule, not all were able to secure the kind of jobs they wanted, as they were discriminated against for not studying in Europe or were perceived as being too radical. Many became champions of American-type education. I will limit my examples to the first half of the twentieth century.

The number of Africans who went to school in the United States began to increase after 1880, encouraged by the few who had gone before and the need to overcome the limitations of higher education in colonial Africa. Many of these Africans distinguished themselves in various careers. The activities of the politicians among them bore a clear imprint of the impact of the United States on their politics and ideology. A large number made contributions as nationalists and community leaders, for example, John Chilembwe, Ndabaningi Sithole, J. E. K. Aggrey, Charlotte and Marshall Maxeke, John Dube, Pixley Ka Izaka Seme, D. S. Malekebu, Franck Osam-Pinanko, Peter Koinange, and A. B. Xuma. Three became heads of states—Kwame Nkrumah of Ghana, Kamuzu Banda of Malawi, and Nnamdi Azikiwe of Nigeria.

The contributions of this group of people were diverse. Among them were church founders and leaders such as Chilembwe and Malekebu; pioneer industrialists such as Malekebwu; and educators such as the famous J. E. K. Aggrey (1875–1921) of Ghana.[33] Aggrey left for the United States in 1898, sponsored by the American Methodist Episcopla (AME) Zion Church, to attend Livingstone College in North Carolina. After his degree, he stayed in the United States where he worked as a newspaper correspondent, schoolteacher, and church minister. He contributed to the demand for higher education in west Africa and served as a mentor to a generation of African students in the United States.

The idea of technical education, as espoused by Booker T. Washington and his Tuskegee Institute, gained considerable influence among Africans who wanted to duplicate it in Africa. Characterized as the "Tuskegee spirit," it was widely believed to be superior to European colonial education in blending agricultural, technical, and liberal education. The belief was that a technical and commercial class would emerge that would give blacks considerable professional and economic power, allowing them to use the skills and capital generated to improve their standards of living and overcome domination by other races. The impact of Washington on Garvey has been mentioned earlier.

As expected, the best known were the politicians. Here, the Atlantic and Pan-Africanist connections are clear. One example was Nnamdi Azikiwe, who started his impressive educational career in West Virginia in 1925, and later attended Howard University in Washington, D.C.[34] Azikiwe was exposed to the ideas of Marcus Garvey and Pan-Africanist principles. At Howard, he became a student of leading African American scholars, such as Ralph Bunche, Leo Hansberry, and Alain Locke. He was also privileged to meet a number of notable visiting scholars, such as the distinguished Trinidadian Pan-Africanist and socialist George Padmore. He moved to Lincoln University in Jefferson City, Missouri, in 1930, where he stayed for four years and criticized the school for its racist policies. Upon his return to Africa, Azikiwe propagated political ideas and publicized Pan-Africanism. Under the umbrella of the National Association for the Advancement of Colored People (NAACP), African American leaders, most notably W. E. B. Du Bois, added the decolonization of Africa to its agenda, thus making statements that future African leaders easily connected to. For instance, Kwame Nkrumah of Ghana enrolled at Lincoln in 1935, and later became a leading Pan-Africanist, the first president of independent Ghana, and a tremendous symbol for African Americans.

Culture and Resistance

Resistance has been part of diaspora from the very beginning, and culture has always been deployed as a strategy to mobilize people, ensure cooperation, prevent the betrayal of fellow members, and generate hope. In important cases, Africans in the diaspora formed ethnic associations to mobilize against their masters or create opportunities for violence and flight. Examples of the linkage between associations and resistance can be found in slave revolts in Cuba. In Havana, Cuba, in 1836, the Abakua society was formed, modeled on the eastern Nigerian Ekpe secret society, to fight against slavery. The secret language of the Abakua society is now part of Cuban popular music.

In Jamaica, Haiti, Cuba, and Santo Domingo, countries with maroon communities, we find examples of fugitive slaves who came together, separated themselves from others, and resorted to cultural identity to create strong bonds among themselves. Living in rural communities, they were able to turn to African values in creating their semi-autonomous societies.

The linkage between culture and resistance survives today. In Jamaica and some Caribbean islands, the Rastafarian movements emerged in part as a culture of protest against the domination of capitalism and race. While Protestantism did spread, many elements were added to it, in particular the idea of the Messiah. Haile Selassie became a god, the Messiah that would deliver many Rastafarians from oppression.

There are several aspects which do not manifest themselves in rebellion or other direct forms of violence, but rather in intellectual ideas, radical leadership, and the belief in a savior. I will provide three examples.

Négritude: Blackness and the Creativity of Resistance

The leading intellectual idea in the Francophone black diaspora during the twentieth century was the cultural concept of a collective black consciousness, known as Négritude. Usually regarded as the cultural side of Pan-Africanism, the intellectual leaders of Négritude include notable Caribbean intellectuals such as Aimé Césaire, Léon Damas, and Jean Price-Mars of Haiti, and the famous poet-politician, Léopold Senghor of Senegal. These men and their ideas connected the black universe in an intellectual affirmation of blackness. Scholarship was connected with identity politics, as the writers sought the means to be politically relevant. Excited by the Harlem Renaissance and eager to support Marcus Garvey and Du Bois, Négritude scholars turned to history, poetry, and other genres to invest culture with political meaning. Senghor and Césaire regarded the diaspora as an indivisible cultural entity, sharing a similar past, common historical traditions, and great dreams about the future. If the Harlem poet, Countee Cullen, posed the question, "What is Africa to me?" in his celebrated poem, "Heritage,"[35] other members of the Harlem group such as Langston Hughes and the Négritude scholars decided to answer the question in an assertive and definitive manner by praising blackness, minimizing or rejecting the relevance of Western civilization, rejecting the idea of white superiority, and calling for black nationalism.

Who is Prester John?

Négritudist imaginations moved from dreams to reality in the symbolism and expression of black unity and consciousness, but more so in the belief that a savior would arise to deliver the black race. The Rastafarians saw in Emperor Haile Selassie of Ethiopia such a savior.[36] The Muslims believed in the Mahdi, a prophet who would emerge to clean the world, reform Islam, bring justice, and restore people's dignity.

Many African Americans are unlikely to imagine, to say nothing of believing, that part of the African millennial tradition was to regard them as saviors. Those seeking an alternative to white missionaries expected black missionaries. According to the Xhosa of South Africa, who lost their land and cattle in the mid-nineteenth century, African Americans would come to their rescue by fighting on their behalf. To those seeking an end to colonial rule, African Americans would come to Africa to form an army that Europeans could not defeat. If there was a shortage of skills and entrepreneurs, why not ask African Americans to return to the homeland? In the apartheid era of the 1920s in South Africa, when Africans were regarded as primitive and incapable of understanding and enjoying the rights and privileges of citizenship, African Americans became examples of modernizers and the role models of radicalism and civility. James Thaele, the Lincoln-trained South African professor, became a prominent member of the radical African National Congress in the 1920s and a firm believer in the capacity of African Americans to lead Africa out of its colonial domination.

There was also the creative invention of prophets, leaders, warriors, and even gods. Bishop Msiqinya, the peripatetic black American, appeared to many in South Africa in the 1910s as a deliverer, and those who offered political deliverance could be regarded as Messiahs. Thus, Marcus Garvey was believed in some parts of South Africa to be semi-divine. Even James Aggrey, the teacher, was welcomed in South Africa as a sign that an army of African Americans would soon arise to save them from European domination.

In his novel, *Prester John,* published in 1910, John Buchan, a white man, explored this millennial theme by creating a fictionalized educated African pastor who emerged from the black community and led a rebellion against white people. For capturing the prevalent view among blacks and the fear of violence among whites, *Prester John* received attention in South Africa. Thirteen years later, another novel with the same theme was written, entitled *Bayete!*, which describes the coming of African Americans to South Africa and also portrays the great fear that whites had that such a migration would prove to be a calamity for them.

The diaspora experience can also be seen among the marginalized blacks of India. Called "untouchables" by the others, but calling themselves the Dalits, they have been able to connect with the African American leadership in the United States, borrowing organizational strategies and political ideas from them, and building bridges to ensure an end to their marginality.[37]

Rastafarianism

"By the rivers of Babylon"—so begins one of the most famous reggae songs of the twentieth century, by Bob Marley, based on the Old Testament Psalm 137. Reggae is not just music for listening pleasure, but is connected to Rastafarianism, a movement which began in Jamaica in the early decades of the twentieth century.[38] It is a resistance movement, one that uses cultural identity to seek an end to the domination and marginalization of its members. To the general public, the "Rastas" are known by their dress and speech—they wear "dreadlocks," ornaments in the colors of Africa (red, green, yellow, black, and gold), and use a "dread talk" language which is a form of creole. The public associates the Rastas with drugs and the use of *ganja* (marijuana), which has made them victims of police harassment.

The public imagery of the Rasta obscures their complex practices, as well as their strong beliefs. The dreadlocks and dread talk help to create a very strong sense of identity and bonding among members. The ritualistic and secular use of drugs is not meant to produce a careless, reckless lifestyle. Indeed, Rasta members are forbidden from consuming alcohol, hard drugs, and unprocessed foods. They are expected to be religious, and to constantly reread the Bible and the speeches of Haile Selassie and Marcus Garvey. They subscribe to a set of religious beliefs: *Ras Tafari* (Haile Selassie of Ethiopia) is a prophet and *Jah* (God) is black. *Ras Tafari* is God incarnate, the Messiah that will save the black people. They see themselves as the descendants of the Israelites of the ancient period, represented in the modern world by the Ethiopian Coptic Church. They see an end to the present world, which will destroy itself and be replaced by a just, new one.[39]

These practices and beliefs are connected to a political agenda and resistance ideology. Like the Nation of Islam discussed below, they attribute the destruction of the black race to Western influences, usually described as evil. For the black race to prevail, it has to deal with this evil. A Messiah will help, and blacks must return to their homeland in Africa. To communicate with one another and reach a larger audience, the Rastas use reggae music, their fashion, *ganja,* and their religious leaders. They have been successful in reaching places outside of Jamaica, including west Africa, New Zealand, Britain, India, Canada, and the United States, where they have appealed to a number of young people. As with the spread of religions and ideas, when they reach new places, they can be "customized" to meet the demands of local cultures and established lifestyles.[40]

As Rastafarianism spreads, its association with identity politics and resistance is clear. It appeals to those who regard their peoples and cultures as having been suppressed by capitalism and Western influence, those who complain against American and Western colonialism; youth dealing with joblessness and urban problems, and those who seek alternative models to the present realities that appear to them to be corrupt and alienating. Rastafarianism is regarded by its members as a source of hope, a way to make life more meaningful in a noncapitalist ideology. Its connection to the African diaspora is also very apparent: the Rastas condemn slavery and exploitation, call for the restoration of African values and cultures among all blacks, advocate emigration to Africa, preach freedom from mental colonization, and affirm the importance of blackness. The scholarship that appeals to members relates to race pride and radicalism, in particular the ideas of Garvey, Du Bois, and Frantz Fanon.

Resistance is much broader than I have presented here. Indeed, the entire Pan-Africanist movement can be interpreted as resistance to colonial domination and racism. "Africa Must Unite," the slogan of Kwame Nkrumah and the title of his famous book, is an affirmation of the power of collective resistance. This idea in turn led to the formation of many socialist-oriented associations (such as the Pan-African Revolutionary Socialist Party in 1983), and regional and continental organizations, notably the Organization of African Unity established in 1963. Resistance can also be reflected in scholarship, as in Afrocentricity, which celebrates black scholarship against the background of Western universalism,[41] or black radical scholarship in general.[42]

Religious Identities and Evangelization

Many religious traditions illustrate the ability and success of religion to create connections and memory among the members of the diaspora. Such

Yoruba gods as Ogun, Yemoja, and Sango have spread beyond their original homeland to North America. Belief in magic and witchcraft is pervasive in many locations. Islamic and Christian missionaries have broadened the scope of religious interactions to respond to local conditions. I will examine these three religions.

Christianity and African Gods

A blending of Catholicism and African gods has taken place in many areas. Voodoo practices are not regarded as any violation of Christian injunctions. Just as a Catholic in west Africa can have two or more wives and still expect salvation, his counterpart in Haiti can take to *orisa*. The Catholic saints and Yoruba *orisa* (gods) are regarded as equals, even with the celebration of *orisa* replacing those of the saints.

The practice of traditional religion can also be influenced by that of Christianity. Catholic sacraments have been incorporated into *orisa* worship to add to the spiritual energy and the rituals. In Brazil, the candomblé and macumba cults have taken elements from other sources such as the Amerindian culture.

Black Evangelism

Traditional religion was not the only basis for maintaining identity. Both Islam and Christianity have contributed to strengthening linkages and promoting affinity among the members of the diaspora. Owing to the conversion of many African Americans to Christianity, it is this religion that has been more important in the cultural traffic and linkages. African Americans have served as missionaries in Africa in an attempt to propagate Christianity.[43] Many worked as missionaries for established mainstream churches, such as the Presbyterian Church, which sent missions to French Cameroon in the 1890s; the Southern Presbyterian Church, with its mission in the Congo also in the 1890s;[44] and the Seventh-Day Adventists, who sent three African Americans to Malawi at the turn of the century.

Black-owned churches and organizations sent their own agents at different periods and to different areas. The Rev. Alexander Crummell was one of the early pioneers who went to west Africa, also serving as the principal of an Episcopal school in Liberia. In 1893, the African Methodist Episcopal (AME) Church organized two conferences, in 1893 and 1895, to discuss the possible contributions of African Americans to Africa. The motives were genuine, and the answers were passionate. Participants at the conferences and many church leaders believed that African Americans owed Africans a duty and needed to evangelize them. Many were to repeat the same ideology of the mid-nineteenth-century white missions of the "Bible and the Plough"—that Africa required Christianity and a new economy to grow and transform itself. Regarding it as a continent with great potential and a great future, Christianity would let Africa discover and actualize itself. In the words of Bishop Turner, the redemption was certain, and the agents were clear: "God brought the Negro to America and Christianized him so that he might go back to Africa and redeem that land."[45] Black missionaries went to various parts of the continent as the agents of missions such as the AME, the African Methodist Episcopal Zion, and the National Baptist Convention.

Their impact was substantial. A number of Africans were drawn into African American-led missions. For instance, in Ghana J. E. K. Aggrey and Franck Osam-Pinanko distinguished themselves and became members of the AME Zion Church. In South Africa the AME had an impact that lasted for a long time in the nineteenth and twentieth centuries. In 1896, the AME was able to create a temporary alliance with the "Ethiopian" Church—a set of African independent churches that broke away from the white-led Wesleyan mission. Through the AME, black South Africans gained some access to the United States, more African American missionaries were sent to South Africa, and a school (the Wilberforce Institution) was later established in 1908. A number of Africans went to school in the United States, sponsored by African American churches. Many others were trained in Africa by African American missionaries and teachers.

Conversion was a process of culture creation and an avenue to empowerment. African Christians, drawing currents from African American churches, tend to be intense in their mode of worship; see the church as an agency to create a social, cultural, and political network; and emphasize passages in the Bible that lend force to the struggles for emancipation and liberation from poverty and injustice imposed by colonial or racial domination.

Very quickly, many Africans, persuaded by African American evangelism, connected race emancipation with Christianity. One of the early remarkable figures was John Chilembwe of Nyasaland, a graduate of the Virginia Theological Seminary, an all-black school. While in the United States he witnessed the 1898 race riots in Wilmington, North Carolina, read a lot of protest literature, and interacted with a number of race-conscious African Americans. When he returned to Africa, he combined mission work with the creation of small industries and an apprenticeship system for the converts,[46] who led an unsuccessful rebellion against the British in 1915.

Black evangelists attuned their followers to the power of Christianity. The church led the attack against the atrocities of the Belgians in the Congo in the 1890s and 1900s, and was consistently critical of minority rule and apartheid in South Africa. Churches became centers of opposition to the colonial governments throughout Africa, their activities explaining why European officers were always suspicious of African American missionaries.

The Nation of Islam

With the spread of Islam to the Americas and Europe, it has become imperative to treat it as an important religion in the diaspora. The literature is still new, and I want to focus only on the Nation of Islam in the United States in relation to the theme of culture and politics. The Nation of Islam offers a case study for understanding militancy, leadership, and political mobilization in some black communities in the United States.

Islam is an old religion in the Americas, although it has attracted fewer people than Christianity.[47] Many more African Americans began to embrace Islam after the 1930s. Although not all Muslims are members of the denomination, much attention on Islam has been focused on the Nation of Islam, whose visibility began in 1934 when Minister Elijah Muhammad became its leader and set up headquarters (Temple Number Two) in Chicago. Membership grew, reaching about 200,000 in the 1980s, with temples in different parts of the country.[48] The figure is now larger, and the Nation of Islam has spread to Africa, Asia, and Europe, thus becoming a truly transnational organization. Minister Louis Farrakhan, the present leader, is treated as a head of state whenever he visits certain countries. The Nation of Islam has also grown financially, benefiting from contributions by its members and a wide range of investments.

The growth in the membership and visibility of the Nation of Islam is connected to the belief that blacks suffer from racism and discrimination. Certainly, such factors as the economic depression of the 1930s, which led to a high rate of unemployment, and the race problems of the 1960s and 1970s led to many African Americans joining the organization. Most members are former Christians who regard Christianity as too closely tied to white power and racism. According to C. Eric Lincoln, the majority of members are young African American men from low-income families, although the Nation's message also reaches people of other classes. The members are prohibited from consuming alcohol, smoking, gambling, premarital sex, and other things considered to be vices.

The Nation of Islam regards religion as an opportunity for political expression, a militant nationalism that seeks to empower blacks. Islam provides an agency of unification, and the majority of the members tend to subscribe to a set of common beliefs, although they may disagree on strategies.[49] Many of the leading beliefs have been altered, but the original leaders believed that Christianity is the creation of the devil, although the Bible is a Holy Book; that Allah is black and black people are the chosen people; and that white domination will end. The Nation of Islam is opposed to the use of violence, but believes that empowerment will come with spiritual power. Some of its members advocate the separation of races, and subscribe to a demand for a separate state for blacks. The ideas of the Nation of Islam on black economic and political power, racial solidarity, and the role of other races in the condition of African Americans have generated controversy in the United States and deepened racial conflicts. Orthodox Muslims who are members of other organizations do not necessarily agree with the message of the Nation of Islam even if they share the goal of race emancipation through religion.

Concluding Remarks

All the issues highlighted above are combined in one aim: the expression of the consciousness of blackness. Multiple media are used to express this consciousness. Cultural survival and adaptation show the power of memory (to retain and to use ideas) as well as the power of articulation (to resort to memory and practices to construct communities and enduring strategies of survival). Shared experiences of exploitation and domination by other races and powers are turned into a cultural presentation of a shared destiny and a vigorous effort to seek redemption.

While culture provides a means of identification, the goal is to translate the consciousness to strength—to convert culture and consciousness to economic and political power. Underlying visions of political emancipation and economic reconstruction are heavily embedded in those of cultural reformation and redemption. The energization of the black race has involved projects of cultural renaissance—even the transfer of skills from one black world to the other was predicated on the assumption of race redemption. There is a political and practical side to projects of cultural solidarity. Culture translates into power; the power of culture is shown in political struggles. Culture and political struggles are interwoven—Kwanza creates an alternative to Christmas and consumerism; voodoo complements

Western medicine; the defense of cultural practices is at the same time a defense of race and identity; political meetings and activities advance cultural interests; reliance on local products and ideas minimize dependence on the West; and breaking with or minimizing the impact of the culture of the colonizer is to empower oneself.

In the linkage between consciousness and power, many expect persecution and tend to use the language of redemption. The expectation of persecution is derived from the historical circumstances of slavery, resistance against slavery, colonial domination and nationalist expression. Thus, in colonial Africa, those who declared themselves as followers of Marcus Garvey, for instance Clements Kadalie and Dr. D. S. Malekebu, experienced discrimination from the government. The Rastafarians claim the same discrimination and accusations of drug trading in their relations with the police. The persecution enhances the visibility of cultural projects, turning their consumption into the articulation of consciousness, the embodiment of resistance, and a powerful statement on race difference and affirmation.

The use of culture and cultural symbols does not mean that there is no tension in the diaspora. There have been African American evangelists who regard Africa as too poor and primitive, and Africans as exotic people requiring civilization. There have been African migrants in the United States who question the integrity and autonomy of African Americans. There have been historical moments when the contingencies of assimilation in new societies have called for a distancing from Africa or even the claim to blackness. Other forces that create divisions between Africans and diasporan Africans are stereotypes, different historical experiences, barriers erected by powerful forces, etc.[50] To limit myself to the United States, African American history and identity have their own complexities, richness, and internal struggles in addition to being connected to Africa. However, as a lived and shared experience, culture and an identity constructed around Africa have also created clearly visible bonds—as in similar physical appearance— and in building bridges between peoples.

The cultural bonds have fostered a feeling of diasporic consciousness, an international identity. International solidarity can be expressed in political ways or in the use of culture to globalize political projects. The strong opposition to the Italian invasion of Ethiopia in 1935, the success of Patrice Lumumba in the independence of the Congo in the 1960s, the FESTAC in 1977, and the end of apartheid in the 1990s are examples of events that show the power of cultural consciousness and solidarity in the diaspora. When notable black American leaders visit Africa, they are treated as heroes, as in the case of Governor Douglas Wilder of Virginia, who led a trade mission to seven African countries in 1992. In grappling with underdevelopment, Africans look to the diasporic blacks for help. Diasporic blacks look to Africa for cultural and racial pride, and for emotional comfort. When cultural identity is linked with politics, one outcome is to create groups in opposition, a subject and an object. Members of the African diaspora regard themselves and their cultures as victims, and they struggle to resolve many of the conflicts and to overcome victimization—real or imagined—by turning to culture as a weapon. Music, art, history, past heroes, etc. can all be used to defend identity and create metaphors for political struggles. A kinship terminology is often used to describe relationships among the members of the diaspora and Africans—the "Ties that Bind," to use the title of one book on the subject. The naming of the race—African Americans, Afro-Cubans, Africans, Afro-Caribbeans, Afro-Latinos and some others—reveals the relevance of identity and the power of culture in a diaspora fostered by the consciousness of a common origin and shared destiny. Perhaps, when more people know about us, both Africans in the homeland and in the diaspora, they will begin the slow process of appreciating us.

Notes

1. The chapter does not examine in any way the creation of the diaspora. For some studies on the history of the African diaspora, see Vincent Bakpetu Thompson, *The Making of the African Diaspora in the Americas 1441–1900* (New York: Longman, 1987); Joseph E. Harris, ed., *Global Dimensions of the African Diaspora,* 2nd ed. (Washington, D.C.: Howard University Press, 1993); Ronald Segal, *The Black Diaspora* (London: Faber and Faber, 1995); and Vincent Bakpetu Thompson, *Africans of the Diaspora: The Evolution of African Consciousness in the Americas (From Slavery to the 1920s)* (Trenton, N.J.: Africa World Press, 2000).

2. In recent time, the field has grown and the interest keeps growing. For recent essays on the subject, see the various issues of *Diaspora: A Journal of Transnational Studies.* In addition, see Paul Gilroy, *The Black Atlantic: Modernity and Double Consciousness* (Cambridge, Mass.: Harvard University Press, 1993); John Thornton, *Africa and Africans in the Making of the Atlantic World* (Cambridge: Cambridge University Press, 1992); Darlene Clark Hine and Jacqueline McLeod, eds., *Crossing Boundaries: Comparative History of Black People in Diaspora* (Bloomington: Indiana University Press, 1989); Isidore Okpewho et al., eds., *The African Diaspora: African Origins and New World Identities* (Bloomington: Indiana University Press, 1999); and Tiffany Ruby Patterson and Robin D. G. Kelley, "Unfinished Migrations: Reflections on the African Diaspora and the Making of the Modern World," *African Studies Review* 43, no. 1 (2000): 11–45.

3. See Adam Potkay and Sandra Burr, eds., *Black Atlantic Writers of the Eighteenth Century* (New York: St. Martin's Press, 1995).

4. My broad understanding notwithstanding, I have concentrated on the Americas, thereby ignoring the Asian and Mediterranean worlds.

5. Ronald W. Walters, *Pan Africanism in the African Diaspora: An Analysis of Modern Afrocentric Political Movements* (Detroit: Wayne State University Press, 1997), 355.

6. Ibid., 387.

7. Ibid., 385.

8. See Sandra T. Barnes, ed., *Africa's Ogun: Old World and New,* 2nd ed. (Bloomington: Indiana University Press, 1997). See also George Brandon, *Santería from Africa to the New World: The Dead Sell Memories* (Bloomington: Indiana University Press, 1993); and Lucie Pradel, *African Beliefs in the New World* (Trenton, N.J.: Africa World Press, 2000).

9. See M. J. Herskovits, *The New World Negro: Selected Papers in Afroamerican Studies* (Bloomington: Indiana University Press, 1966); and E. F. Frazier, *The Negro in the United States* (New York: Macmillan, 1949).

10. Roger Bastide, *Les Amériques noires: Les civilisations africaines dans le Nouveau Monde* (Paris: Payot, 1967), 199.

11. R. D. Ralston, "Africa and the New World," in *Unesco General History of Africa,* vol. 7, *Africa under Colonial Domination,* ed. A. Adu Boahan (Berkeley: University of California Press, 1985), 775–76.

12. (1941; reprint, Boston: Beacon Press, 1958)

13. E. Franklin Frazier, *The Negro Church in America* (New York: Schocken Books, 1963).

14. See Sidney Mintz and Richard Price, *The Birth of African American Culture: An Anthropological Perspective* (Boston: Beacon Press, 1992).

15. See Michael Mullin, *Africa in the America: Slave Acculturation and Resistance in the American South and the British Caribbean, 1736–1831* (Urbana: University of Illinois Press, 1992).

16. For a brief review of this literature, see Joseph E. Holloway, ed., *Africanisms in American Culture* (Bloomington and Indianapolis: Indiana University Press, 1990), xi-xii.

17. Ibid.

18. See Joseph E. Holloway and Winifred K. Vass, *The African Heritage of America English* (Bloomington: Indiana University Press, 1993).

19. Ibid, xlv.

20. Jessie Gaston Mulira, "The Case of Voodoo in New Orleans," in Holloway, ed., *Africanisms,* 34–68.

21. Robert L. Hall, "African Religious Retentions in Florida," in Holloway, ed., *Africanisms,* 98–118.

22. Melville Herskovits, "What Has Africa Given America?" *New Republic* 84, 1083 (1935): 92–94; reprinted in Frances S. Herskovits, ed., *The New World Negro* (Bloomington: Indiana University Press, 1966), 168–74.

23. Philips, "The African Heritage of White America," in Holloway, ed., *Africanisms,* 229.

24. Cornel West, *Race Matters* (New York: Vintage Books, 1994), 156.

25. For the literature which has examined this, see J. A. Rogers, *The World's Great Men of Color* (New York: Macmillan, 1972); W. E. Brown, ed., *Africa and the American Negro* (Atlanta, Ga.: Atlanta University, 1896); John P. Davis, ed., *Africa as Seen by American Negroes* (Paris: Présence Africaine, 1958); W. E. B. Du Bois, *The Souls of Black Folk* (New York: Penguin Books, 1989); W. E. B. Du Bois, *The World and Africa: An Inquiry into*

the Part African Has Played in World History (New York: International Publishers, 1965); Adelaide C. Hill and Martin Kislon, eds., *Apropos of Africa: Afro-American Leaders and the Romance of Africa* (New York: Doubleday, 1971); Okon Uya, *Black Brotherhood: Afro-Americans and Africa* (Boston: D. C. Heath and Co., 1971); Robert G. Weisbord, *Ebony Kinship: Africa, Africans, and the Afro-Americans* (Westport, Conn.: Greenwood Press, 1973); Chancellor Williams, *The Destruction of Black Civilization* (Chicago: Third World Press, 1974); and Carter G. Woodson, *The African Background Outlined* (Washington, D.C.: Negro Universities Press, 1968).

26. See Bernard Makhosezwe Magubane, *The Ties That Bind: African-American Consciousness of Africa* (Trenton, N.J.: Africa World Press, 1987); Carlos Moore et al, eds., *African Presence in the Americas* (Trenton, N.J.: Africa World Press, 1995); and Harris, ed., *Global Dimensions of the African Diaspora,* 1–82.

27. For some useful literature on the subject of emigration, see Howard Brotz, ed., *Negro Social and Political Thought: 1850–1920* (New York: Basic Books, 1966); and Floyd J. Miller, *The Search for a Black Nationality: Black Emigration and Colonization 1787–1863* (Chicago: University of Illinois Press, 1975).

28. A. C. Hill and M. Kilson, eds., *Apropos of Africa: Sentiments of Negro American Leaders on Africa from the 1800s to the 1950s* (New York: Anchor, 1971), 192–94.

29. See A. J. Garvey, ed., *Philosophy and Opinions of Marcus Garvey* (London: Frank Cass, 1967); A. J. Garvey, *Garvey and Garveyism* (Kingston: United Printers, 1963).

30. See M. B. Akpan, "Liberia and the Universal Negro Improvement Association: The Background to the Abortion of Garvey's Scheme for African Colonization," *Journal of African History* 14, no. 1 (1973): 105–27. Robert Hill has also edited Garvey's papers.

31. Quoted in R. D. Ralston, "Africa and the New World," in *Unesco General History,* vol. 7, 747.

32. Quoted in E. D. Cronon, *Black Moses: The Story of Marcus Garvey and the Universal Negro Improvement Association* (Madison: University of Wisconsin Press, 1962), 65.

33. For details of his career, see E. Smith, *Aggrey of Africa: A Study in Black and White* (London: SCM Press, 1929).

34. For his memoir, see *My Odyssey: An Autobiography* (London: Hurst, 1970).

35. For the full poem, cited below, see Countee Cullen, *On These I Stand: An Anthology of Selected Poems* (New York: Harper and Brothers, 1947).

> What is Africa to me:
> Copper sun or scarlet sea,
> Jungle star or jungle track,
> Strong bronzed men, or regal black
> Women from whose loins I sprang
> When the birds of Eden sang?
> One three centuries removed
> From the scenes his father told
> Spring grove, cinnamon tree
> What is Africa to me?

36. See Robert Hill, "Leonard P. Howell and Millenarian Visions in Early Rastafari," *Epoche (Journal of the History of Religions)* 9 (1981): 30–71.

37. See V. T. Rajshekar, *Dalit: The Black Untouchables of India* (Atlanta, Ga.: Clarity Press, 1995).

38. For details on this movement, see Leonard Barrett, *The Rastafarians: Sounds of Cultural Dissonance* (Boston: Beacon Press, 1977).

39. For an elaboration of the belief system of the Rastas, see Peter B. Clarke, *Black Paradise: The Rastafarian Movement* (London: The Aquarian Press, 1986).

40. See Neil J. Savishinsky, "Rastafari in the Promised Land: The Spread of a Jamaican Socioreligious Movement among the Youth of West Africa," *African Studies Review* 37, no. 3 (December 1994): 19–50.

41. See Molefi Kete Asante, *Afrocentricity* (Trenton, N.J.: Africa World Press, 1988).

42. See Kinfe Abraham, *Politics of Black Nationalism: From Harlem to Soweto* (Trenton, N.J.: Africa World Press, 1991). See also Cedric Robinson, *Black Marxism: The Making of the Black Radical Tradition* (London: Zed, 1983).

43. See Walter L. Williams, *Black Americans and the Evangelization of Africa, 1877–1900* (Madison: The University of Wisconsin Press, 1982).

44. C. Clendenen, R. Collins, and P. Duignan, *Americans in Africa, 1865–1900* (Stanford, Calif.: Hoover Institution Press, 1966), 63.

45. M. M. Ponton, *Life and Times of Henry M. Turner* (Atlanta, Ga.: A. B. Caldwell, 1917), 77.

46. For his impressive career, see G. Shepperson and T. Price, *Independent African: John Chilembwe and the Origins, Setting and Significance of the Nyasaland Native Uprising of 1915* (Edinburgh: Edinburgh University Press, 1958).

47. See Yvonne Haddad, ed., *The Muslims in America* (New York: Oxford University Press, 1991); Yvonne Haddad, *Islamic Values in the United States: A Comparative Study* (New York: Oxford University Press, 1987); and Earl Waugh et al., eds., *The Muslim Community in North America* (Alberta, Canada: The University of Alberta Press, 1983).

48. On the Nation of Islam, see C. Eric Lincoln, *The Black Muslims in America,* 3rd edition (Trenton, N.J.: Africa World Press, 1994).

49. When Elijah Muhammad died in 1975, there was a leadership struggle between the representatives of the conservatives and the radicals. Before then, Malcom X, a well-known defender of the Nation, was expelled in 1964, and he founded his own organizations: the Muslim Mosque, Inc, and the Organization of Afro-American Unity (OAAU) based on the OAU, which had been founded the year before, where he preached radicalism until his assassination in 1965. Wallace Muhammad, who succeeded his father in 1975, changed the organization's name to The World Community of Islam in the West, but this did not last. Some relaxation of some of the early rules on dress code, eating, drinking, and voting, and Wallace's attempt to move the organization closer to orthodox Islam created a split among the leaders. Louis Farrakhan eventually emerged as a leader—he regards himself as the rightful successor to Elijah Muhammad and he retains the name of the Nation of Islam as well as many of the original ideas. In recent times, the Nation is again relaxing some of its ideas and tenets.

50. On the tension, see F. Ugboaja Ohaegbulam, "Continental Africans and Africans in America: The Progression of a Relationship," in *Africana Studies: A Survey of Africa and the African Diaspora,* ed. Mario Azevado (Durham, N.C.: Carolina Academic Press, 1993), 219–42. For a recent pessimistic view of Africa by an African American, see Keith B. Richburg, *Out of America: A Black Man Confronts Africa* (New York: Basic Books, 1997).

BIBLIOGRAPHY

The bibliography indicates the extensive range of materials consulted by the author, and offers a useful list to those interested in African studies.

Abdul-Raheem, Tajudeen. *Pan Africanism: Politics, Economy and Social Change in the Twenty-First Century.* New York: New York University Press, 1996.
———, and Adebayo Olukoshi. "The Left in Nigerian Politics and the Struggle for Socialism, 1945–1985," *Review of African Political Economy* 38 (1986): 64–80.
Abimbola, Wande. *Ifa: An Exposition of Ifa Literary Corpus.* Ibadan: University Press, 1976.
Abraham, Kinfe. *Politics of Black Nationalism: From Harlem to Soweto.* Trenton, N.J.: Africa World Press, 1991.
Abraham, W. E. *The Mind of Africa.* Chicago: University of Chicago Press, 1962.
Abubakar, Sa'ad. "Amina of Zazzau: Exploits and Impact in the Savanna Region of Nigeria," *Kano Studies* 2 (1981): 99–109.
Achebe, Chinua. "The African Writer and the English Language," *Transition* 4, no. 18, 1965.
———. *Morning Yet on Creation Day.* London and Ibadan: Heinemann, 1975.
———. *Things Fall Apart.* London: Heinemann, 1958.
———. *The Trouble with Nigeria.* Enugu: Fourth Dimension Publishers, 1983.
———, Goran Hyden, Achola Pala Okeyo, and Christopher Magadza, eds. *Beyond Hunger: Conventional Wisdom and a Vision of Africa in 2057.* London: James Currey, 1990.
Adamu, Mahdi. *The Hausa Factor in West African History.* Zaria: Ahmadu Bello University Press, 1978.
Adebayo, Augustus. *White Man in Black Skin.* Ibadan: Spectrum, 1981.
Adebayo, A. G. *Embattled Federalism: History of Revenue Allocation in Nigeria, 1946–1990.* New York: Peter Lang, 1993.
Adedeji, Adebayo, and United Nations Economic Commission for Africa, *African Charter for Popular Participation in Development and Transformation.* Arusha, Tanzania: UNECA, 1987.
———, ed. *Africa within the World: Beyond Dispossession and Dependence.* London: Zed Books in association with African Centre for Development and Strategic Studies, Ijebu-Ode, Nigeria, 1993.
Adegbola, Adenipekun. *Why Africans Grumble.* Ibadan: self-published, 1950.
Adejuyigbe, O. *Boundary Problems in Western Nigeria: A Geographical Analysis.* Ile-Ife: University of Ife Press, 1975.

Aderinwale, A., ed. *Corruption, Democracy and Human Rights in Southern Africa.* Abeokuta, Nigeria: African Leadership Forum, 1995.

Adetugbo, A. "The Development of English in Nigeria up to 1914: A Sociolinguistic Appraisal," *Journal of the Historical Society of Nigeria 9*, no. 2 (1978).

Adeyemo, O. A. *Women in Development.* Ibadan, Nigeria: National Centre for Economic Management and Administration, 1991.

Adi, Hakim. "Bandele Omoniyi: A Neglected Nigerian Nationalist," *African Affairs* 90 (1991): 581–65.

———. *West Africans in Britain, 1900–1960: Nationalism, Pan-Africanism, and Communism.* London: Lawrence and Wishart, 1998.

Afonja, Simi et al., eds. *Nigerian Women in Social Change.* Ile-Ife, Nigeria: Obafemi Awolowo University Press, 1995.

Africa Watch. *Conspicuous Destruction: War, Famine and the Reform Process in Mozambique.* New York: Human Rights Watch, 1992.

Ahmed An-Na'im, Abdullahi, ed. *Proselytization and Communal Self-Determination in Africa.* New York: Orbis, 1999.

Aig-Imoukhuede, F. *Pidgin Stew and Sufferhead.* Ibadan: Heinemann, 1982.

Ajayi, J. F. Ade. "Africa in Perspective." In *Encyclopaedia of Africa South of the Sahara,* edited by John Middleton, 1:xix–xxv. New York: Charles Scribner's Sons, 1997.

———. *Christian Missions in Nigeria, 1841–1891: The Making of a New Elite* (London: Longman, 1966).

———. "Nineteenth Century Origins of Nigerian Nationalism." In *Tradition and Change in Africa: The Essays of J. F. Ade Ajayi,* edited by Toyin Falola, 69–84. Trenton, N.J.: Africa World Press, 2000.

———, ed. *UNESCO General History of Africa,* vol. 6, *Africa in the Nineteenth Century until the 1880s.* Paris and Berkeley: UNESCO and University of California Press, 1989.

———, and R. S. Smith. *Yoruba Warfare in the Nineteenth Century* (Cambridge: Cambridge University Press, 1964).

———, Ali A. Mazrui, and Dudley Thompson. *Pan-Africanism and the Crusade for Reparation.* Ibadan: Occasional Publication No. 2 of the Research and Documentation Committee of the O.A.U. Group of Eminent Persons for Reparation, n.d..

———, Lameck K. H. Goma, and G. Ampah Johnson. *The African Experience with Higher Education.* Accra, London, and Athens: The Association of African Universities in association with James Currey and Ohio University Press, 1996.

Ake, Claude. *Democracy and Development in Africa,* Washington, D.C.: The Brookings Institution, 1996.

———. *A Political Economy of Africa.* Harlow, United Kingdom: Longman, 1981.

———. *Social Science as Imperialism: The Theory of Political Development.* Ibadan: Ibadan University Press, 1982.

Akindele, R. A., and Bassey E. Ate, eds. *Nigeria's Economic Relations with the Major Developed Market-Economy Countries, 1960–1985.* Lagos: Nelson and NIIA, 1988.

Akinsanya, Adeoye. *The Expropriation of Multinational Properties in the Third World.* New York: Praeger, 1980.

Akinyemi, Bolaji. ed. *Nigeria and the World: Reading in Nigerian Foreign Policy.* Lagos: Nigeria Institute of International Affairs, 1978.

Akinsola Akiwowo. "The Place of Mojola Agbebi in the African Nationalist Movements: 1890–1917," *Phylon* (Atlanta) 26 (1965): 122–39.

———. "Racialism and Shifts in the Mental Orientation of Black People in West Africa and the Americas, 1856 to 1956," *Phylon* (Atlanta) 31 (1970): 256–64.

Akpan, M. B. "Liberia and the Universal Negro Improvement Association: The background to the abortion of Garvey's scheme for African colonization," *Journal of African History* 14, no. 1 (1973): 105–27.

Alden, Patricia, David Lloyd, and Ahmed Samatar. *African Studies and the Undergraduate Curriculum.* Boulder, Colo.: Lynne Rienner Publishers, 1994.

Ali, Z.A., ed. *African Unity: The Cultural Foundations.* Lagos: Centre for Black and African Arts and Civilization, 1988.

Altbach, Philip G., and Salah M. Hassan, eds. *The Muse of Modernity: Essays on Culture as Development in Africa.* Trenton, N.J.: Africa World Press, 1996.

Aluko, Olajide, ed. *The Foreign Policies of African States.* London: Hodder and Stoughton, 1977.

Alvarez, Sonia E., Evelina Dagnino, and Arturo Escobar, eds. *Cultures of Politics, Politics of Cultures: Re-Visioning Latin American Social Movements.* Boulder, Colo.: Westview Press, 1998.

Amadiume, Ife. *Male Daughters, Female Husbands: Gender and Sex in an African Society.* London: Zed, 1987.

———. *Reinventing Africa: Matriarchy, Religion and Culture.* London: Zed, 1997.

Andreski, Stanislav. *The African Predicament.* New York: Atherton Press, 1969.

Anifowose, R. *Violence and Politics in Nigeria: The Tiv and Yoruba Experience.* New York: Nok, 1982.

Appiah, Kwame. *In My Father's House: Africa in the Philosophy of Culture.* New York: Oxford University Press, 1992.

Apter, Andrew. *Black Critics and Kings: The Hermeneutics of Power in Yoruba Society.* Chicago: University of Chicago Press, 1992.

Apter, David E., and Carl G. Rosberg, eds. *Political Development and the New Realism in Sub-Saharan Africa.* Charlottesville: University of Virginia Press, 1994.

Arhin, Kwame. *Traditional Rule in Ghana: Past and Present.* Accra, Ghana: Sedco Publishing Ltd., 1985.

Arifalo, S. O. "Ethnic Political Consciousness in Nigeria, 1947–1951," *Geneve-Afrique* 34, no. 1 (1986): 7–34.

Arnold, S. and A. Nitecki, eds. *Culture and Development in Africa.* Trenton, N.J.: Africa World Press, 1990.

Arnoldi, Mary, Christraud M. Geary, and Kris I. Hardin, eds. *African Material Culture.* Bloomington and Indianapolis: Indiana University Press, 1996.

Asante, Molefi Kete. *The Afrocentric Idea.* Philadelphia: Temple University Press, 1984.

———. *Afrocentricity.* Trenton, N.J.: Africa World Press, 1990.

———. *Afrocentricity: The Theory of Social Change.* Buffalo, N.Y.: Amulefi, 1980.

———. *Kemet, Afrocentricity, and Knowledge.* Trenton, N.J.: Africa World Press, 1990.

————. *Malcolm X as Cultural Hero and other Afrocentric Essays.* Trenton, N.J.: Africa World Press, 1993.

————, and Abu S. Abarry, eds. *African Intellectual Heritage: A Book of Sources.* Philadelphia: Temple University Press, 1996.

————, and Kariamu Welsh Asante, eds. *African Culture: The Rhythms of Unity.* Trenton, N.J.: Africa World Press, 1990.

Ashcroft, Bill, Gareth Griffiths, and Helen Tiffin. *The Empire Writes Back: Theory and Practice in Post-Colonial Literatures.* New York: Routledge, 1989.

Assensoh, A. B. *African Political Leadership: Jomo Kenyatta, Kwame Nkrumah, and Julius K. Nyerere.* Malabar, Fla.: Krieger, 1998.

Atanda, J. A. *The New Oyo Empire: Indirect Rule and Change in Western Nigeria, 1894–1934.* London: Longman, 1973.

Awe, Bolanle. "The Iyalode in the Traditional Yoruba Political System." In *Social Stratification: A Cross-Cultural View,* edited by Alice Schlegel, 144–95. New York: Columbia University Press, 1977.

————, ed. *Nigerian Women in Historical Perspective.* Ibadan, Nigeria: Sankore, 1992.

Awolowo, Obafemi. *Awo: The Autobiography of Chief Obafemi Awolowo.* Cambridge: Cambridge University Press, 1960.

————. *Path to Nigerian Freedom.* London: Faber, 1947.

————. *The Strategy and Tactics of the People's Republic of Nigeria.* London: Macmillan, 1970.

Awonusi, V. O. "The Americanization of Nigerian English." *World Englishes* 13, no. 1 (1994): 75–82.

Ayandele, E. A. *The Educated Elite in the Nigerian Society.* Ibadan: Ibadan University Press, 1974.

————. *Holy Johnson: Pioneer African Nationalism.* London: Frank Cass, 1970.

————. *The Missionary Impact on Modern Nigeria, 1842–1914: A Social and Political Analysis.* London: Longman, 1966.

————. *A Visionary of the African Church: Mojola Agbebi, 1860–1917.* Nairobi: East Africa Publishing House, 1971.

Ayittey, George B. N., *Africa Betrayed.* New York: St. Martins, 1992.

————. *Africa in Chaos.* New York: St Martin's Griffin, 1998.

Ayoade, John A. A. "Party and Ideology in Nigeria: A Case Study of the Action Group," *Journal of Black Studies* 16, no. 2 (1985): 9–188.

————, and Adigun A. B. Agbaje, eds. *African Traditional Political Thought and Institutions.* Lagos: Centre for Black and African Arts and Civilization, 1989.

Ayoob, Mohammed. *Third World Security Predicament.* Boulder, Colo.: Lynne Rienner, 1995.

Azevedo, Mario. *Africana Studies.* Durham: Carolina Academic Press, 1993.

Azikiwe, Nnamdi. *My Odyssey: An Autobiography.* New York: Praeger, 1970.

————. *Renascent Africa.* London: Frank Cass, 1968.

————. *Zik: A Selection from the Speeches of Nnamdi Azikiwe.* Cambridge: Cambridge University Press, 1961.

Babalola, Adeboye. *Not Vernaculars, But Languages!* Inaugural Lecture. Lagos: University of Lagos, 1974.

Babatope, Ebenezer. *The Abacha Regime and the June 12 Crisis.* Lagos: self-published, 1995.

————. *Student Power in Nigeria, 1956–1980*. Lagos: Ebino Topsy, 1991.

Babu, A. *African Socialism or Socialist Africa?* London: Zed Books, 1981.

Badru, Pade. *Imperialism and Ethnic Politics in Nigeria*. Trenton, N.J.: Africa World Press, 1998.

Bamgbose, Ayo. *Linguistics in a Developing Country*. Inaugural Lecture. Ibadan: University of Ibadan Press, 1972.

Bamiro, E., "Nigerian Englishes in Nigerian Literature," *World Englishes* 10, no. 1 (1991): 7–17.

Banks, Williams M. *Black Intellectuals: Race and Responsibility in American Life*. New York: Norton, 1996.

Baran, Paul A. *The Political Economy of Growth*. London: Cox and Wyman, 1978.

Barber, Karin, and P. F. de Moraes Farias, eds. *Self-Assertion and Brokerage: Early Cultural Nationalism in West Africa*. Birmingham, England: Birmingham University Center of African Studies, 1990.

Bardhan, P. "Corruption and Development: A Review of the Issues," *Journal of Economic Literature* 35 (1997): 1320–46.

Barkindo, B. "Growing Islamism in Kano City since 1970." In *Muslim Identity and Social Change in Sub-Saharan Africa*, edited by Louise Breener. Bloomington: Indiana University Press, 1993.

Barnes, Sandra T., ed. *Africa's Ogun: Old World and New*. 2nd edition. Bloomington: Indiana University Press, 1997.

Barret, David B. *Schism and Renewal in Africa*. Nairobi: Oxford University Press, 1968.

Barret, Leonard. *The Rastafarians: Sounds of Cultural Dissonance*. Boston: Beacon Press, 1977.

Bascom, W. R., and M. J. Herskovits, eds. *Continuity and Change in African Cultures*. Chicago: University of Chicago Press, 1959.

Bassey, Magnus O. *Missionary Rivalry and Educational Expansion in Nigeria, 1885–1945*. New York: Peter Lang, 1999.

Bastide, Roger. *African Civilizations in the New World*. New York: Harper and Row, 1973.

————. *African Religions in Brazil*. Translated by Helen Sebba. 2nd edition. Baltimore, Md.: Johns Hopkins University Press, 1978.

————. *Les Amériques noires: Les civilisations africaines dans le Nouveau Monde*. Paris: Payot, 1967.

Bates, Robert H., V. Y. Mudimbe, and Jean O'Barr. *Africa and the Disciplines*. Chicago: University Chicago Press, 1993.

Bath, Frederick, ed. *Ethnic Groups and Boundaries*. Boston: Little, Brown, 1969.

Bayart, Francois Jean, *The State in Africa: The Politics of the Belly* (London: Longman, 1994).

Bayley, D. H., "The Effects of Corruption in a Developing Nation," *The Western Political Science Quarterly*, 19, 1996, pp. 719–732.

Baylis, John and Steve Smith, eds., *The Globalization of World Politics: an Introduction to International Relations* (New York: Oxford University, 1999).

Beckett, P., and C. Young, eds. *Dilemmas of Democracy in Nigeria* (Rochester, N.Y.: University of Rochester Press, 1997).

Beckman, Bjorn. "Imperialism and the 'National Bourgeoisie,'" *Review of African Political Economy* 22 (1981): 5–19.

———, and Segun Osoba. "The Deepening Crisis of the Nigerian National Bourgeoisie," *Review of African Political Economy* 13 (1978): 63–77.

Behrend, Heike. "'Is Alice Lakwena a Witch?': The Holy Spirit Movement and Its Fight against Evil in the North." In *Changing Uganda: The Dilemmas of Social Adjustment and Revolutionary Change,* edited by Holger Bernt Hansen and Michael Twaddle, 162–77. London: James Currey, 1991.

Beir, Ulli. *The Return of the Gods: The Sacred Art of Susanne Wenger.* Oxford: Oxford University Press, 1959.

Bell, Morag. *Contemporary Africa.* New York: John Wiley and Sons, 1986.

Bello S., and Y. Nasidi, eds. *Culture, Economy and National Development.* Lagos, Nigeria: National Council for Arts and Culture, 1991.

Bender, G. J. *Angola under the Portuguese.* London: Heinemann, 1978.

Bennet, Oliver. *Cultural Pessimism: Narratives of Decline in the Postmodern World.* Edinburgh: Edinburgh University Press, 2001.

Benson, G. C. S., S. A. Maaranen, and A. Heslop. *Political Corruption in America.* Lexington, Mass.: Lexington Books, 1978.

Benson, Peter. *"Black Orpheus," "Transition," and Modern Cultural Awakening in Africa.* Berkeley and Los Angeles: University of California Press, 1986.

Berg, Robert J., and Jennifer S. Whitaker, eds. *Strategies for African Development.* Berkeley: University of California Press, 1986.

Berger, Iris, and E. Frances White. *Women in Sub-Saharan Africa.* Bloomington and Indianapolis: Indiana University Press, 1999.

Berman, B., and J. Lonsdale. *Unhappy Valley: Conflict in Kenya*: Book 1, *State and Class*; Book 2, *Violence and Ethnicity.* London: James Currey, 1992.

Bernal, Martin. *Black Athena: The Afroasiatic Roots of Classical Civilization*: Vol. 1: *The Fabrication of Ancient Greece, 1785–1985.* New Brunswick, N.J.: Rutgers University Press, 1987.

———. *Black Athena: The Afroasiatic Roots of Classical Civilization*: Vol. 2: *The Archaeological and Documentary Evidence.* New Brunswick, N.J.: Rutgers University Press, 1991.

Berridge, G. R. *International Politics: States, Power and Conflict since 1945.* New York: St. Martins Press, 1987.

Berthélemy, Jean-Claude, and Ludvig Söderling. *Emerging Africa.* Washington, D.C.: Organization for Economic Cooperation and Development, 2001.

Bhabha, Homi. *The Location of Culture.* London: Routledge, 1994.

Bienen, Henry. *Political Conflict and Economic Change in Nigeria.* London: Frank Cass, 1985.

Biersteker, Thomas J. *Multinationals, The State, and Control of the Nigerian Economy.* Princeton, N.J.: Princeton University Press, 1987.

Birai, U. M. "Islamic Tajdid and the Political Process in Nigeria." In *Fundamentalisms and the States,* edited by Martin E. Marty and R. Scott Appleby. Chicago: University of Chicago Press, 1993.

Blakely, Thomas D., Walter E. A. van Beek, and Dennis L. Thomson, eds. *Religion in Africa.* Portsmouth, N.H.: Heinemann, 1994.

Blumenfeld, Jesmond. *Economic Interdependence in Southern Africa: From Conflict to Cooperation.* Cape Town: Oxford University Press, 1992.

Blyden, Edward Wilmot, *African Life and Customs.* London: African Publication Society, 1969.

Boahen, Adu. *African Perspectives on Colonialism.* Baltimore, Md.: Johns Hopkins Press, 1987.

———. *Ghana: Evolution and Change in Nineteenth and Twentieth Centuries.* London: Longman, 1975.

Boas, Franz. "Fallacies of Racial Inferiority," *Current History* 25 (February 1927): 672–82.

Bolt, Christine. *Victorian Attitudes to Race.* Toronto: University of Toronto Press, 1971.

Bonnell, Victoria E., and Lynn Hunt, eds. *Beyond the Cultural Turn.* Berkeley: University of California Press, 1999.

Boserup, Ester. *Women's Role in Economic Development.* Aldershot, England: Gower, 1986.

Boularès, Habib. *Islam: the Fear and the Hope.* London: Zed, 1990.

Boyd, Jean. *The Caliph's Sister: Nana Asma'u, 1793–1865: Teacher, Poet and Islamic Leader.* London: Frank Cass, 1989.

Brandon, George. *Santería from Africa to the New World: The Dead Sell Memories.* Bloomington: Indiana University Press, 1993.

Bratton, Michael. *Democratic Experiences in Africa.* Cambridge: Cambridge University Press, 1997.

Breuilly, John. *Nationalism and the State.* Manchester, England: Manchester University Press, 1982.

Brotz, Howard, ed. *Negro Social and Political Thought, 1850–1920.* New York: Basic Books, 1966.

Brown, W. E., ed. *Africa and the American Negro.* Atlanta, Ga.: Atlanta University, 1896.

Brzezinski, Zbigniew, ed. *Africa and the Communist World.* Stanford, Calif.: Stanford University Press, 1963.

Buijtenhuijs, Rob, and Celine Thiriot. *Democratization in Sub-Saharan Africa, 1992–1995: An Overview of the Literature.* Leiden: African Studies Center, 1995.

Bull, Hedley. *The Anarchical Society: A Study of Order in World Politics.* London, Basignstoke: Macmillan, 1977.

Bush, Rod. *We Are Not What We Seem: Black Nationalism and Class Struggle in the American Century.* New York: New York University Press, 1999.

Busia, Kofi Abrefa. *The Position of the Chief in the Modern Political System of Ashanti.* London: Oxford University Press, 1951.

———. *Purposeful Education for Africa.* The Hague: Mouton, 1968.

Cabral, Amilcar. *Return to the Source: Selected Speeches by Amilcar Cabral.* New York: Monthly Review Press, 1973.

———. *Revolution in Guinea: An African People's Struggle.* London: Stage 1, 1965.

Cabral, A., L. Njinya-Mujinya, and P. Habomugisha. "Published or Rejected? African Intellectuals' Scripts and Foreign Journals, Publishers and Editors" *Nordic Journal of African Studies* 7, no. 2 (1998): 83–94.

Callaghy, Thomas M. *The State-Society Struggle: Zaire in Comparative Perspective*. New York: Columbia University Press, 1984.

Carey, Alexander T. *Colonial Students: A Study of the Social Adaptation of Colonial Students in London*. London: Secker and Warburg, 1956.

Carr, H. *The System of Education in Lagos*. London: Education Office, 1901.

Carr-Saunders, A. M. *New Universities Overseas*. London: George Allen and Unwin, 1961.

Carter, Gwendolen, M., ed. *National Unity and Regionalism in Eight African Countries*. Ithaca, N.Y.: Cornell University Press, 1966.

Carter, Gwendolen, M., and Patrick O'Meara, eds. *African Independence: The First Twenty-Five Years*. Bloomington: Indiana University Press, 1986.

Chabal, Patrick. *Power in Africa: An Essay in Political Interpretation*. New York: St. Martin's Press, 1992.

———, and Jean-Pascal Deloz, eds. *Africa Works: Disorder as Political Instrument*. Oxford: James Currey, 1999.

Chazan, Naomi, Robert Mortimer, John Ravenhill and Donald Rothchild, *Politics and Society in Contemporary Africa*. Boulder, Colo.: Lynne Riener Publishers, 1992.

Chernoff, John Miller. *African Rhythm and African Sensibility: Aesthetics and Social Action in African Musical Idioms*. Chicago: The University of Chicago Press, 1979.

Chidester, David. *Savage Systems: Colonialism and Comparative Religion in Southern Africa*. Charlottesville and London: University Press of Virginia, 1996.

Chinweizu. *The West and the Rest of Us*. New York: Random House, 1974.

Chinweizu et al. *Toward the Decolonization of African Literature*. Enugu: Fourth Dimension, 1980.

Chizea, Dora Obi, and Juliet Njoku. *Nigerian Women and the Challenges of Our Time*. Lagos, Nigeria: Malthouse, 1991.

Cilliers, Jakkie, and Christian Dietrich, eds. *Angola's War Economy: The role of Oil and Diamonds*. Pretoria: ISS, 2000.

Cilliers, Jakkie, and Greg Mills, eds. *From Peacekeeping to Complex Emergencies: Peace Support Missions in Africa*. Johannesburg: SIIA and ISS, 1999.

Cilliers, Jakkie, and Peggy Mason, eds. *Peace, Profit or Plunder: The Privatisation of Security in War Torn African Societies*. Midrand: ISS, 1999.

Clapham, Christopher. *Africa and the International System*. Cambridge: Cambridge University Press, 1996.

———. "Democratisation in Africa: Obstacles and Prospects," *Third World Quarterly* 14 (1993): 423–38.

Clark, John F. *Africans at the Crossroads: Notes for African World Revolution*. Trenton, N.J.: Africa World Press, 1991.

Clark, John F., and David E. Gardinier, eds. *Political Reform in Francophone Africa*. Boulder, Colo.: Westview, 1997.

Clarke, Peter B. *Black Paradise: The Rastafarian Movement*. London: The Aquarian Press, 1986.

Clarke, Peter B., and Ian Linden. *Islam in Modern Nigeria: A Study of a Muslim Community in a Post-Independent State, 1960–1983*. Mainz and Munich: Grunewald-Kaiser, 1984.

Clarke, M., ed. *Corruption: Causes, Consequences and Control*. New York: St. Martin's Press, 1983.

Clendenen, C., R. Collins, and P. Duignan. *Americans in Africa, 1865–1900.* Stanford: Hoover Institution Press, 1966.

Coetzee S. F., B. Turok, and E. P. Beukes. *Transition to Democracy: Breaking out of Apartheid.* London: Institute for African Alternatives, 1994.

Cohen, David William, and E. S. Atieno Odhiambo, *Burying SM: The Politics of Knowledge and the Sociology of Power in Africa.* Portsmouth, N.H.: Heinemann, 1992.

Cohen, Dennis L., and John Daniel, eds. *Political Economy of Africa.* London: Longman, 1981.

Cohen, William B. *The French Encounter with Africans: White Response to Blacks, 1530–1880.* Bloomington: Indiana University Press, 1980.

Cole, Patrick. *Modern and Traditional Elites in the Politics of Lagos.* Cambridge: Cambridge University Press, 1975.

Coleman, James Smoot. *Nationalism and Development in Africa: Selected Essays.* Edited by James Sklar. Berkeley: University of California Press, 1994.

———. *Nigeria: Background to Nationalism.* Berkeley: University of California Press, 1958.

———, ed. *Education and Political Development.* Princeton, N.J.: Princeton University Press, 1965.

Coleman, James Smoot, and J. D. Court. *University Development in the Third World.* London: Perzanon Press, 1993.

———, and Gabriel Almond, eds. *The Politics of Developing Areas.* Princeton, N.J.: Princeton University Press, 1960.

Coleman, James Smoot, and Carl Rosberg, Jr., eds. *Political Parties and National Integration in Tropical Africa.* Berkeley: University of California Press, 1964.

Comaroff, Jean, and John Comaroff. *Of Revelation and Revolution: Christianity, Colonialism, and Consciousness in South Africa.* Vol. 1. Chicago: University of Chicago Press, 1991.

Conyers, James L. *Africana Studies.* Jefferson: Mofarland & Co., 1997.

Cooper, Brenda, and Andrew Steyn. *Transgressing Boundaries: New Directions in the Study of Culture in Africa.* Athens: Ohio University Press, 1996.

Cooper, Frederick. "What is the Concept of Globalization Good For?: An African Perspective," *African Affairs* 100 (2001): 189–213.

Cooper, Frederick, Allan F. Isaacman, Florencia E. Mallon, William Roseberry, and Steve J. Stern. *Confronting Historical Paradigms.* Madison: University of Wisconsin Press, 1993.

Coquery-Vidrovitch, Catherine. *African Women: A Modern History.* Boulder, Colo.: Westview, 1994.

Coran, B., A. Gboyega, and E. Osaghae, eds. *Democratic Transition in Africa.* Ibadan: Credu, Institute of African Studies, University of Ibadan, 1992.

Cornwell, R. "War and Decline in Africa," *Africa Insight* (Joahnnesburg) 21 (1991): 74–77.

Cox, Thomas. *Civil-Military Relations in Sierra Leone: A Case Study of African Soldiers in Politics.* Cambridge, Mass.: Harvard University Press, 1976.

Cronje, Suzanne. *The World and Nigeria: The Diplomatic History of the Biafra War, 1967–1970.* London: Sidgwick & Jackson, 1972.

Cronon, Edmund D. *Black Moses: Marcus Garvey and the Universal Negro Im-*

provement Association. Madison: University of Wisconsin Press, 1955, reprint 1962.

Crowder, Michael, and Obaro Ikime, eds. *West African Chiefs: Their Changing Status under Colonial Rule and Independence.* Ile-Ife, Nigeria: University of Ife Press, 1970.

Crummell, Alexander. *The Future of Africa, Being Addresses, Sermons, Etc., Delivered in the Republic of Liberia.* 1861, reprint, New York: Negro University Press, 1969.

Cullen, Countee. *On These I Stand: An Anthology of Selected Poems.* New York: Harper and Brothers, 1947.

Cummings-John, Constance Agatha. *Memoirs of a Krio Leader.* Edited by LaRay Denzer. Ibadan, Nigeria: Sam Bookman, 1995.

Cunard, Nancy, ed. *Negro Anthology.* 1934, reprint, New York: Negro University Press, 1969.

Curle, Adam. *The Role of Education in Developing Societies.* Legon: Ghana University Press, 1961.

Curtin, Philip D. *The Image of Africa: British Ideas and Action, 1780–1850.* Madison: University of Wisconsin Press, 1964.

———, ed. *Africa and the West: Intellectual Responses to European Culture.* Madison: Wisconsin University Press, 1972.

Cutrufelli, Maria R. *Women of Africa: Roots of Oppression.* London: Zed, 1983.

Davidson, Basil. *African Civilization Revisited.* Trenton, N.J.: Africa World Press, 1991).———. *The African Past.* London: Longman, 1964.

———. *The Black Man's Burden: Africa and the Curse of the Nation-State.* New York: Times Book, 1992.

———. *Black Star: A View of the Life and Times of Kwame Nkrumah.* Boulder, Colo.: Westview, 1989.

———. *Let Freedom Come: Africa in Modern History.* Boston: The Atlantic Monthly Press, 1978.

———. *The Liberation of Guinea.* Harmondsworth: Penguin, 1969.

———. *Modern Africa.* London: Longman, 1983.

———. *The People's Cause: A History of Guerillas in Africa.* London and New York: Longman, 1981.

Davis, John. *Pan-Africanism Reconsidered.* Berkeley: University of California Press, 1962.

———, ed. *Africa as Seen by American Negroes.* Paris: Présence Africaine, 1958.

———, ed. *The American Negro Reference Book.* Englewood Cliffs, N.J.: Prentice Hall, 1966.

Davis, W. T. "Our Image of God and Our Image of Women." *Orita: Ibadan Journal of Religious Studies* 10, no. 2 (Dec. 1976): 123–28.

Davison, Jean, "Who Owns What? Land Registration and Tensions in Gender Relations of Production in Kenya" in *Agriculture, Women, and Land: The African Experience,* ed. Jean Davison, 157–76. Boulder, Colo.: Westview, 1988.

Decalo, Samuel. *Coups and Army Rule in Africa: Studies in Military Style.* New Haven, Conn.: Yale University Press, 1976).

———. "Modalities of Civil-Military Stability in Africa," *Journal of Modern African Studies* 27 (1989): 547–78.

————. *Psychoses of Power: African Personal Dictatorships.* Boulder, Colo.: Westview, 1989.

DeGraft-Johnson, J. C. *African Glory: The Story of Vanished Negro Civilization.* Baltimore, Md.: Black Classic Press, 1954; reprint, 1986.

Dia, Mamadou. *The African Nations and World Solidarity.* New York: Frederick A. Praeger, 1960.

Diamond, Larry. "Nigeria: The Uncivic Society and the Descent into Praetorianism." In *Politics in Developing Countries,* edited by Larry Diamond, Juan J. Linz, and Seymour Martin Lispet. Boulder, Colo.: Lynne Rienner, 1995.

Diamond, Larry, and Marc F. Plattner, eds. *Democratization in Africa.* Baltimore, Md.: Johns Hopkins University Press, 1999.

————, eds. *Economic Reform and Democracy.* Baltimore, Md.: Johns Hopkins University Press, 1995.

Diamond, Larry, A. Kirk-Greene, and O. Oyediran, eds. *Transition without End.* Boulder, Colo.: Lynne Rienner, 1997.

Diawara, Manthia. *In Search of Africa.* Cambridge, Mass.: Harvard University Press, 1998.

Dike, K. O. "African History and Self-Government," *West Africa* 37 (February/March 1953): 177–78, 225–26. Reprinted in *Issues in African Studies and National Education: Selected Works of Kenneth Onwuka Dike,* edited by Chieka Ifemesia, 71–79. Awka, Nigeria: K. O. Dike Centre, 1988.

————. *A Hundred Years of British Rule in Nigeria.* Ibadan: Ibadan University Press, 1957.

————. "The Importance of African Studies." In *The Proceedings of the First International Congress of Africanists,* edited by Lalage Bown and Michael Crowder, 19–29. London: Longmans, Green and International Congress of Africanists, 1964.

————. *The Origins of the Niger Mission.* Ibadan: Ibadan University Press, 1958.

————. *Trade and Politics in the Niger Delta, 1830–1885: An Introduction to the Economic and Political History of Nigeria.* Oxford: Clarendon Press, 1956.

————, ed., *Eminent Nigerians of the Nineteenth Century.* Cambridge: Cambridge University Press, 1960.

Diop, Cheikh Anta. *The African Origin of Civilization: Myth or Reality.* Edited and translated by Mercer Cook. Chicago: Lawrence Hill, 1974.

————. *Civilization or Barbarism: An Authentic Anthropology.* Translated by Yaa-Lengi Meema Ngemi, Harold J. Salemson, and Marjolijn de Jager. Chicago: Lawrence Hill, 1981.

————. *Precolonial Black Africa.* Translated by Harold Salemson. Chicago: Lawrence Hill, 1987.

Dirks, Nicholas B., ed., *Colonialism and Culture.* Ann Arbor: University of Michigan Press, 1992.

Dompere, K. K. *Africentricity and African Nationalism.* Langley Park, Md.: I.A.A.S. Publishers, 1992.

Douglas, Mary, and Phyllis M. Kaberry, eds. *Man in Africa.* Urbana: University of Illinois Press, 1967.

Drake, S. C. "Diasporan Studies and Pan-Africanism." In *Global Dimensions of the African Diaspora,* edited by J. E. Harris, 341–402. Washington, D.C.: Howard University Press, 1993.

Du Bois, W. E. B. *The Souls of Black Folk.* New York: Penguin Books, 1989.

———. *The World and Africa: An Inquiry Into the Part African Has Played in World History.* New York: International Publishers, 1965.

Dudley, B. J. *Instability and Political Order: Politics and Crisis in Nigeria.* Ibadan: Ibadan University Press, 1973.

———. *An Introduction to Nigerian Government and Politics.* Bloomington: Indiana University Press, 1982.

———. *Parties and Politics in Nigeria.* London: Macmillan, 1968.

Dumont, René. *False Start in Africa.* London: Deutsch, Ltd., 1966.

Dunstan, E. *Twelve Nigerian Languages: A Handbook on Their Sound Systems for Teachers of English.* London: Longman, 1969.

Dzidzienyo, Anani. *The Position of Blacks in Brazilian and Cuban Society.* London: Minority Rights Groups, 1979.

———. *The Position of Blacks in Brazilian Society.* London: Minority Rights Group, 1971.

Echeruo, Michael J. C. *Victorian Lagos: Aspects of Nineteenth Century Lagos Life.* London: Macmillan, 1977.

Edunam, Effiong E. B. "Unaccredited Ambassadors: Nigerian Students as Africa's Spokesmen in the United States, 1920–1950," *Calabar Historical Journal* 3 (1985): 136–53.

Effah-Attoe, Stella A., and Solomon Odini Jaja. *Margaret Ekpo: Lioness in Nigerian Politics.* Abeokuta, Nigeria: ALF Publications, 1993.

Egbe Omo Yoruba. *Family Handbook and National Blueprint.* Washington, D.C.: Egbe Omo Oduduwa, 1996.

Ekeh, Peter. *Colonialism and Social Structure.* Inaugural Lecture, University of Ibadan, 1980. Ibadan: University of Ibadan Press, 1983.

———. "The Scope of Culture in Nigeria." In *Nigeria since Independence: The First Twenty-Five Years,* Vol. 7: *Culture,* edited by Peter P. Ekeh and Garba Ashiwaju, 1–17. Ibadan: Heinemann).

Ekwekwe, H. *Class and State in Nigeria.* Lagos: Longman, 1986.

Elliot, K. A. ed. *Corruption and the Global Economy.* Washington, D.C.: Institute for International Economics, 1997.

Elugbe, B. O. "National Language and National Development." In *Multilingualism, Minority Languages, and Language Policy in Nigeria,* edited by E. N. Emenanjo. Agbor, Nigeria: Central Books Limited in collaboration with the Linguistic Association of Nigeria, 1990.

Elugbe, B. O., and A. P. Omamor. *Nigerian Pidgins: Background and Prospects.* Ibadan: Heinemann, 1991.

Elwert, Georg, Stephan Feuchtwang, and Dieter Neuberts, eds. *Dynamics of Violence.* Berlin: Duncker and Humbolt, 1999.

Emenanjo, E. N., ed. *Multilingualism, Minority Languages, and Language Policy in Nigeria.* Agbor, Nigeria: Central Books Limited in collaboration with the Linguistic Association of Nigeria, 1990.

Emerson, Rupert. *From Empire to Nation: The Rise to Self-Assertion of Asian and African Peoples.* Boston: Beacon, 1960.

————, and Martin Kilson, eds. *The Political Awakening of Africa.* Englewood Cliffs, N.J.: Prentice-Hall, 1965.

Engberg-Pedersen, P., P. Gibbon, P. Raikes, and L. Udholt, eds. *Limits of Adjustment in Africa.* London: James Currey, 1996.

Enwerem, I. M. *A Dangerous Awakening: The Politicization of Religion in Nigeria.* Ibadan, Nigeria: IFRA, 1995.

Epega, Afolabi A., and Philip Neimark. *The Sacred Ifa Oracle.* New York: Athelia Henrietta Press, 1995.

Epstein, Edmund L., and Robert Cole, eds. *The Language of African Literature.* Trenton, N.J.: Africa World Press, 1998.

Erekosima, B. *African Proverbs in Special English.* Port Harcourt: Rivers State Newspaper Corporation, 1987.

Ergas, Zaki, ed. *The African State in Transition.* New York: St Martin's Press, 1987.

Essenstadt, Stuart N., and René Lemarchand. *Political Clintelism, Patronage and Development.* Beverly Hills, Calif.: Sage Publication, 1981).

Eze, Emmanuel Chukwudi, ed. *African Philosophy: An Anthology.* Oxford: Blackwell, 1998.

————, ed. *Postcolonial African Philosophy: A Critical Reader.* Oxford: Blackwell, 1997.

Fafunwa, A. Babs. "The Importance of the Mother Tongue as Medium of Instruction," *Nigeria Magazine* 102 (1969).

Fage, J. D. *A History of Africa.* London: Hutchinson University Library for Africa, 1978.

Falola, Toyin. "Africa." In *Cambridge Illustrated History of the British Empire,* edited by P. J. Marshall, 34–56. Cambridge: Cambridge University Press, 1996.

————. *Colonial Africa, 1885–1939.* Durham: Carolina Academic Press, 2002.

————. *Decolonization and Development Planning in Nigeria.* Gainesville: University Press of Florida, 1996.

————. "Elite Networking: Traditional Chiefs in Modern Nigeria." In *African Networks, Exchange and Spatial Dynamics,* edited by Laurence Marfaing and Brigitte Reinwald, 269–80. Berlin: Lit Verlag, 2001.

————. *The History of Nigeria.* Westport, Conn.: Greenwood Press, 1999.

————. *Nationalism and African Intellectuals.* Rochester, N.Y.: University of Rochester Press, 2001.

————. *The Political Economy of a Pre-Colonial African State: Ibadan, 1830–1900.* Ile-Ife: University of Ife Press, 1984.

————. "Power Drift in the Political System of Southwestern Nigeria in the Nineteenth Century," *ODU: A Journal of West African Studies* 21 (January/July, 1981): 109–27.

————. *Violence in Nigeria: The Crisis of Religious Politics and Secular Ideologies.* Rochester, N.Y.: University of Rochester Press, 1998.

————. *Yoruba Gurus: Indigenous Production of Knowledge in Africa.* Trenton, N.J.: Africa World Press, 2000.

————, ed. *African Cultures and Societies before 1885.* Durham: Carolina Academic Press, 2000.

———, ed. *African Historiography: Essays in Honour of J. F. Ade Ajayi.* London: Longman, 1993.

———, ed. *African Politics in Postimperial Times: The Essays of Richard L. Sklar.* Trenton, N.J.: Africa World Press, 2002.

———, ed., *Britain and Nigeria: Exploitation or Development?* London: Zed, 1987.

———, ed. *Pioneer, Patriot and Patriarch: Samuel Johnson and the Yoruba People.* Madison: University of Wisconsin-Madison, African Studies Program, 1993.

———, ed. *Tradition and Change in Africa: The Essays of J. F. Ade Ajayi.* Trenton, N.J.: Africa World Press, 2000.

———, ed. *Yoruba Historiography.* Madison: University of Wisconsin-Madison, African Studies Program, 1991.

———, and A. G. Adebayo. *Culture, Politics and Money among the Yoruba.* New Brunswick, N.J.: Transaction, 2000.

———, and Hassan Mathew Kukah. *Religious Militancy and Self-Assertion: Islam and Politics in Nigeria.* London: Avebury, 1996.

———, and Paul Lovejoy. *Pawnship in Africa: Debt Bondage in Historical Perspective.* Boulder, Colo.: Westview Press, 1994.

———, and Dare Oguntomisin. *The Military in Nineteenth Century Yoruba Politics.* Ile-Ife: University of Ife Press, 1984.

———, and Dare Oguntomisin. *Yoruba Warlords of the Nineteenth Century.* Trenton, N.J.: Africa World Press, 2002.

———, and J. K. Olupona. *Religion and Society in Nigeria: Historical and Comparative Perspectives.* Ibadan: Spectrum, 1991.

———, and E. S. Atieno-Odhiambo, eds. *The Challenges of History and Leadership in Africa: The Essays of Bethwell Allan Ogot.* Trenton, N.J.: Africa World Press, 2002.

———, et al. *Chief Obafemi Awolowo: The End of an Era?* Ile-Ife: Obafemi Awolowo University Press, 1988.

———, et al. *The Military Factor in Nigeria.* Lewiston, N.Y.: Edwin Mellen Press, 1994.

Fanon, Frantz. *Black Skins, White Masks.* New York: Grove Press, 1967.

———. *The Damned.* Translated by Constance Farrington. Paris: Présence Africaine, 1963.

———. *Toward the African Revolution: Political Essays.* Translated by Haakon Chevalier. New York: Grove Press, 1964.

———. *The Wretched of the Earth.* New York: Grove Press, 1968.

Fatton, Robert Jr.. *Predatory Rule: State and Civil Society in Africa.* Boulder, Colo.: Lynne Rienner, 1992.

———. "The State of African Studies and the Studies of the African State: The Theoretical Softness of the 'Soft State,'" *Journal of Asian and African Studies* 24 (1989): 170–87.

Fatunde, Tunde. *No Food No Country.* Benin, Nigeria: Adena Publishers, 1985.

———. *Oga Na Tief Man.* Benin, Nigeria: Adena Publishers, 1986.

Feierman, Steven. *Peasant Intellectuals: Anthropology and History in Tanzania.* Madison: University of Wisconsin Press, 1990.

Feinstein, Alan. *African Revolutionary: The Life and Times of Nigeria's Aminu Kano.* Enugu: Fourth Dimension, 1987.

Fieldhouse, D. K. *Black Africa 1945–1980: Economic Decolonization and Arrested Development*. London: Allen and Unwin, 1989.

Fierce, Milfred C., *African Studies Outside the United States: Africa, Brazil, the Caribbean* (Ithaca: Africana Studies and Research Center, 1991).

Finch, Charles. *The African Background to Medical Science: Essays on African History, Science and Civilizations*. London: Karnak, 1990.

Finnegan, William. *A Complicated War: The Harrowing of Mozambique*. Berkeley and Los Angeles: University of California Press, 1992.

Flitch, Bob, and Mary Oppenheimer. *Ghana: End of an Illusion*. New York: Monthly Review Press, 1966.

Forrest, T. *Politics and Economic Development in Nigeria*. 2nd edition. Boulder, Colo.: Westview Press, 1995.

Fortes, M., and G. Dieterlen, eds. *African Systems of Thought*. London: Oxford University Press, 1965.

Frazier, E. Franklin. *The Negro Church in America*. New York: Schocken Books, 1963.

———. *The Negro in the United States*. New York: Macmillan, 1949.

Fredland, Richard A. *Understanding Africa: A Political Economy Perspective*. Chigaco: Burnham, 2001.

Fukuyama, Francis. *The End of History and the Last Man*. New York: Free Press, 1992.

Fyfe, Christopher. *African Medicine in the Modern World*. Edinburgh: Center of African Studies, 1986.

———. *Africanus Horton, 1835–1883: West African Scientist and Patriot*. New York: Oxford University Press, 1972.

———, ed. *African Studies Since 1945: A Tribute to Basil Davidson*. London: Longman, 1976.

Galli, Rosemary, and Jocelyn Jones. *Guinea-Bissau: Politics, Economics, and Society*. London: Frances Pinter Publishers, 1987.

Gann, L. H., and Peter Duignan. *Burden of Empire: An Appraisal of Western Colonialism in Africa South of the Sahara*. Stanford: Hoover Institution, 1971.

Garique, Philip, "The West African Students' Union," *Africa*, 23, Jan. 1953, pp. 55–69.

Garvey, A. J. *Garvey and Garveyism*. Kingston: United Printers, 1963.

———, ed. *Philosophy and Opinions of Marcus Garvey*. London: Frank Cass, 1967.

Geertz, C., ed. *Old Societies and New States*. New York: The Free Press, 1963.

Gifford, P., and W. R. Louis, eds. *Decolonization and African Independence*. New Haven and London: Yale, 1988.

Gillespie, K., and G. Okruhlik. "The Political Dimensions of Corruption Cleanup: A Framework for Analysis," *Comparative Politics* 24 (1991): 77–97.

Gilroy, Paul. *The Black Atlantic: Modernity and Double Consciousness*. Cambridge, Mass.: Harvard University Press, 1993.

Glassman, Jonathon. *Feasts and Riot: Revelry, Rebellion, and Popular Consciousness on the Swahili Coast, 1856–1888*. Portsmouth, N.H.: Heinemann, 1995.

Glauke, Claris Obiageli. *Zik's Kingdom: Dr Nnamdi Azikiwe, Nigerian Politics, 1960–1996*. Berlin: Wissenschaft und Technik Verlag, 1997.

Gleason, Judith. *Orisha: The Gods of Yorubaland.* New York: Atheneum, 1971.

Goldthorpe, J. E. *An African Elite: Makerere College Students, 1922–1969.* Nairobi: Oxford University Press, 1965.

Gordon, April, and Donald L. Gordon. *Understanding Contemporary Africa.* Boulder, Colo.: Lynne Rienner, 1992.

Gould, D. J. *Bureaucratic Corruption and Underdevelopment in the Third World: The Case of Zaire.* New York: Pergamon Press, 1980.

———, and T. B. Mukendi. "Bureaucratic Corruption in Africa: Causes, Consequences and Remedies," *International Journal of Public Administration* 13 (1989): 427–57.

Gray, Martin, and Robin Law, eds. *Images of Africa: The Depiction of Pre-Colonial Africa in Creative Literature.* Stirling: Centre of Commonwealth Studies, University of Stirling, Occasional Paper No. 1, 1990.

Greenbaum, S. "Standard English and the International Corpus of English," *New Englishes* 1, no. 9 (1990): 79–83.

Greene, Sandra E. *Sacred Sites and the Colonial Encounter: A History of Meaning and Memory in Ghana.* Bloomington: Indiana University Press, 2002.

Grinker, Roy Richard, and Christopher B. Steiner, eds. *Perspectives on Africa: A Reader in Culture, History, and Representations.* London: Blackwell, 1997.

Grosh, B., and R. S. Mukandala, eds. *State-Owned Enterprises in Africa.* Boulder, Colo.: Lynne Rienner, 1994.

Gundara, J. S., and I. Duffield, eds. *Essays on the History of Blacks in Britain.* Aldershot, England: Avebury, 1992.

Guyer, Jane I. *Family and Farm in Southern Cameroon.* Boston: Boston University African Studies Center, 1984.

Gyekye, Kwame. *Tradition and Modernity: Philosophical Reflections on the African Experience.* New York: Oxford University Press, 1997.

Haddad, Yvonne. *Islamic Values in the United States: A Comparative Study.* New York: Oxford University Press, 1987.

———, ed. *The Muslims in America.* New York: Oxford University Press, 1991.

Hafkin, M. J., and Edna C. Bay, eds. *African Women in Changing Perspective.* Stanford, Calif.: Stanford University Press, 1977.

Hall, Robert L. "African Religious Retentions in Florida." In *Africanisms in American Culture,* ed. Holloway, 98–118. Bloomington and Indianapolis: Indiana University Press, 1990.

Hallen, Barry. *The Good, the Bad and the Beautiful: Discourse about Values in Yoruba Culture.* Bloomington: Indiana University Press, 2000.

Hallgren, Roland. *The Good Things in Life: A Study of the Traditional Religious Culture of the Yoruba People.* Löberöd, Sweden: Plus Ultra, 1988.

Hamilton, Carolyn. *Terrific Majesty: The Powers of Shaka Zulu and the Limits of Historical Invention.* Cambridge, Mass: Harvard University Press, 1998).

Hanlon, J. *Beggar Your Neighbours: Apartheid Power in Southern Africa.* Bloomington: Indiana University Press, 1986.

Harbeson, John W., and Donald Rothchild, eds. *Africa in World Politics: The African State System in Flux.* Boulder, Colo.: Westview Press, 2000.

Haring, Lee. *Verbal Arts in Madagascar: Performance in Historical Perspective.* Philadelphia: University of Pennsylvania Press, 1992.

Hansberry, William Leo. "Howard's Supreme Opportunity," *Howard University Record* 18, no. 8 (July 1923): 416–18.

———. "Material Culture of Ancient Nigeria," *Journal of Negro History* 6 (July, 1921): 261–95.

Hansen, Holger Bernt, and Michael Twaddle, eds. *Religion and Politics in East Africa.* Athens: Ohio University Press, 1995.

Hargreaves, J. D. *Decolonization in Africa.* London and New York: Longman, 1988.

Harman, Marylen E. *Infusion of African and African American Studies into the Curriculum.* Roanoke, Va.: Absolute LTD, 1991.

Harris, Joseph E. "Africa and Its Diaspora since 1935." In *UNESCO General History of Africa,* VIII, *Africa since 1935,* edited by Ali A. Mazrui. Berkeley: University of California Press, 1993.

———. *Africans and Their History.* New York: Mentor, 1972.

———. *Global Dimensions of the African Diaspora.* Washington, D.C.: Howard University Press, 1982; 2nd ed., 1993.

———. *Pillars in Ethiopian History: The William Leo Hansberry African History Notebook,* Vol. 1. Washington, D.C.: Howard University Press, 1974.

Harsch, E. "Accumulators and Democrats: Challenging State Corruption in Africa," *The Journal of Modern African Studies* 31 (1993): 31–48.

Hastings, Adrian. *African Christianity.* New York: Seabury, 1976.

Haugerud, Angelique, ed. "The Future of Regional Studies," *Africa Today* [Special Edition]. Boulder, Colo.: Lynne Rienner, 1997.

Hayford, J. E. Casely. *Ethiopia Unbound: Studies in Race Emancipation.* 1911, 2nd ed., with an introduction by F. Nnabuenyi Ugonna. London: Cass, 1969.

Haynes, Jeff. *Religion and Politics in Africa.* London: Zed, 1996.

Hayward, Fred M., ed. *Elections in Independent Africa.* Boulder, Colo.: Westview, 1987.

Herbert, Eugenia W. *Iron, Gender, and Power: Rituals of Transformation in African Societies.* Bloomington: Indiana University Press, 1993.

Herskovits, Melville, "What Has Africa Given America?" *New Republic* 84, 1083 (1935): 92–94; reprinted in Frances S. Herskovits, ed., *The New World Negro: Selected Papers in Afroamerican Studies.* Bloomington: Indiana University Press, 1966, 168–74.

Heidenheimer, A., M. Johnson, and V. T. LeVine, eds. *Political Corruption: A Handbook.* New Brunswick, N.J.: Transaction Publishers, 1990.

Henderson, H. "Ritual Roles of Women in Onitsha Ibo Society," Ph.D. dissertation, University of California at Berkeley, 1969.

Henriksen, Thomas, H. "African Intellectual Influences of Black Americans: The Role of Edward Blyden," *Phylon* 36, no. 3 (1975): 279–90.

Hill, Adelaide C., and Martin Kilson, eds. *Apropos of Africa: Afro-American Leaders and the Romance of Africa.* New York: Doubleday, 1971.

Hill, Robert. "Leonard P. Howell and Millenarian Visions in Early Rastafari." *Epoche (Journal of the History of Religions)* 9 (1981): 30–71.

Hine, Darlene Clark, and Jacqueline McLeod, eds. *Crossing Boundaries: Com-*

parative History of Black People in Diaspora. Bloomington: Indiana University Press, 1989.

Hobsbawn, Eric, and Terence Ranger, eds. *The Invention of Tradition.* Cambridge: Cambridge University Press, 1983.

Hochschild, Adam. *King Leopold's Ghost.* Boston: Houghton Mifflin Co., 1998.

Hodgkin, Thomas. *Nationalism in Colonial Africa.* London: Mueller, 1956.

Hodder-Williams, Richard. *An Introduction to the Politics of Tropical Africa.* London: George Allen and Unwin, 1984.

Hoehler-Fatton, Cynthia. *Women of Fire and Spirit: History, Faith, and Gender in Roho Religion in Western Kenya.* New York: Oxford University Press, 1996.

Holden, Edith. *Blyden of Liberia.* New York: Vantage, 1966.

Holloway, Joseph E., ed. *Africanisms in American Culture.* Bloomington and Indianapolis: Indiana University Press, 1990.

———, and Winifred K. Vass. *The African Heritage of America English.* Bloomington: Indiana University Press, 1993.

Hope, S K.R., and B. C. Chikulo, eds. *Corruption and Development in Africa: Lessons from Country Case Studies.* London: MacMillan, 2000.

Horton, Robin. "African Coversion," *Africa* 41, no. 2 (1971): 81–108.

Horowitz, Donald L. *Ethnic Groups in Conflict.* Berkeley: University of California Press, 1985.

Hoskyns, C. *The Congo since Independence.* Oxford: Oxford University Press, 1965.

Hountodji, Pauline. *African Philosophy: Myth and Reality.* Bloomington: Indiana University Press, 1983.

Huntington, Samuel P. *The Clash of Civilizations and the Remaking of World Order.* New York: Simon and Schuster, 1996.

Hunwick, John O. *Religion and National Integration in Africa: Islam, Christianity, and Politics in the Sudan and Nigeria.* Evanston, Ill.: Northwestern University Press, 1992.

Hurley, E. Anthony, Renée Larrier, and Joseph McLaren, eds. *Migrating Words and Worlds: Pan-Africanism Updated.* Trenton, N.J.: Africa World Press, 1999.

Hyden, Goran, and Michael Bratton, eds. *Governance and Politics in Africa.* Boulder, Colo.: Lynne Rienner, 1992.

Hymans, Jacques Louis. *Leopold Sedar Senghor: An Intellectual Biography.* Edinburgh: Edinburgh University Press, 1971.

Ibrahim, Jibrin. "Religion and Political Turbulence in Nigeria," *Journal of Modern African Studies* 29, no. 1 (1991): 115–37.

Idowu, E. Bolaji. *African Traditional Religion: A Definition.* London: SCM, 1973.

———. *Olodumare: God in Yoruba Belief.* London: Longman, 1962.

Igwe, Agbafor. *Nnamdi Azikiwe: The Philosopher of Our Time.* Enugu, Nigeria: Fourth Dimension Publishing Co., 1992.

Ikime, Obaro. *The Isoko People: A Historical Survey.* Ibadan: Ibadan University Press, 1972.

———. *Through Changing Scenes: Nigerian History Yesterday, Today and Tomorrow.* Ibadan: University of Ibadan, Inaugural Lecture, 1979.

Iliffe, John. *The African Poor.* Cambridge: Cambridge University Press, 1987.

Imam, Ayesha, and Amina Mama Fatou Sow, eds. *Engendering African Social Sciences.* Dakar, Senegal: Codesria, 1997.

Imasogie, O. *African Traditional Religion.* Ibadan, Nigeria: Ibadan University Press, 1982.

Inikori, J. E. *The Chaining of a Continent: Export Demand for Captives and the History of Africa South of the Sahara, 1450–1870.* Mona, Jamaica: Institute of Social and Economic Research, University of the West Indies, 1992.

———. *Forced Migration: The Impact of the Export Slave Trade on West African Societies.* New York: Africana Publishing Company, 1982.

Irele, Abiola. *The African Experience in Literature and Ideology.* Bloomington: Indiana University Press, 1981.

———. "The African Scholar: Is Black Africa Entering the Dark Ages of Scholarship?" *Transition* 51 (1991): 56–69.

———. "In Praise of Alienation," Inaugural Lecture. University of Ibadan, 22 November 1982.

———, ed., *Selected Poems of Leopold Sedar Senghor.* Cambridge: Cambridge University Press, 1977.

Isaacman, A., and N. Isaacman. *Mozambique: From Colonialism to Revolution.* Boulder, Colo.: Westview, 1983.

Isichei, Elizabeth. *A History of Christianity in Africa.* Trenton, N.J.: Africa World Press, 1995.

Iweriebor, Ehiedu E. G. *The Age of Neocolonialism in Africa.* Ibadan: African Book Builders, 1997.

———. *Radical Politics in Nigeria, 1945–1950: The Significance of the Zikist Movement.* Zaria, Nigeria: Ahmadu Bello University Press, 1996.

Jabbra, J. G. "Bureaucratic Corruption in the Third World: Causes and Remedies," *Indian Journal of Public Administration* 22 (1976): 673–91.

Jackson, John G. *Introduction to African Civilizations.* Seacaucus, N.J.: Carol, 1997.

Jackson, Richard L. *The Black Image in Latin American Literature.* Albuquerque: University of New Mexico Press, 1976.

Jackson, R. H., and C. G. Rosberg. *Personal Rule in Black Africa.* Berkeley: University of California Press, 1982.

Jahn, Janheinz. *Muntu: African Culture and the Western World.* London: Faber and Faber, 1961; reprint, New York: Grove Weidenfeld, 1990.

Jalloh, Alusine. *African Entrepreneurship: Muslim Fula Merchants in Sierra Leone.* Monograph in International Studies, Africa Series No. 71. Athens: Ohio University Center for International Studies, 1999.

Jalloh, Alusine, and David E. Skinner, eds. *Islam and Trade in Sierra Leone.* Trenton, N.J.: Africa World Press, 1997.

Jay, Margaret Jean, and Sharon Stichter, eds. *African Women South of the Sahara.* 2nd ed. London: Longman, 1995.

Jaycox, E.V.K. *The Challenges of African Development.* Washington, D.C.: World Bank, 1992.

Jenkins, Paul, ed. *The Recovery of the West African Past: African Pastors and African History in the Nineteenth Century: C. C. Reindorf and Samuel Johnson.* Basel: Basler Afrika Bibliographien, 1998.

Johnson, Samuel, *The History of the Yorubas*. Lagos: C.M.S., 1921.

Johnson, William John, Thomas A. Hale, and Stephen Belcher, eds. *Oral Epics from Africa: Vibrant Voices Form a Vast Continent*. Bloomington and Indianapolis: Indiana University Press, 1997.

Johnson-Odim, Cheryl, and Nina Emma Mba. *For Women and The Nation: Funmilayo Ransome-Kuti of Nigeria*. Urbana and Chicago: University of Illinois Press, 1997.

Joseph, R. A. "Class, State, and Prebendal Politics in Nigeria," *Journal of Commonwealth and Comparative Politics* 21 (1983): 21–38.

———. *Democracy and Prebendal Politics in Nigeria*. Cambridge: Cambridge University Press, 1987.

Jowitt, D. *Nigerian English Usage: An Introduction*. Lagos: Routledge, 1991.

July, Robert W. *A History of the African People*. 2nd ed. New York: Charles Scribner's Sons, 1974.

———. *The Origins of Modern African Thought: Its Development in West Africa during the Nineteenth and Twentieth Centuries*. New York: Praeger, 1967.

———, and Peter Benson, eds., *African Culture and Intellectual Leaders and the Development of the New African Nations*. New York: Rockefeller Foundation, 1982.

Kaba, Lansine. "Historical Consciousness and Politics in Africa," In *Black Studies*, edited by Talmage Anderson. 43–51. Pullman, Wash.: University of Washington Press, 1990.

Kachru, Braj. Foreword to *New Englishes: A West African Perspective*, edited by Ayo Bamgbose, Ayo Banjo, and Andrew Thomas, iii-iv. Trenton, N.J.: Africa World Press, 1997.

———. *The Other Tongue: English across Cultures*. Urbana: University of Illinois Press, 1982.

———. "Toward Expanding the English Canon: Raja Rao's 1938 Credo for Creativity," *World Literature Today* 4, no. 4 (1988): 582–86.

———. "World Englishes: Approaches, Issues, and Resources," *Language Teaching* 25, no. 1 (1992): 1–4.

Kaplan, Robert D. *The Ends of the Earth: A Journey at the Dawn of the 21st Century*. New York: Random House, 1996.

Karenga, Maulana. *Essays on Struggle: Positions and Analysis*. San Diego: Kawaida Publications, 1978.

Karp, Ivan, and Charles S. Bird, eds. *Explorations in African Systems of Thought*. Washington, D.C.: Smithsonian Institution Press, 1987.

Kastfelt, Niels, *Religion and Politics in Nigeria: A Study in Middle Belt Christianity*. London: British Academic Press, 1994.

Kato, C. Tsehloane. *The African Centered Perspective of History*. London: Kamak, 1994.

Kayode, J. O. *Understanding African Traditional Religion*. Ile-Ife, Nigeria: University of Ife Press, 1984.

Kayongo-Male, Diane, and Philista Onyango. *The Sociology of the African Family*. New York: Longman, 1984.

Kenyatta, Jomo. *Facing Mount Kenya: The Tribal Life of the Gikuyu*. London, 1938; reprint, New York: Vintage Books, 1965.

Keohane, Robert O. *After Hegemony: Cooperation and Discord in the World Political Economy.* Princeton, N.J.: Princeton University Press, 1984.

Kilson, Martin. *Political Change in Sierra Leone.* Cambridge, Mass.: Harvard University Press, 1966.

Kimble, David. *A Political History of Ghana: The Rise of Gold Coast Nationalism, 1850–1928.* Oxford: Clarendon Press, 1965.

King, Bruce, and Kolawole Ogungbesan. *A Celebration of Black and African Writing.* Zaria and Ibadan: Ahmadu Bello Univesity Press and Oxford University Press, 1977.

Koelle, S. W. *Polyglotta Africana or a Comparative Vocabulary of Nearly 300 Words and Phrases in More Than One Hundred District African Languages.* London: C.M.S., 1963; originally published in 1853.

Kohn, Hans, and Wallace Sokolsky. *African Nationalism in the Twentieth Century.* Princeton, N.J.: Van Nostraud, 1965.

Komolafe, Kolawole. *African Traditional Religion: Understanding Ogboni Fraternity.* Lagos: self-published, 1995.

Kopytoff, Igor, ed. *The African Frontier: The Reproduction of Traditional African Societies.* Bloomington: Indiana University Press, 1987.

Kopytoff, Jean Herskovits. *A Preface to Modern Nigeria: The "Sierra Leonians" in Yoruba, 1830–1890.* Madison: University of Wisconsin Press, 1965.

Krueger, A. O. "The Political Economy of Rent-Seeking Society," *American Economic Review* 64 (1974): 291–301.

Kujore, O. *English Usage: Some Notable Nigerian Variations.* Ibadan: Evans, 1985.

Kukah, M. H. *Religion, Politics and Power in Northern Nigeria.* Ibadan: Spectrum, 1993.

———, and Toyin Falola. *Religious Militancy and Self-Assertion: Islam and Politics in Nigeria.* London: Avebury, 1996.

Kuper, Leo, and M. G. Smith, eds. *Pluralism in Africa.* Berkeley: University of California Press, 1969.

Kurfi, Amadu. *Election Contest: Candidate's Companion.* Ibadan: Spectrum, 1989.

Laitin, David D. *Hegemony and Culture: Politics and Religious Change among the Yoruba.* Chicago: University of Chicago Press, 1986.

Lan, David. *Guns and Rain: Guerrillas and Spirit Mediums in Zimbabwe.* London: James Currey, 1985.

Langley, J. A. "Garveyism and African Nationalism," *Race* 11 (1969): 157–72.

———. *Ideologies of Liberation in Black Africa, 1856–1970.* London: Rex Collins, 1979.

———. *Pan-Africanism and Nationalism in West Africa 1900–1945: A Study in Ideology and Social Classes.* London: Oxford University Press, 1973.

Langley, Philip. "A Preliminary Approach to Women and Development: Getting a Few Facts Right." In *The Roles of Women in the Process of Development,* edited by Gerard M. Ssenkoloto, 79–100. Doula, Cameroon: Pan African Institute for Development, 1983.

Lapping, Brian. *Apartheid: A History.* London: Paladin Books, 1987.

Last, Murray, and G. L. Chevunduka, *The Professionalisation of African Medicine.* Manchester: Manchester University Press, 1986.

Leatt, James, et al. *Contending Ideologies in South Africa.* Cape Town and Johannesburg: David Philip, 1986.

Legum, Colin. *The Battlefronts of Southern Africa.* New York: Africana Publishing Company, 1988.

Lemarchand, R. *Political Awakening in the Belgian Congo.* Berkeley: University of California Press, 1964.

Levtzion, Nehemia, and Randall L. Pouwels, eds. *The History of Islam in Africa.* Athens: Ohio University Press, 2000.

LeVine, V. T. *Political Corruption: The Ghanaian Case.* Stanford, Calif.: Hoover Institution, 1975.

Lewis, David Levering. *W.E.B. Du Bois: The Fight for Equality, 1919–1963.* New York: Henry Holt, 2000.

Lewis, Peter. *Africa: Dilemmas of Development and Change.* Boulder, Colo.: Westview, 1998.

Liebenow, J. Gus. *African Politics: Crises and Challenges.* Bloomington: Indiana University Press, 1986.

Lincoln, C. Eric. *The Black Muslims in America.* 3rd edition. Trenton, N.J.: Africa World Press, 1994.

Little, Kenneth. *African Women in Towns.* Cambridge: Cambridge University Press, 1973.

Livingston, Thomas W. *Education and Race: A Biography of Edward Wilmot Blyden.* San Francisco: Glendessary, 1975.

Lloyd, Peter C., ed. *The New Elites of Tropical Africa.* London: Oxford University Press, 1964.

Loimeier, R. *Islamic Reform and Political Change in Nigeria.* Evanston, Ill.: Northwestern University Press, 1997.

Lorimer, Douglas A. *Colour, Class and the Victorians: English Attitudes to the Negro in the Mid Nineteenth Century.* Leicester, England: Leicester University Press, 1978.

Lovejoy, Paul, "Interregional Monetary Flows in the Precolonial Trade of Nigeria," *Journal of African History* 15 (1974): 536–85.

Lovett, Margot. "Gender Relations, Class Formation, and the Colonial State in Africa." In *Women and the State in Africa,* edited by Jane L. Parpart and Kathleen A. Staudt, 23–46. Boulder, Colo.: Lynne Rienner, 1989.

Louw, Leon, and Kendall Frances. *South Africa: The Solution.* Bisho: Amagi, 1986.

Lowe, Christopher C. "Unexamined Consequences of Academic Globalism in African Studies," *Africa Today* 44, no. 3 (1997): 297–307.

Lubeck, P. M. "Islamic Political Movements in Northern Nigeria: The Problem of Class Analysis." In *Islamic Politics and Social Movements,* edited by Edmund Burkell and Ira M. Lapidus. Berkeley: University of California Press, 1988.

———. "Islamic Protest under Semi-Industrial Capitalism: 'Yan Tatsine' Explained," *Africa* 55, no. 4 (1985): 369–89.

Luckham, Robin. "The Military, Militarization and Democratization in Africa," *African Studies Review* 37 (1994): 13–75.

Lynch, Hollis R. *Black Spokesman: Selected Published Writings of Edward Wilmot Blyden.* London: Cass, 1971.

———. *Edward Wilmot Blyden: Pan-Negro Patriot, 1832–1912.* London: Oxford University Press, 1967.

MacGaffey, Wyatt. *Kongo Political Culture: The Conceptual Challenge of the Particular*. Bloomington: Indiana University Press, 1993.

Mackenzie, A. Fiona D., *Land, Ecology and Resistance in Kenya, 1880–1952*. Portsmouth, N.H.: Heinemann, 1998.

MacKintosh, John P. *Nigerian Government and Politics*. Evanston, Ill.: Northwestern University Press, 1966.

Macridis Roy C., ed. *Foreign Policy in World Politics*. New York: Prentice-Hall, 1972.

Maddieson, Ian, and Thomas J. Hineebusch, eds. *Language History and Linguistic Description in Africa*. Trenton, N.J.: Africa World Press, 1998.

Maghan, Keita. *Race and the Writing of History*. Oxford: Oxford University Press, 2000.

Magnus, J. Sampson, ed. *West African Leadership*. London: Frank Cass, 1969; originally published 1951.

Magubane, Bernard Makhosezwe. *African Sociology: Towards a Critical Perspective: The Collected Essays of Bernard Makhosezwe Magubane*. Trenton, N.J.: Africa World Press, 2000.

———. *The Ties That Bind: African-American Consciousness of Africa*. Trenton, N.J.: Africa World Press, 1987.

Makinde, M. Akin. *African Philosophy, Culture, and Traditional Medicine*. Monographs in International Studies, No. 53. Athens: Ohio University Center for International Studies, 1988.

Malinowski, Bronislaw. *The Dynamics of Culture Change: An Inquiry in Race Relations in Africa*. New Haven, Conn.: Yale University Press, 1961.

Mamdani, Mahmood. *Citizen and Subject: Contemporary Africa and the Legacy of Late Colonialism*. Princeton, N.J.: Princeton University Press, 1996.

———. "A Glimpse at African Studies, Made in USA," *CODESRIA Bulletin* 2 (1990): 7–11.

Manganyi, N. C. *Being-Black-in-the World*. Johannesburg: Ravan, 1973.

Mann, Kristin. *Marrying Well: Marriage, Status, and Social Change among the Educated Elite in Colonial Lagos*. Cambridge: Cambridge University Press, 1985.

Manning, Patrick. *Francophone Sub-Saharan Africa, 1880–1985*. New York: Cambridge University Press, 1988.

Markakis, J. *National and Class Conflict in the Horn of Africa*. Cambridge: Cambridge University Press, 1987.

Marke, Charles. *Africa and the Africans*. Freetown: self-published, 1881.

Markovitz, Irving Leonard. *Léopold Sédar Sénghor and the Politics of Negritude*. New York: Atheneum, 1969.

———. *Power and Class in Africa*. Englewood Cliffs, N.J.: Prentice-Hall, 1977.

Martey, Emmanuel. *African Theology: Inculturation and Liberation*. New York: Orbis, 1993.

Martin, D., and P. Johnson. *The Struggle for Zimbabwe*. London: Faber, 1981.

Masolo, D. A. *African Philosophy in Search of Identity*. Bloomington: Indiana University Press, 1994.

Mason, R. J. *British Education in Africa*. Oxford: Oxford University Press, 1959.

Mathurin, Owen Charles. *Henry Sylvester Williams and the Origins of the Pan-African Movement, 1869–1911*. Westport, Conn.: Greenwood, 1976.

Maquet, J. *Africanity: The Cultural Unity of Black Africa.* New York: Oxford University Press, 1972.

Maxwell, Joseph Renner. *The Negro Question or Hints for the Physical Improvement of the Negro.* London: T. F. Unwin, 1892.

Mazrui, Ali A. *The African Condition.* Cambridge: Cambridge University Press, 1980.

———. *Cultural Engineering and Nation Building in East Africa.* Evanston, Ill: Northwestern Press, 1973.

———. *Cultural Forces in World Politics.* London: James Currey, 1990.

———. "From Slave Ship to Space Ship: Africa between Marginalization and Globalization," *African Studies Quarterly* 2, no. 4 (1999).

———. "Global Africa: From Abolitionists to Reparationists." In *Pan Africanism: Politics, Economy and Social Change in the Twenty-First Century,* edited by Tajudeen Abdul-Raheem, 123–44. New York: New York University Press, 1996.

———. "On the Concept 'We are all Africans!'" *American Political Science Review* 42 (1963): 88–97.

———. *The Political Sociology of the English Language: An African Perspective.* The Hague: Mouton, 1975.

———. *Political Values and the Educated Class in Africa.* London: Heinemann, 1978.

———. *Towards a Pax Africana.* Worcester and London: Ebenezer Baylis and Sons, Ltd., and the Trinity Press, 1967.

———, ed. *UNESCO General History of Africa,* vol. 8, *Africa since 1935.* Paris: UNESCO; Ibadan, Nairobi: Heinemann; California: University of California Press, 1993.

———, and Alamin M. Mazrui. *The Power of Babel: Language and Governance in the African Experience.* Chicago: University of Chicago Press, 1998.

———, and Hasu H. Patel. *Africa: The Next Thirty Years.* London: Davison Publishing, 1974.

———, and Michael Tidy. *Nationalism and New States in Africa: From about 1935 to the Present.* Nairobi: Heinemann, 1984.

———, and Tobi Kleban Levine. *The Africans: A Reader.* New York: Praeger, 1986.

Mba, Nina Emma. *Nigerian Women Mobilized: Women's Political Activity in Southern Nigeria, 1900–1965.* Berkeley: University of California Institute of International Studies, 1982.

Mbaku, John M. *Bureaucratic and Political Corruption in Africa: The Public Choice Perspective.* Malabar, Fla.: Krieger, 2000.

———. "Bureaucratic Corruption as Rent-Seeking Behavior," *Konjunkturpolitik* (Berlin) 4, no. 38 (1992): 247–65.

———. *Institutions and Reform in Africa: The Public Choice Perspective.* Westport, Conn: Praeger, 1997.

———. "Military Coups as Rent-Seeking Behavior," *Journal of Political and Military Sociology* 22 (1994): 241–84.

———. "State Control, Economic Planning and Competition among Interest Groups for Government Transfers in Africa," *The Journal of Social, Political and Economic Studies* 16 (1991): 181–94.

————, ed. *Corruption and the Crisis of Institutional Reforms in Africa*. Lewiston, N.Y.: Edwin Mellen Press, 1998.

Mbiti, John S. *African Religion and Philosophy*. London: Heinemann, 1969.

————. *Concepts of God in Africa*. London: S.P.C.K., 1982.

————. *Introduction to African Traditional Religion*. London: Heinemann, 1975.

————. *New Testament Eschatology in an African Background*. Oxford: Oxford University Press, 1971.

McGowan, Pat, and Thomas H. Johnson. "African Military Coups d'Etat and Underdevelopment: A Quantitative Historical Analysis," *Journal of Modern African Studies* 22 (1984): 633–66.

McMullan, M., "A Theory of Corruption," *Sociological Review*, 9, 1961, pp. 181–201.

Meier, August, and Elliott Rudwick. *Black History and the Historical Profession, 1915–1980*. Urbana and Chicago: University of Illinois Press, 1986.

Melson, R., and H. Wolpe, eds. *Nigeria: Modernization and the Politics of Communalism*. Lansing: Michigan State University Press, 1971.

Middleton, John, ed. *Black Africa: Its Peoples and Their Cultures Today*. London: Macmillan, 1970.

Miles, William. *Elections in Nigeria: A Grassroots Perspective*. Boulder, Colo.: Lynne Rienner, 1988.

Miller, Christopher. *Theories of Africans: Francophone Literature and Anthropology in Africa*. Chicago: University of Chicago Press, 1990.

Miller, Floyd J. *The Search for A Black Nationality: Black Emigration and Colonization 1787–1863*. Chicago: University of Illinois Press, 1975.

Miller, Joseph C. "History and Africa/Africa and History," *American Historical Review* 104, no. 1 (February 1999).

Mills, Greg, ed. *From Pariah To Participant: South Africa's Evolving Foreign Relations, 1990–1994*. Johannesburg: SIIA, 1994.

Mintz, Sidney, and Richard Price. *The Birth of African American Culture: An Anthropological Perspective*. Boston: Beacon Press, 1992.

Mkandawire, Thandika, and Charles C. Soludo, eds. *Our Continent Our Future: African Perspectives on Structural Adjustment*. Trenton, N.J.: Africa World Press, 1999.

Modibbo Ahmed Mohammed, ed. *A Giant of a Man: Tributes to Professor Abdullahi Smith (1920–1984)*. Kaduna: Abdullahi Smith Centre for Historical Research, 1986.

Moon, Henry Lee, ed. *Emerging Thought of W. E. B. Du Bois: Essays and Editorials From the Crisis*. New York: Simon and Schuster, 1972.

Moore, Carlos, et al., eds. *African Presence in the Americas*. Trenton, N.J.: Africa World Press, 1995.

Moraes Farias, Paulo Fernando de, and Karin Barber, eds. *Self-Assertion and Brokerage: Early Cultural Nationalism in West Africa*. African Studies Series No. 2. Birmingham, England: Centre of West African Studies, 1990.

Mowoe, Isaac J., ed. *The Performance of Soldiers as Governors*. Washington, D.C.: University Press of America, 1980.

————, and Richard Bjornson, eds. *Africa and the West: The Legacy of Empire*. New York: Greenwood, 1986.

Mudimbe, V. Y. *The Invention of Africa: Gnosis, Philosophy and the Order of Knowledge.* Bloomington: Indiana University Press, 1988.

Mullin, Michael. *Africa in the America: Slave Acculturation and Resistance in the American South and the British Caribbean, 1736–1831.* Urbana: University of Illinois Press, 1992.

Munford, Clarence J. *Race and Reparations: A Black Perspective for the 21st Century.* Trenton, N.J.: Africa World Press, 1996.

Munnion, Christopher. *Banana Sunday: Datelines from Africa.* Rivonia: William Waterman, 1995.

Munslow, B. *Mozambique: The Revolution and Its Origins.* London and New York: Longman, 1983.

Murphy, Joseph M., and Mei-Mei Sanford, eds. *Osun across the Waters: A Yoruba Goddess in Africa and the Americas.* Bloomington: Indiana University Press, 2001.

Museveni, Yoweri Kaguta. *Sowing The Mustard Seed: The Struggle for Freedom and Democracy in Uganda.* London and Basingstoke: Macmillan, 1997.

Nantambu, K. "Pan-Africanism versus Pan-African Nationalism: An Afrocentric Analysis," *Journal of Black Studies* 28, no.5 (1998): 561–74.

Nduka, Otonti. *Western Education and the Nigerian Cultural Background.* Ibadan: Ibadan University Press, 1965.

Neale, Caroline. *Writing "Independent" History: African Historiography, 1960–1980.* Westport, Conn.: Greenwood, 1985.

Neimark, Philip John. *The Way of the Orisa: Empowering Your Life through the Ancient African Religion of Ifa.* New York: Harper San Francisco, 1993.

Nel, Philip, and Patrick J. McGowan, eds. *Power, Wealth, and the Global Order.* Cape Town: University of Cape Town Press, 1999.

Newsum, H. E. (Ikechukwu Okafor). *Class, Language, and Education: Class Struggle and Sociolinguistics in an African Situation.* Trenton, N.J.: Africa World Press, 1990.

Ngubane, H. *Body and Mind in Zulu Medicine: An Ethnography of Health and Disease in Nynowa Zulu Thought and Practice.* London: Academic Press, 1977.

Nicol, Davidson, ed. *Black Nationalism in Africa,1867: Extracts from the Political, Educational, Scientific, and Medical Writings of Africanus Horton.* New York: Africana, 1969.

Nkrumah, Kwame. *Africa Must Unite.* London: Heinemann, 1963; reprint, New York: International Publishers, 1972.

———. *The Autobiography of Kwame Nkrumah.* New York: International Publishers, 1971.

———. *Axioms of Kwame Nkrumah.* London: Panaf Books, 1967. ———. *Class Struggle in Africa.* New York: International Publishers, 1970.

———. *Consciencism: Philosophy and Ideology of Decolonization.* London: Heinemann, 1964.

———. *I Speak of Freedom.* London: Panaf, 1962.

———. *Neo-Colonialism: The Last Stage of Imperialism.* New York: International Publishers, 1965.

———. *Revolutionary Path.* New York: International Publishers, 1973.

———. *The Struggle Continues.* London: Panaf Books Ltd. 1973.

————. *Towards Colonial Freedom*. London: Panaf Books, 1962.

Nnaemeka, Obioma. *Sisterhood: Feminisms and Power from Africa to the Diaspora*. Trenton, N.J.: Africa World Press, 1998.

Nnoli, Okwudiba. *Ethnic Politics in Nigeria*. Enugu, Nigeria: Fourth Dimension, 1980.

————. *Ethnicity and Development in Nigeria*. Aldershot: Avebury, 1995.

————, ed. *Path to Nigerian Development*. Dakar: Codesria, 1981.

Nore, Peter, and Terisa Turner, eds. *Oil and Class Struggle*. London: Zed, 1980.

Northrup, David. *Africa's Discovery of Europe, 1450–1850*. New York: Oxford University Press, 2002.

Nwala, T. *Igbo Philosophy*. Lagos: Lanern Books, 1985.

Nwankwo, Arthur A. *African Dictators: The Logic of Tyranny and Lessons from History*. Enugu: Fourth Dimension, 1990.

————. *The African Possibility in Global Power Struggle*. Enugu: Fourth Dimension, 1995.

————. *National Consciousness for Nigeria*. Enugu: Fourth Dimension Publishers, 1985.

Nwauwa, Apollos. *Imperialism, Academe and Nationalism: Britain and University Education for Africans, 1860–1960*. London: Frank Cass, 1996.

Nyamnjoh, Francis B. "Expectations of Modernity in Africa or a Future in the Rearview Mirror?" *Journal of Southern African Studies* 27, no. 2 (2001): 364–66.

Nye, Joseph S. "Corruption and Political Development: A Cost-Benefit Analysis," *American Political Science Review* 61, no. 2 (1967): 417–27.

Nyerere, Mwalimu Julius K. "Africa: The Current Situation," *African Philosophy* 11, no. 1 (June 1998): 7–12.

————. *The Arusha Declaration: Ten Years After*. Dar-es Salaam: Government Printer, 1977.

————. *Reflections on Africa and Its Future*. Public Lecture. Lagos: Nigerian Institute of International Affairs, 1987.

————. *Ujamaa: Essays on Socialism*. Dar Es Salaam: Oxford University Press, 1968.

Obasanjo, Olusegun, ed. *African Perspectives: Myth and Realities*. Washington, D.C.: Council on Foreign Relations, 1988.

Obbo, Christine. *African Women: Their Struggle for Economic Independence*. London: Zed, 1980.

Obee, Ruth. *Mphahlele: Themes of Alienation and African Humanism*. Athens: Ohio University Press, 1999.

Obemeata, J. O. *Language and the Intelligence of the Black Man*. Ibadan: Inaugural Lecture, University of Ibadan, 1992.

Obenga, Theophile. *African Philosophy in World History*. Princeton, N.J.: Sungai, 1998.

OECD and African Development Bank. *African Economic Outlook*. Washington, D.C..: The Organization for Economic Cooperation and Development, 2002.

————. *Reform and Growth in Africa*. Washington, D.C..: The Organization for Economic Cooperation and Development, 2000.

Offiong, Daniel A. *Imperialism and Dependency.* Enugu: Fourth Dimension, 1980.

Ogali, O. A. *Veronica My Daughter.* Ontisha: Appolos Brothers Press, n.d.

Ogbomo, Onaiwu W., *When Men and Women Mattered: A History of Gender Relations among the Owan of Nigeria.* Rochester, N.Y.: University of Rochester Press, 1997.

Ohaegbulam, F. Ugboaja. "Continental Africans and Africans in America: The Progression of a Relationship." In *Africana Studies: A Survey of Africa and the African Diaspora,* edited by Mario Azevado, 219–42. Durham, N.C.: Carolina Academic Press, 1993.

Ojike, Mbonu. *My Africa.* New York: John Day, 1946.

Okadigbo, C. *Consciencism in African Political Philosophy: Nkrumah's Critique.* Enugu, Nigeria: Fourth Dimension Publishers, 1985.

Okolo, Amechi. *Foreign Capital in Nigeria: Roots of Underdevelopment.* Lagos: Heartland Publishing House, 1987.

Okonkwo, Rina L. "The Garvey Movement in British West Africa," *Journal of African History* 21 (1980): 105–17.

———. *Heroes of West African Nationalism.* Enugu, Nigeria: Delta, 1985.

Okpewho, Isidore, et al., eds. *The African Diaspora: African Origins and New World Identities.* Bloomington: Indiana University Press, 1999.

Olalokun F. A., F. O. Fajana. et al., eds. *Structure of the Nigerian Economy.* Ibadan and Lagos: Macmillan and University of Lagos Press, 1984.

Olorunsola, Victor O., ed. *The Politics of Cultural Sub-Nationalism in Africa: Africa and the Problems of "One State, Many Nationalisms."* New York: Anchor Books, 1972.

Olukoshi, Adebayo O. *The Politics of Opposition in Contemporary Africa.* Uppsala, Sweden: Nordiska Afrikainstutet, 1998.

Olupona, J. K., ed. *African Traditional Religions in Contemporary Society.* New York: Paragon, 1991.

Olurode, 'Lai. *A Political Economy of Nigeria's 1983 Elections.* Lagos: John West, 1990.

———, ed. *Women and Social Change in Nigeria.* Lagos: Unity Publishing and Research Co., 1990.

Omari, T. Peter. *Kwame Nkrumah: The Anatomy of an African Dictatorship.* New York: African Publishing Corp., 1970.

Onimode, Bade. *Imperialism and Underdevelopment in Nigeria.* London: Macmillan, 1983.

———. *A Political Economy of African Crisis.* London: Zed Books, 1988.

Onwujeogwu, M. A. *An Igbo Civilization: Nri Kingdom and Hegemony.* Benin: Ethiope, 1985.

Onyioha, K. O. K. *African Godianism.* New York: self published, 1980.

Opoku, Kofi Asare. *West African Traditional Religion.* Accra: FEP International Private, 1978.

Osaghae, Eghosa E. *Crippled Giant: Nigeria since Independence.* London and Bloomington: Hurst and Indiana University Press, 1998.

———, ed. *Between the State and Civil Society in Africa.* Dakar: Codesria, 1994.

Osoba, Segun. "The Transition to Neo-Colonialism." In *Britain and Nigeria: Exploitation or Development?* edited by Toyin Falola, 223–48. London: Zed, 1987.

Othman, S. "Classes, Crises and Coup: The Demise of Shagari's Regime," *African Affairs* 83, no. 333 (1984): 441–61.

Otite, Onigu, ed. *African Social and Political Thought*. Enugu: Fourth Dimension Publishers, 1978.

Owoeye, Jide, ed. *Understanding the New World Order*. Ibadan: College Press, 1993.

Oyebade, Adebayo, and Abiodun Alao, eds. *Africa after the Cold War: The Changing Perspectives on Security*. Trenton, N.J.: Africa World Press, 1998.

Oyediran, Oyeleye, ed. *The Nigerian 1979 Elections*. London: Macmillan, 1981.

Oyejide, T. A., A. Soyode, and M. O. Kayode. *Nigeria and the IMF*. Ibadan: Heinemann, 1985.

Oyewumi, Oyeronke. *The Invention of Women: Making an African Sense of Western Gender Discourses*. Minneapolis: University of Minnesota Press, 1997.

Oyugi, Walter O., et al., eds. *Democratic Theory and Practice in Africa*. Portsmouth, N.H.: Heinemann, 1988.

Packard, Randall M. *Chiefship and Cosmology: An Historical Study of Political Competition*. Bloomington: Indiana University Press, 1981.

Paden, J. N. *Ahmadu Bello: Sardauna of Sokoto*. London: Hodder and Stoughton, 1986.

———. *Religion and Political Culture in Kano*. Berkeley: University of California Press, 1973.

———, and Edward Soja, eds. *The African Experience*, vol. 1, *Essays*. Evanston, Ill.: Northwestern University Press, 1970.

Panter-Brick, Keith. *Soldiers and Oil: The Political Transformation of Nigeria*. London: Frank Cass, 1978.

———, ed. *Nigerian Politics and Military Rule*. London: Athlone Press, 1970.

Parker, Aida. *The Citizen Secret U.S. War against South Africa*. Johannesburg: South Africa Today, 1977.

Parrinder, E. G. *African Traditional Religion*. London: S.P.C.K., 1968.

———. *West African Religion*. London: Epworth Press, 1961.

Patterson, Tiffany Ruby, and Robin D. G. Kelley. "Unfinished Migrations: Reflections on the African Diaspora and the Making of the Modern World," *African Studies Review* 43, no. 1 (2000): 11–45.

Peek, Philip M. *African Divination Systems: Ways of Knowing*. Bloomington: Indiana University Press, 1991.

Peel, J. D. Y. *Aladura: A Religious Movement among the Yoruba*. London, 1968.

———. *Religious Encounter and the Making of the Yoruba*. Bloomington: Indiana University Press, 2000.

Pemberton III, John, and Funso S. Afolayan. *Yoruba Sacred Kingship: "A Power Like That of the Gods."* Washington, D.C.: Washington Institution Press, 1996.

Peters, Jimi. *The Nigerian Military and the State*. London: I. B. Tauris, 1997.

Peters, Pauline E. *Dividing the Commons: Politics, Policy, and Culture in Botswana*. Charlottesville: University Press of Virginia, 1994.

Peterson, Bhekizizwe. *Monarchs, Missionaries and African Intellectuals: African*

Theatre and the Unmaking of Colonial Marginality. Trenton, N.J.: Africa World Press, 2000.

Ponton, M. M. *Life and Times of Henry M. Turner.* Atlanta: A. B. Caldwell, 1917.

Potkay, Adam, and Sandra Burr, eds. *Black Atlantic Writers of the Eighteenth Century.* New York: St. Martin's Press, 1995.

Pradel, Lucie. *African Beliefs in the New World.* Trenton, N.J.: Africa World Press, 2000.

Rajshekar, V. T. *Dalit: The Black Untouchables of India.* Atlanta: Clarity Press, 1995.

Ralston, R. D. "Africa and the New World." in A. Adu Boahen, ed., *Unesco General History of Africa,* vol. 7, *Africa under Colonial Domination.* Berkeley: University of California Press, 1985.

Ranger, Terence. "The Invention of Tradition in Colonial Africa." In *The Invention of Tradition,* edited by Eric Hobsbawm and Terence Ranger, 211–62. Cambridge: Cambridge University Press, 1983.

———, and I. Kimambo, eds. *The Historical Study of African Traditional Religion.* London: Heinemann, 1972.

Rasmussen, Lissi. *Christian-Muslim Relations in Africa.* London: British Academic Press, 1993.

Richards, Melsome Nelsone. *Poverty of Philosophy in African Studies.* Lawrenceville, N.J.: Brunswick Publishing Corporation, 1990.

Richburg, Keith B. *Out of America: A Black Man Confronts Africa.* New York: Basic Books, 1997.

Robinson, Cedric. *Black Marxism: The Making of the Black Radical Tradition.* London: Zed, 1983.

Rodney, Walter. *How Europe Underdeveloped Africa.* London: Bogle-l'Ouverture Publications, 1972.

Rogers, J. A. *Africa's Gift to Humanity.* New York: H. M. Rogers, 1961.

———. *The World's Great Men of Color.* New York: Macmillan, 1972.

Rose-Ackerman, S. *Corruption: A Study in Political Economy.* New York: Academic Press, 1978.

Rotberg, Robert I., and Ali Mazrui, eds. *Protest and Power in Black Africa.* New York: Oxford University Press, 1970.

Rothschild, Donald *Racial Bargaining in Independent Kenya.* London: Oxford University Press, 1973.

———, and Naomi Chazan, eds. *The Precarious Balance: State and Society in Africa.* Boulder, Colo.: Westview, 1988.

Rothchild, Joseph. *Ethnopolitics.* New York: Cambridge University Press, 1981.

Rowe, Cyprian Lamar. *Crisis in African Studies: The Birth of the African Heritage Studies Association.* Buffalo, N.Y.: Black Academy Press, 1970.

Ruch, E. A., and K. C. Anyawu. *African Philosophy.* Rome: Catholic Book Agency, 1981.

Rugumamu, Severine M. *Lethal Aid: The Illusion of Socialism and Self-Reliance in Tanzania.* Trenton, N.J.: Africa World Press, 1997.

Said, Abdul Aziz. *The African Phenomenon.* Boston: Allyn and Bacon, 1966.

Said, Edward, W. *Culture and Imperialism.* New York: Vintage, 1994.

Sanneh, Lamin. *Abolitionists Abroad: American Blacks and the Making of Modern West Africa.* Cambridge, Mass.: Harvard University Press, 1999.

————. *Christianity in West Africa: The Religious Impact.* Maryknoll, N.Y.: Orbis, 1983.

————. *The Crown and the Turban: Muslims and West African Pluralism.* Boulder, Colo.: Westview, 1997.

Sarbah, John Mensah. *Fanti National Constitution: A Short Treatise on the Constitution and Government of the Fanti, Asanti, and Other Akan Tribes of West Africa.* 2nd ed., with new introduction by H. R. Lynch. London: Cass, 1968.

Saro-Wiwa, Ken. *Sozaboy: A Novel in Rotten English.* Port-Harcourt, Nigeria: Saros International Publishers, 1985.

Saul, Mahir, and Patrick Royer. *West African Challenge to Empire: Culture and History in the Volta-Bani Anticolonial.* Athens and Oxford: Ohio University Press and James Currey, 2001.

Savishinsky, Neil J. "Rastafari in the Promised Land: The Spread of a Jamaican Socioreligious Movement among the Youth of West Africa," *African Studies Review* 37, no. 3 (December 1994): 19–50.

Segal, Ronald. *The Black Diaspora.* London: Faber and Faber, 1995.

Seidman, Ann, and Frederick Anang, eds. *Towards a New Vision of Self-Sustainable Development.* Trenton, N.J.: Africa World Press, 1992.

Sénghor, Léopold Sédar. *Selected Poems.* Translated by John Reed and Clive Wake. New York: Atheneum, 1964.

————. "What is Négritude?" *West Africa* 4 (November 1961): 1211.

Serequeberhan, Tsenay., ed. *African Philosophy: The Essential Readings.* New York: Paragon, 1991.

Sesay, Amadu, and Adetanwa Odebiyi, eds. *Nigerian Women in Society and Development.* Ibadan, Nigeria: Dokun Publishing House, 1998.

Shaw, Timothy M., and Aluko Olajide, eds. *The Political Economy of African Foreign Policy: Comparative Analysis.* Aldershot, U.K.: Gower, 1984.

Shepperson, George W. *The Politics of African Nationalism.* New York: Praeger, 1962.

————, and T. Price. *Independent African: John Chilembwe and the Origins, Setting and Significance of the Nyasaland Native Uprising of 1915.* Edinburgh: Edinburgh University Press, 1958.

Sherwood, M. *Kwame Nkrumah: The Years Abroad, 1935–1947.* Legon, Ghana: Freedom Publications, 1996.

Sigmund, Paul E. *The Ideologies of the Developing Nations.* New York: Praeger, 1963.

Sithole, N. *African Nationalism.* New York: Oxford University Press, 1968.

Sivonen, Seppo. *White Collar or Hoe Handle? African Education under British Colonial Policy, 1920–1945.* Bibliotheca Historica No. 4. Helsinki: Suomen Historiallen Seura, 1995).

Sklar, Richard L. *Nigerian Political Parties: Power in an Emergent African Nation.* Princeton, N.J.: Princeton University Press, 1963; reprint, Enugu: Nok, 1997.

———, and C. S. Whitaker. *African Politics and Problems in Development*. Boulder, Colo.: Westview, 1991.

Skurnick, W. A. "Léopold Sédar Sénghor and African Socialism," *Journal of Modern African Studies* 3, no. 3 (1965): 321–71.

Smith, E. *Aggrey of Africa: a Study in Black and White*. London: SCM Press, 1929.

Smith, Robert S. *Warfare and Diplomacy in Pre-Colonial West Africa*. London: Methuen, 1976.

Smock, David R. *Making War and Waging Peace: Foreign Intervention in Africa*. Washington, D.C.: United States Institute of Peace, 1993.

———, and K. Bentsi-Enchill. *The Search For National Integration in Africa*. New York: The Free Press, 1975.

Smythe, Hugh H., and Mabel M. Smythe. *The New Nigerian Elite*. Stanford, Calif.: Stanford University Press, 1960.

Sobande, O. A. "Path to Unity and Culture: Being a Comprehensive Survey of Principles and Practices of Egbe Omo Oduduwa," Mimeo. Lagos, 1952.

Sofola, J. A. *African Culture and the African Personality: What Makes an African Person African*. Ibadan: African Resorces Pubishers, 1973.

———. *Dynamism in African Leadership: The American Influence*. Ibadan: Daystar, 1981.

Sogolo, Godwin. *Foundations of African Philosophy: A Definitive Analysis of Conceptual Issues in African Thought*. Ibadan: Ibadan University Press, 1993.

Sola-Onifade, Bosede. *The Nigerian Woman*. Lagos: Julia Virgo, n.d. [1980s?].

Soyinka, Wole. *Art, Dialogue and Outrage: Essays on Literature and Culture*. New York: Pantheon Books, 1993.

———. *The Burden of Memory, the Muse of Forgiveness*. New York: Oxford University Press, 1999.

———. *Myth, Literature and the African World*. Cambridge: Cambridge University Press, 1976.

———. *The Open Sore of a Continent: A Personal Narrative of the Nigerian Crisis*. New York: Oxford University Press, 1996.

Spear, Thomas, and Isaria N. Kimambo, eds. *East African Expressions of Christianity*. Athens: Ohio University Press, 1999.

Spence, J. E. *Republic under Pressure: A Study of South African Foreign Policy*. London: Oxford University Press, 1965.

Spencer, J., ed. *The English Language in West Africa*. London: Longman, 1971.

Spiller, G., ed. *Inter-racial Problems*. London: P.S. King, 1911.

Stachan, Colin, and Lionel Cliffe. *Zimbabwe: Politics, Economics, and Society*. London: Pinter Publishers 1989.

Staudt Kathleen. "Women's Politics, the State, and Capitalist Transformations in Africa." In *Studies in Power and Class in Africa*, edited by Irvin L. Markovitz. New York: Oxford University Press, 1987.

Stein, Judith. *The World of Marcus Garvey: Race and Class in Modern Society*. Baton Rouge: Louisiana State University Press, 1986.

Steward, Alexander. *The World, the West and Pretoria*. New York: David McKay, 1977.

Sticher, Sharon B., and Jane L. Parpart, eds. *Patriarchy and Class: African Women in the Home and Workforce*. Boulder, Colo.:Westview, 1988.

Stocking, George, Jr., ed. *Colonial Situations*. Madison: University of Wisconsin Press, 1991.

Stockwell, Sarah. *The Business of Decolonization: British Business Strategies in the Gold Coast*. Oxford: Oxford University Press, 2000.

Suliman, Mohamed, ed. *Alternative Development Strategies for Africa*. 2 vols. London: The Institute for African Alternatives, 1991, 1995.

Takaya, B. J., and S. G. Tyoden. *The Kaduna Mafia: A Study of the Rise, Development and Consolidation of a Nigerian Power Elite*. Jos: Jos University Press, 1987.

Tempels, P. *Bantu Philosophy*. Paris: Présence Africaine, 1959.

Thiong'O, Ngugi wa. *Decolonising the Mind: The Politics of Language in African Literature*. London: James Currey, 1986.

Thompson, Vincent Bakpetu. *Africans of the Diaspora: The Evolution of African Consciousness in the Americas (from Slavery to the 1920s)*. Trenton, N.J.: Africa World Press, 2000.

———. *The Making of the African Diaspora in the Americas, 1441–1900*. New York: Longman, 1987.

Thornton, John K. *Africa and Africans in the Making of the Atlantic World*. Cambridge: Cambridge University Press, 1992.

———. *The Kongolese Saint Anthony: Dona Beatriz Kimpa Vita and the Antonian Movement, 1684–1706*. Cambridge: Cambridge University Press, 1998.

Tordoff, William. *Government and Politics in Africa*. Bloomington: Indiana University Press, 1984.

Touré, A. S. "A Call for Revolutionary Pan-Africanism," *Africa and the World*, July 1988, 39–44.

Turner, John W. *Continent Ablaze: The Insurgency Wars in Africa, 1960 to the Present*. London: Arms and Armour Press, 1998.

Turok, Ben, ed. *Debt and Democracy: Alternative Strategies for Africa*, vol. 3. London: Institute for Alternative Africa, 1991.

Tutuola, Amos. *My Life in the Bush of Ghosts*. London: Faber and Faber, 1955.

———. *The Palm-Wine Drinkard and His Dead Palm-Wine Tapster in the Dead's Town*. London: Faber and Faber, 1952.

UNDP. *Human Development Report*. New York: Oxford University Press, 2000.

Ungar, Sanford, J. *Africa: The People and Politics of an Emerging Continent*. 3rd ed. New York: Simon and Schuster, 1989.

Unoh, S. O., ed. *Cultural Development and Nation Building*. Ibadan: Spectrum, 1986.

Urnov, Andrei. *South Africa against Africa, 1966–86*. Moscow: Progress Publishers, 1988.

Uya, Okon. *Black Brotherhood: Afro-Americans and Africa*. Boston: D. C. Heath and Co., 1971.

Van den Berghe, Pierre L. *Power and Privilege at an African University*. Cambridge, Mass.: Schenkman, 1973.

Vandenbosch, Amry. *South Africa and the World: The Foreign Policy of Apartheid*. Lexington: University Press of Kentucky. 1970.

Van Der Hoeven, Rolph, and Fred Van Der Kraaij, eds. *Structural Adjustment and Beyond in Sub-Saharan Africa*. London: James Currey, 1994.

Vasta, M. J. *Tori for Geti Bow Leg*. Lagos: Cross Continental Press, 1981.

Vaughan, Olufemi. *Nigerian Chiefs: Traditional Power in Modern Politics, 1890s–1990s*. Rochester, N.Y.: University of Rochester Press, 2000.

Venter, Lester. *When Mandela Goes: The Coming of South Africa's Second Revolution*. London: Transworld Publisher, 1997.

Viereck, W., and W. D. Bald, eds. *English in Contact with Other Languages*. Budapest: Akadamiai Kiado, 1986.

Wallerstein, Immanuel. *Africa and the Modern World*. Trenton, N.J.: Africa World Press, 1986.

———. *Africa, the Politics of Independence: An Interpretation of Modern African History*. New York: Vintage Books, 1961.

———. *Geopolitics and Geoculture: Essays on the Changing World System*. Cambridge: Cambridge University Press, 1991.

———. "Pan-Africanism as Protest." In *The Revolution in World Politics*, edited by Morton A. Kaplan. New York: Wiley, 1962.

Walters, Ronald W. *Pan Africanism in the African Diaspora: An Analysis of Modern Afrocentric Political Movements*. Detroit: Wayne State University Press, 1997.

Washington, Booker T. *The Story of the Negro*. 2 vols. New York: Outlook, 1909; reprint, Gloucester, Mass: Peter Smith, 1969.

Waugh, Earl, et al., eds. *The Muslim Community in North America*. Edmonton, Alberta, Canada: University of Alberta Press, 1983.

Webster, James B. *The African Churches among the Yoruba, 1888–1922*. Oxford: Clarendon Press, 1964.

Weigert, Stephen L. *Traditional Religion and Guerilla Warfare in Modern Africa*. New York: St. Martin's Press, 1996.

Weisbord, Robert G. *Ebony Kinship: Africa, Africans and the Afro-American*. Westport, Conn.: Greenwood, 1973.

Welch, Claude E. Jr., ed. *Soldier and State in Africa: A Comparative Analysis of Military Intervention and Political Change*. Evanston, Ill.: Northwestern University Press, 1970.

Werlin, H. H. "The Consequences of Corruption: The Ghanaian Experience," *Political Science Quarterly* 88 (1973): 71–85.

West, Cornel. *Race Matters*. New York: Vintage Books, 1994.

Whitaker, Jennifer. *How Can Africa Survive?* New York: Harper and Row, 1988.

Whitaker, C. S. *The Politics of Tradition: Continuity and Change in Northern Nigeria, 1946–66*. Princeton, N.J.: Princeton University Press, 1970.

White, Luise. *Speaking with Vampires: Rumor and History in Colonial Africa*. Berkeley: University of California Press, 2000.

Wiley, David and Marylee Crofts, *The Third World: Africa* (Guilford, CT: Dushkin Publishing Company, 1988).

Williams, Chancellor. *The Destruction of Black Civilization: Great Issues of a Race from 4500 BC to 2000 AD*. Chicago: Third World Press, 1974.

Williams, Pat, and Toyin Falola, *Religious Impact on the Nation State: The Nigerian Predicament*. London: Avebury, 1995.

Williams, R. *Political Corruption in Africa*. Brookfield, Vt.: Gover, 1987.

Williams, Walter L. *Black Americans and the Evangelization of Africa, 1877–1900*. Madison: University of Wisconsin Press, 1982.

———. "Black Journalism's Opinions about Africa during the Late Nineteenth Century," *Phylon* 34, no. 3 (1973): 224–35.

Wilson, Bryan. *Religion in Sociological Perspectives.* Oxford: Oxford University Press, 1982.

Wilson, Henry S., ed. *Origins of West African Nationalism.* London: Macmillan, 1969.

Wilson, J. Moses. *Alexander Crummell: A Study in Civilization and Discontent.* Oxford: Oxford University Press, 1989.

Wiredu, Kwesi. *Philosophy and an African Culture.* New York: Cambridge University Press, 1980.

Wise, Collin G. *A History of Education in West Africa.* London: Longman, 1956.

Wright, Stephen. *Nigeria: Struggle for Stability and Status.* Boulder, Colo.: Westview, 1998.

———, and Julius Emeka Okolo. *African Foreign Policies.* Boulder, Colo.: Westview, 1999.

Wright, W. D. *Black Intellectuals, Black Cognition and Black Aesthetic.* Westport: Greenwood Publishing Group, Inc., 1997.

Woodson, Carter G. *The African Background Outlined.* Washington, D.C.: Negro Universities Press, 1968.

———. *The Miseducation of the Negro.* Washington, D.C.: Associated Press, 1933.

World Bank. *African Development Indicators, 1996.* Washington, D.C.: World Bank, 1996.

———. *Human Development Report, 2000.* New York: Oxford University Press, 2000.

———. *Sub-Saharan Africa: From Crisis to Sustainable Growth: A Long-Term Perspective Study.* Washington, D.C.: World Bank, 1989.

Wunsch, James S., and Dele Olowu. *The Failure of the Centralized State: Institutions and Self-Governance in Africa.* Boulder, Colo.: Westview, 1990).

Yakubu, M. *An Aristocracy in Political Crisis: The End of Indirect Rule and the Emergence of Party Politics in the Emirates of Northern Nigeria.* Aldershot: Ashgate Publishing Ltd., 1996.

Youé, Chris, and Tim Stapleton, eds. *Agency and Action in Colonial Africa.* New York: Palgrave, 2001.

Young, Crawford. *The African Colonial State in Comparative Perspective.* New Haven, Conn.: Yale University Press, 1994.

———. *Ideology and Development in Africa.* New Haven, Conn.: Yale University Press, 1982.

———, ed. *The Politics of Cultural Pluralism.* Madison: University of Wisconsin Press, 1976.

———, and Thomas Turner. *The Rise and Decline of the Zairian State.* Madison: University of Wisconsin Press, 1985.

Zachernuk, Philip S. *Colonial Subjects: An African Intelligentsia and Atlantic Ideas.* Charlottesville: University Press of Virginia, 2000.

Zakaria, Rafiq. *The Struggle within Islam.* London: Penguin, 1988.

Zartman, William, ed. *Collapsed States: The Disintegration and Restoration of Legitimate Authority.* Boulder, Colo.: Lynne Rienner, 1995.

———, ed. *The Political Economy of Nigeria.* New York: Praeger, 1983.

Zeleza, Paul Tiyambe. *Manufacturing African Studies and Crises.* Dakar: Codesria, 1997.

Zolberg, Astride. *Creating Political Order: The Party States of West Africa.* Chicago: Rand McNally, 1966.

INDEX